CONFIDENTIAL
CONFESSIONS

ALSO AVAILABLE FROM TOKYOPOP®

CONFIDENTIAL CONFESSIONS

Volume Three
by Reiko Momochi

TOKYOPOP®

Los Angeles • Tokyo • London

Translator - Amy Forsyth
English Adaptation - Marion Brown
Copy Editor - Amy Court Kaemon
Retouch and Lettering - Angie Lee
Cover Artist - Aaron Suhr

Editor - Julie Taylor
Managing Editor - Jill Freshney
Production Coordinator - Antonio DePietro
Production Manager - Jennifer Miller
Art Director - Matt Alford
Editorial Director - Jeremy Ross
VP of Production - Ron Klamert
President & C.O.O. - John Parker
Publisher & C.E.O. - Stuart Levy

Email: editor@TOKYOPOP.com
Come visit us online at www.TOKYOPOP.com

A  Manga

TOKYOPOP Inc.
5900 Wilshire Blvd. Suite 2000
Los Angeles, CA 90036

CONFIDENTIAL CONFESSIONS VOLUME 3

ISBN: 1-59182-395-1

First TOKYOPOP® printing: November 2003

10 9 8 7 6 5 4 3 2 1

Printed in the USA

\<Contents\>

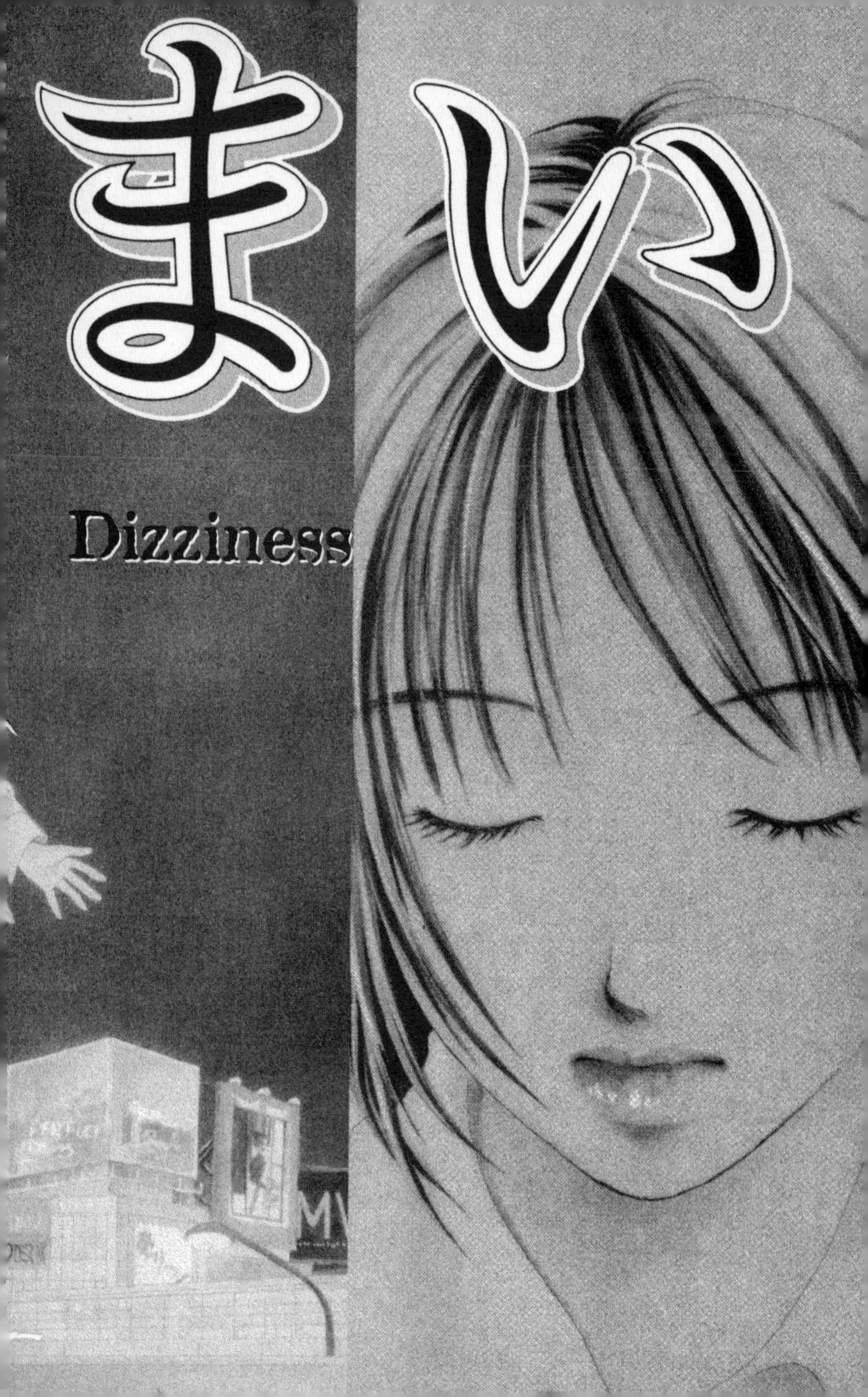
めまい
Dizziness

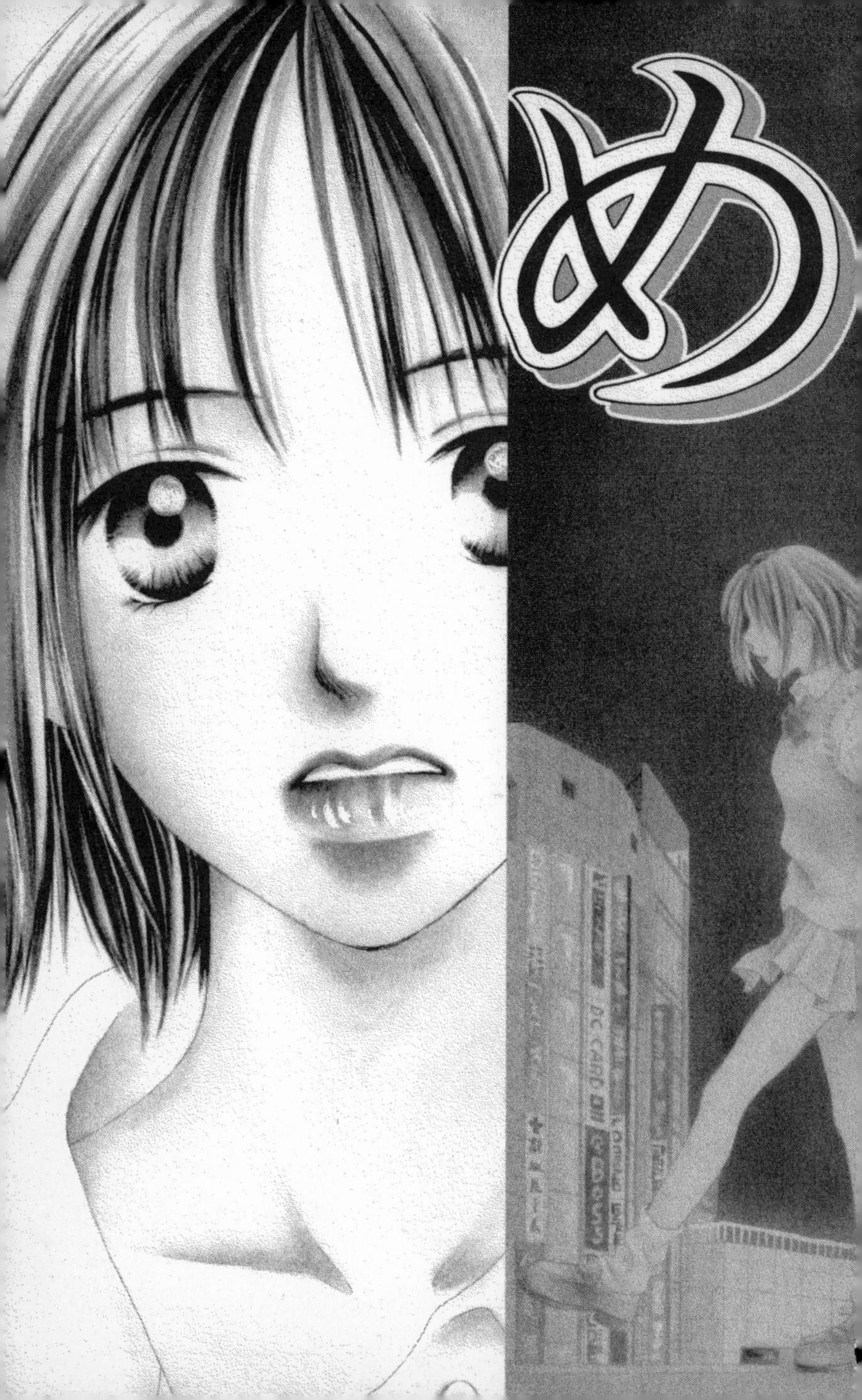

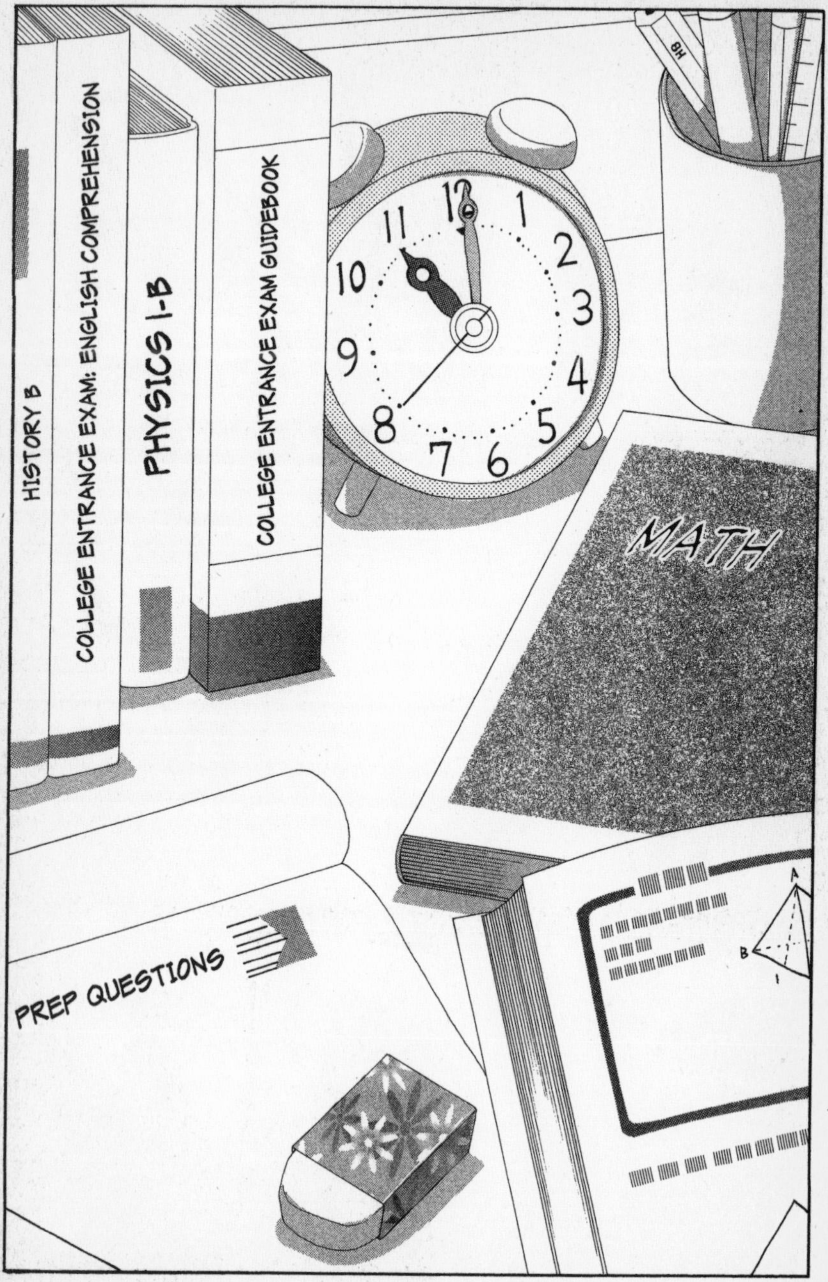
HB
MATH
COLLEGE ENTRANCE EXAM GUIDEBOOK
PHYSICS I-B
COLLEGE ENTRANCE EXAM: ENGLISH COMPREHENSION
HISTORY B
A
B
PREP QUESTIONS

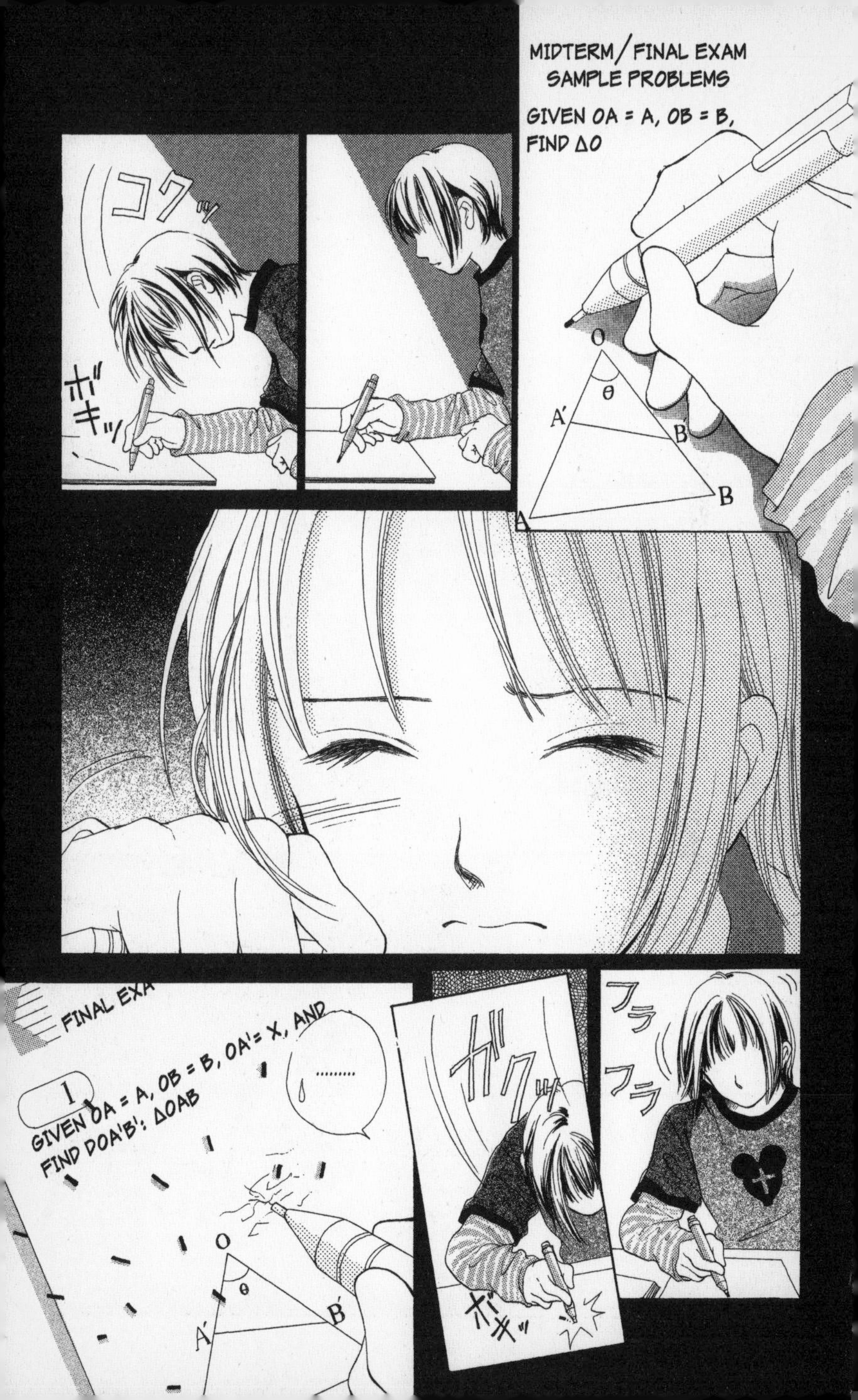
MIDTERM / FINAL EXAM
SAMPLE PROBLEMS
GIVEN OA = A, OB = B,
FIND ΔO
O
θ
A′
B′
B
A
コクッ
ボキッ
フラ
フラ
ガクッ
ボキッ
FINAL EXA
1
GIVEN OA = A, OB = B, OA'= X, AND
FIND ΔOA'B': ΔOAB
....
O
θ
B′
A′

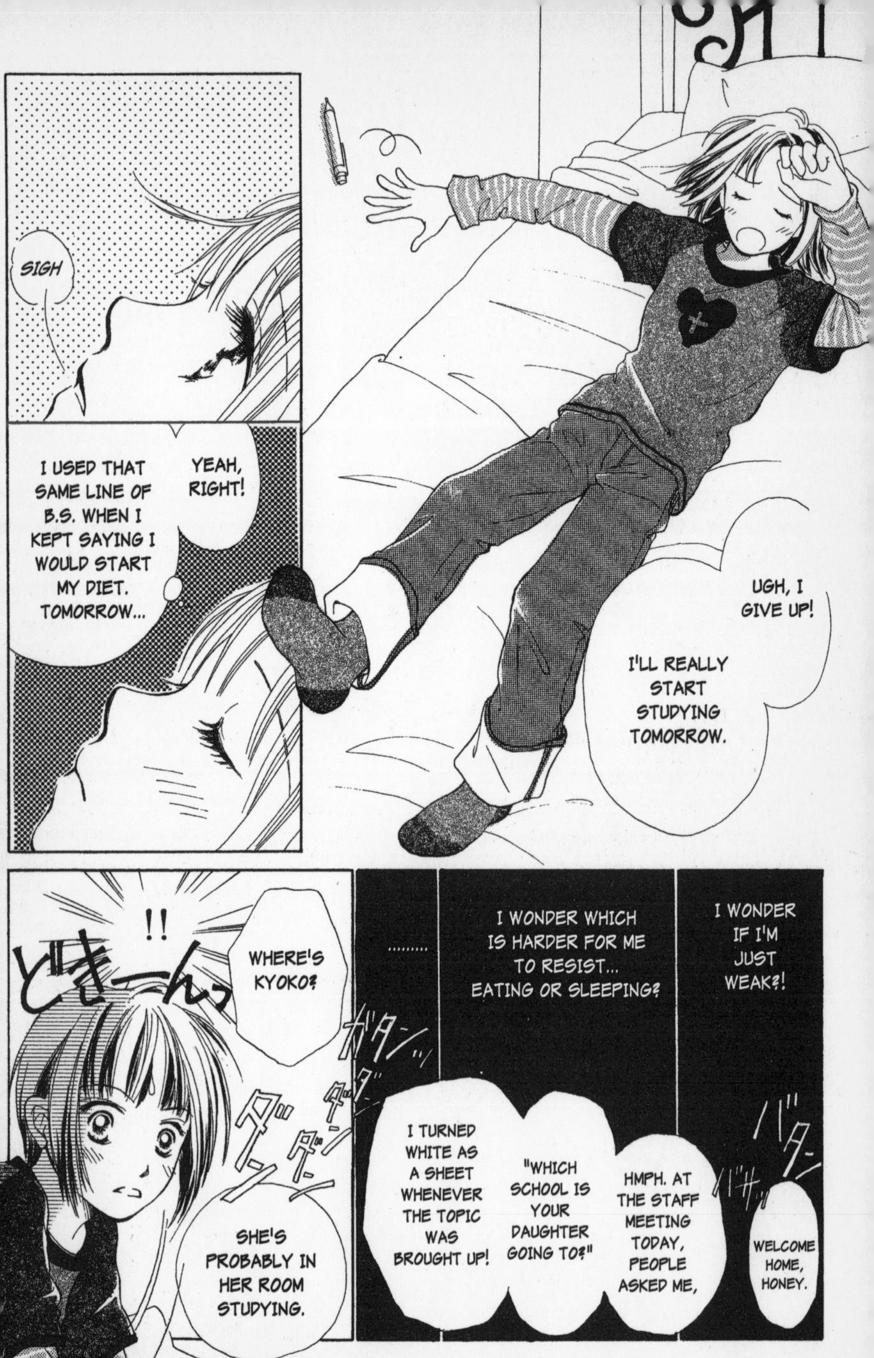
UGH, I GIVE UP!
I'LL REALLY START STUDYING TOMORROW.
SIGH
YEAH, RIGHT!
I USED THAT SAME LINE OF B.S. WHEN I KEPT SAYING I WOULD START MY DIET. TOMORROW...
I WONDER IF I'M JUST WEAK?!
WELCOME HOME, HONEY.
I WONDER WHICH IS HARDER FOR ME TO RESIST... EATING OR SLEEPING?
HMPH. AT THE STAFF MEETING TODAY, PEOPLE ASKED ME,
"WHICH SCHOOL IS YOUR DAUGHTER GOING TO?"
I TURNED WHITE AS A SHEET WHENEVER THE TOPIC WAS BROUGHT UP!
....
どきーんっ
!!
WHERE'S KYOKO?
SHE'S PROBABLY IN HER ROOM STUDYING.

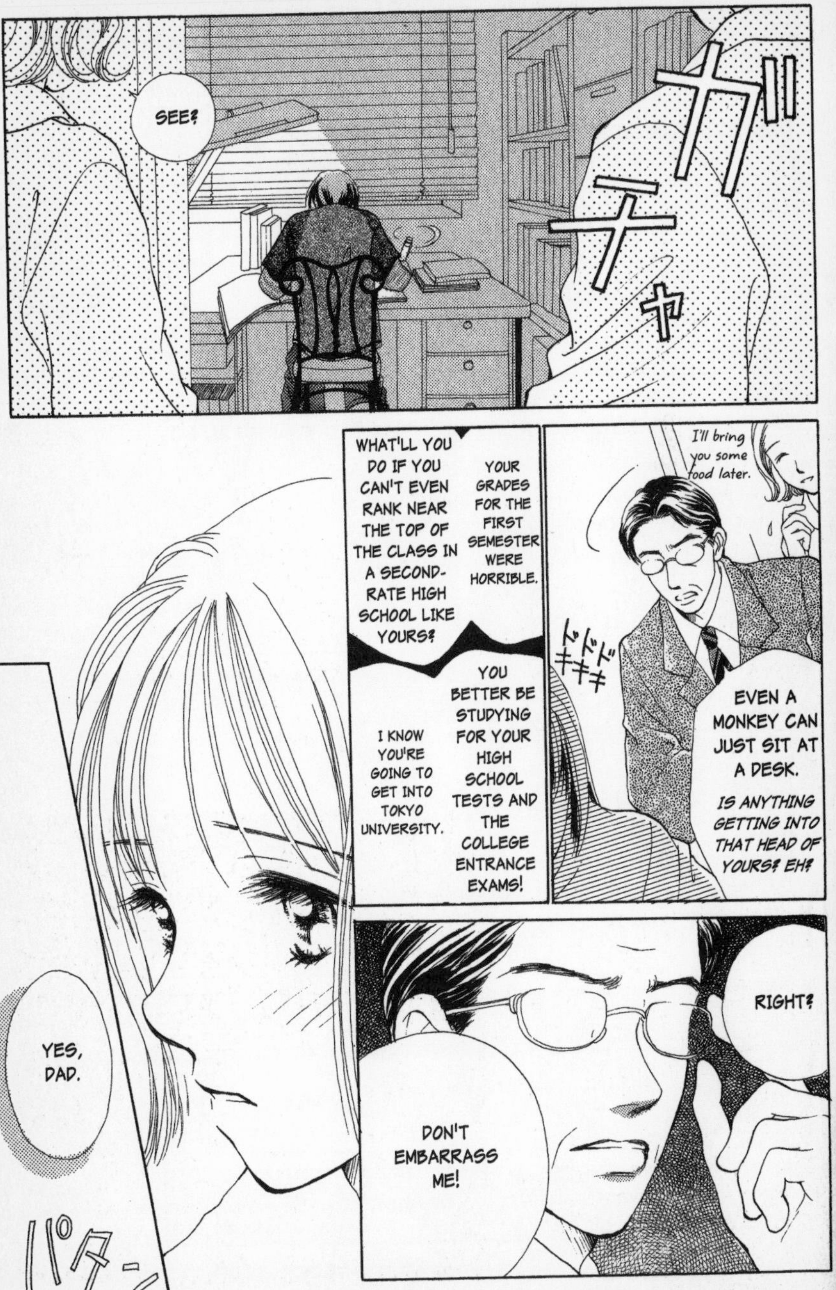
ガチャ
SEE?
I'll bring you some food later.
EVEN A MONKEY CAN JUST SIT AT A DESK.
IS ANYTHING GETTING INTO THAT HEAD OF YOURS? EH?
YOUR GRADES FOR THE FIRST SEMESTER WERE HORRIBLE.
WHAT'LL YOU DO IF YOU CAN'T EVEN RANK NEAR THE TOP OF THE CLASS IN A SECOND-RATE HIGH SCHOOL LIKE YOURS?
YOU BETTER BE STUDYING FOR YOUR HIGH SCHOOL TESTS AND THE COLLEGE ENTRANCE EXAMS!
I KNOW YOU'RE GOING TO GET INTO TOKYO UNIVERSITY.
RIGHT?
DON'T EMBARRASS ME!
YES, DAD.

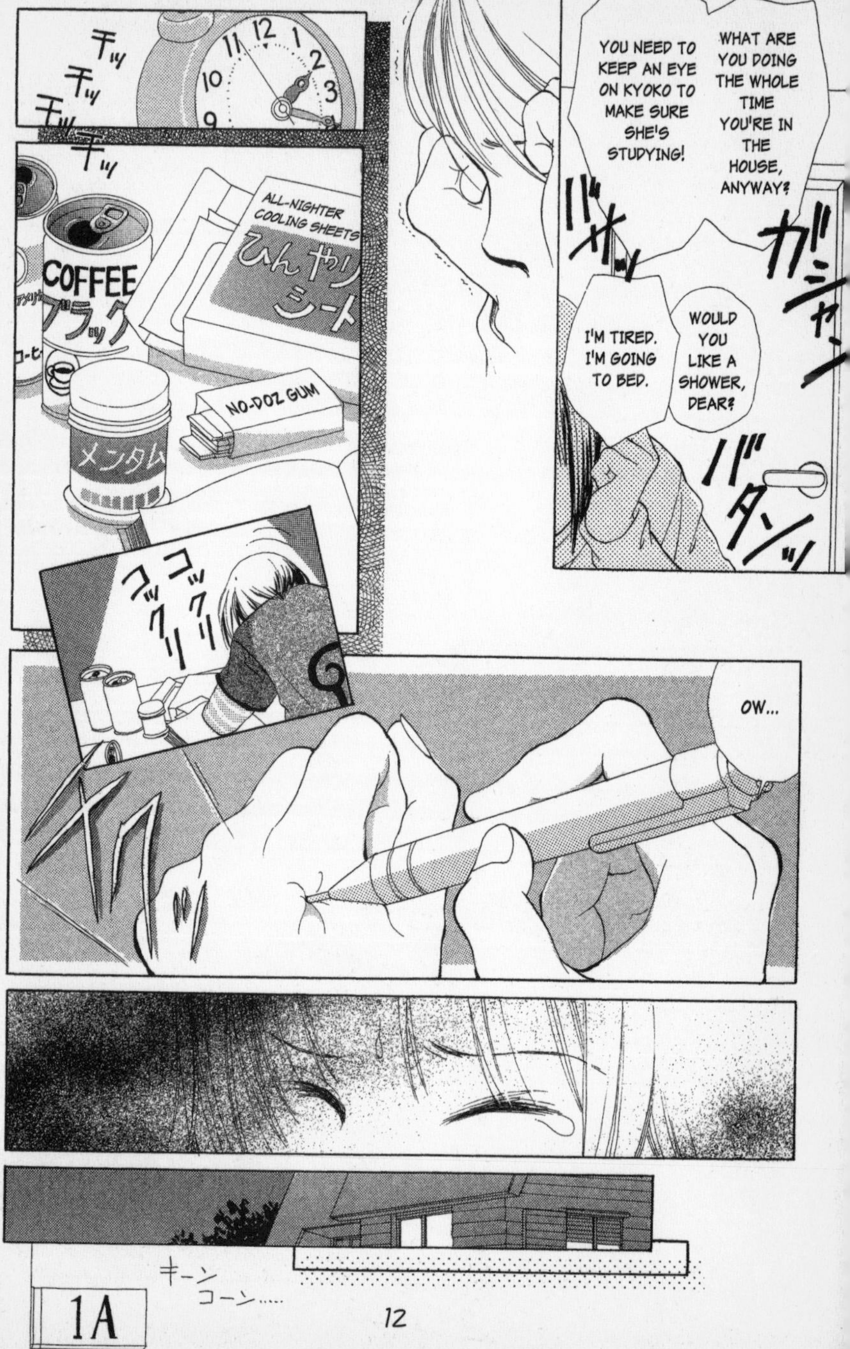
WHAT ARE YOU DOING THE WHOLE TIME YOU'RE IN THE HOUSE, ANYWAY?
YOU NEED TO KEEP AN EYE ON KYOKO TO MAKE SURE SHE'S STUDYING!
ガシャン
WOULD YOU LIKE A SHOWER, DEAR?
I'M TIRED. I'M GOING TO BED.
バタンッ
チッ
チッ
チッ
チッ
ALL-NIGHTER COOLING SHEETS
ひんやりシート
COFFEE
ブラック
NO-DOZ GUM
メンタム
コックリ コックリ
OW...
キーン
コーン……
1A

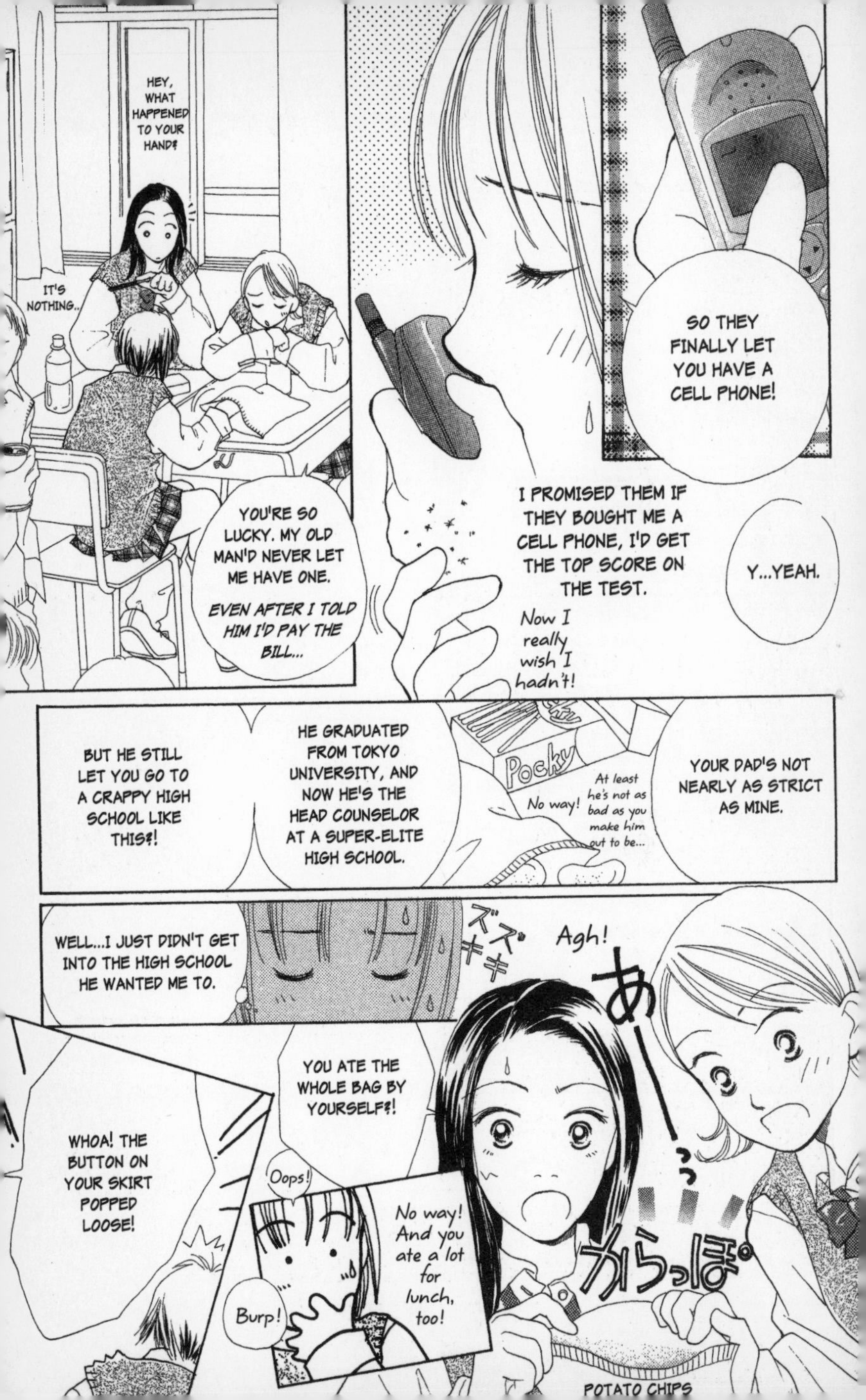
SO THEY FINALLY LET YOU HAVE A CELL PHONE!
Y...YEAH.
I PROMISED THEM IF THEY BOUGHT ME A CELL PHONE, I'D GET THE TOP SCORE ON THE TEST.
Now I really wish I hadn't!
HEY, WHAT HAPPENED TO YOUR HAND?
IT'S NOTHING..
YOU'RE SO LUCKY. MY OLD MAN'D NEVER LET ME HAVE ONE.
EVEN AFTER I TOLD HIM I'D PAY THE BILL...
YOUR DAD'S NOT NEARLY AS STRICT AS MINE.
At least he's not as bad as you make him out to be...
No way!
Pocky
HE GRADUATED FROM TOKYO UNIVERSITY, AND NOW HE'S THE HEAD COUNSELOR AT A SUPER-ELITE HIGH SCHOOL.
BUT HE STILL LET YOU GO TO A CRAPPY HIGH SCHOOL LIKE THIS?!
Agh!
ズキズキ
あーっ
からっぽ
YOU ATE THE WHOLE BAG BY YOURSELF?!
POTATO CHIPS
Oops!
No way! And you ate a lot for lunch, too!
Burp!
WELL...I JUST DIDN'T GET INTO THE HIGH SCHOOL HE WANTED ME TO.
WHOA! THE BUTTON ON YOUR SKIRT POPPED LOOSE!

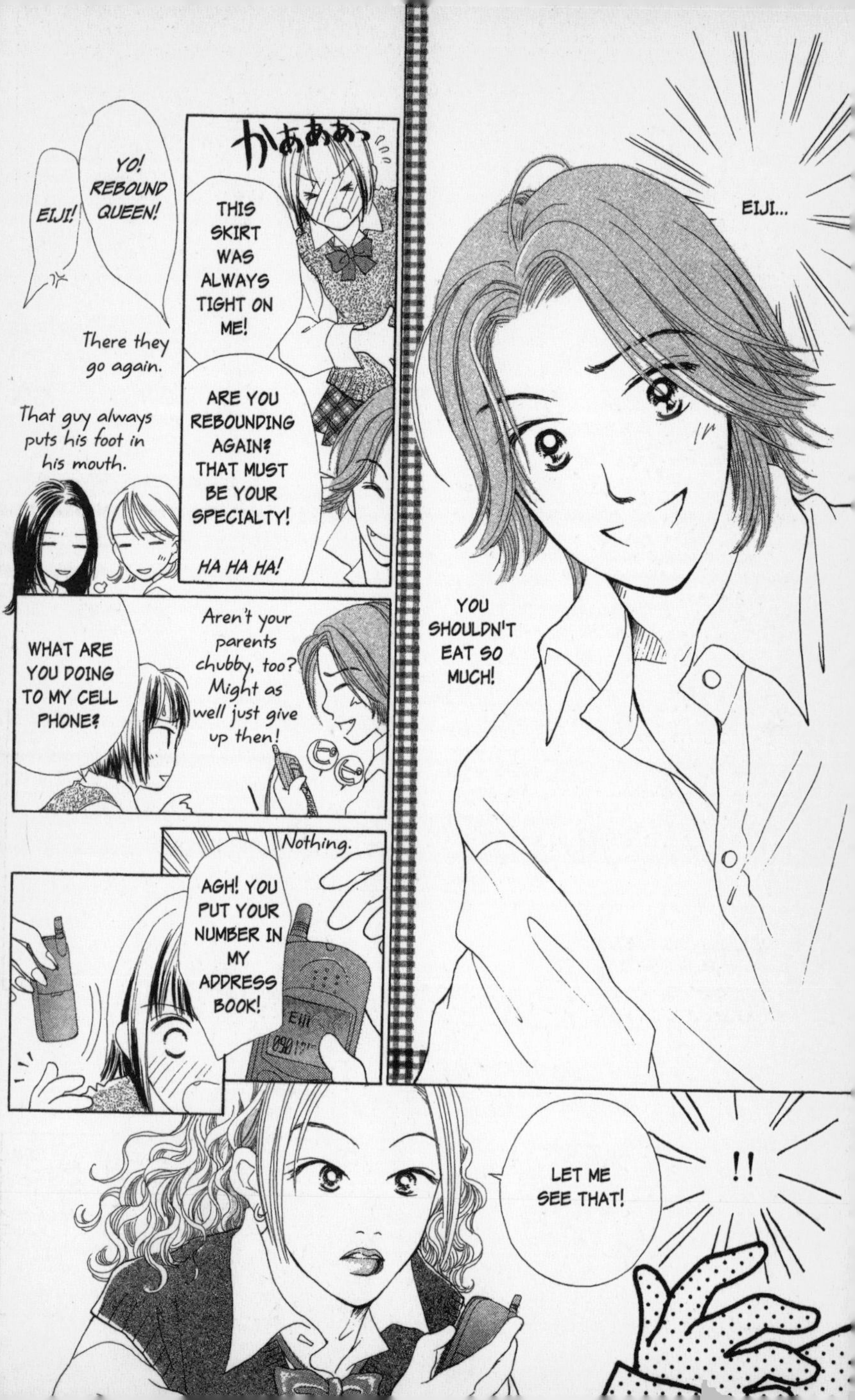
EIJI...
YOU SHOULDN'T EAT SO MUCH!
かあああっ
THIS SKIRT WAS ALWAYS TIGHT ON ME!
ARE YOU REBOUNDING AGAIN? THAT MUST BE YOUR SPECIALTY!
HA HA HA!
YO! REBOUND QUEEN!
EIJI!
There they go again.
That guy always puts his foot in his mouth.
Aren't your parents chubby, too? Might as well just give up then!
WHAT ARE YOU DOING TO MY CELL PHONE?
Nothing.
AGH! YOU PUT YOUR NUMBER IN MY ADDRESS BOOK!
!!
LET ME SEE THAT!

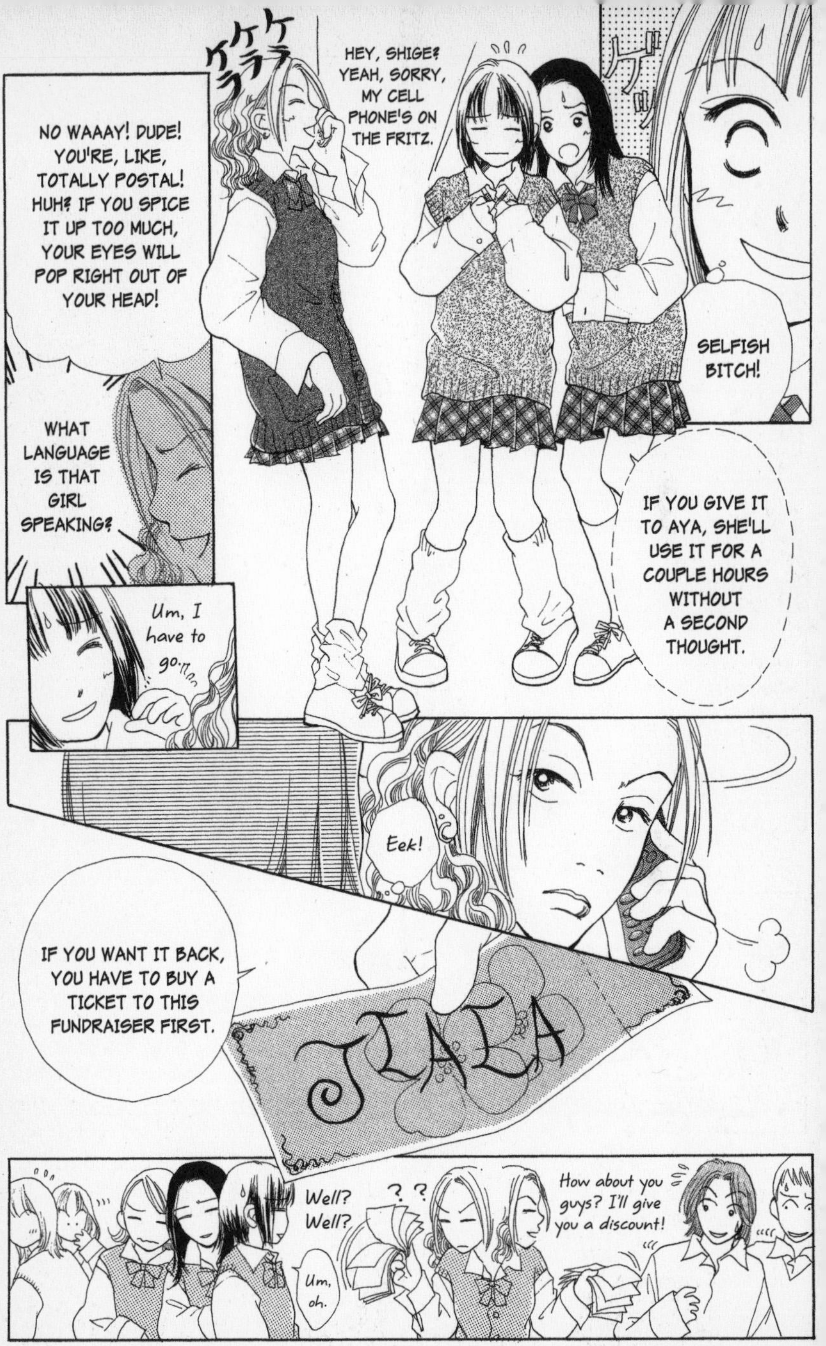
ゲゲッ
SELFISH BITCH!
ケラケラ
HEY, SHIGE? YEAH, SORRY, MY CELL PHONE'S ON THE FRITZ.
IF YOU GIVE IT TO AYA, SHE'LL USE IT FOR A COUPLE HOURS WITHOUT A SECOND THOUGHT.
NO WAAAY! DUDE! YOU'RE, LIKE, TOTALLY POSTAL! HUH? IF YOU SPICE IT UP TOO MUCH, YOUR EYES WILL POP RIGHT OUT OF YOUR HEAD!
WHAT LANGUAGE IS THAT GIRL SPEAKING?
Um, I have to go.
Eek!
IF YOU WANT IT BACK, YOU HAVE TO BUY A TICKET TO THIS FUNDRAISER FIRST.
TIALA
How about you guys? I'll give you a discount!
? ?
Well? Well?
Um, oh.

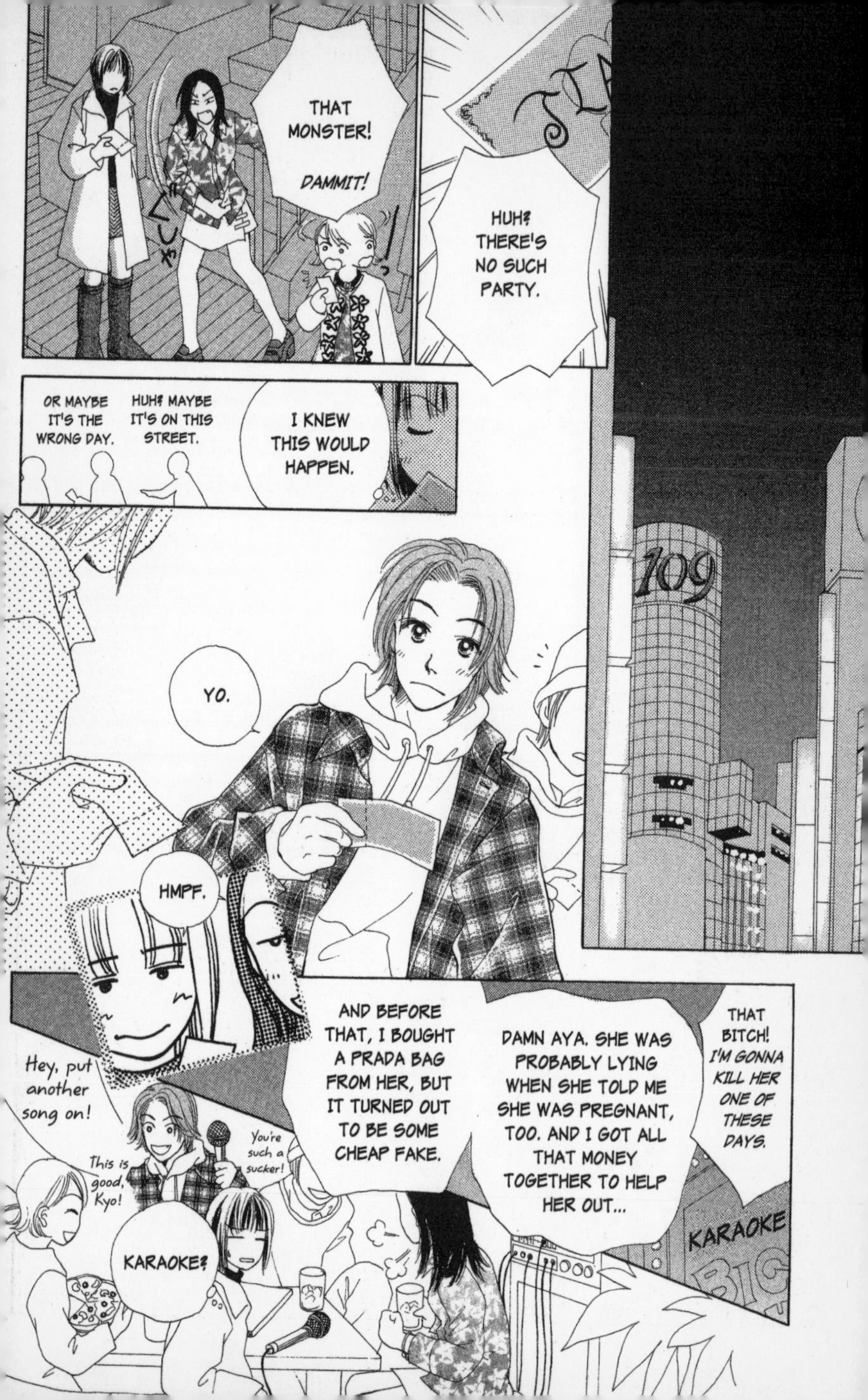
HUH? THERE'S NO SUCH PARTY.
THAT MONSTER!
DAMMIT!
109
I KNEW THIS WOULD HAPPEN.
HUH? MAYBE IT'S ON THIS STREET.
OR MAYBE IT'S THE WRONG DAY.
YO.
HMPF.
THAT BITCH! I'M GONNA KILL HER ONE OF THESE DAYS.
KARAOKE
DAMN AYA. SHE WAS PROBABLY LYING WHEN SHE TOLD ME SHE WAS PREGNANT, TOO. AND I GOT ALL THAT MONEY TOGETHER TO HELP HER OUT...
AND BEFORE THAT, I BOUGHT A PRADA BAG FROM HER, BUT IT TURNED OUT TO BE SOME CHEAP FAKE.
You're such a sucker!
This is good, Kyo!
Hey, put another song on!
KARAOKE?

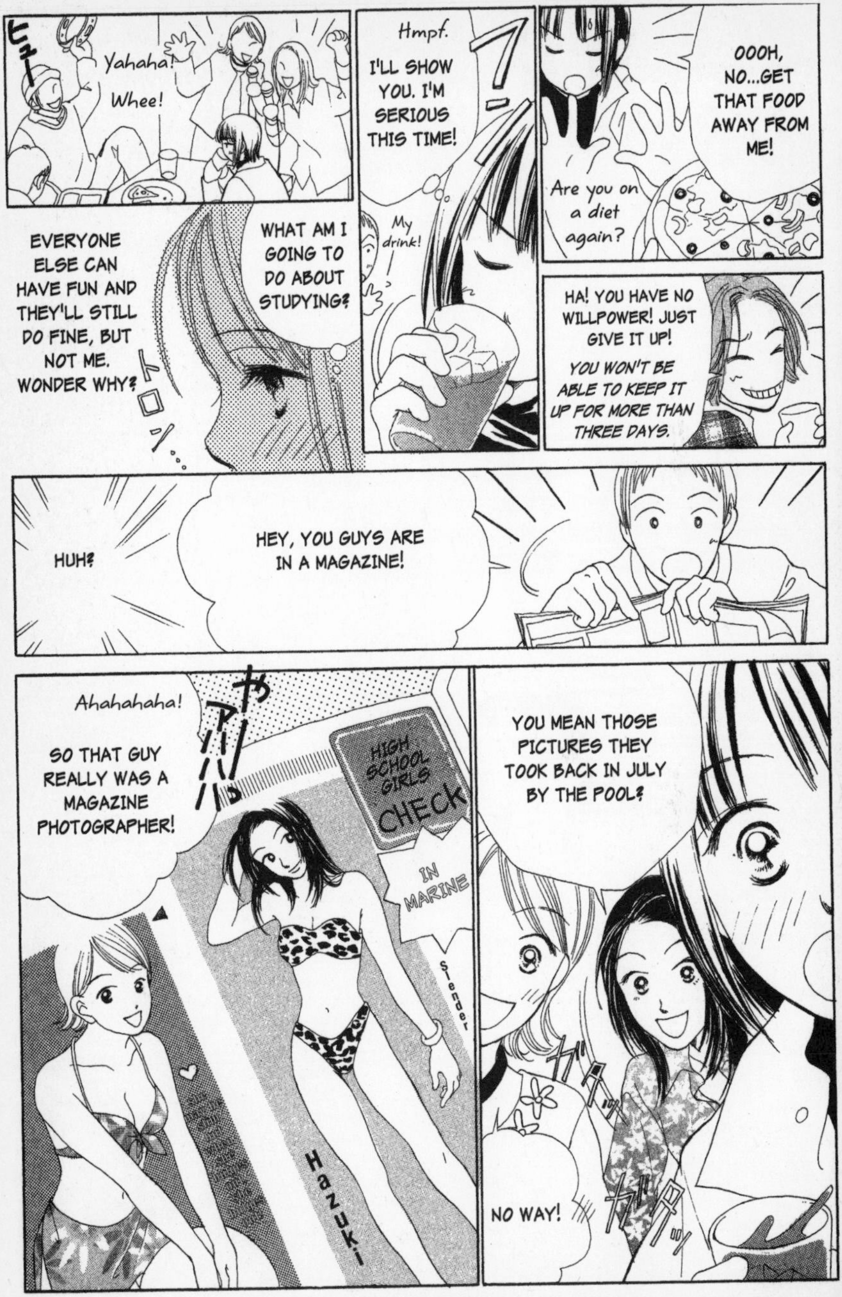
OOOH, NO...GET THAT FOOD AWAY FROM ME!
Are you on a diet again?
HA! YOU HAVE NO WILLPOWER! JUST GIVE IT UP!
YOU WON'T BE ABLE TO KEEP IT UP FOR MORE THAN THREE DAYS.
Hmpf.
I'LL SHOW YOU. I'M SERIOUS THIS TIME!
My drink!
Yahaha!
Whee!
WHAT AM I GOING TO DO ABOUT STUDYING?
EVERYONE ELSE CAN HAVE FUN AND THEY'LL STILL DO FINE, BUT NOT ME. WONDER WHY?
HEY, YOU GUYS ARE IN A MAGAZINE!
HUH?
YOU MEAN THOSE PICTURES THEY TOOK BACK IN JULY BY THE POOL?
NO WAY!
Ahahahaha!
SO THAT GUY REALLY WAS A MAGAZINE PHOTOGRAPHER!
HIGH SCHOOL GIRLS CHECK
IN MARINE
Slender
Hazuki

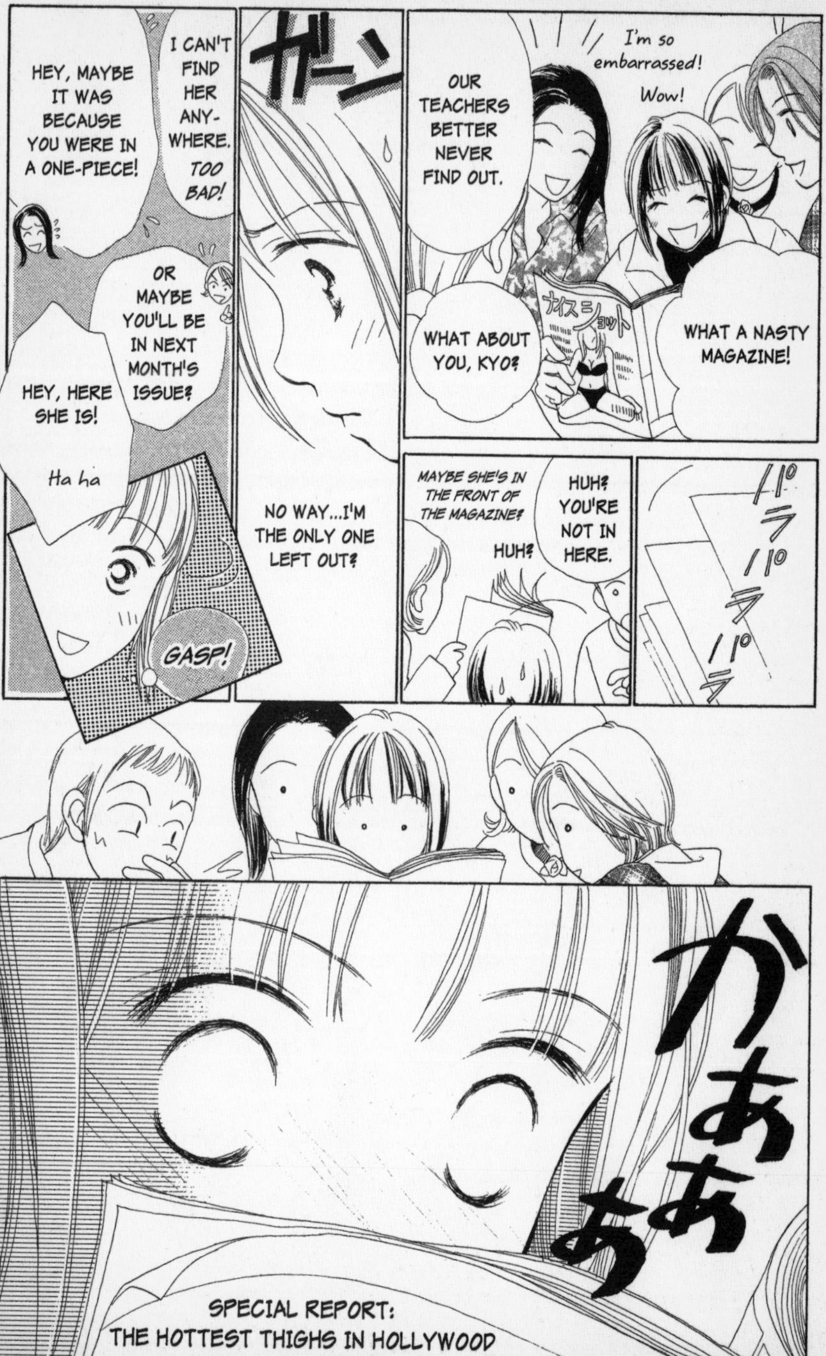
I'm so embarrassed!
Wow!
OUR TEACHERS BETTER NEVER FIND OUT.
WHAT A NASTY MAGAZINE!
ナイスショット
WHAT ABOUT YOU, KYO?
パラパラパラパラ
HUH? YOU'RE NOT IN HERE.
MAYBE SHE'S IN THE FRONT OF THE MAGAZINE?
HUH?
ガーン
NO WAY...I'M THE ONLY ONE LEFT OUT?
I CAN'T FIND HER ANYWHERE. TOO BAD!
HEY, MAYBE IT WAS BECAUSE YOU WERE IN A ONE-PIECE!
OR MAYBE YOU'LL BE IN NEXT MONTH'S ISSUE?
HEY, HERE SHE IS!
Ha ha
GASP!
かあああ
SPECIAL REPORT: THE HOTTEST THIGHS IN HOLLYWOOD

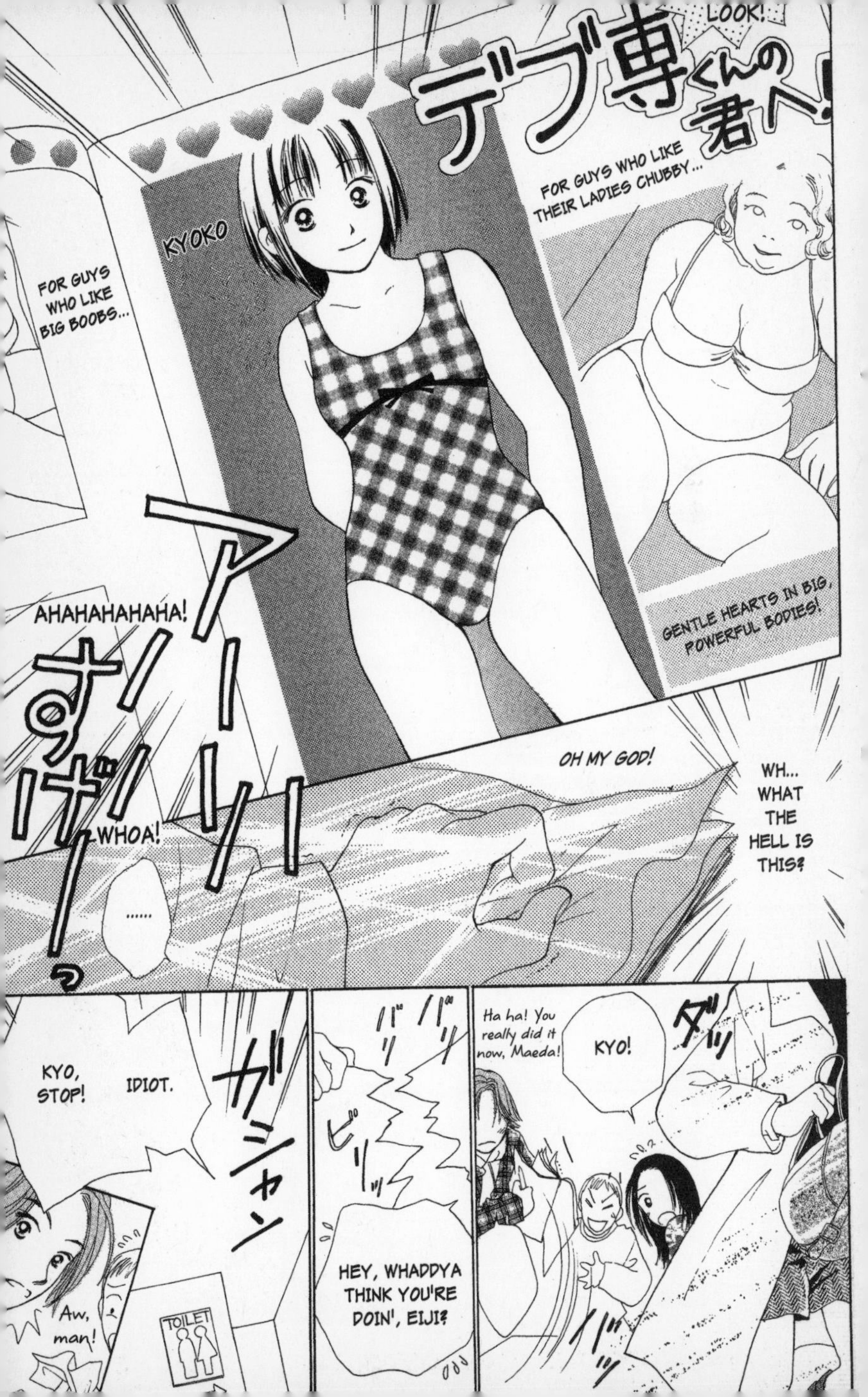
LOOK!
デブ専くんの君へ!
FOR GUYS WHO LIKE THEIR LADIES CHUBBY...
GENTLE HEARTS IN BIG, POWERFUL BODIES!
KYOKO
FOR GUYS WHO LIKE BIG BOOBS...
WH... WHAT THE HELL IS THIS?
OH MY GOD!
AHAHAHAHAHA!
WHOA!
......
ダッ
KYO!
Ha ha! You really did it now, Maeda!
バリ バリ
ビリッ
HEY, WHADDYA THINK YOU'RE DOIN', EIJI?
ガシャン
IDIOT.
KYO, STOP!
Aw, man!
TOILET

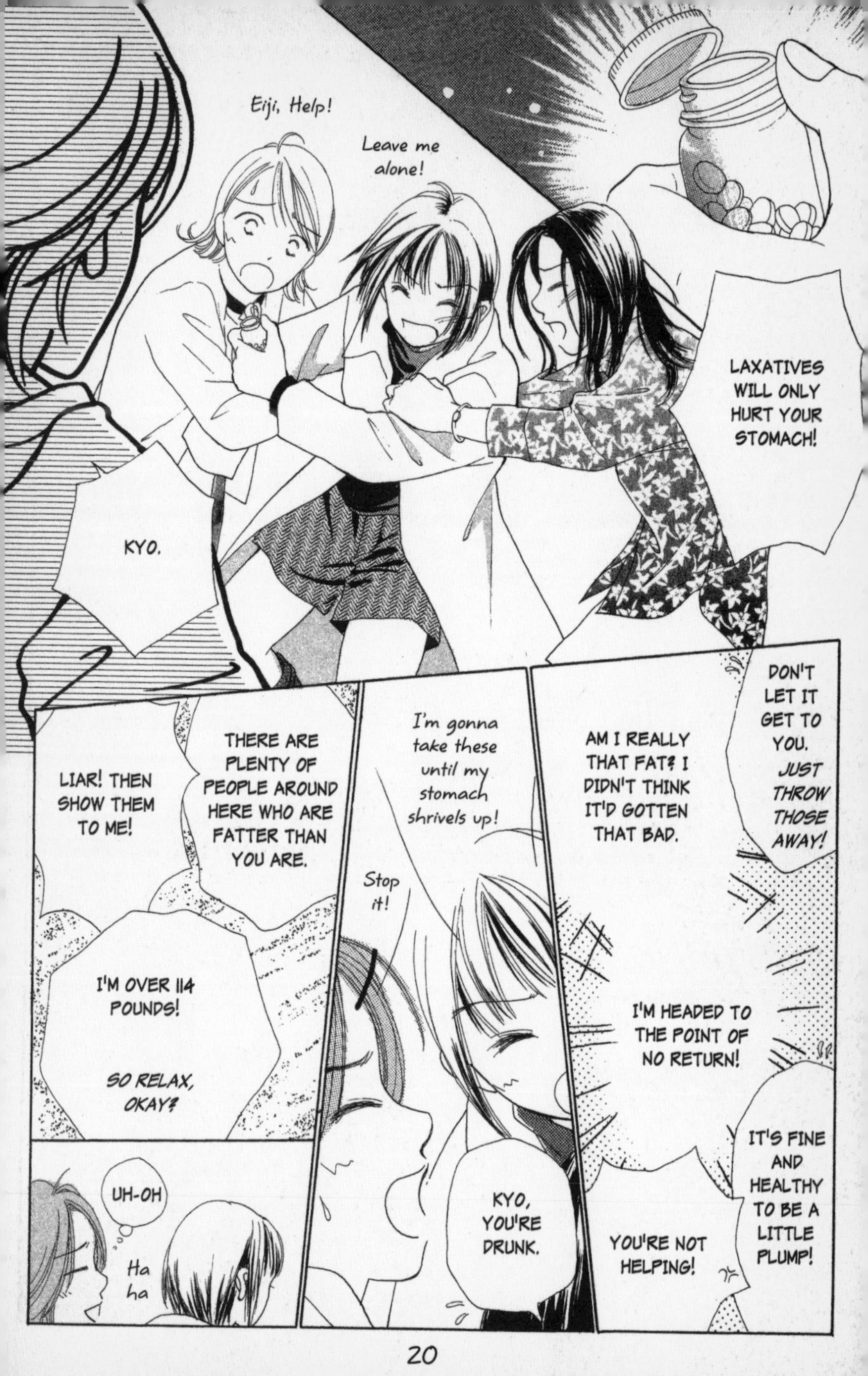
Eiji, Help!
Leave me alone!
LAXATIVES WILL ONLY HURT YOUR STOMACH!
KYO.
DON'T LET IT GET TO YOU. JUST THROW THOSE AWAY!
AM I REALLY THAT FAT? I DIDN'T THINK IT'D GOTTEN THAT BAD.
I'M HEADED TO THE POINT OF NO RETURN!
IT'S FINE AND HEALTHY TO BE A LITTLE PLUMP!
YOU'RE NOT HELPING!
I'm gonna take these until my stomach shrivels up!
Stop it!
KYO, YOU'RE DRUNK.
THERE ARE PLENTY OF PEOPLE AROUND HERE WHO ARE FATTER THAN YOU ARE.
LIAR! THEN SHOW THEM TO ME!
I'M OVER 114 POUNDS!
SO RELAX, OKAY?
UH-OH
Ha ha

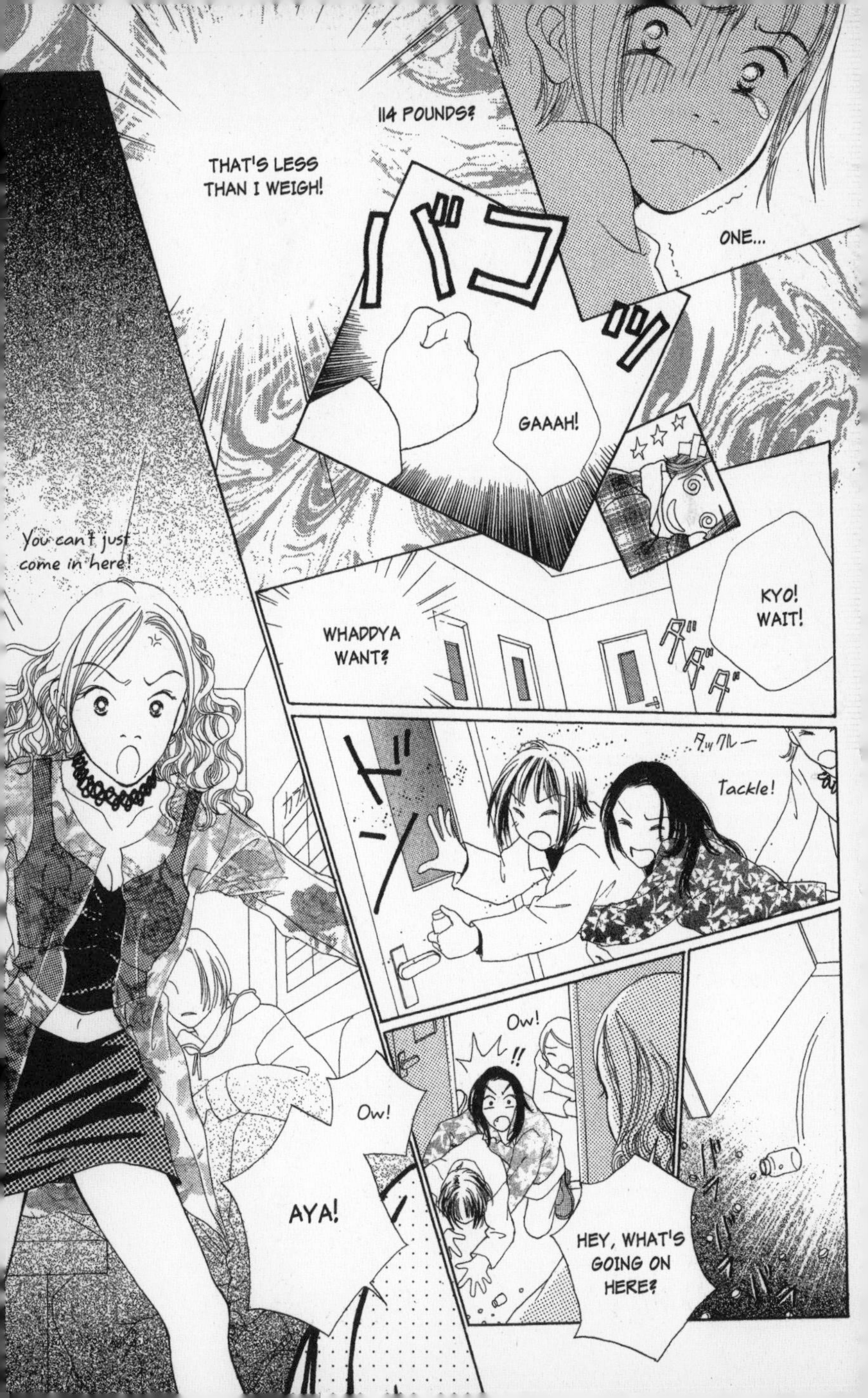
ONE...
114 POUNDS?
THAT'S LESS THAN I WEIGH!
バコッ
GAAAH!
KYO! WAIT!
ダダダ
WHADDYA WANT?
タックルー
Tackle!
HEY, WHAT'S GOING ON HERE?
Ow! !!
Ow!
AYA!
You can't just come in here!

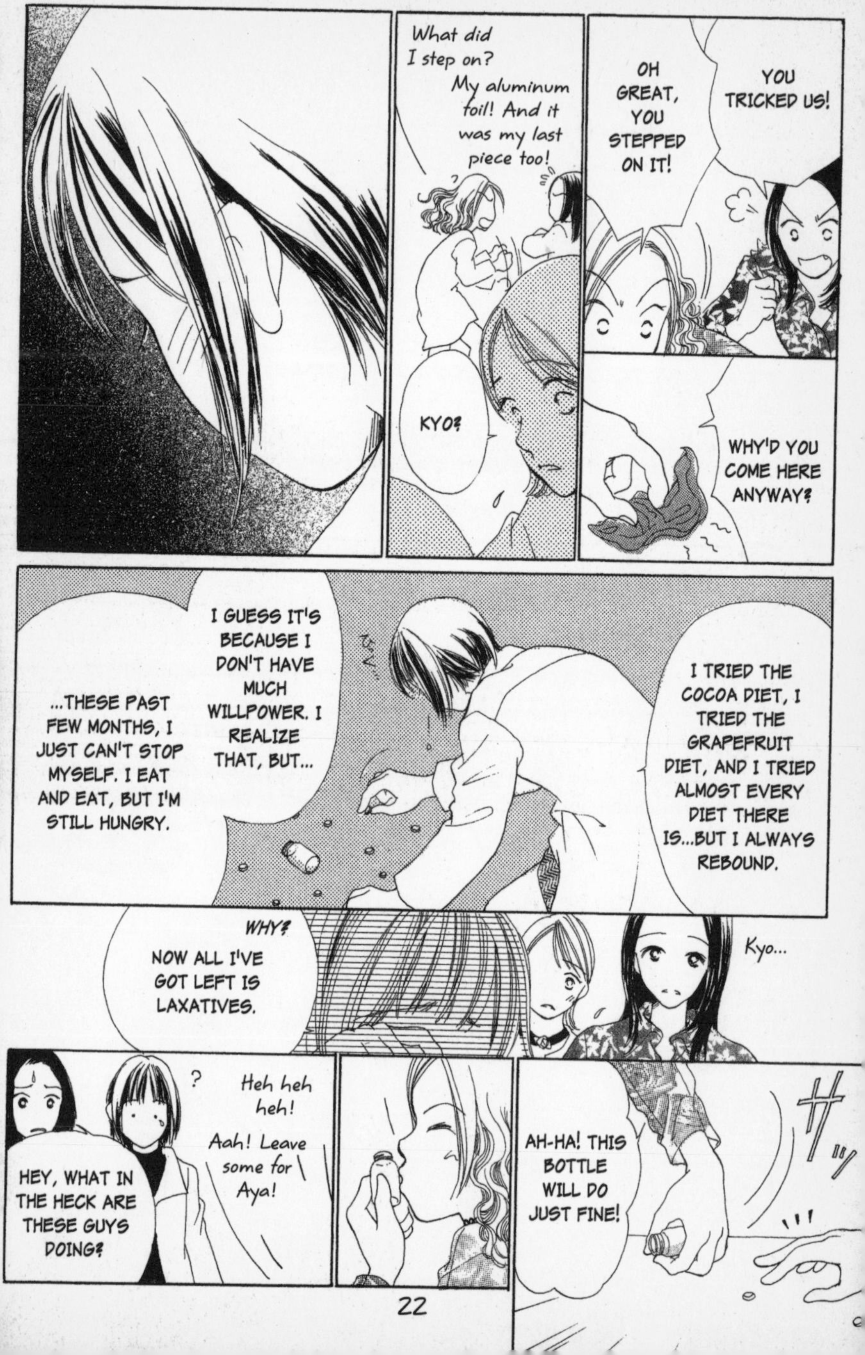
YOU TRICKED US!
OH GREAT, YOU STEPPED ON IT!
WHY'D YOU COME HERE ANYWAY?
What did I step on?
My aluminum foil! And it was my last piece too!
KYO?
I TRIED THE COCOA DIET, I TRIED THE GRAPEFRUIT DIET, AND I TRIED ALMOST EVERY DIET THERE IS...BUT I ALWAYS REBOUND.
I GUESS IT'S BECAUSE I DON'T HAVE MUCH WILLPOWER. I REALIZE THAT, BUT...
...THESE PAST FEW MONTHS, I JUST CAN'T STOP MYSELF. I EAT AND EAT, BUT I'M STILL HUNGRY.
Kyo...
WHY?
NOW ALL I'VE GOT LEFT IS LAXATIVES.
AH-HA! THIS BOTTLE WILL DO JUST FINE!
Heh heh heh!
Aah! Leave some for Aya!
?
HEY, WHAT IN THE HECK ARE THESE GUYS DOING?

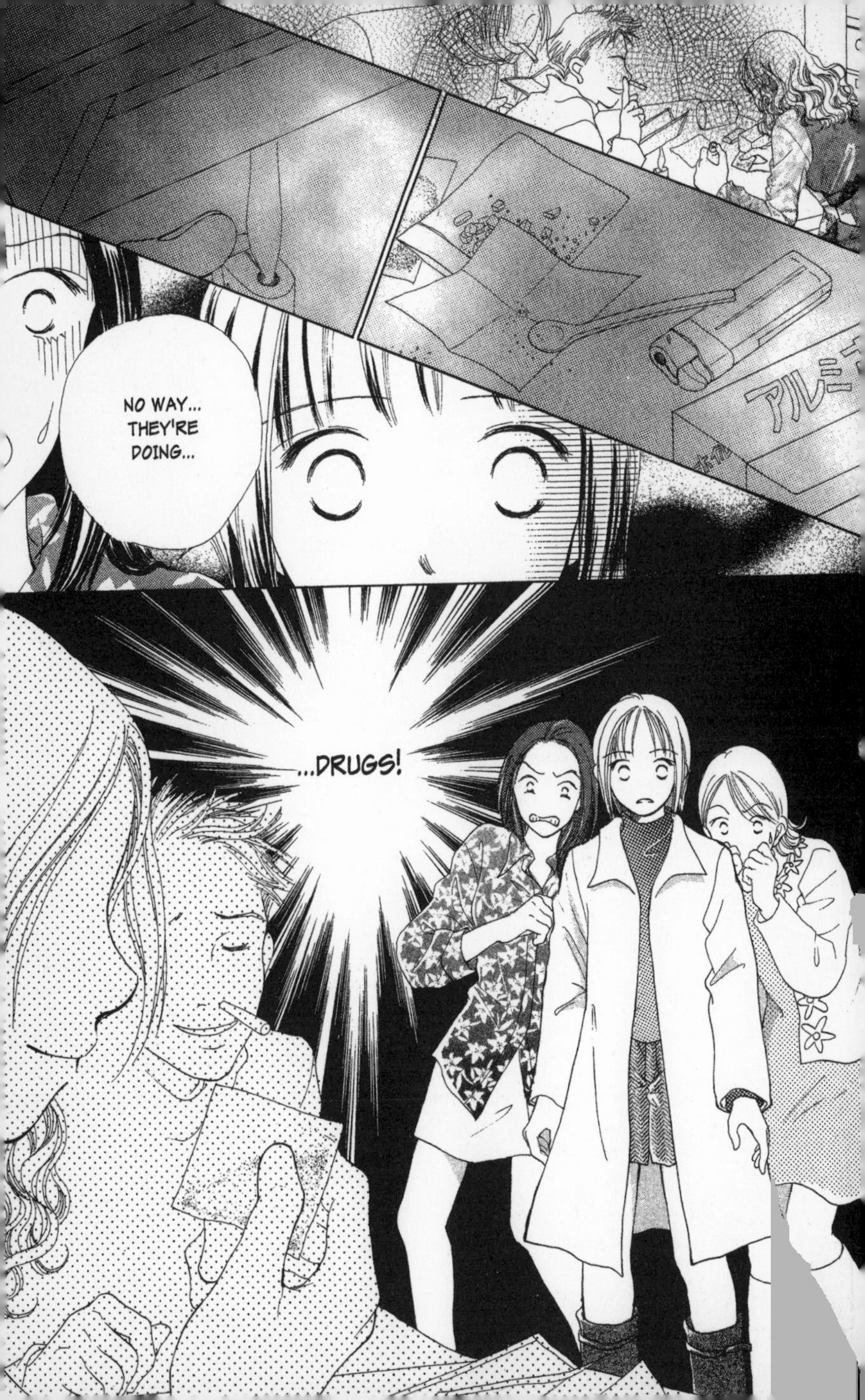
NO WAY... THEY'RE DOING...
...DRUGS!

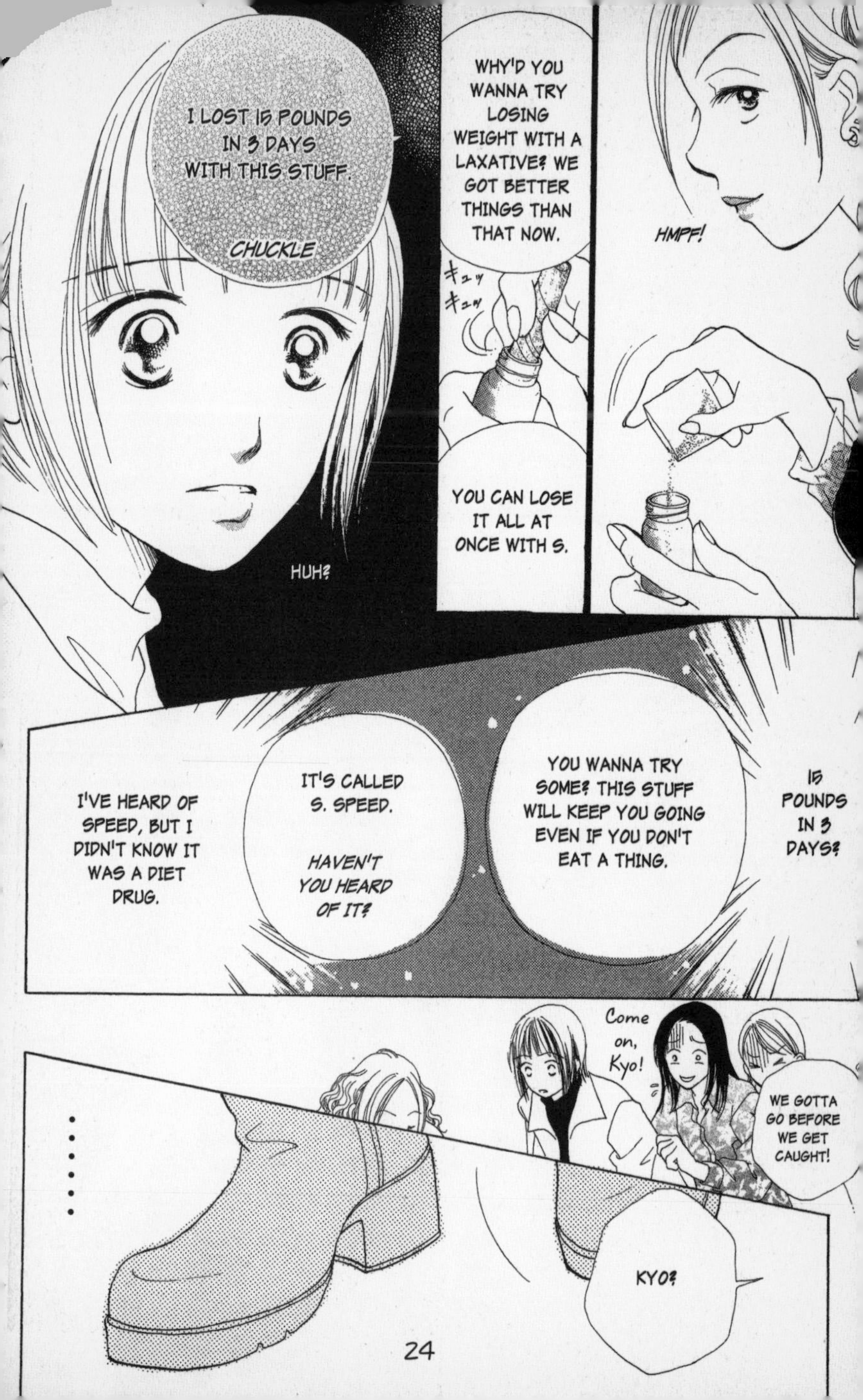
HMPF!
WHY'D YOU WANNA TRY LOSING WEIGHT WITH A LAXATIVE? WE GOT BETTER THINGS THAN THAT NOW.
キュッ キュッ
YOU CAN LOSE IT ALL AT ONCE WITH S.
I LOST 15 POUNDS IN 3 DAYS WITH THIS STUFF.
CHUCKLE
HUH?
15 POUNDS IN 3 DAYS?
YOU WANNA TRY SOME? THIS STUFF WILL KEEP YOU GOING EVEN IF YOU DON'T EAT A THING.
IT'S CALLED S. SPEED.
HAVEN'T YOU HEARD OF IT?
I'VE HEARD OF SPEED, BUT I DIDN'T KNOW IT WAS A DIET DRUG.
WE GOTTA GO BEFORE WE GET CAUGHT!
Come on, Kyo!
KYO?
......

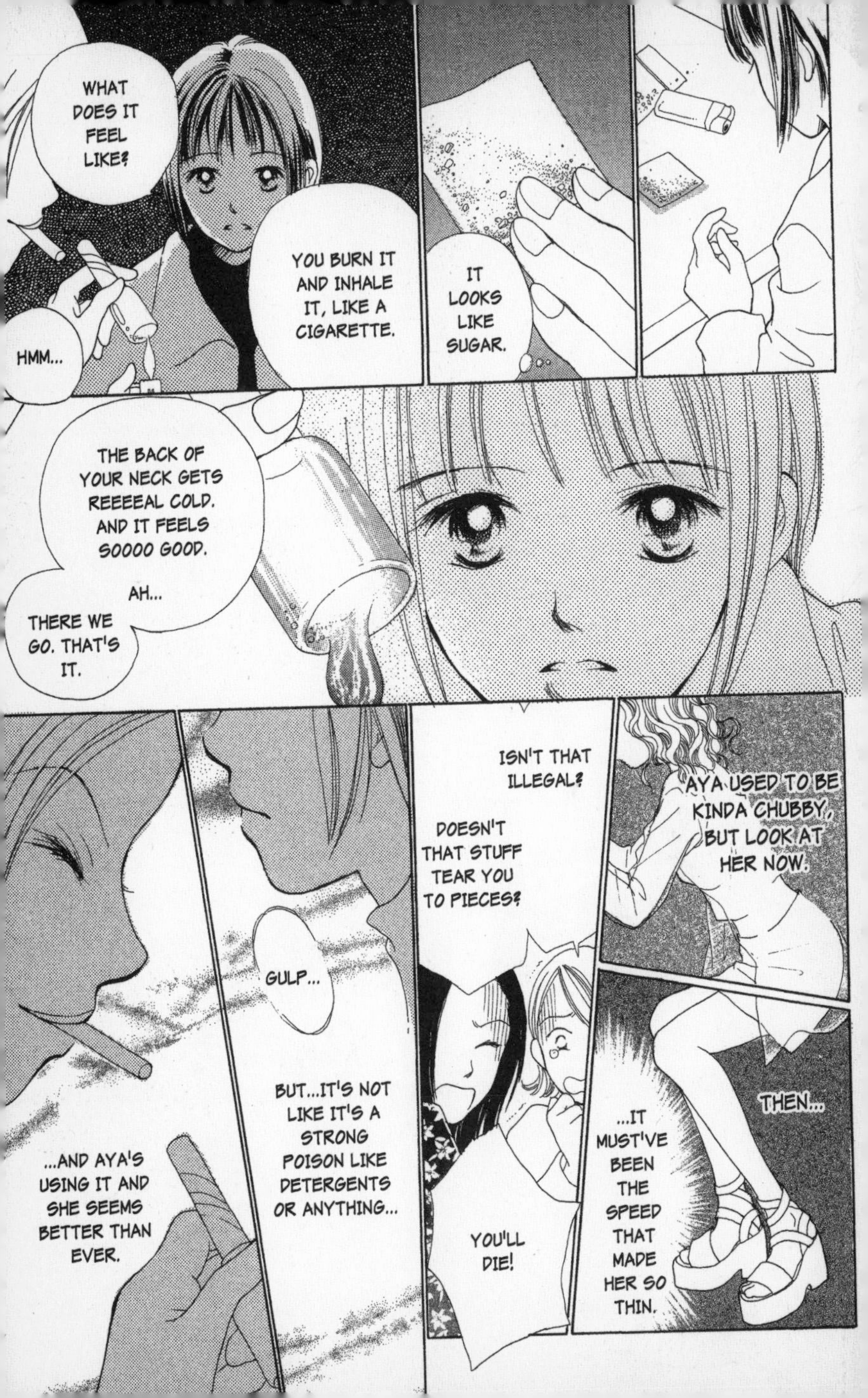

IT LOOKS LIKE SUGAR.
WHAT DOES IT FEEL LIKE?
YOU BURN IT AND INHALE IT, LIKE A CIGARETTE.
HMM...
THE BACK OF YOUR NECK GETS REEEEAL COLD. AND IT FEELS SOOOO GOOD.
AH...
THERE WE GO. THAT'S IT.
AYA USED TO BE KINDA CHUBBY, BUT LOOK AT HER NOW.
THEN...
...IT MUST'VE BEEN THE SPEED THAT MADE HER SO THIN.
ISN'T THAT ILLEGAL?
DOESN'T THAT STUFF TEAR YOU TO PIECES?
YOU'LL DIE!
GULP...
BUT...IT'S NOT LIKE IT'S A STRONG POISON LIKE DETERGENTS OR ANYTHING...
...AND AYA'S USING IT AND SHE SEEMS BETTER THAN EVER.

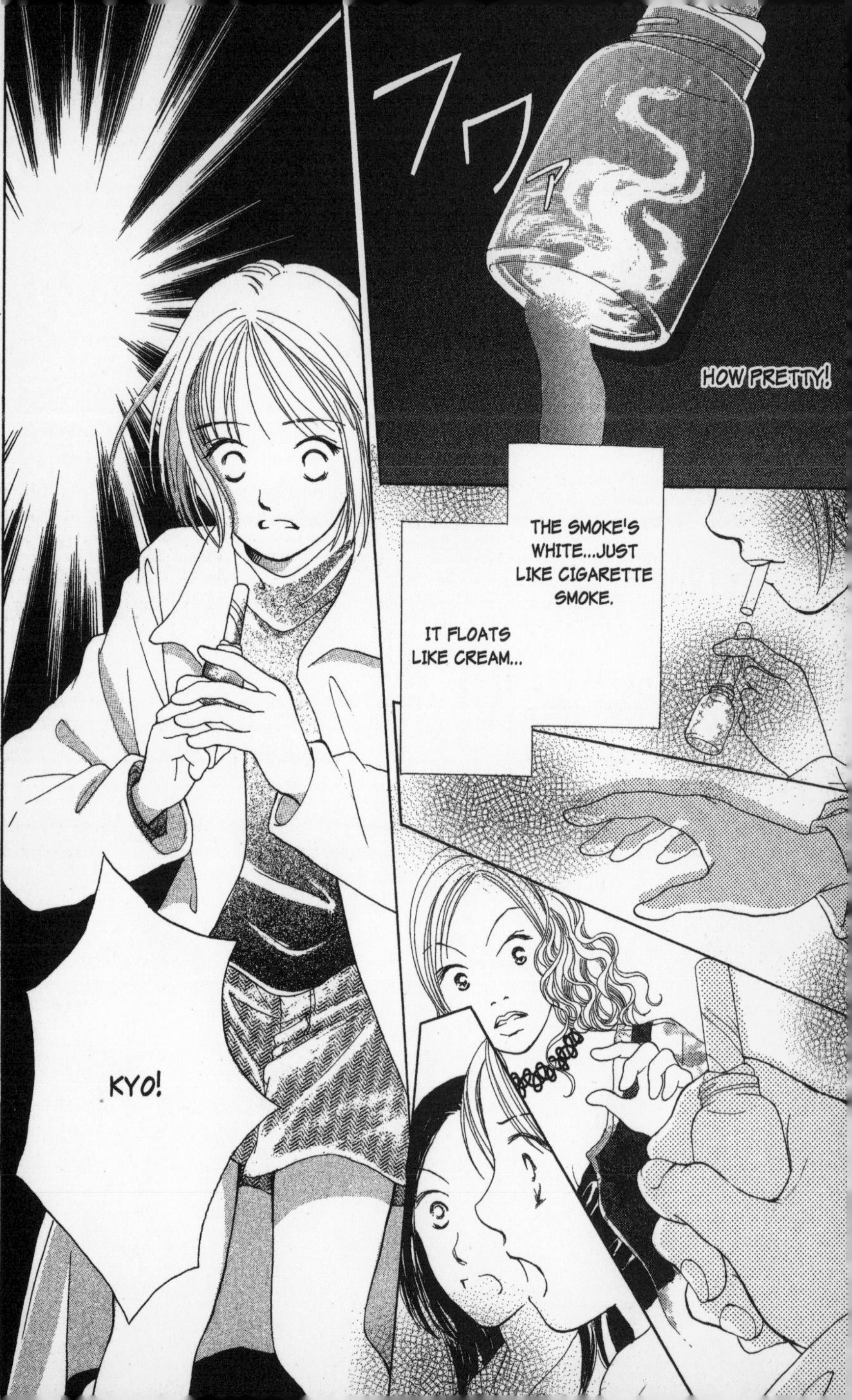
フワァ
HOW PRETTY!
THE SMOKE'S WHITE...JUST LIKE CIGARETTE SMOKE.
IT FLOATS LIKE CREAM...
KYO!

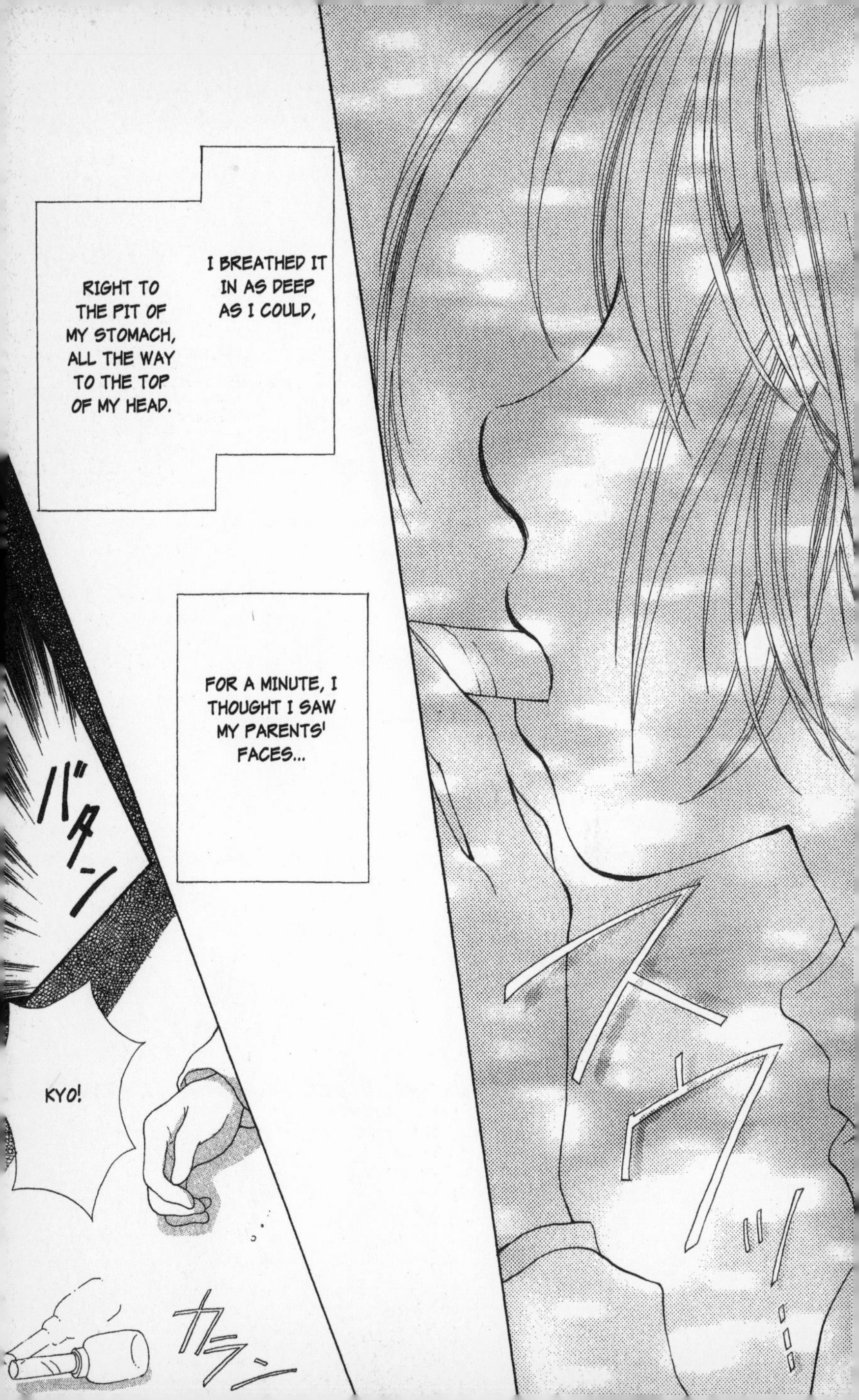

I BREATHED IT IN AS DEEP AS I COULD,
RIGHT TO THE PIT OF MY STOMACH, ALL THE WAY TO THE TOP OF MY HEAD.
FOR A MINUTE, I THOUGHT I SAW MY PARENTS' FACES...
バタン
KYO!
カラン

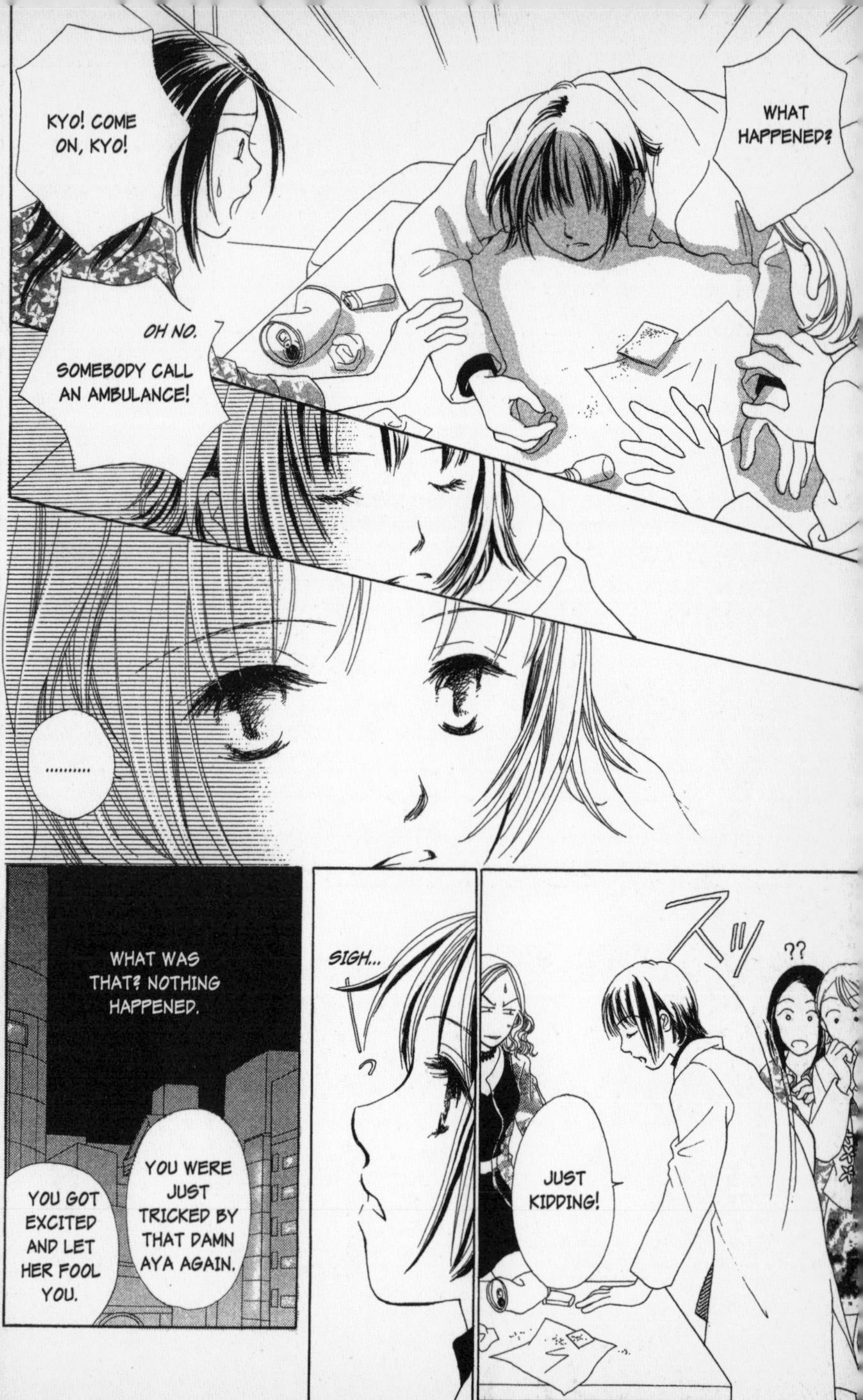
WHAT HAPPENED?
KYO! COME ON, KYO!
OH NO.
SOMEBODY CALL AN AMBULANCE!
....
??
スッ
JUST KIDDING!
SIGH...
WHAT WAS THAT? NOTHING HAPPENED.
YOU WERE JUST TRICKED BY THAT DAMN AYA AGAIN.
YOU GOT EXCITED AND LET HER FOOL YOU.

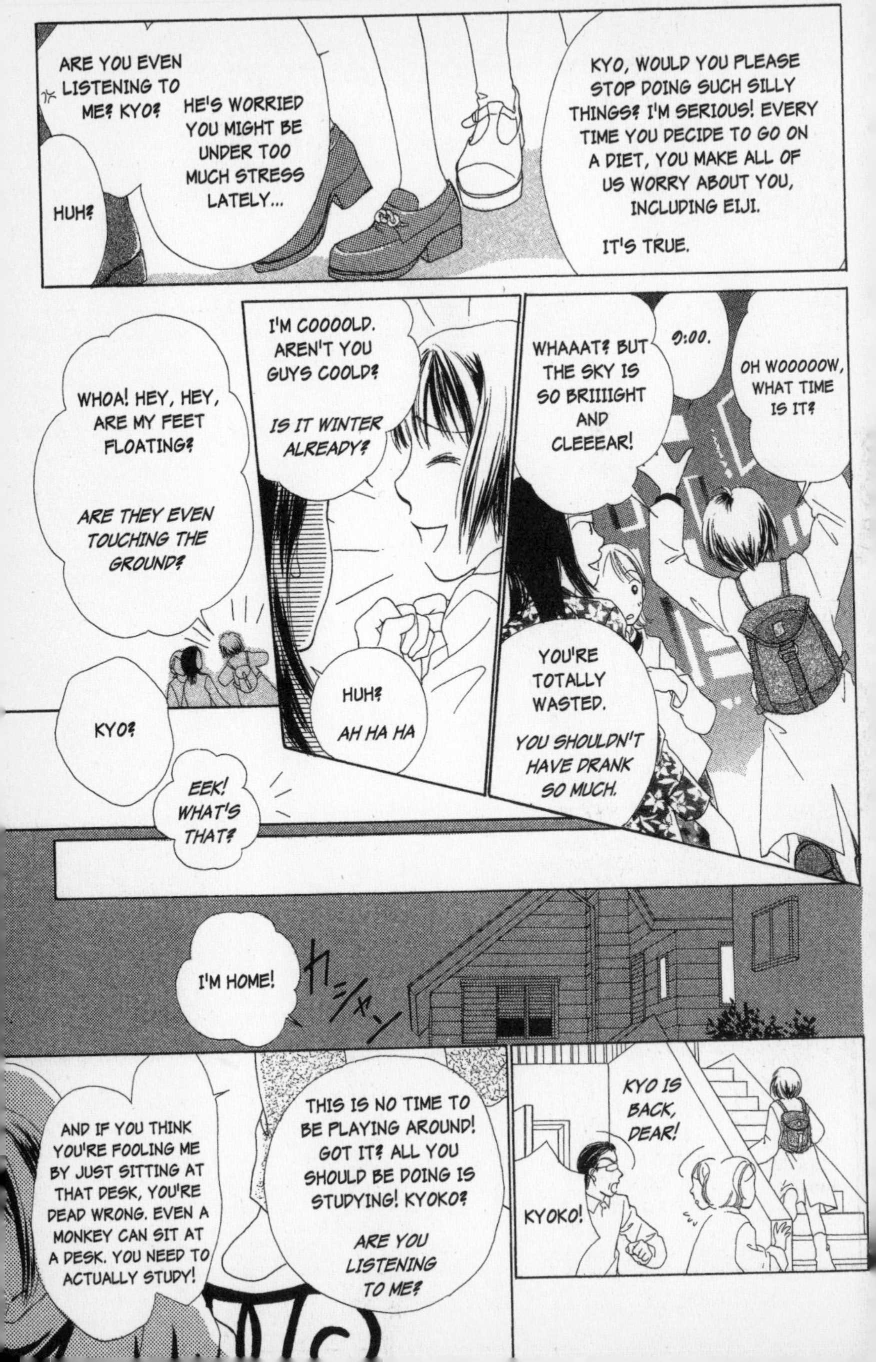
KYO, WOULD YOU PLEASE STOP DOING SUCH SILLY THINGS? I'M SERIOUS! EVERY TIME YOU DECIDE TO GO ON A DIET, YOU MAKE ALL OF US WORRY ABOUT YOU, INCLUDING EIJI.
IT'S TRUE.
ARE YOU EVEN LISTENING TO ME? KYO?
HE'S WORRIED YOU MIGHT BE UNDER TOO MUCH STRESS LATELY...
HUH?
OH WOOOOW, WHAT TIME IS IT?
9:00.
WHAAAT? BUT THE SKY IS SO BRIIIIGHT AND CLEEEAR!
YOU'RE TOTALLY WASTED.
YOU SHOULDN'T HAVE DRANK SO MUCH.
I'M COOOOLD. AREN'T YOU GUYS COOLD?
IS IT WINTER ALREADY?
HUH?
AH HA HA
WHOA! HEY, HEY, ARE MY FEET FLOATING?
ARE THEY EVEN TOUCHING THE GROUND?
KYO?
EEK! WHAT'S THAT?
I'M HOME!
KYO IS BACK, DEAR!
KYOKO!
THIS IS NO TIME TO BE PLAYING AROUND! GOT IT? ALL YOU SHOULD BE DOING IS STUDYING! KYOKO?
ARE YOU LISTENING TO ME?
AND IF YOU THINK YOU'RE FOOLING ME BY JUST SITTING AT THAT DESK, YOU'RE DEAD WRONG. EVEN A MONKEY CAN SIT AT A DESK. YOU NEED TO ACTUALLY STUDY!

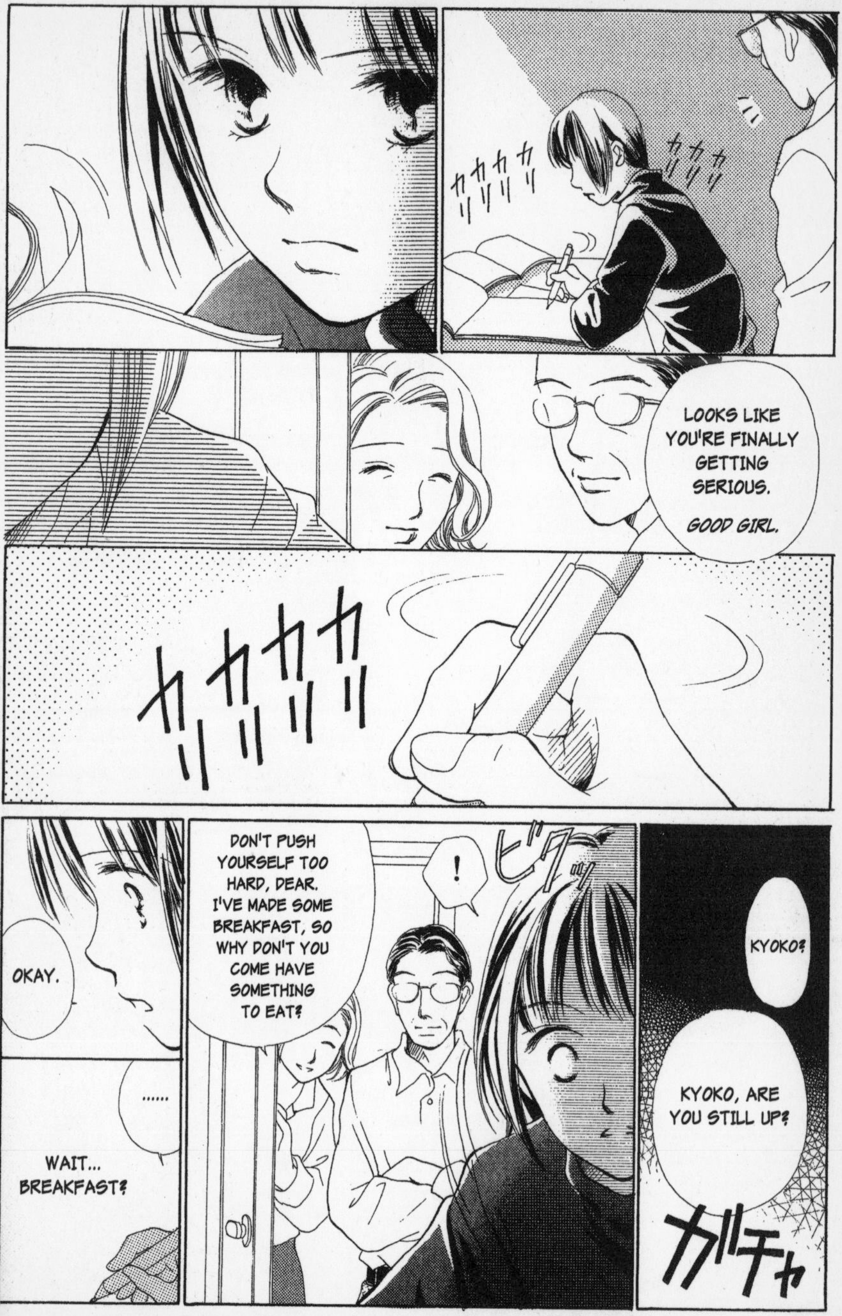
LOOKS LIKE YOU'RE FINALLY GETTING SERIOUS.
GOOD GIRL.
KYOKO?
KYOKO, ARE YOU STILL UP?
!
DON'T PUSH YOURSELF TOO HARD, DEAR. I'VE MADE SOME BREAKFAST, SO WHY DON'T YOU COME HAVE SOMETHING TO EAT?
OKAY.
......
WAIT... BREAKFAST?

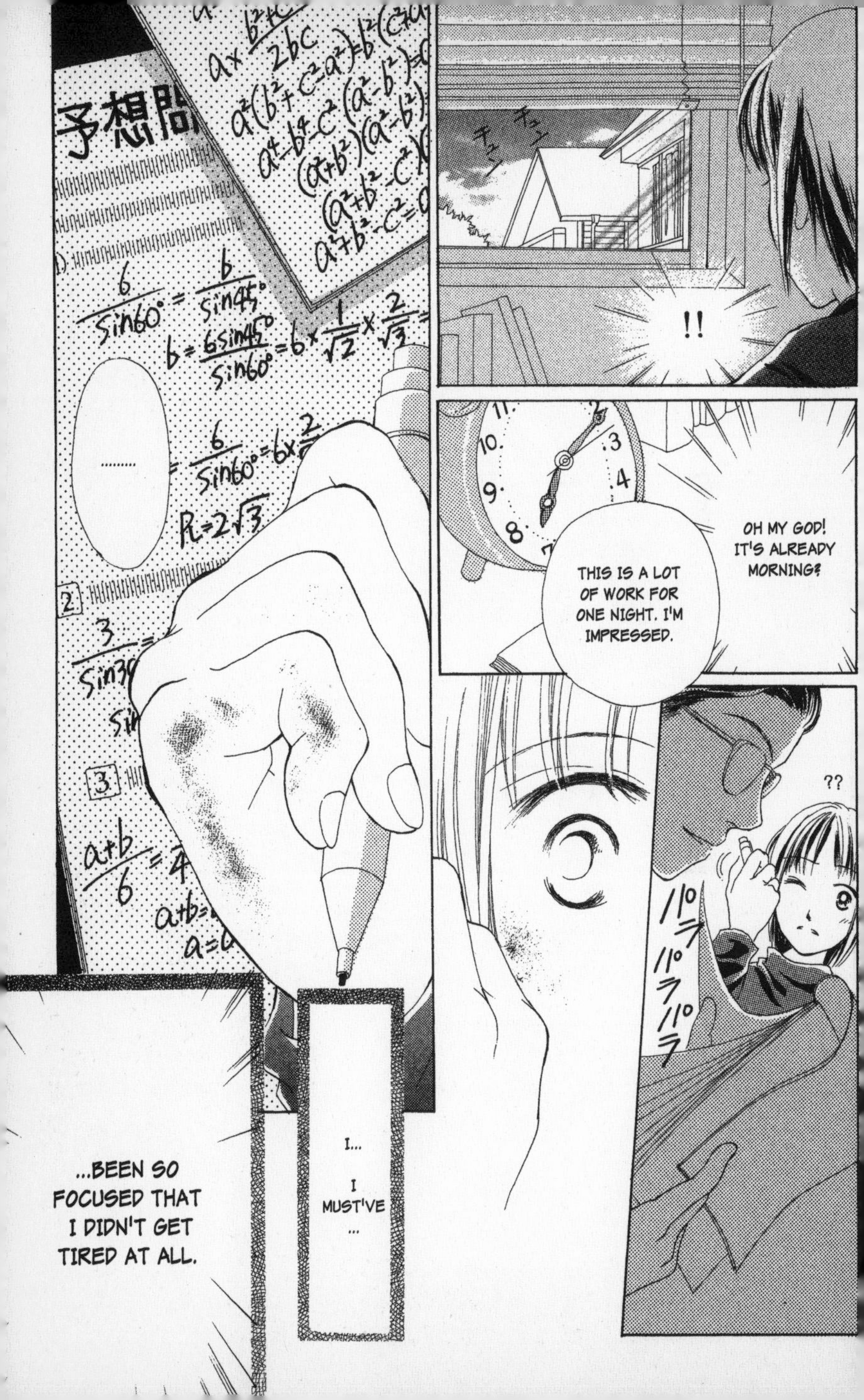

チュン
チュン
!!
OH MY GOD! IT'S ALREADY MORNING?
THIS IS A LOT OF WORK FOR ONE NIGHT. I'M IMPRESSED.
??
パラ
パラ
パラ
予想問
......
I...
I MUST'VE...
...BEEN SO FOCUSED THAT I DIDN'T GET TIRED AT ALL.

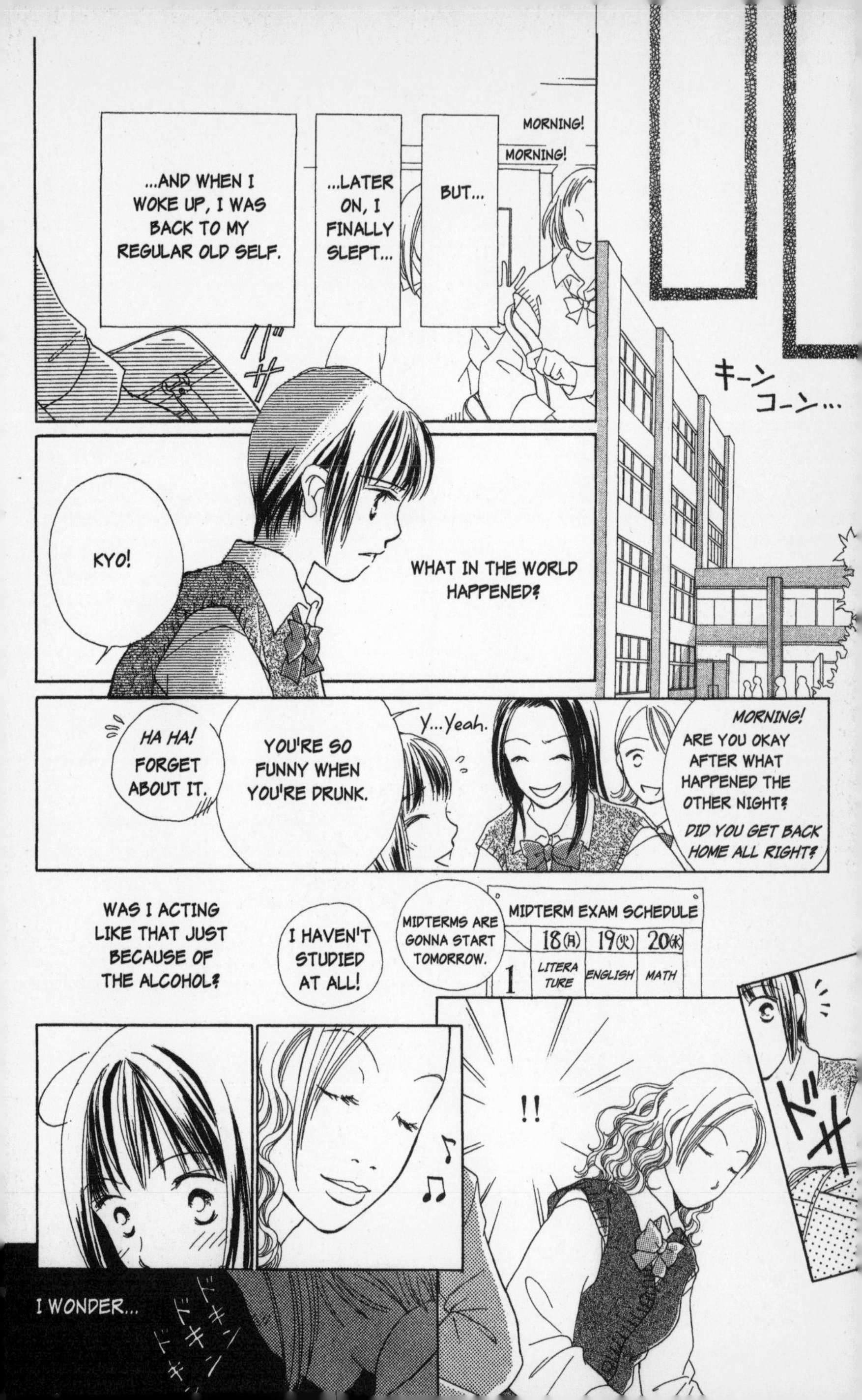
キーン
コーン…
MORNING!
MORNING!
BUT...
...LATER ON, I FINALLY SLEPT...
...AND WHEN I WOKE UP, I WAS BACK TO MY REGULAR OLD SELF.
バサ
WHAT IN THE WORLD HAPPENED?
KYO!
MORNING!
ARE YOU OKAY AFTER WHAT HAPPENED THE OTHER NIGHT?
DID YOU GET BACK HOME ALL RIGHT?
Y...Yeah.
YOU'RE SO FUNNY WHEN YOU'RE DRUNK.
HA HA! FORGET ABOUT IT.
MIDTERM EXAM SCHEDULE
18(月) 19(火) 20(水)
1 LITERATURE ENGLISH MATH
MIDTERMS ARE GONNA START TOMORROW.
I HAVEN'T STUDIED AT ALL!
WAS I ACTING LIKE THAT JUST BECAUSE OF THE ALCOHOL?
ドキ
!!
I WONDER...
ドキン
ドキン
ドキン

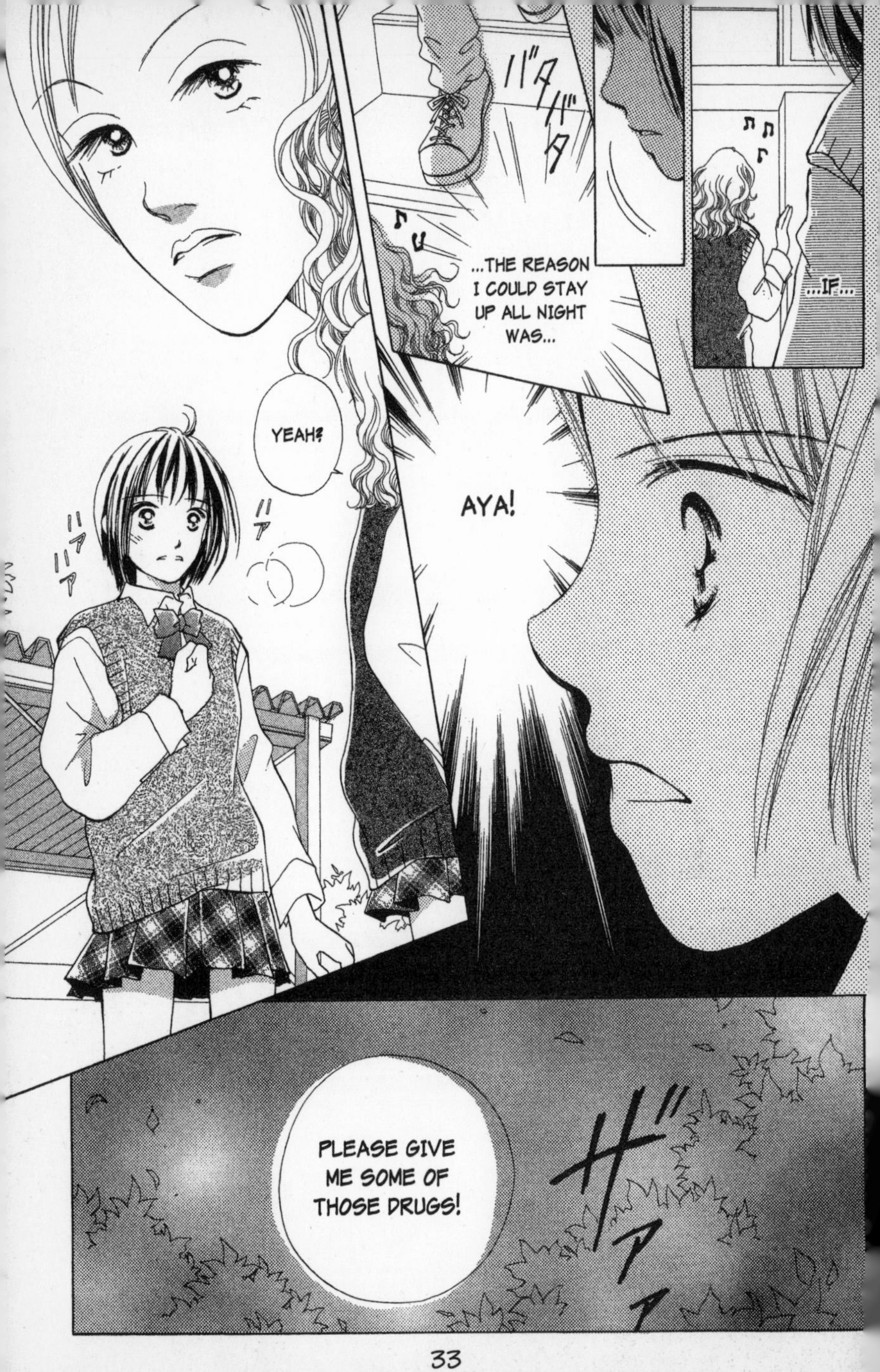
...IF...
...THE REASON I COULD STAY UP ALL NIGHT WAS...
AYA!
YEAH?
PLEASE GIVE ME SOME OF THOSE DRUGS!

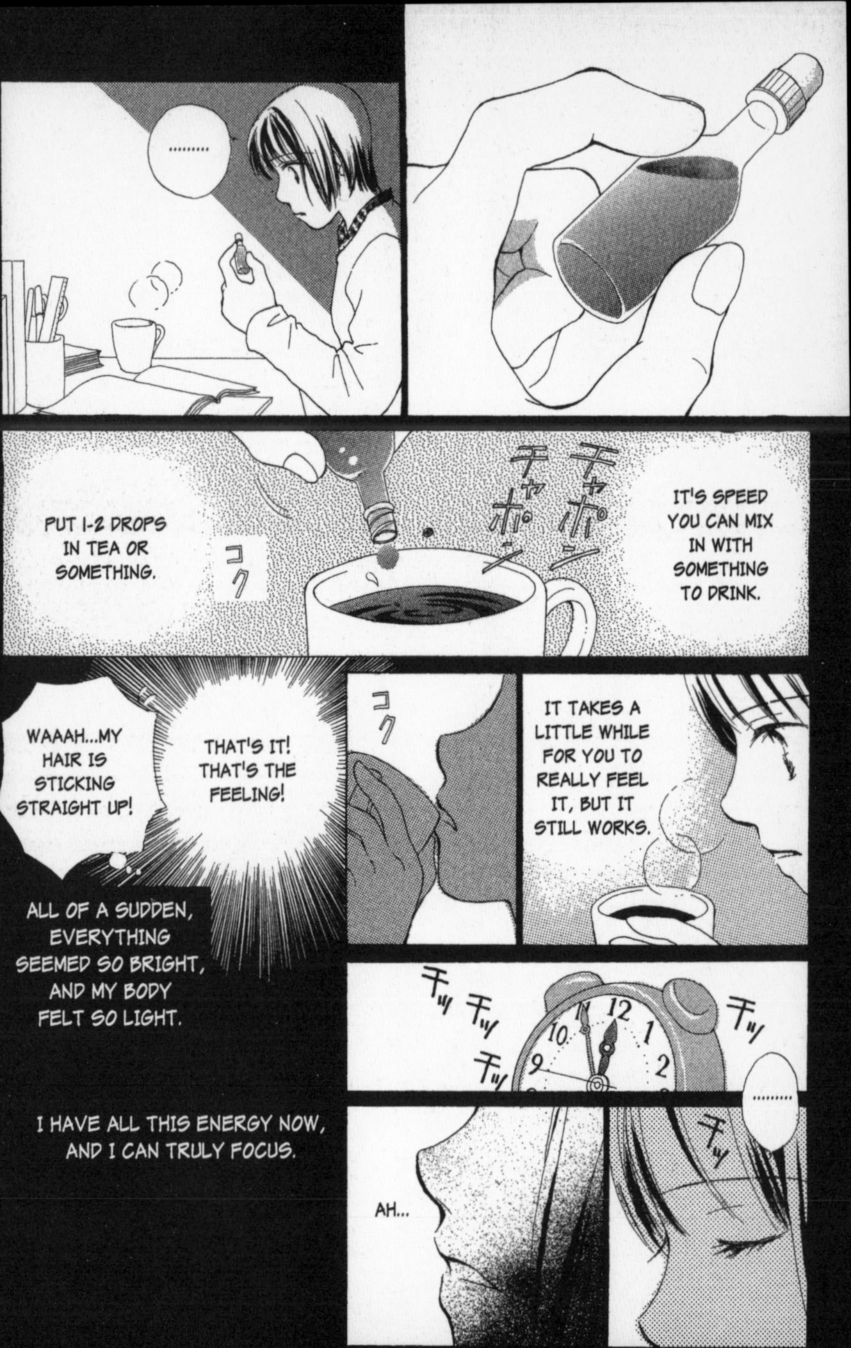
....
IT'S SPEED YOU CAN MIX IN WITH SOMETHING TO DRINK.
チャポン
チャポン
コク
PUT 1-2 DROPS IN TEA OR SOMETHING.
IT TAKES A LITTLE WHILE FOR YOU TO REALLY FEEL IT, BUT IT STILL WORKS.
コク
THAT'S IT! THAT'S THE FEELING!
WAAAH...MY HAIR IS STICKING STRAIGHT UP!
ALL OF A SUDDEN, EVERYTHING SEEMED SO BRIGHT, AND MY BODY FELT SO LIGHT.
チッ
チッ
チッ
チッ
....
チッ
AH...
I HAVE ALL THIS ENERGY NOW, AND I CAN TRULY FOCUS.

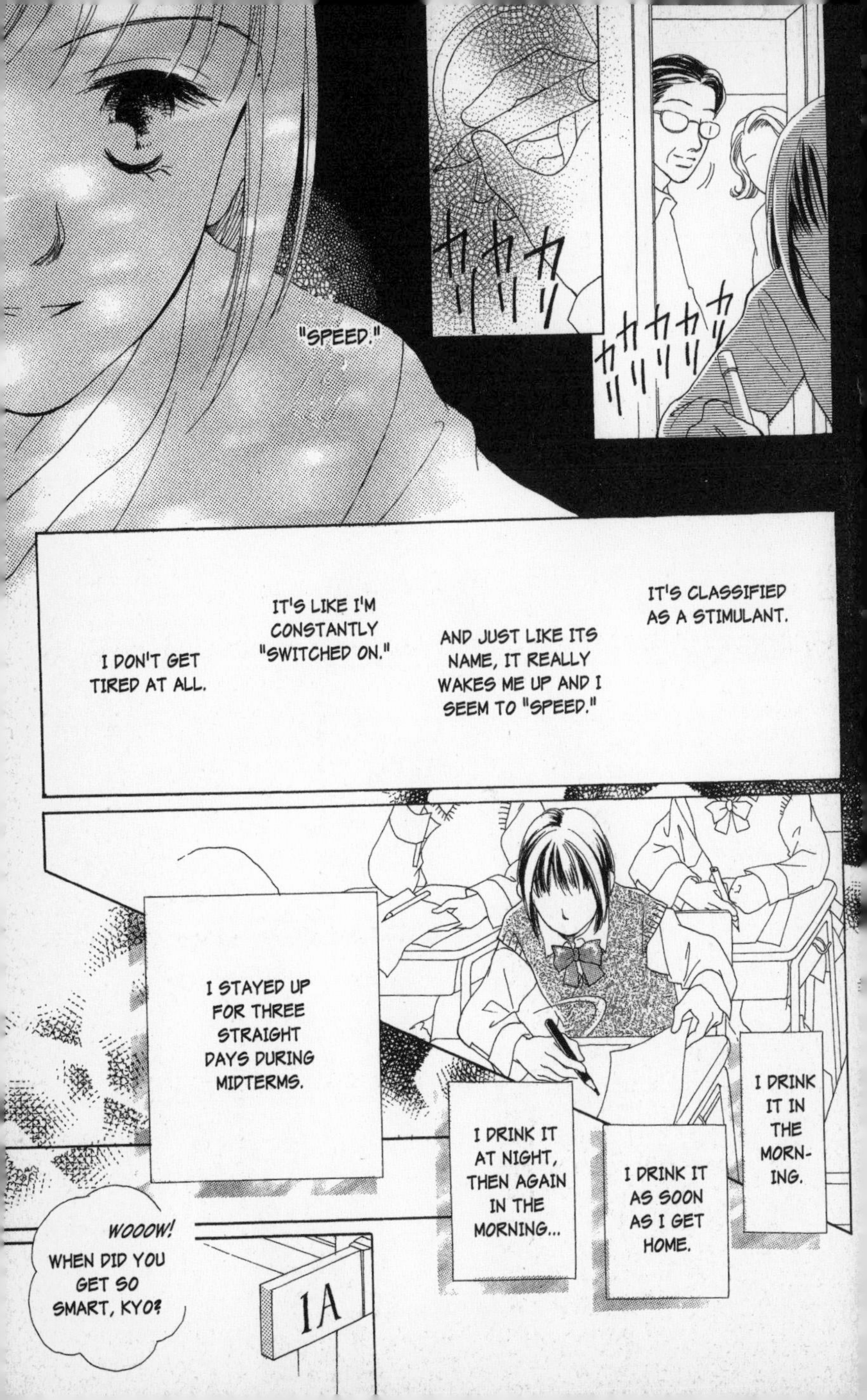
"SPEED."
IT'S CLASSIFIED AS A STIMULANT.
AND JUST LIKE ITS NAME, IT REALLY WAKES ME UP AND I SEEM TO "SPEED."
IT'S LIKE I'M CONSTANTLY "SWITCHED ON."
I DON'T GET TIRED AT ALL.
I DRINK IT IN THE MORN-ING.
I DRINK IT AS SOON AS I GET HOME.
I DRINK IT AT NIGHT, THEN AGAIN IN THE MORNING...
I STAYED UP FOR THREE STRAIGHT DAYS DURING MIDTERMS.
WOOOW! WHEN DID YOU GET SO SMART, KYO?
1A

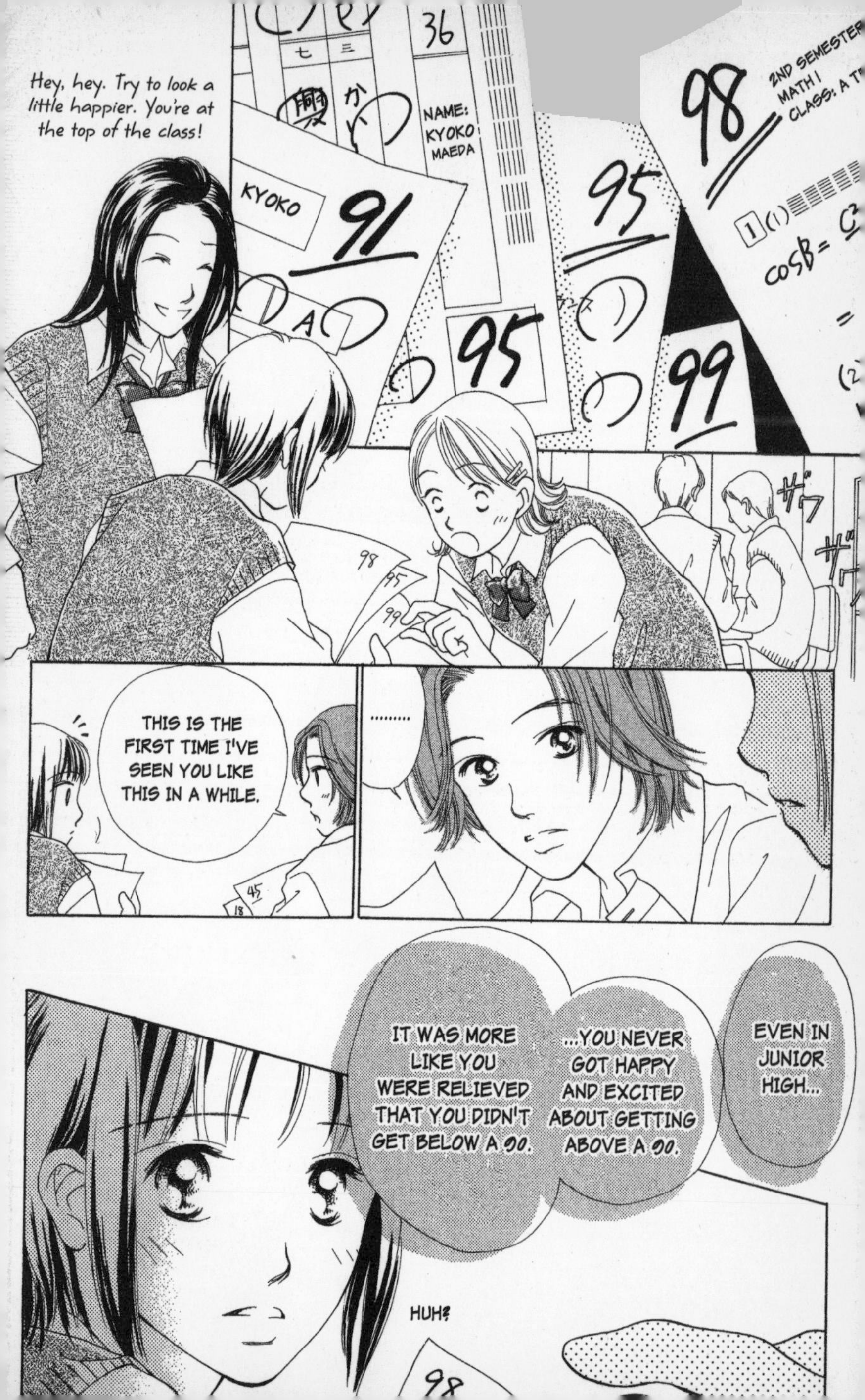
2ND SEMESTER MATH I CLASS: A
98
95
99
NAME: KYOKO MAEDA
95
KYOKO
91
Hey, hey. Try to look a little happier. You're at the top of the class!
....
THIS IS THE FIRST TIME I'VE SEEN YOU LIKE THIS IN A WHILE.
EVEN IN JUNIOR HIGH...
...YOU NEVER GOT HAPPY AND EXCITED ABOUT GETTING ABOVE A 90.
IT WAS MORE LIKE YOU WERE RELIEVED THAT YOU DIDN'T GET BELOW A 90.
HUH?

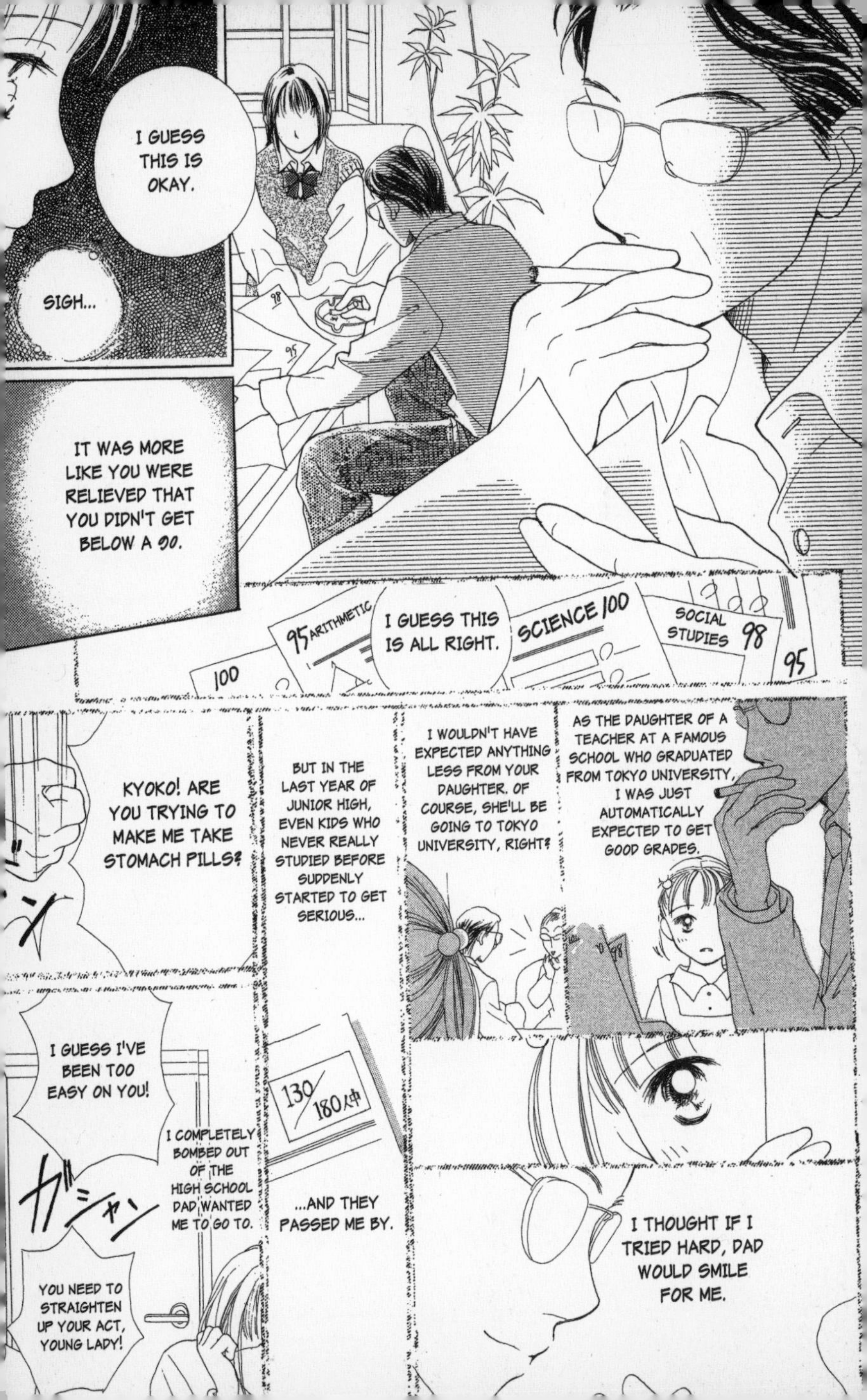
I GUESS THIS IS ALL RIGHT.
SCIENCE 100
SOCIAL STUDIES 98
95 ARITHMETIC
I GUESS THIS IS OKAY.
SIGH...
IT WAS MORE LIKE YOU WERE RELIEVED THAT YOU DIDN'T GET BELOW A 90.
AS THE DAUGHTER OF A TEACHER AT A FAMOUS SCHOOL WHO GRADUATED FROM TOKYO UNIVERSITY, I WAS JUST AUTOMATICALLY EXPECTED TO GET GOOD GRADES.
I WOULDN'T HAVE EXPECTED ANYTHING LESS FROM YOUR DAUGHTER. OF COURSE, SHE'LL BE GOING TO TOKYO UNIVERSITY, RIGHT?
I THOUGHT IF I TRIED HARD, DAD WOULD SMILE FOR ME.
BUT IN THE LAST YEAR OF JUNIOR HIGH, EVEN KIDS WHO NEVER REALLY STUDIED BEFORE SUDDENLY STARTED TO GET SERIOUS...
130/180人中
...AND THEY PASSED ME BY.
I COMPLETELY BOMBED OUT OF THE HIGH SCHOOL DAD WANTED ME TO GO TO.
KYOKO! ARE YOU TRYING TO MAKE ME TAKE STOMACH PILLS?
I GUESS I'VE BEEN TOO EASY ON YOU!
ガシャン
YOU NEED TO STRAIGHTEN UP YOUR ACT, YOUNG LADY!

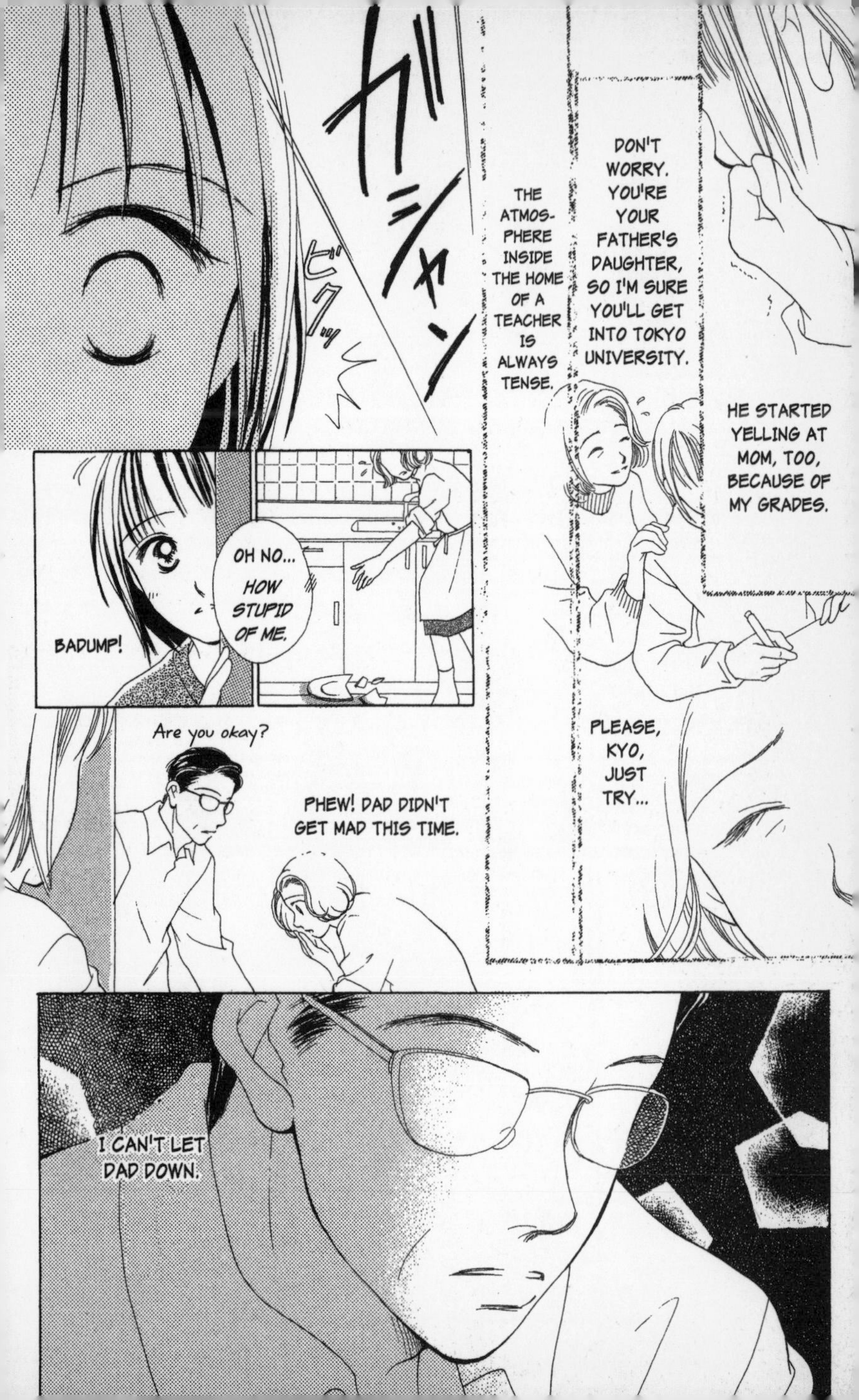
THE ATMOSPHERE INSIDE THE HOME OF A TEACHER IS ALWAYS TENSE.
DON'T WORRY. YOU'RE YOUR FATHER'S DAUGHTER, SO I'M SURE YOU'LL GET INTO TOKYO UNIVERSITY.
HE STARTED YELLING AT MOM, TOO, BECAUSE OF MY GRADES.
PLEASE, KYO, JUST TRY...
ガシャン
ビクッ
OH NO... HOW STUPID OF ME.
BADUMP!
Are you okay?
PHEW! DAD DIDN'T GET MAD THIS TIME.
I CAN'T LET DAD DOWN.

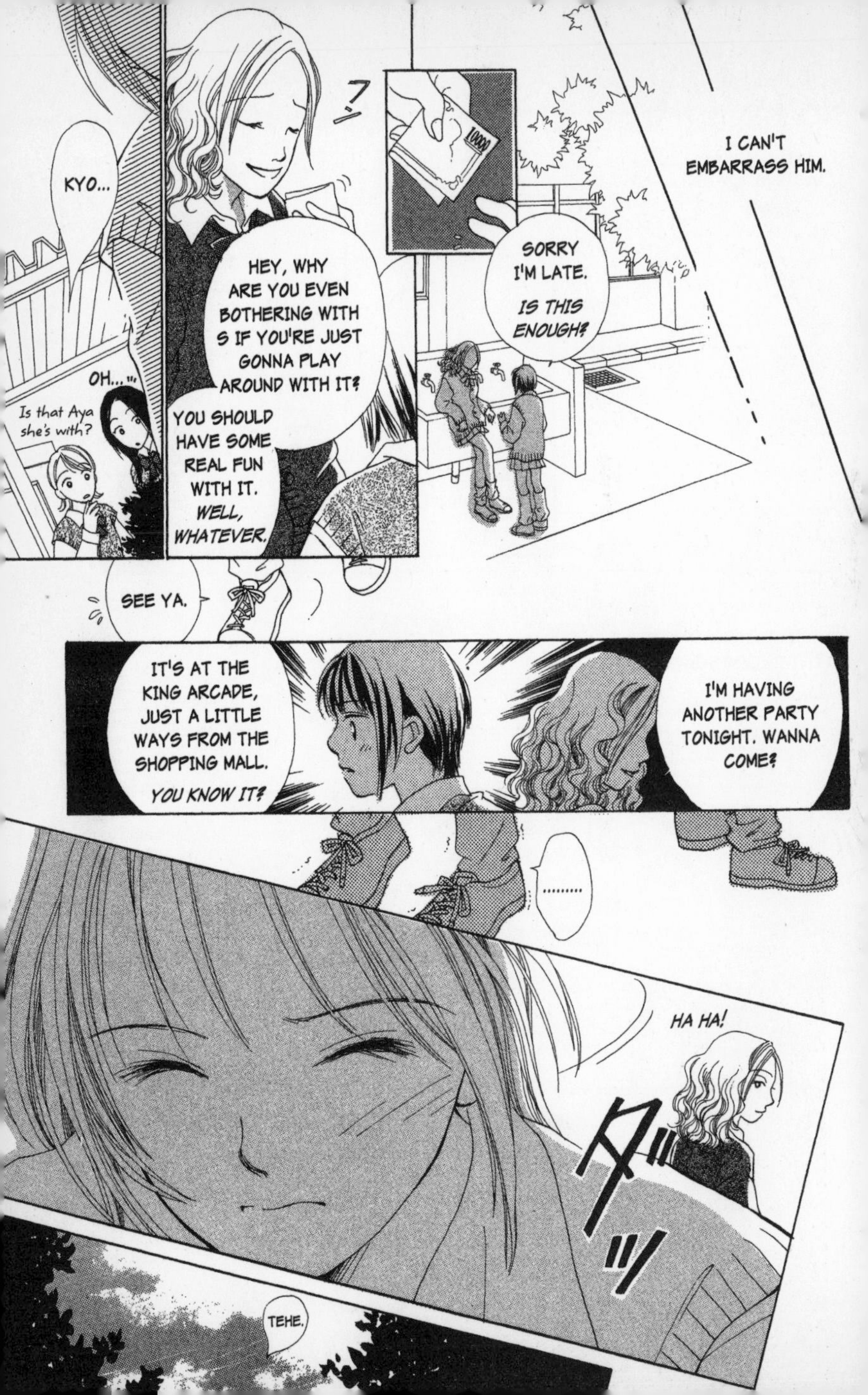
I CAN'T EMBARRASS HIM.
SORRY I'M LATE. IS THIS ENOUGH?
HEY, WHY ARE YOU EVEN BOTHERING WITH S IF YOU'RE JUST GONNA PLAY AROUND WITH IT?
YOU SHOULD HAVE SOME REAL FUN WITH IT. WELL, WHATEVER.
KYO...
OH...
Is that Aya she's with?
SEE YA.
I'M HAVING ANOTHER PARTY TONIGHT. WANNA COME?
IT'S AT THE KING ARCADE, JUST A LITTLE WAYS FROM THE SHOPPING MALL. YOU KNOW IT?
....
HA HA!
TEHE.

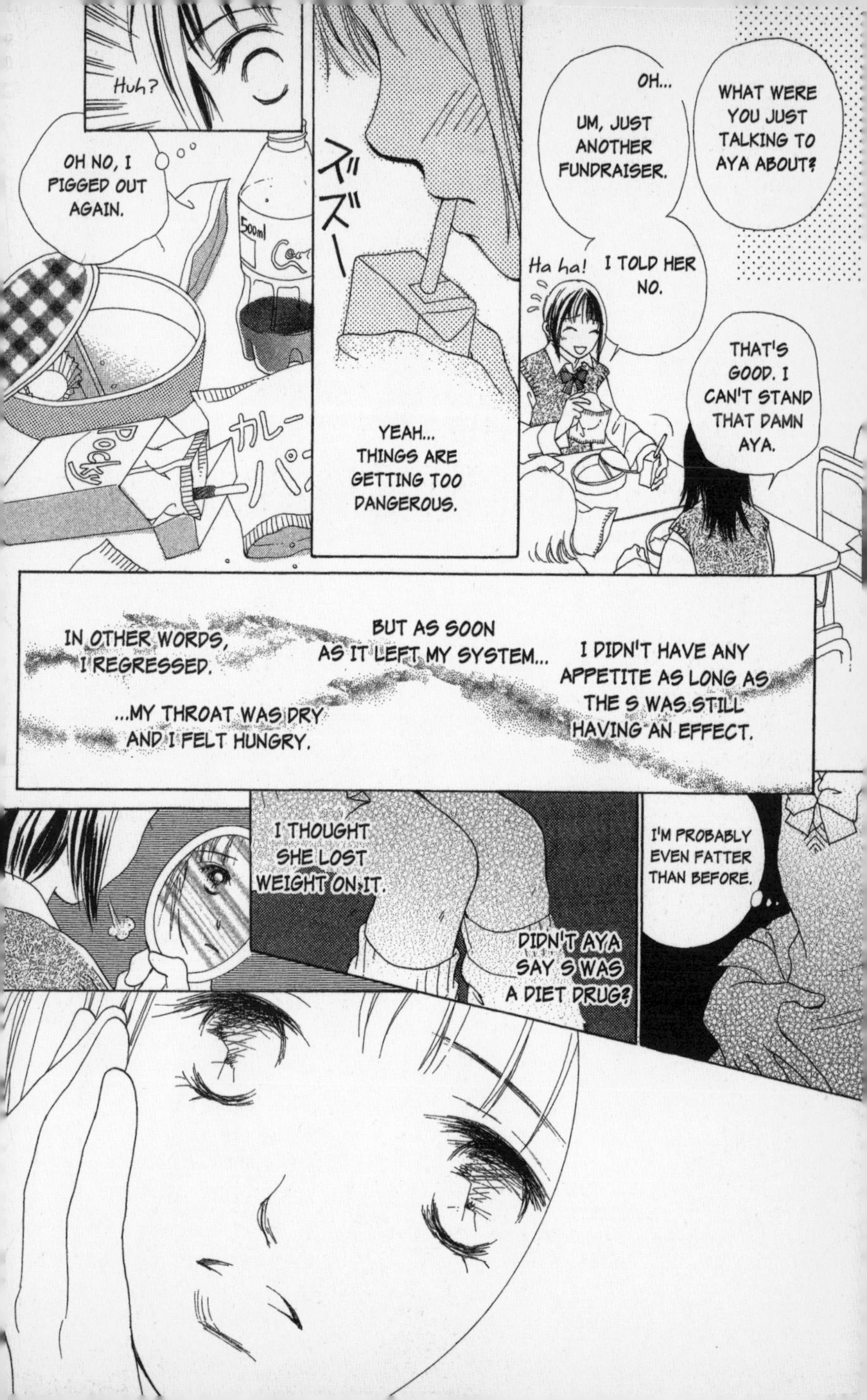
WHAT WERE YOU JUST TALKING TO AYA ABOUT?
OH... UM, JUST ANOTHER FUNDRAISER.
Ha ha! I TOLD HER NO.
THAT'S GOOD. I CAN'T STAND THAT DAMN AYA.
ズズー
YEAH... THINGS ARE GETTING TOO DANGEROUS.
Huh?
OH NO, I PIGGED OUT AGAIN.
500ml
Pocky
I DIDN'T HAVE ANY APPETITE AS LONG AS THE S WAS STILL HAVING AN EFFECT.
BUT AS SOON AS IT LEFT MY SYSTEM...
...MY THROAT WAS DRY AND I FELT HUNGRY.
IN OTHER WORDS, I REGRESSED.
I'M PROBABLY EVEN FATTER THAN BEFORE.
DIDN'T AYA SAY S WAS A DIET DRUG?
I THOUGHT SHE LOST WEIGHT ON IT.

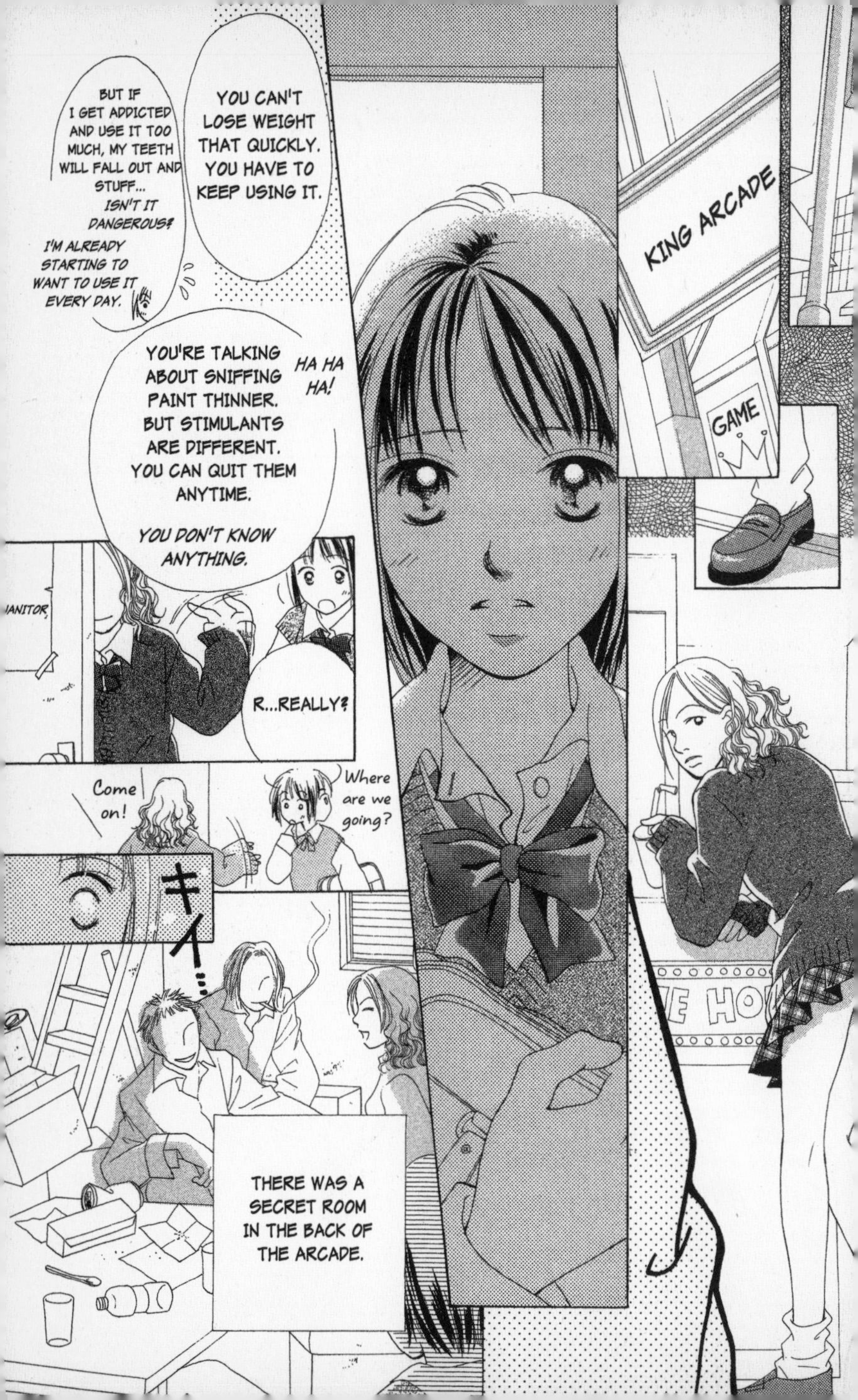
KING ARCADE
GAME
YOU CAN'T LOSE WEIGHT THAT QUICKLY. YOU HAVE TO KEEP USING IT.
BUT IF I GET ADDICTED AND USE IT TOO MUCH, MY TEETH WILL FALL OUT AND STUFF... ISN'T IT DANGEROUS?
I'M ALREADY STARTING TO WANT TO USE IT EVERY DAY.
HA HA HA!
YOU'RE TALKING ABOUT SNIFFING PAINT THINNER. BUT STIMULANTS ARE DIFFERENT. YOU CAN QUIT THEM ANYTIME.
YOU DON'T KNOW ANYTHING.
R...REALLY?
Where are we going?
Come on!
キィ...
THERE WAS A SECRET ROOM IN THE BACK OF THE ARCADE.

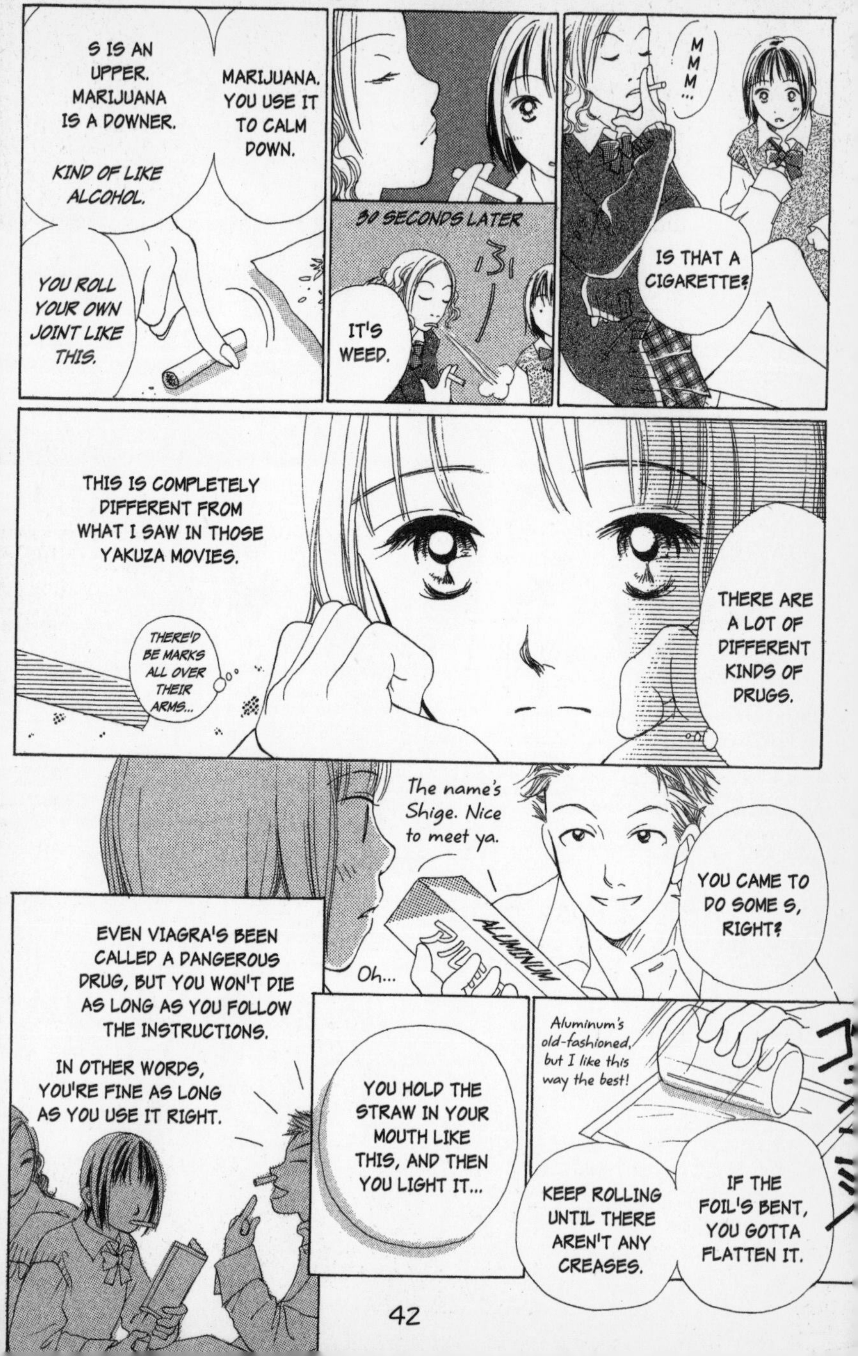
MMM...
IS THAT A CIGARETTE?
30 SECONDS LATER
IT'S WEED.
MARIJUANA. YOU USE IT TO CALM DOWN.
S IS AN UPPER. MARIJUANA IS A DOWNER.
KIND OF LIKE ALCOHOL.
YOU ROLL YOUR OWN JOINT LIKE THIS.
THERE ARE A LOT OF DIFFERENT KINDS OF DRUGS.
THIS IS COMPLETELY DIFFERENT FROM WHAT I SAW IN THOSE YAKUZA MOVIES.
THERE'D BE MARKS ALL OVER THEIR ARMS...
The name's Shige. Nice to meet ya.
YOU CAME TO DO SOME S, RIGHT?
ALUMINUM
Oh...
Aluminum's old-fashioned, but I like this way the best!
IF THE FOIL'S BENT, YOU GOTTA FLATTEN IT.
KEEP ROLLING UNTIL THERE AREN'T ANY CREASES.
YOU HOLD THE STRAW IN YOUR MOUTH LIKE THIS, AND THEN YOU LIGHT IT...
EVEN VIAGRA'S BEEN CALLED A DANGEROUS DRUG, BUT YOU WON'T DIE AS LONG AS YOU FOLLOW THE INSTRUCTIONS.
IN OTHER WORDS, YOU'RE FINE AS LONG AS YOU USE IT RIGHT.

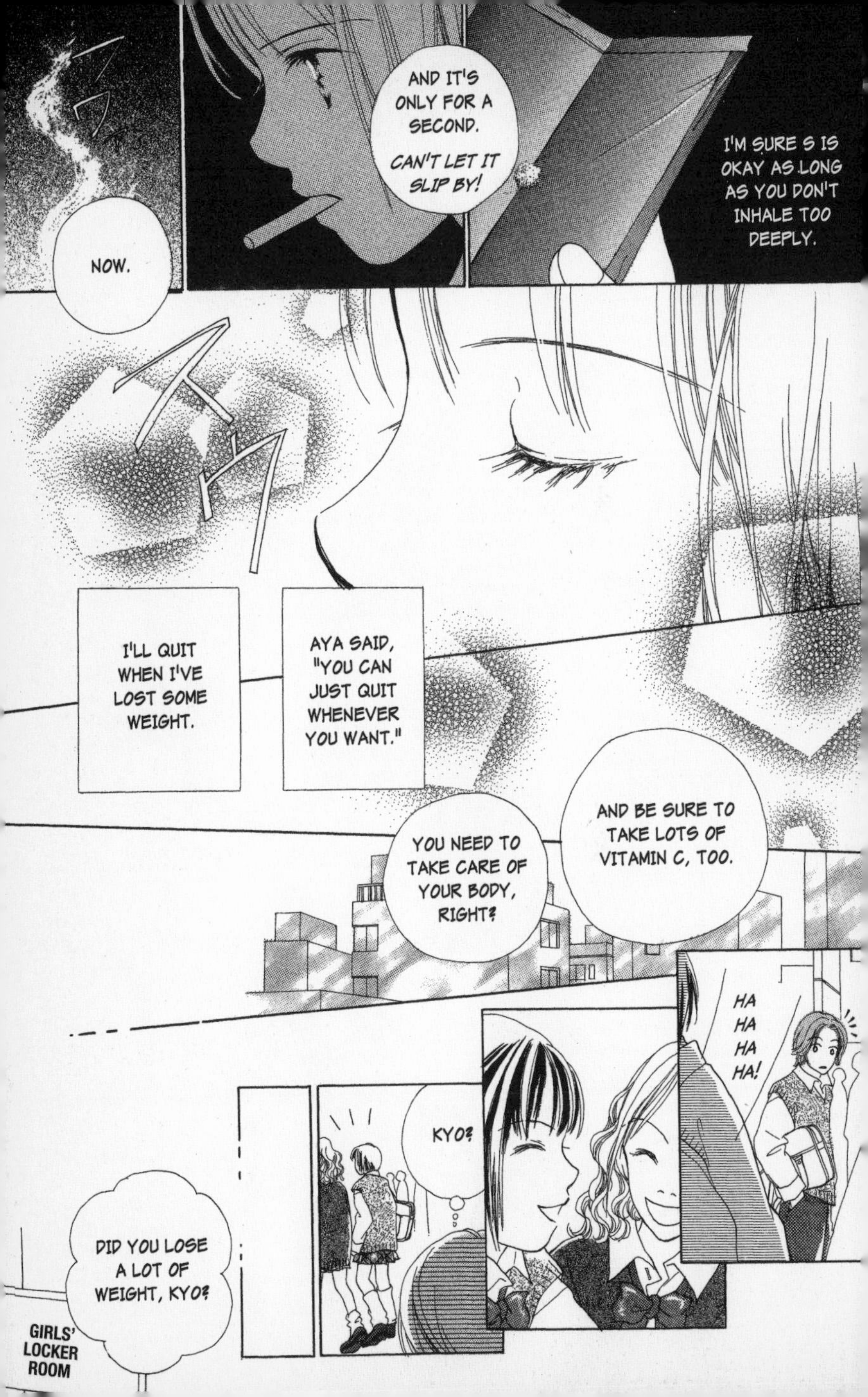
I'M SURE S IS OKAY AS LONG AS YOU DON'T INHALE TOO DEEPLY.
AND IT'S ONLY FOR A SECOND.
CAN'T LET IT SLIP BY!
NOW.
AYA SAID, "YOU CAN JUST QUIT WHENEVER YOU WANT."
I'LL QUIT WHEN I'VE LOST SOME WEIGHT.
AND BE SURE TO TAKE LOTS OF VITAMIN C, TOO.
YOU NEED TO TAKE CARE OF YOUR BODY, RIGHT?
HA HA HA HA!
KYO?
DID YOU LOSE A LOT OF WEIGHT, KYO?
GIRLS' LOCKER ROOM

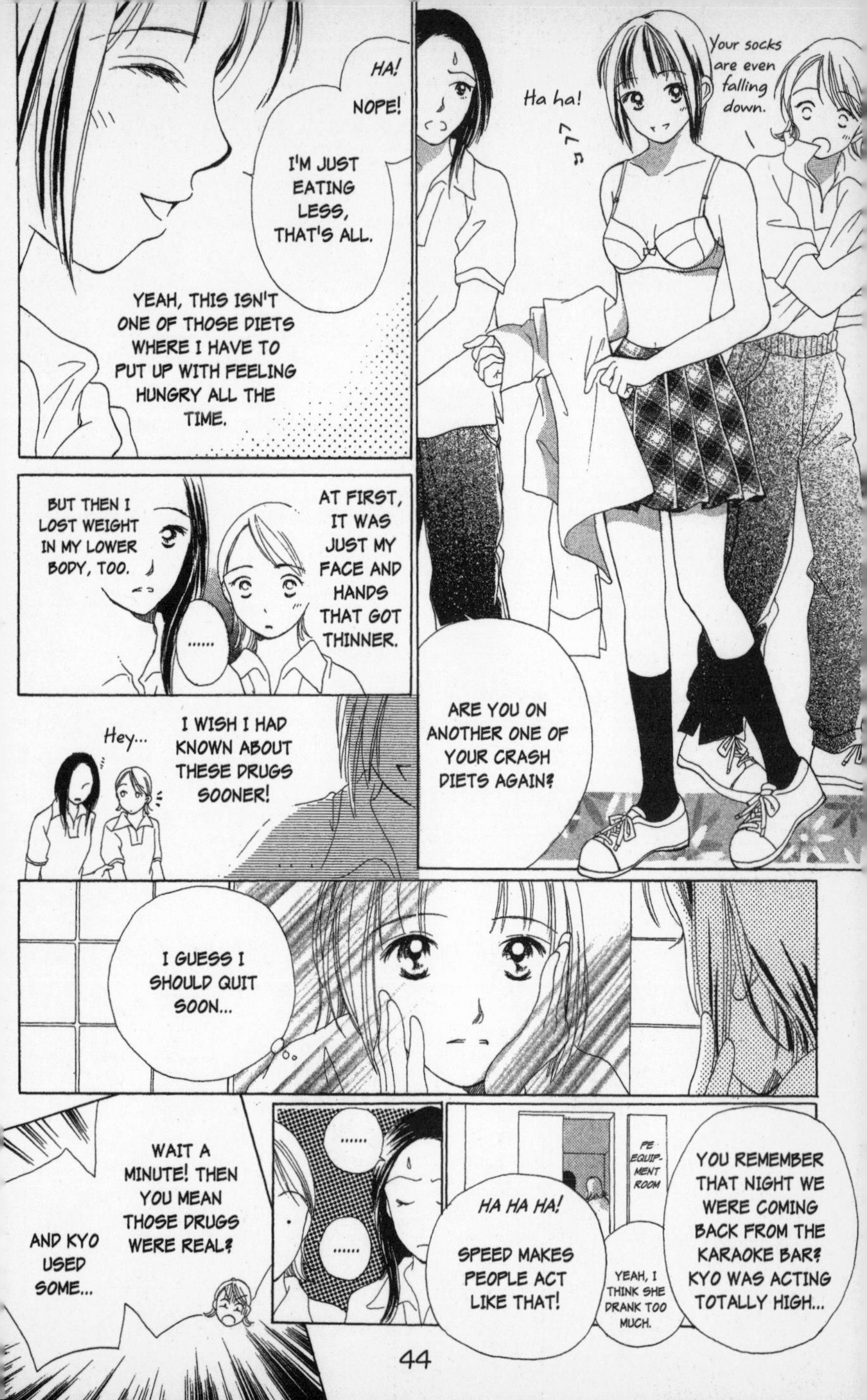
Your socks are even falling down.
Ha ha!
ARE YOU ON ANOTHER ONE OF YOUR CRASH DIETS AGAIN?
HA! NOPE!
I'M JUST EATING LESS, THAT'S ALL.
YEAH, THIS ISN'T ONE OF THOSE DIETS WHERE I HAVE TO PUT UP WITH FEELING HUNGRY ALL THE TIME.
AT FIRST, IT WAS JUST MY FACE AND HANDS THAT GOT THINNER.
BUT THEN I LOST WEIGHT IN MY LOWER BODY, TOO.
......
I WISH I HAD KNOWN ABOUT THESE DRUGS SOONER!
Hey...
I GUESS I SHOULD QUIT SOON...
YOU REMEMBER THAT NIGHT WE WERE COMING BACK FROM THE KARAOKE BAR? KYO WAS ACTING TOTALLY HIGH...
YEAH, I THINK SHE DRANK TOO MUCH.
PE EQUIPMENT ROOM
HA HA HA!
SPEED MAKES PEOPLE ACT LIKE THAT!
......
......
WAIT A MINUTE! THEN YOU MEAN THOSE DRUGS WERE REAL?
AND KYO USED SOME...

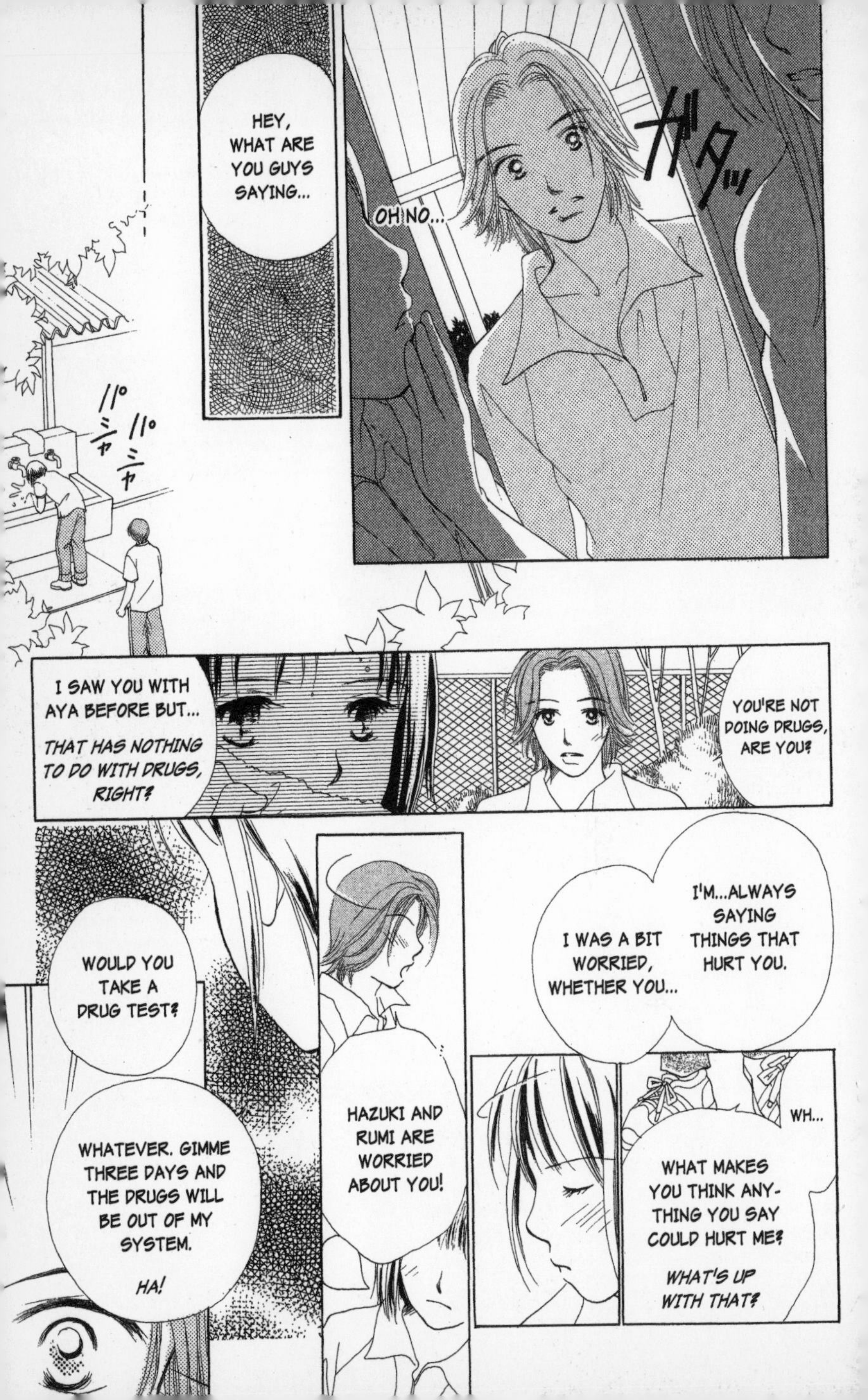
ガタッ
OH NO...
HEY, WHAT ARE YOU GUYS SAYING...
パシャ パシャ
YOU'RE NOT DOING DRUGS, ARE YOU?
I SAW YOU WITH AYA BEFORE BUT...
THAT HAS NOTHING TO DO WITH DRUGS, RIGHT?
I'M...ALWAYS SAYING THINGS THAT HURT YOU.
I WAS A BIT WORRIED, WHETHER YOU...
WH...
WHAT MAKES YOU THINK ANY-THING YOU SAY COULD HURT ME?
WHAT'S UP WITH THAT?
HAZUKI AND RUMI ARE WORRIED ABOUT YOU!
WOULD YOU TAKE A DRUG TEST?
WHATEVER. GIMME THREE DAYS AND THE DRUGS WILL BE OUT OF MY SYSTEM.
HA!

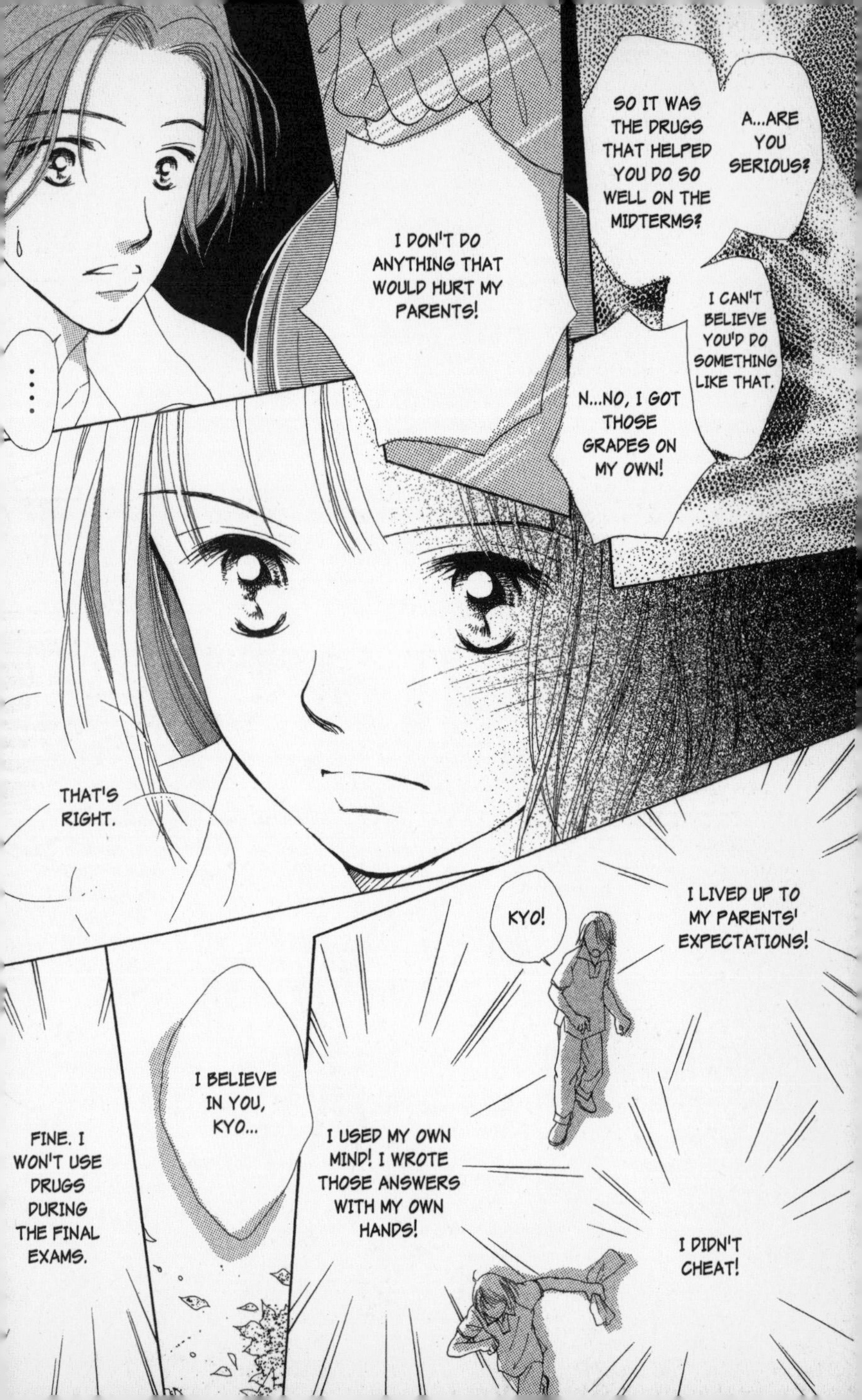
A...ARE YOU SERIOUS?
SO IT WAS THE DRUGS THAT HELPED YOU DO SO WELL ON THE MIDTERMS?
I CAN'T BELIEVE YOU'D DO SOMETHING LIKE THAT.
N...NO, I GOT THOSE GRADES ON MY OWN!
I DON'T DO ANYTHING THAT WOULD HURT MY PARENTS!
....
THAT'S RIGHT.
I LIVED UP TO MY PARENTS' EXPECTATIONS!
KYO!
I DIDN'T CHEAT!
I USED MY OWN MIND! I WROTE THOSE ANSWERS WITH MY OWN HANDS!
I BELIEVE IN YOU, KYO...
FINE. I WON'T USE DRUGS DURING THE FINAL EXAMS.

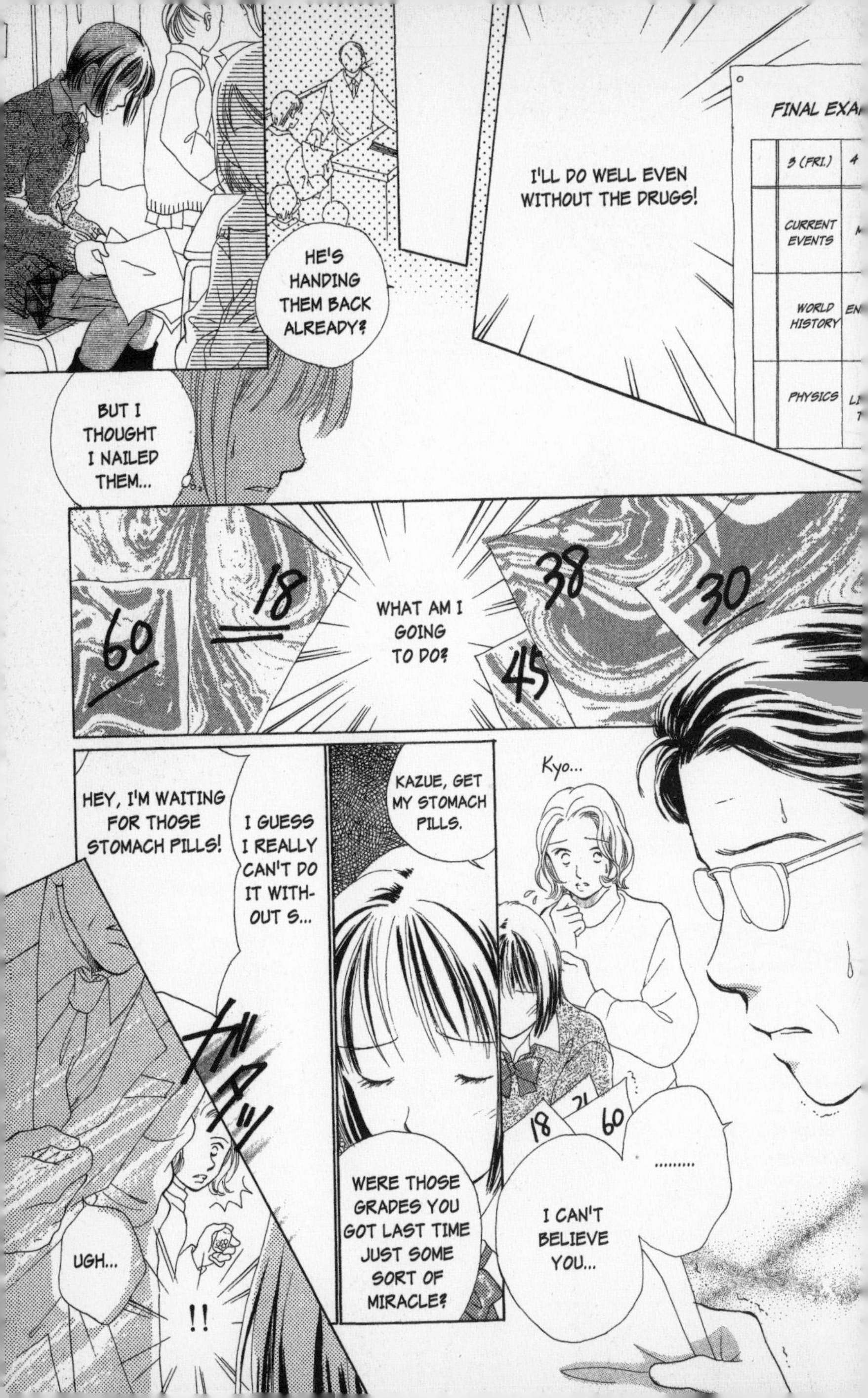
3 (FRI.)
CURRENT EVENTS
WORLD HISTORY
PHYSICS
I'LL DO WELL EVEN WITHOUT THE DRUGS!
HE'S HANDING THEM BACK ALREADY?
BUT I THOUGHT I NAILED THEM...
30
38
45
WHAT AM I GOING TO DO?
18
60
Kyo...
KAZUE, GET MY STOMACH PILLS.
....
I CAN'T BELIEVE YOU...
18
60
WERE THOSE GRADES YOU GOT LAST TIME JUST SOME SORT OF MIRACLE?
I GUESS I REALLY CAN'T DO IT WITHOUT S...
HEY, I'M WAITING FOR THOSE STOMACH PILLS!
UGH...
!!

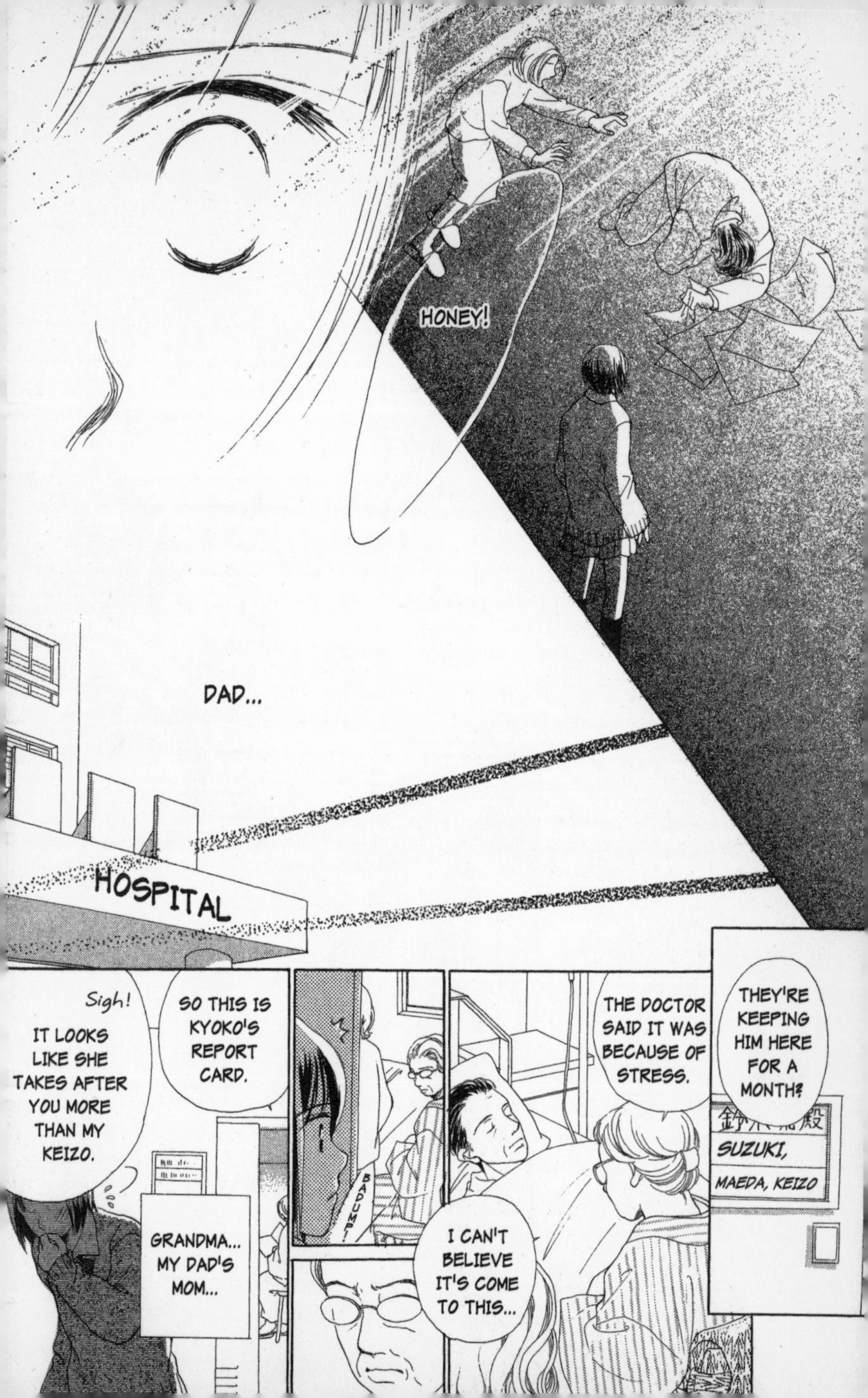
HONEY!
DAD...
HOSPITAL
THEY'RE KEEPING HIM HERE FOR A MONTH?
SUZUKI,
MAEDA, KEIZO
THE DOCTOR SAID IT WAS BECAUSE OF STRESS.
I CAN'T BELIEVE IT'S COME TO THIS...
BADUMP!
SO THIS IS KYOKO'S REPORT CARD.
Sigh!
IT LOOKS LIKE SHE TAKES AFTER YOU MORE THAN MY KEIZO.
GRANDMA... MY DAD'S MOM...

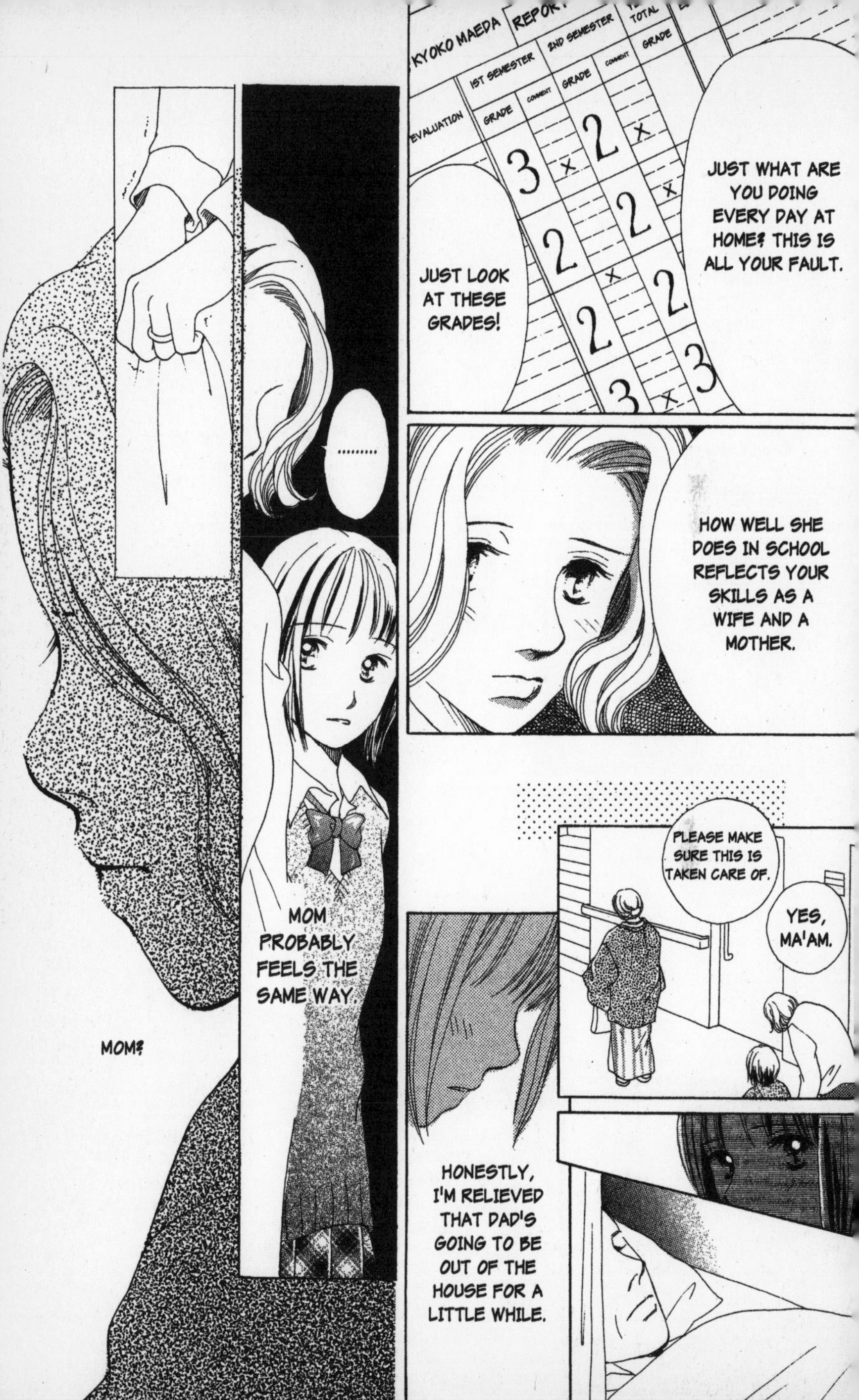
KYOKO MAEDA
EVALUATION
1ST SEMESTER
2ND SEMESTER
TOTAL
GRADE
COMMENT
JUST WHAT ARE YOU DOING EVERY DAY AT HOME? THIS IS ALL YOUR FAULT.
JUST LOOK AT THESE GRADES!
HOW WELL SHE DOES IN SCHOOL REFLECTS YOUR SKILLS AS A WIFE AND A MOTHER.
PLEASE MAKE SURE THIS IS TAKEN CARE OF.
YES, MA'AM.
HONESTLY, I'M RELIEVED THAT DAD'S GOING TO BE OUT OF THE HOUSE FOR A LITTLE WHILE.
....
MOM PROBABLY FEELS THE SAME WAY.
MOM?

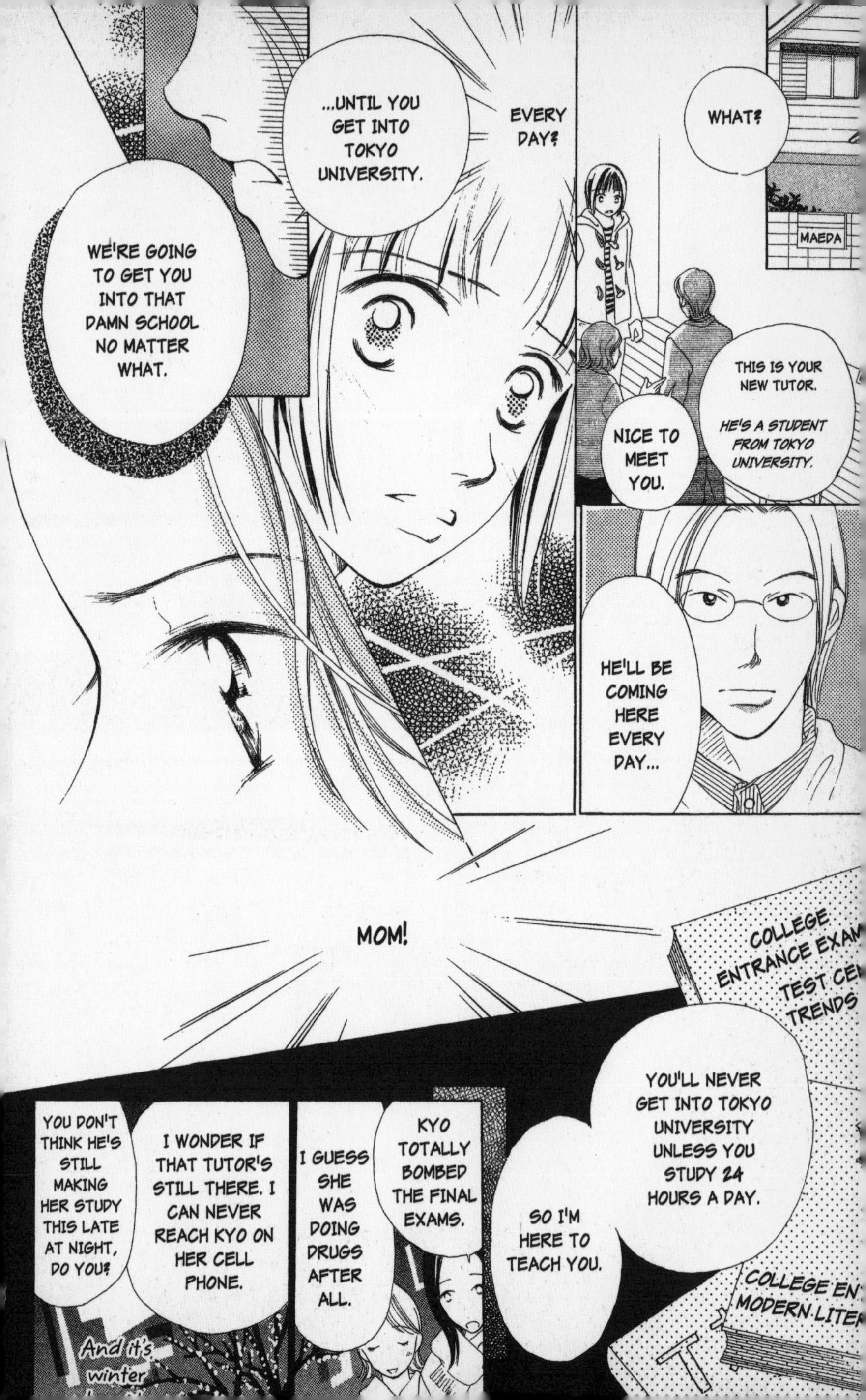
WHAT?
MAEDA
THIS IS YOUR NEW TUTOR.
HE'S A STUDENT FROM TOKYO UNIVERSITY.
NICE TO MEET YOU.
HE'LL BE COMING HERE EVERY DAY...
EVERY DAY?
...UNTIL YOU GET INTO TOKYO UNIVERSITY.
WE'RE GOING TO GET YOU INTO THAT DAMN SCHOOL NO MATTER WHAT.
MOM!
COLLEGE ENTRANCE EXAM TEST CE TRENDS
YOU'LL NEVER GET INTO TOKYO UNIVERSITY UNLESS YOU STUDY 24 HOURS A DAY.
SO I'M HERE TO TEACH YOU.
COLLEGE EN MODERN LITE
KYO TOTALLY BOMBED THE FINAL EXAMS.
I GUESS SHE WAS DOING DRUGS AFTER ALL.
I WONDER IF THAT TUTOR'S STILL THERE. I CAN NEVER REACH KYO ON HER CELL PHONE.
YOU DON'T THINK HE'S STILL MAKING HER STUDY THIS LATE AT NIGHT, DO YOU?
And it's winter

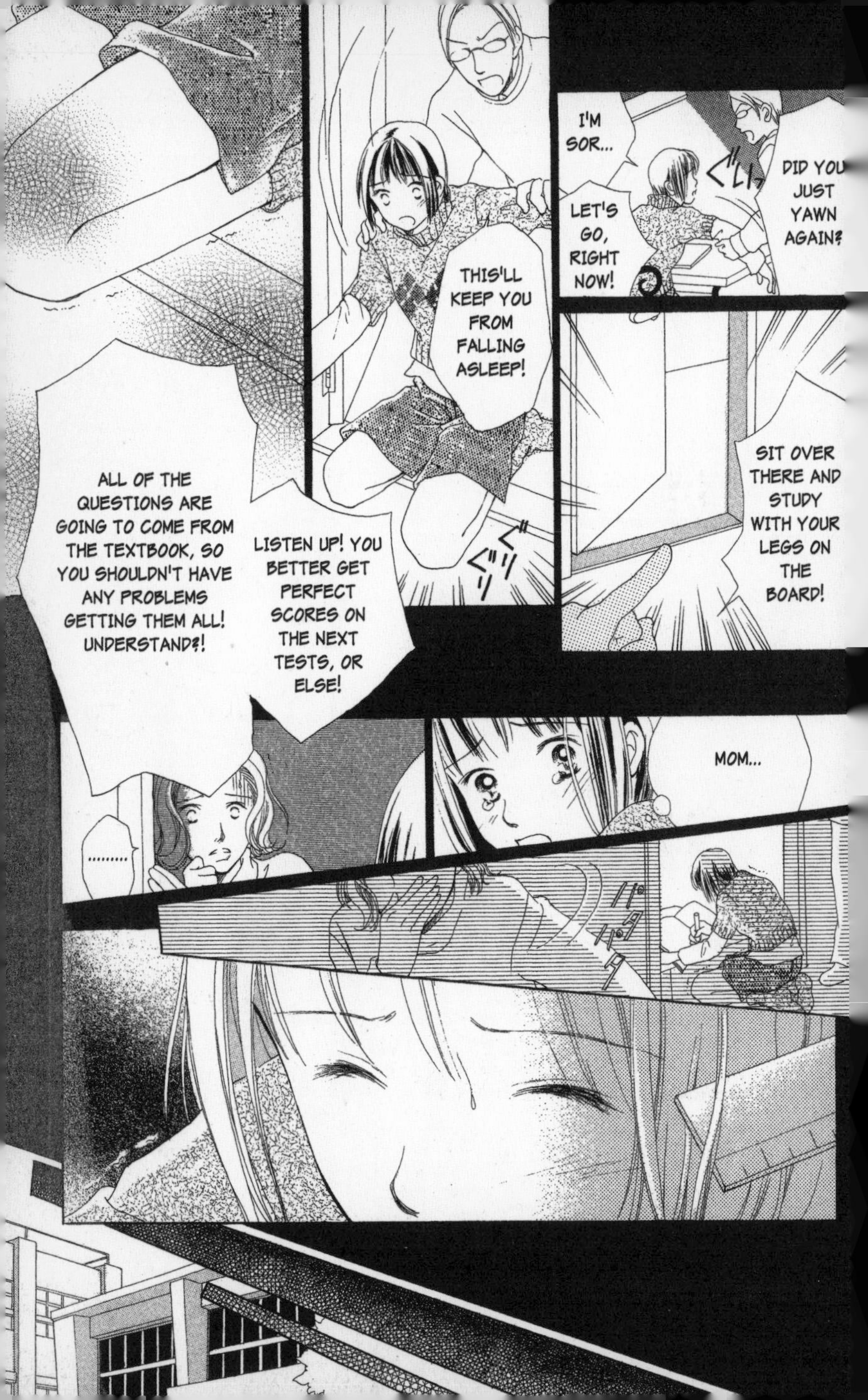
DID YOU JUST YAWN AGAIN?
I'M SOR...
LET'S GO, RIGHT NOW!
SIT OVER THERE AND STUDY WITH YOUR LEGS ON THE BOARD!
THIS'LL KEEP YOU FROM FALLING ASLEEP!
LISTEN UP! YOU BETTER GET PERFECT SCORES ON THE NEXT TESTS, OR ELSE!
ALL OF THE QUESTIONS ARE GOING TO COME FROM THE TEXTBOOK, SO YOU SHOULDN'T HAVE ANY PROBLEMS GETTING THEM ALL! UNDERSTAND?!
MOM...
....

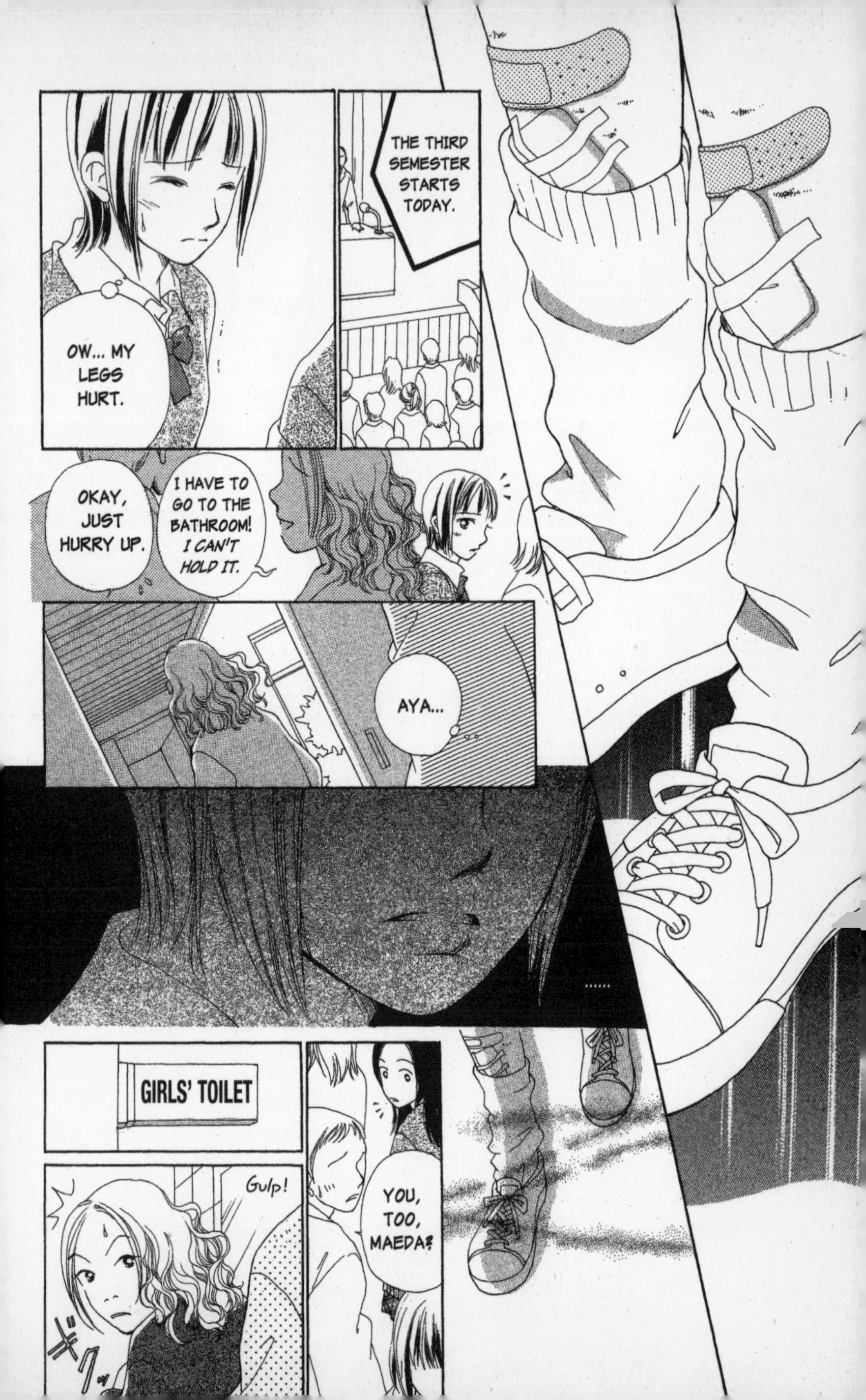
THE THIRD SEMESTER STARTS TODAY.
OW... MY LEGS HURT.
I HAVE TO GO TO THE BATHROOM! I CAN'T HOLD IT.
OKAY, JUST HURRY UP.
AYA...
......
YOU, TOO, MAEDA?
GIRLS' TOILET
Gulp!

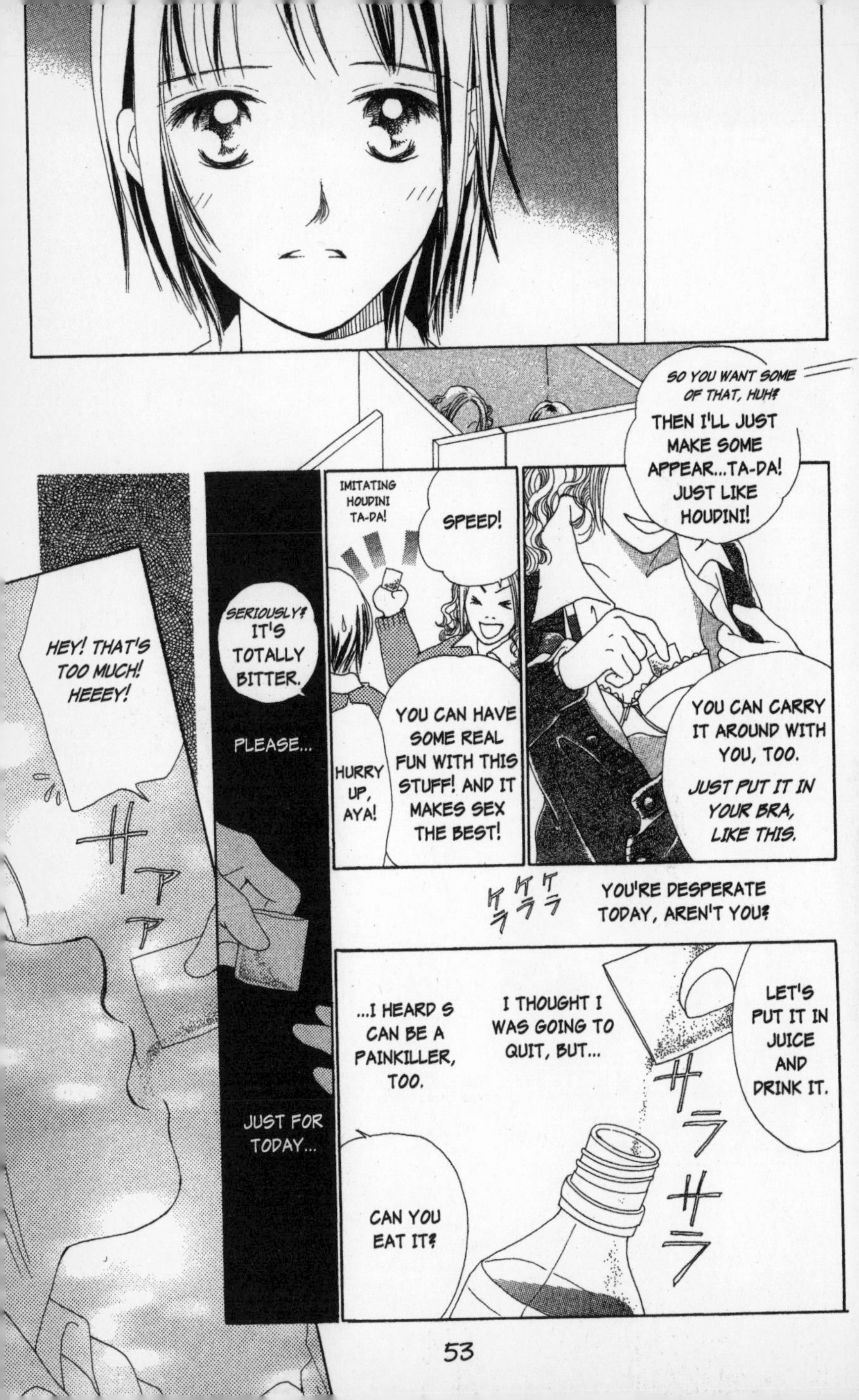
SO YOU WANT SOME OF THAT, HUH?
THEN I'LL JUST MAKE SOME APPEAR...TA-DA! JUST LIKE HOUDINI!
YOU CAN CARRY IT AROUND WITH YOU, TOO.
JUST PUT IT IN YOUR BRA, LIKE THIS.
IMITATING HOUDINI TA-DA!
SPEED!
YOU CAN HAVE SOME REAL FUN WITH THIS STUFF! AND IT MAKES SEX THE BEST!
HURRY UP, AYA!
ケラケラケラ
YOU'RE DESPERATE TODAY, AREN'T YOU?
LET'S PUT IT IN JUICE AND DRINK IT.
サラサラ
I THOUGHT I WAS GOING TO QUIT, BUT...
...I HEARD S CAN BE A PAINKILLER, TOO.
CAN YOU EAT IT?
SERIOUSLY? IT'S TOTALLY BITTER.
PLEASE...
JUST FOR TODAY...
HEY! THAT'S TOO MUCH! HEEEY!
サァァ

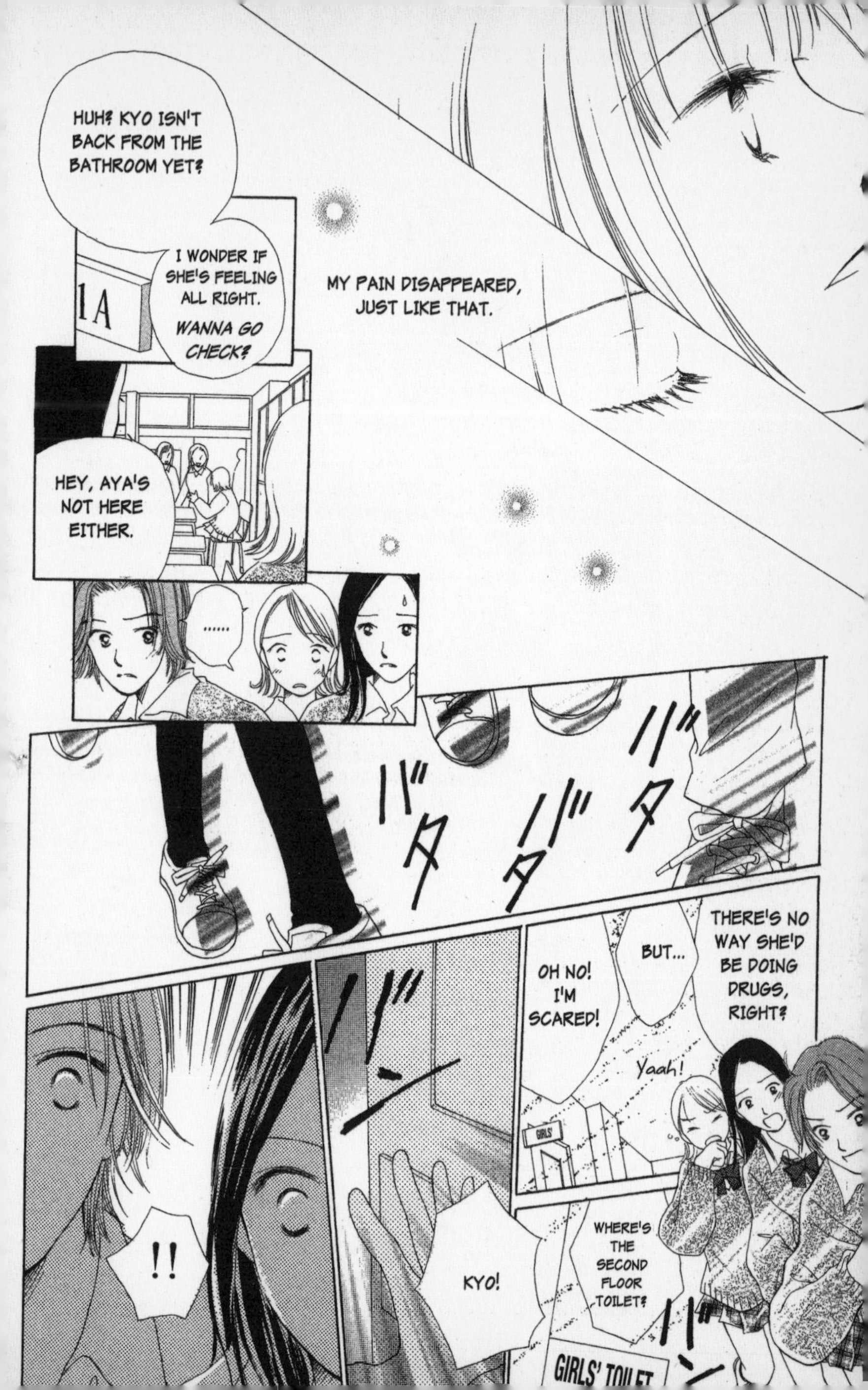
MY PAIN DISAPPEARED, JUST LIKE THAT.
HUH? KYO ISN'T BACK FROM THE BATHROOM YET?
1A
I WONDER IF SHE'S FEELING ALL RIGHT. WANNA GO CHECK?
HEY, AYA'S NOT HERE EITHER.
......
バタ
バタ
バタ
THERE'S NO WAY SHE'D BE DOING DRUGS, RIGHT?
BUT...
OH NO! I'M SCARED!
Yaah!
GIRLS'
WHERE'S THE SECOND FLOOR TOILET?
GIRLS' TOILET
KYO!
!!

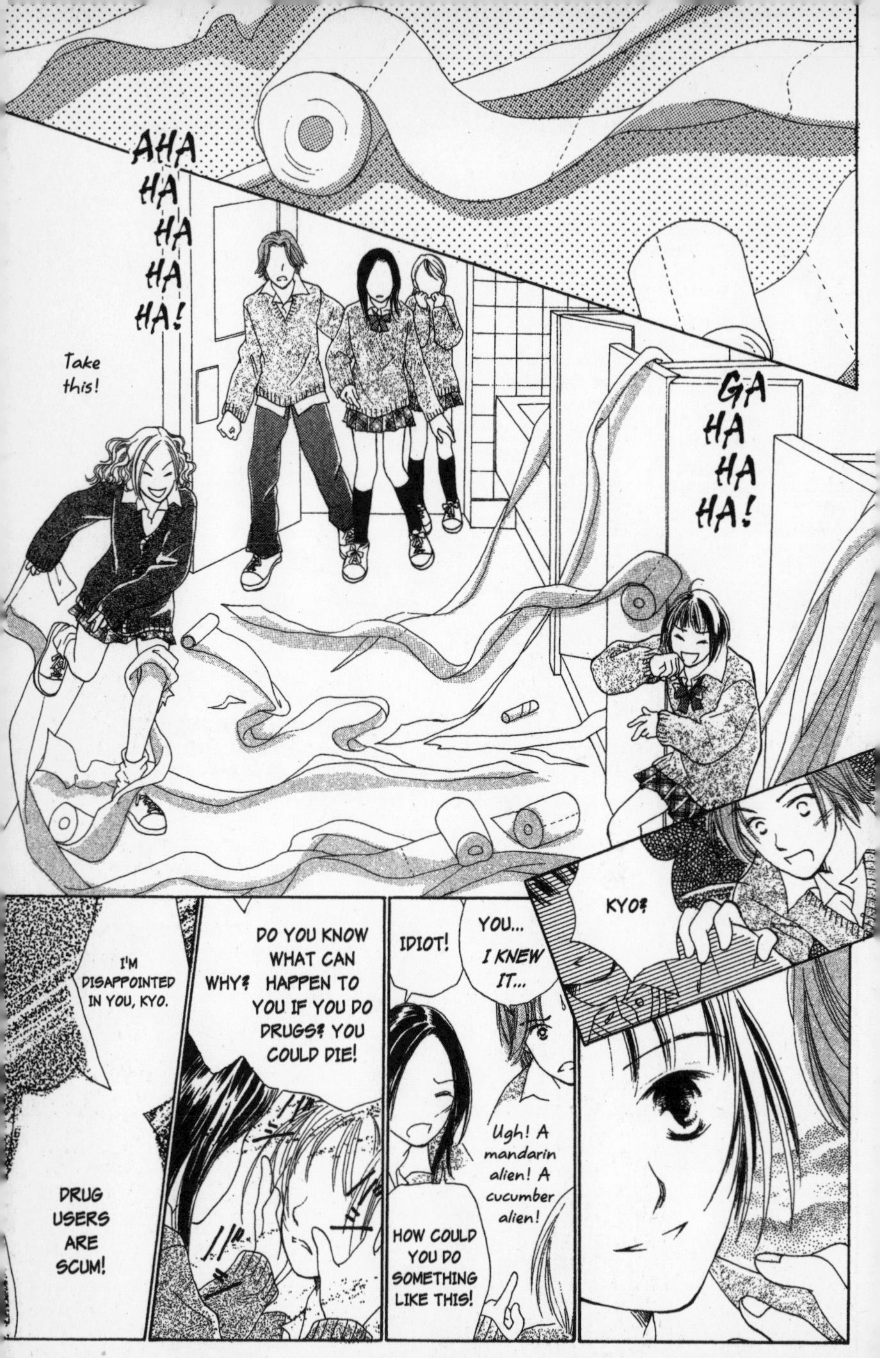
GA HA HA HA HA!
AHA HA HA HA HA!
Take this!
KYO?
YOU... I KNEW IT...
IDIOT!
Ugh! A mandarin alien! A cucumber alien!
HOW COULD YOU DO SOMETHING LIKE THIS!
DO YOU KNOW WHAT CAN HAPPEN TO YOU IF YOU DO DRUGS? YOU COULD DIE!
WHY?
I'M DISAPPOINTED IN YOU, KYO.
DRUG USERS ARE SCUM!

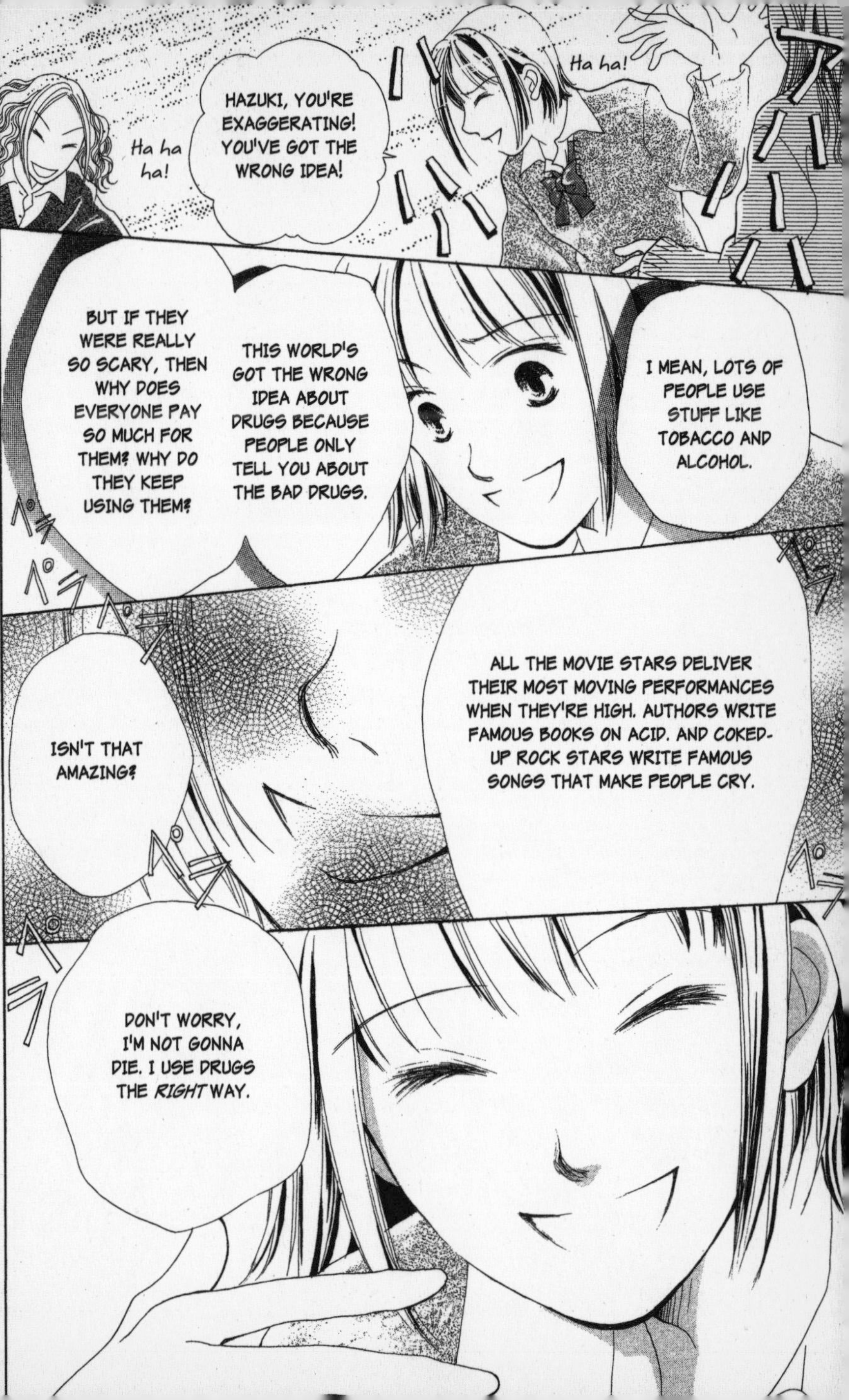
Ha ha!
HAZUKI, YOU'RE EXAGGERATING! YOU'VE GOT THE WRONG IDEA!
Ha ha ha!
I MEAN, LOTS OF PEOPLE USE STUFF LIKE TOBACCO AND ALCOHOL.
THIS WORLD'S GOT THE WRONG IDEA ABOUT DRUGS BECAUSE PEOPLE ONLY TELL YOU ABOUT THE BAD DRUGS.
BUT IF THEY WERE REALLY SO SCARY, THEN WHY DOES EVERYONE PAY SO MUCH FOR THEM? WHY DO THEY KEEP USING THEM?
ALL THE MOVIE STARS DELIVER THEIR MOST MOVING PERFORMANCES WHEN THEY'RE HIGH. AUTHORS WRITE FAMOUS BOOKS ON ACID. AND COKED-UP ROCK STARS WRITE FAMOUS SONGS THAT MAKE PEOPLE CRY.
ISN'T THAT AMAZING?
DON'T WORRY, I'M NOT GONNA DIE. I USE DRUGS THE *RIGHT* WAY.

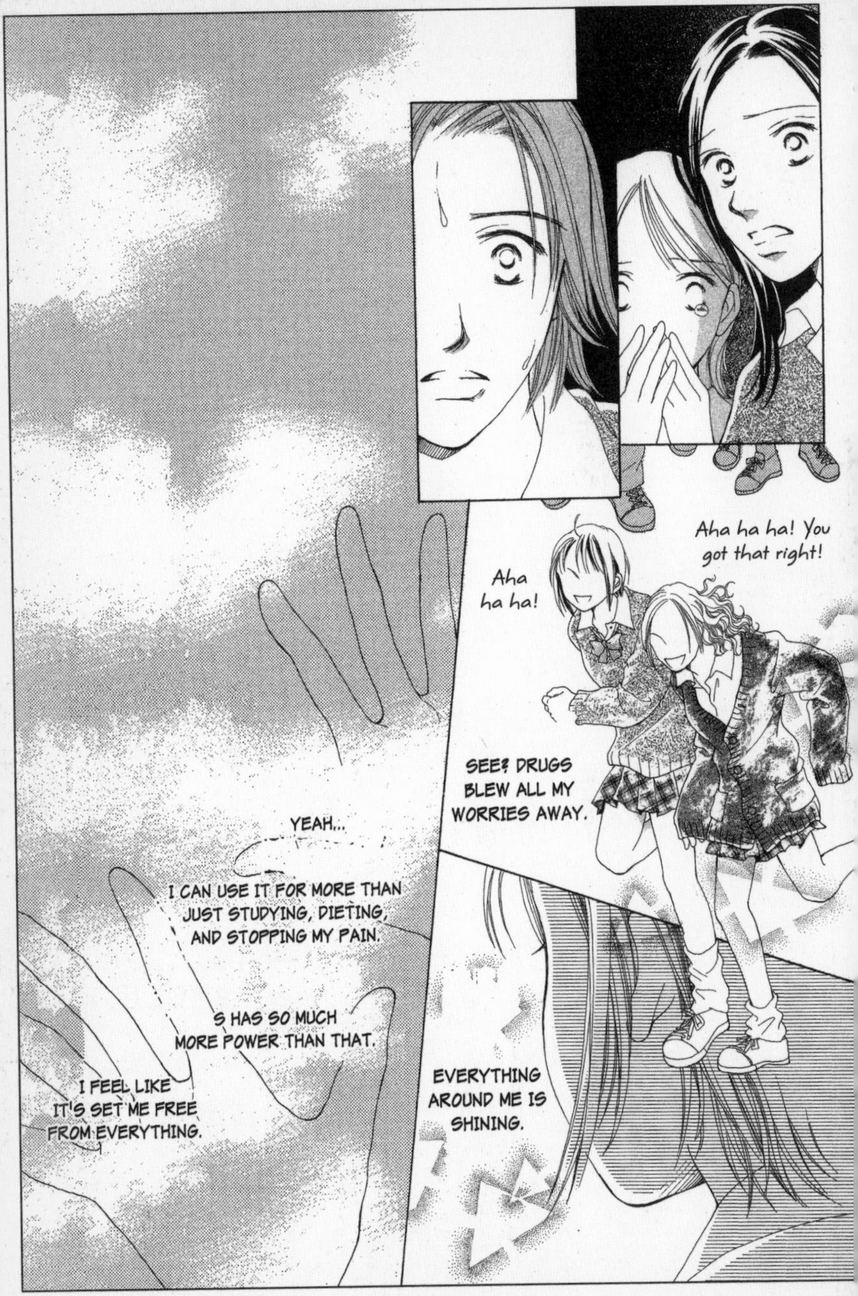
Aha ha ha! You got that right!
Aha ha ha!
SEE? DRUGS BLEW ALL MY WORRIES AWAY.
EVERYTHING AROUND ME IS SHINING.
YEAH...
I CAN USE IT FOR MORE THAN JUST STUDYING, DIETING, AND STOPPING MY PAIN.
S HAS SO MUCH MORE POWER THAN THAT.
I FEEL LIKE IT'S SET ME FREE FROM EVERYTHING.

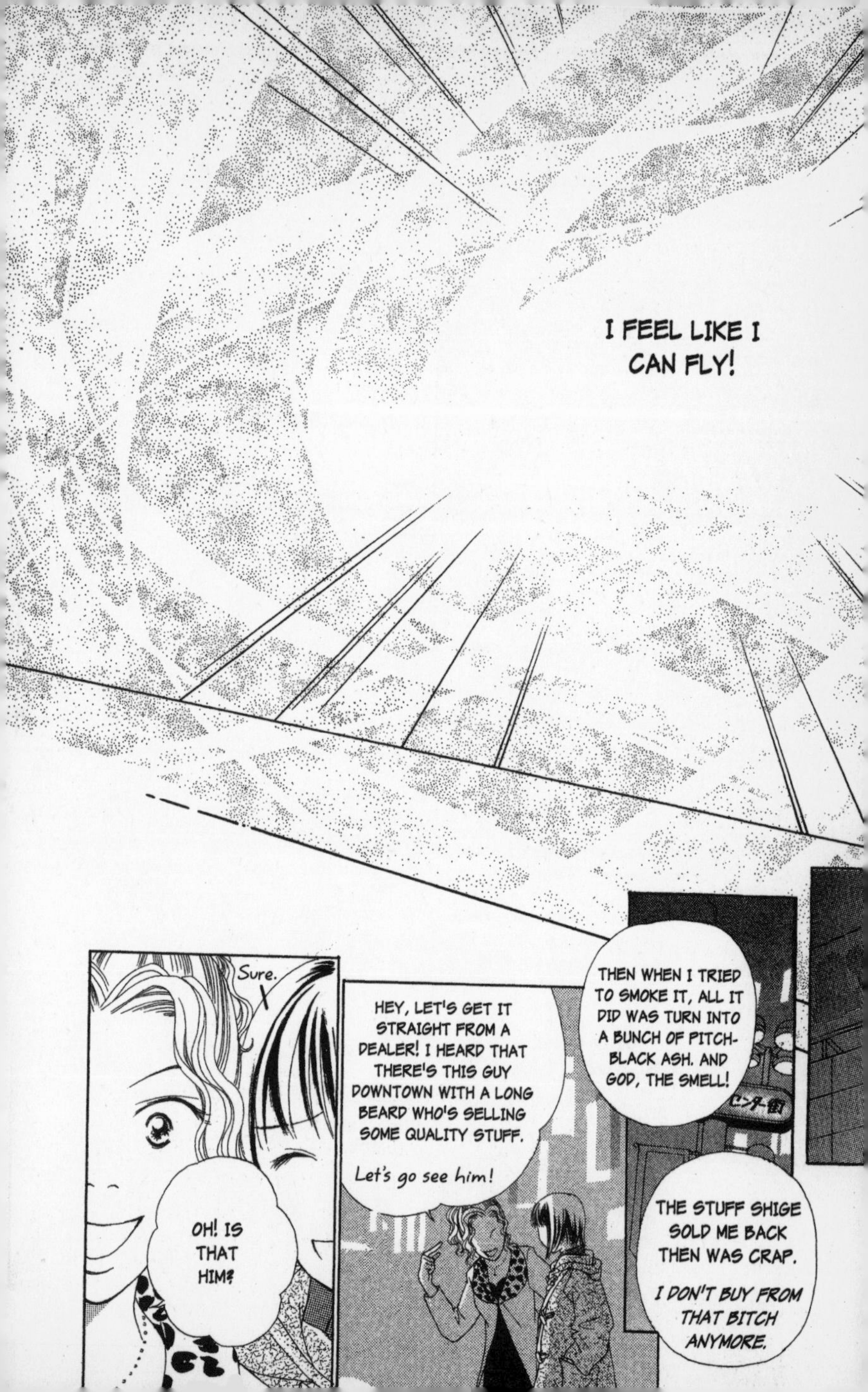
I FEEL LIKE I CAN FLY!
THEN WHEN I TRIED TO SMOKE IT, ALL IT DID WAS TURN INTO A BUNCH OF PITCH-BLACK ASH. AND GOD, THE SMELL!
センター街
THE STUFF SHIGE SOLD ME BACK THEN WAS CRAP.
I DON'T BUY FROM THAT BITCH ANYMORE.
HEY, LET'S GET IT STRAIGHT FROM A DEALER! I HEARD THAT THERE'S THIS GUY DOWNTOWN WITH A LONG BEARD WHO'S SELLING SOME QUALITY STUFF.
Let's go see him!
Sure.
OH! IS THAT HIM?

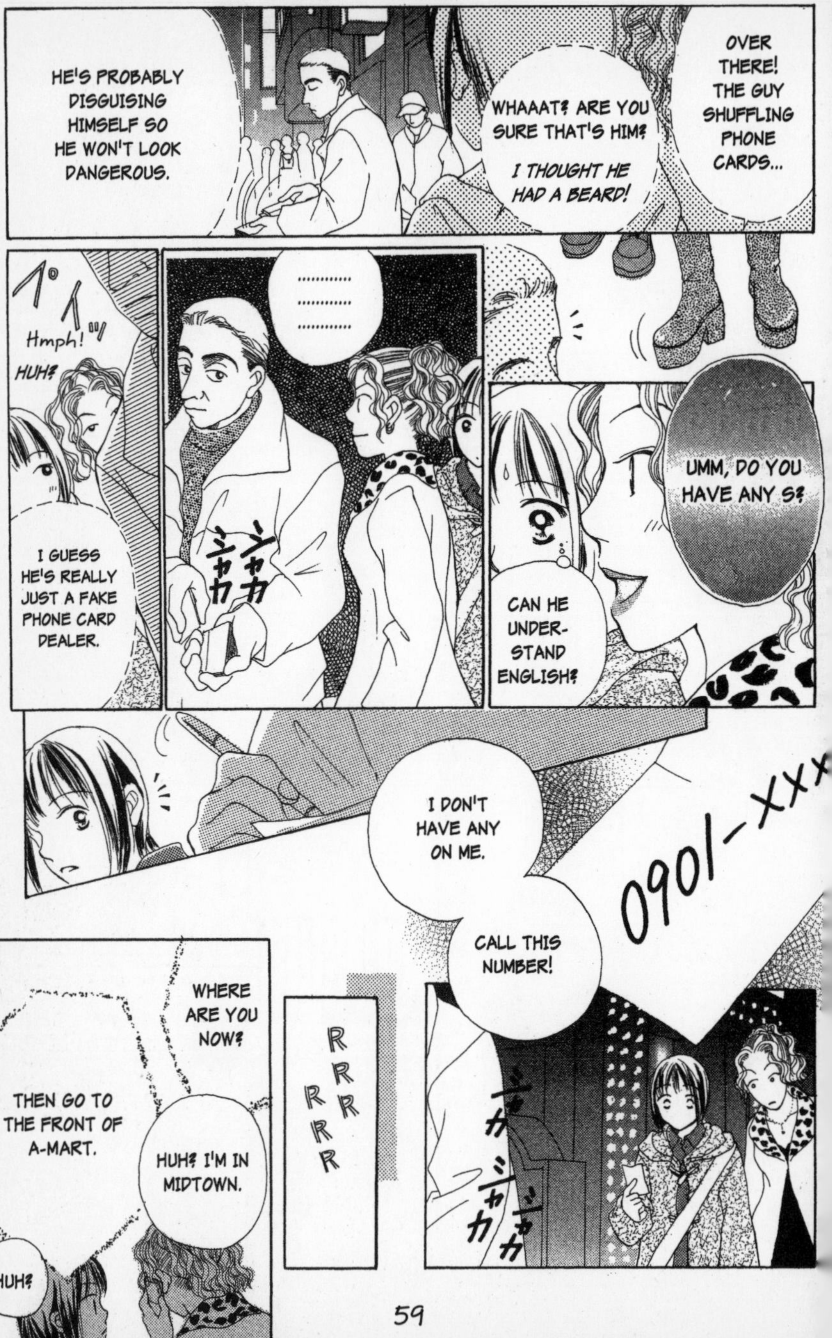
OVER THERE! THE GUY SHUFFLING PHONE CARDS...
WHAAAT? ARE YOU SURE THAT'S HIM?
I THOUGHT HE HAD A BEARD!
HE'S PROBABLY DISGUISING HIMSELF SO HE WON'T LOOK DANGEROUS.
UMM, DO YOU HAVE ANY S?
CAN HE UNDER-STAND ENGLISH?
....
....
....
シャカシャカ
ペイッ
Hmph!
HUH?
I GUESS HE'S REALLY JUST A FAKE PHONE CARD DEALER.
0901-XXX
I DON'T HAVE ANY ON ME.
CALL THIS NUMBER!
シャカシャカシャカ
RRRRRRR
WHERE ARE YOU NOW?
THEN GO TO THE FRONT OF A-MART.
HUH? I'M IN MIDTOWN.
HUH?

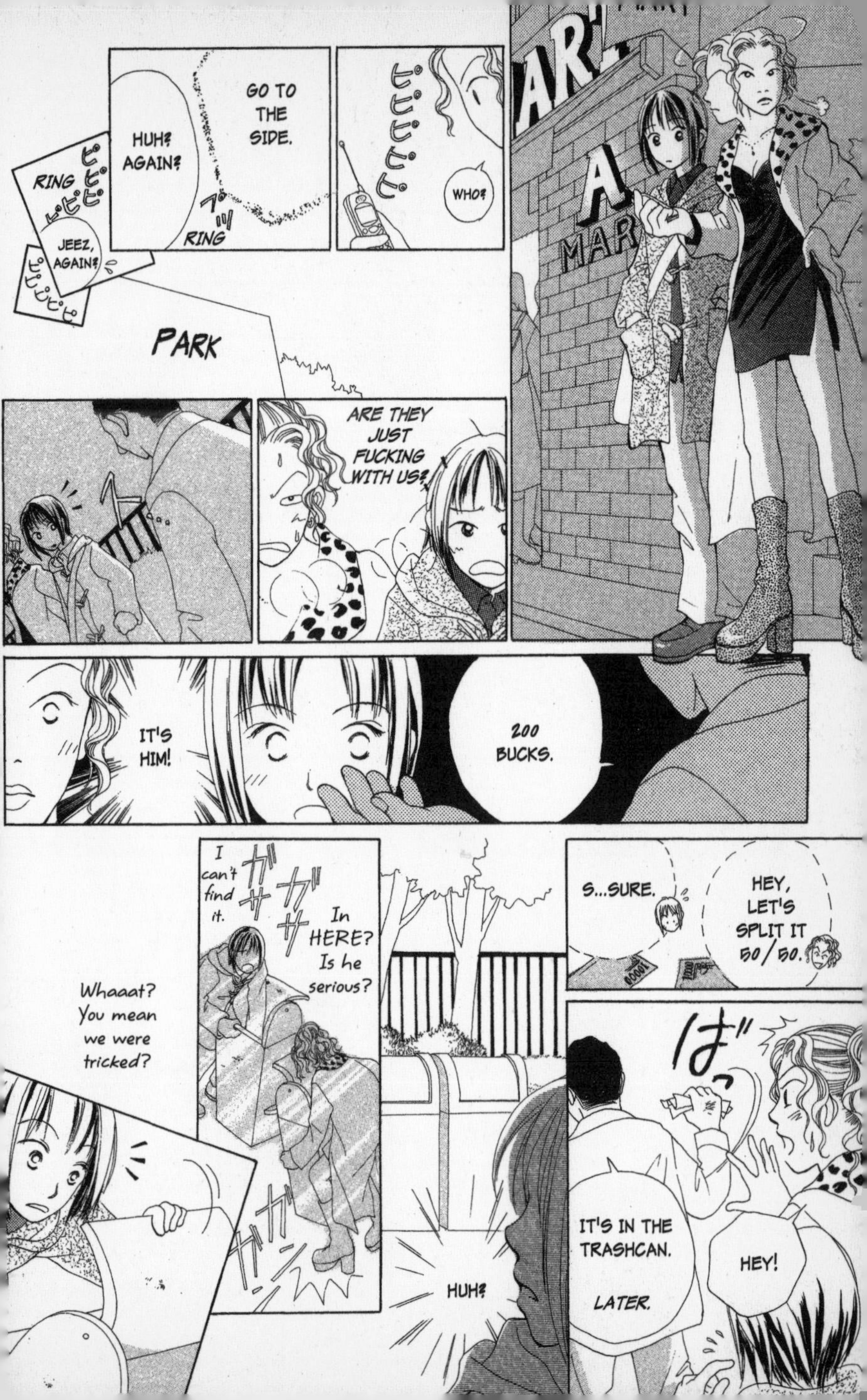

MAR
ピピピピピ
WHO?
GO TO THE SIDE.
HUH? AGAIN?
プツ
RING
ピピピ
RING
JEEZ, AGAIN?
ピピピピピ
PARK
ARE THEY JUST FUCKING WITH US?
200 BUCKS.
IT'S HIM!
HEY, LET'S SPLIT IT 50/50.
S...SURE.
ばっ
HEY!
IT'S IN THE TRASHCAN.
LATER.
HUH?
I can't find it.
ガサ ガサ
In HERE? Is he serious?
ガガー
Whaaat? You mean we were tricked?

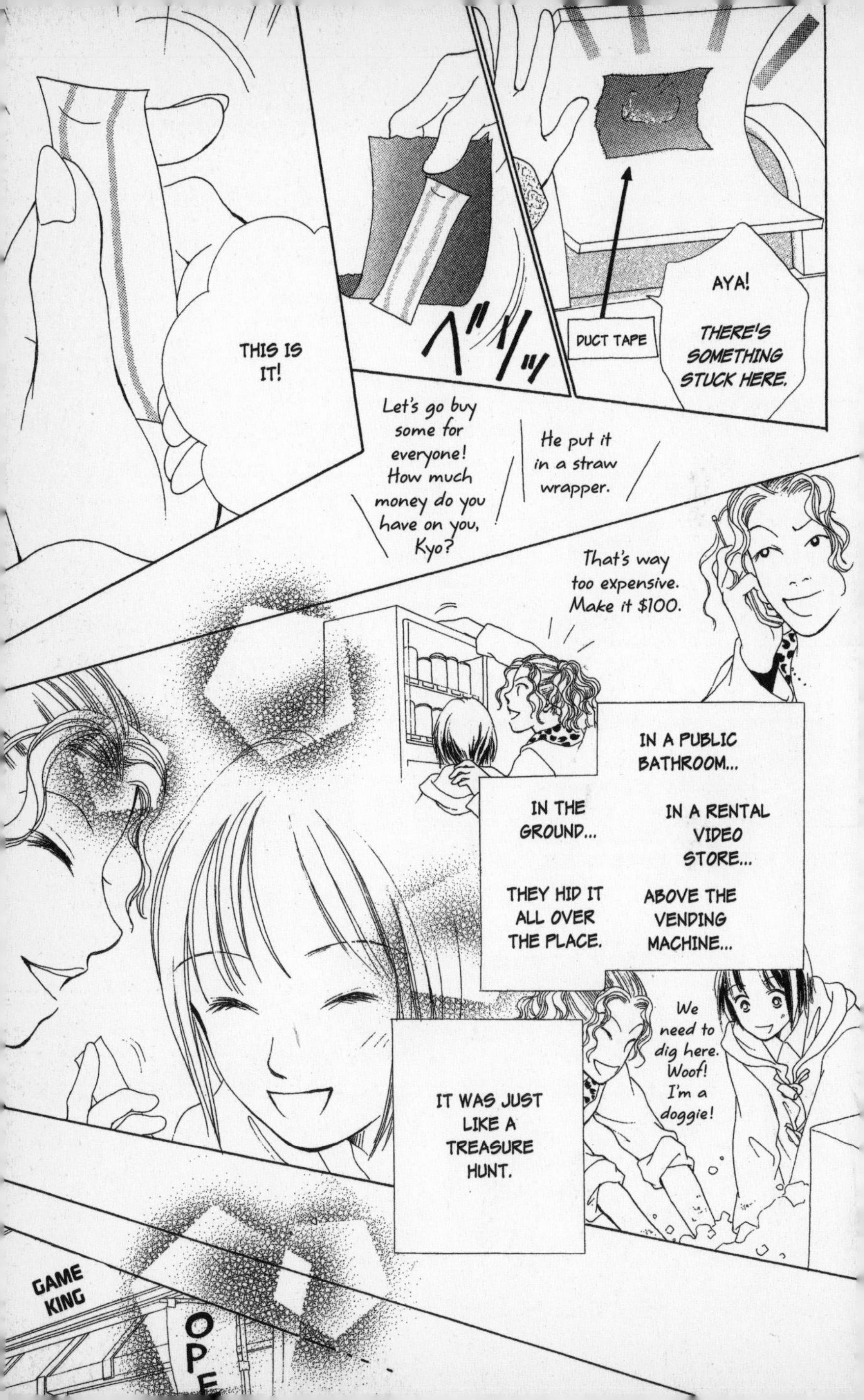
AYA!
THERE'S SOMETHING STUCK HERE.
DUCT TAPE
THIS IS IT!
He put it in a straw wrapper.
Let's go buy some for everyone! How much money do you have on you, Kyo?
That's way too expensive. Make it $100.
IN A PUBLIC BATHROOM...
IN A RENTAL VIDEO STORE...
IN THE GROUND...
ABOVE THE VENDING MACHINE...
THEY HID IT ALL OVER THE PLACE.
We need to dig here. Woof! I'm a doggie!
IT WAS JUST LIKE A TREASURE HUNT.
GAME KING
OPE

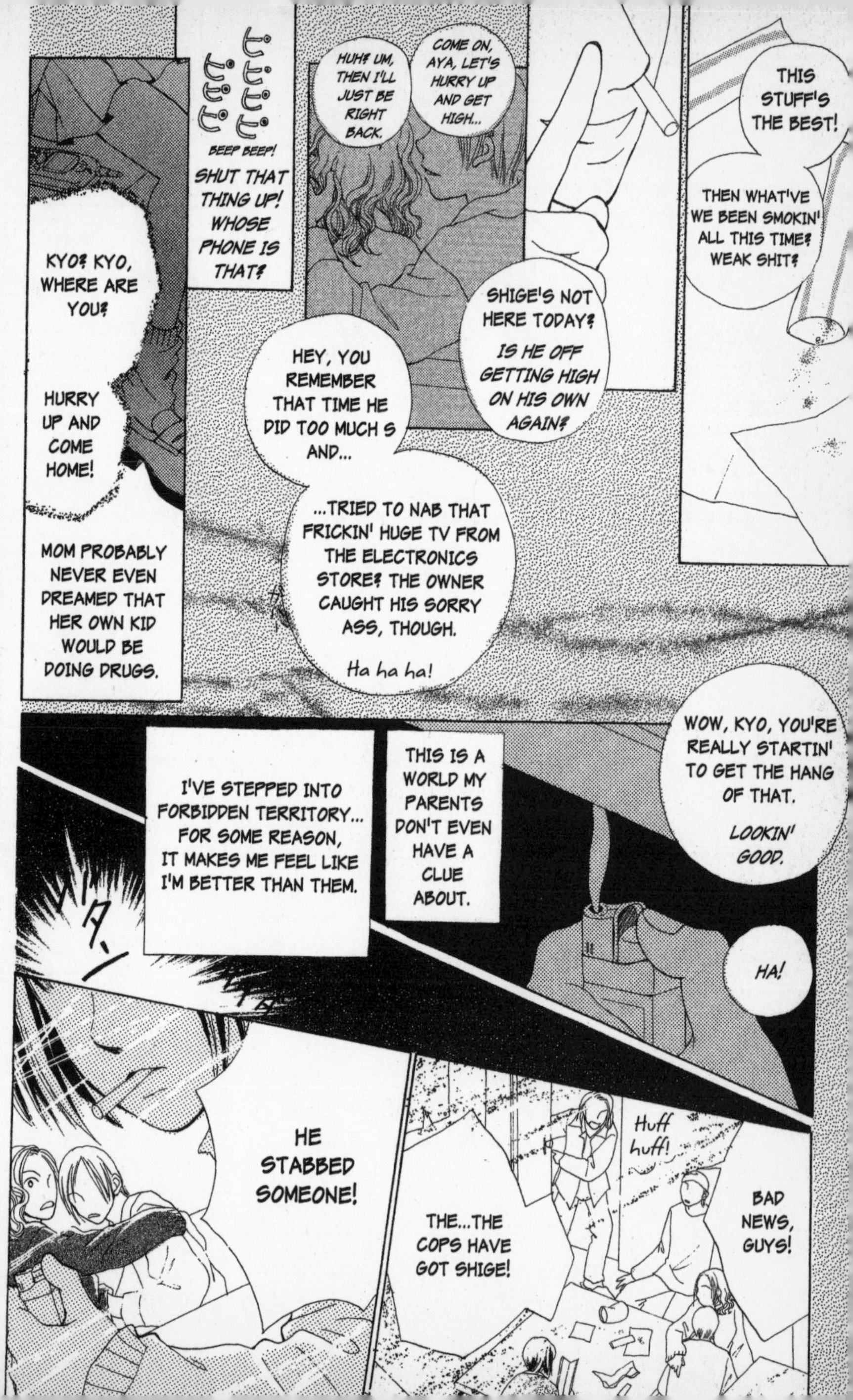
THIS STUFF'S THE BEST!
THEN WHAT'VE WE BEEN SMOKIN' ALL THIS TIME? WEAK SHIT?
COME ON, AYA, LET'S HURRY UP AND GET HIGH...
HUH? UM, THEN I'LL JUST BE RIGHT BACK.
ピピピ ピピピ
BEEP BEEP!
SHUT THAT THING UP! WHOSE PHONE IS THAT?
KYO? KYO, WHERE ARE YOU?
HURRY UP AND COME HOME!
SHIGE'S NOT HERE TODAY?
IS HE OFF GETTING HIGH ON HIS OWN AGAIN?
HEY, YOU REMEMBER THAT TIME HE DID TOO MUCH S AND...
...TRIED TO NAB THAT FRICKIN' HUGE TV FROM THE ELECTRONICS STORE? THE OWNER CAUGHT HIS SORRY ASS, THOUGH.
Ha ha ha!
MOM PROBABLY NEVER EVEN DREAMED THAT HER OWN KID WOULD BE DOING DRUGS.
WOW, KYO, YOU'RE REALLY STARTIN' TO GET THE HANG OF THAT.
LOOKIN' GOOD.
HA!
THIS IS A WORLD MY PARENTS DON'T EVEN HAVE A CLUE ABOUT.
I'VE STEPPED INTO FORBIDDEN TERRITORY... FOR SOME REASON, IT MAKES ME FEEL LIKE I'M BETTER THAN THEM.
BAD NEWS, GUYS!
Huff huff!
THE...THE COPS HAVE GOT SHIGE!
HE STABBED SOMEONE!

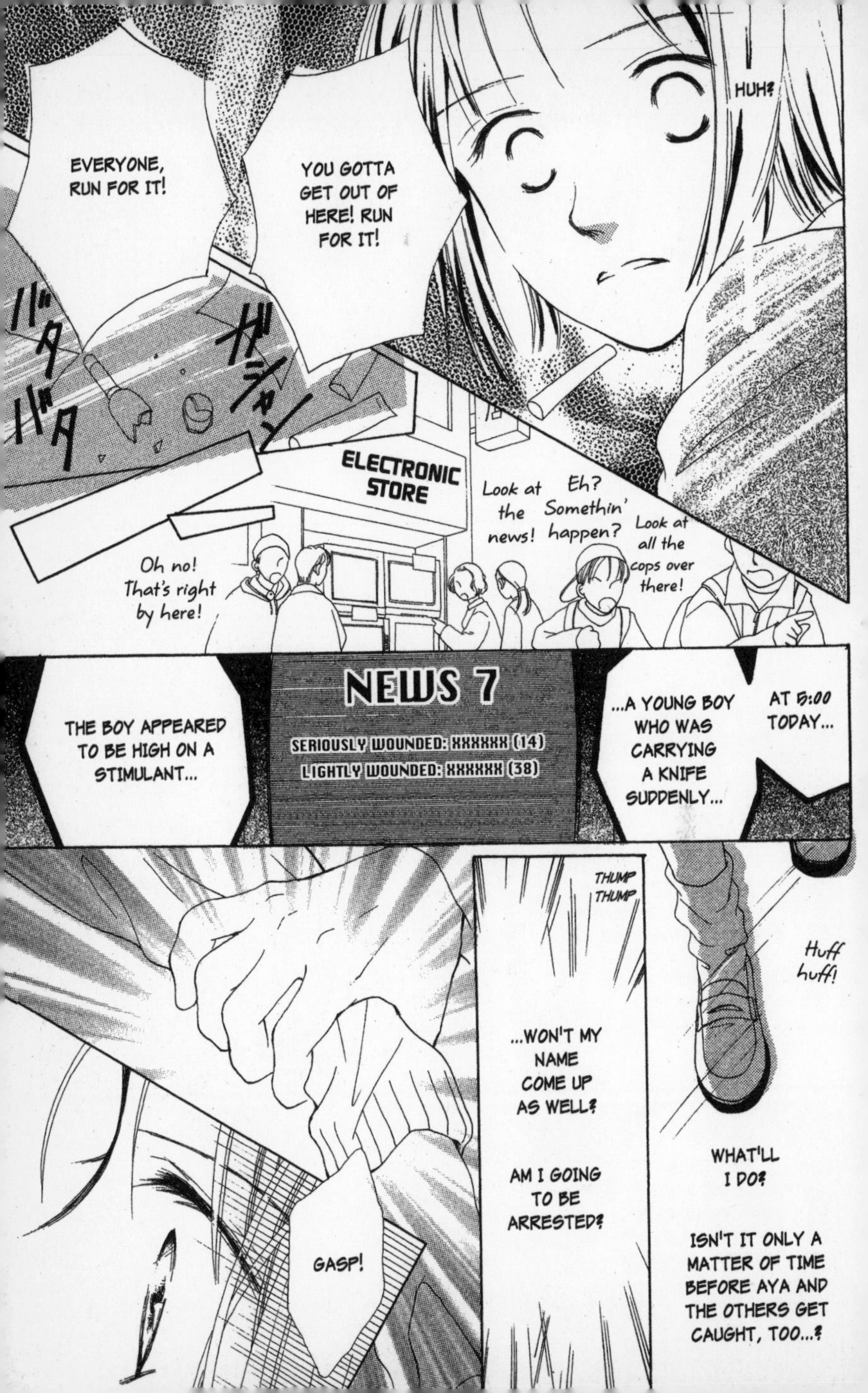
HUH?
YOU GOTTA GET OUT OF HERE! RUN FOR IT!
EVERYONE, RUN FOR IT!
ガシャン
バタバタ
Look at all the cops over there!
Eh? Somethin' happen?
Look at the news!
ELECTRONIC STORE
Oh no! That's right by here!
AT 5:00 TODAY...
...A YOUNG BOY WHO WAS CARRYING A KNIFE SUDDENLY...
NEWS 7
SERIOUSLY WOUNDED: XXXXXX (14)
LIGHTLY WOUNDED: XXXXXX (38)
THE BOY APPEARED TO BE HIGH ON A STIMULANT...
Huff huff!
WHAT'LL I DO?
ISN'T IT ONLY A MATTER OF TIME BEFORE AYA AND THE OTHERS GET CAUGHT, TOO...?
THUMP THUMP
...WON'T MY NAME COME UP AS WELL?
AM I GOING TO BE ARRESTED?
GASP!

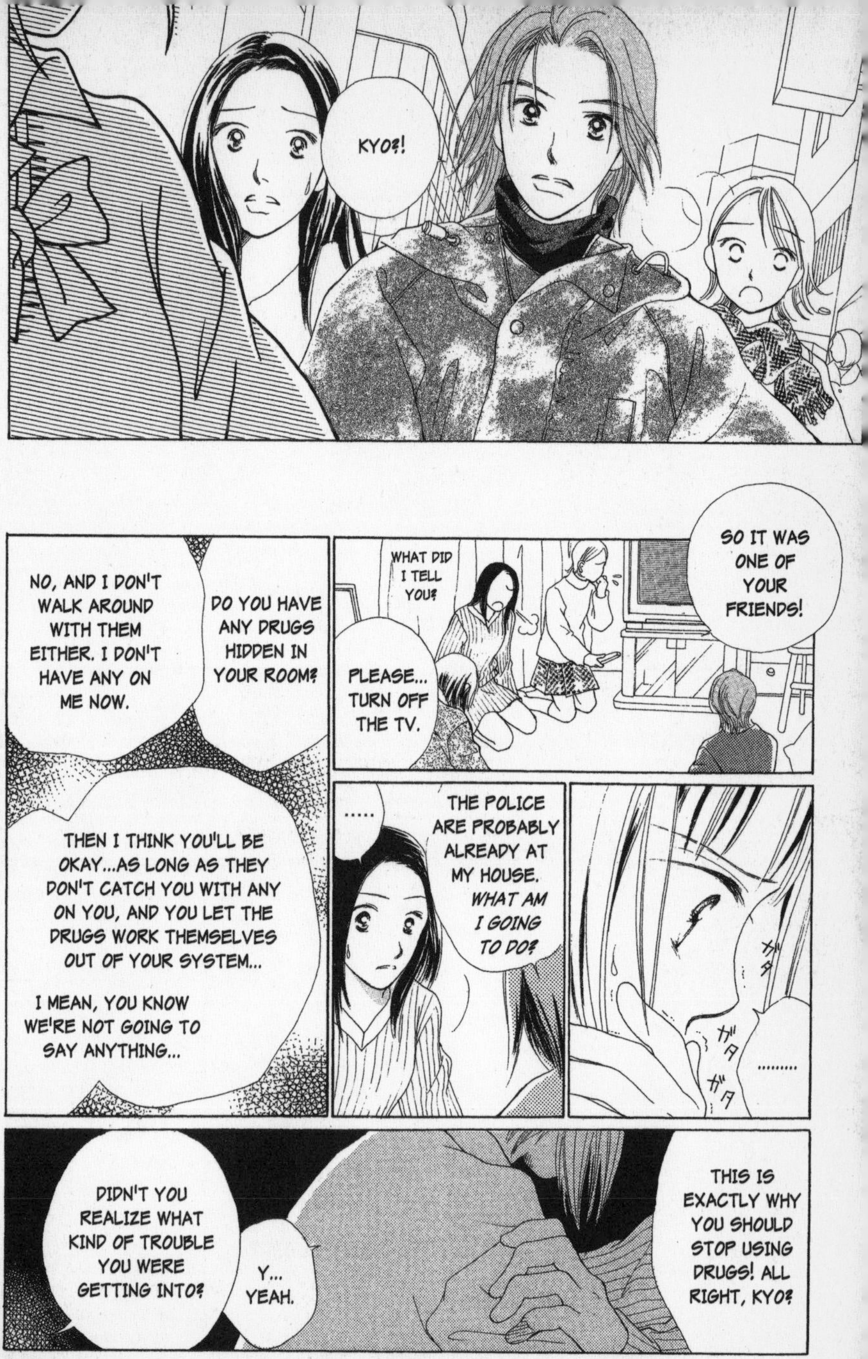
KYO?!
SO IT WAS ONE OF YOUR FRIENDS!
WHAT DID I TELL YOU?
PLEASE... TURN OFF THE TV.
ガタ
ガタ
ガタ
....
THE POLICE ARE PROBABLY ALREADY AT MY HOUSE. WHAT AM I GOING TO DO?
.....
DO YOU HAVE ANY DRUGS HIDDEN IN YOUR ROOM?
NO, AND I DON'T WALK AROUND WITH THEM EITHER. I DON'T HAVE ANY ON ME NOW.
THEN I THINK YOU'LL BE OKAY...AS LONG AS THEY DON'T CATCH YOU WITH ANY ON YOU, AND YOU LET THE DRUGS WORK THEMSELVES OUT OF YOUR SYSTEM...
I MEAN, YOU KNOW WE'RE NOT GOING TO SAY ANYTHING...
THIS IS EXACTLY WHY YOU SHOULD STOP USING DRUGS! ALL RIGHT, KYO?
Y... YEAH.
DIDN'T YOU REALIZE WHAT KIND OF TROUBLE YOU WERE GETTING INTO?

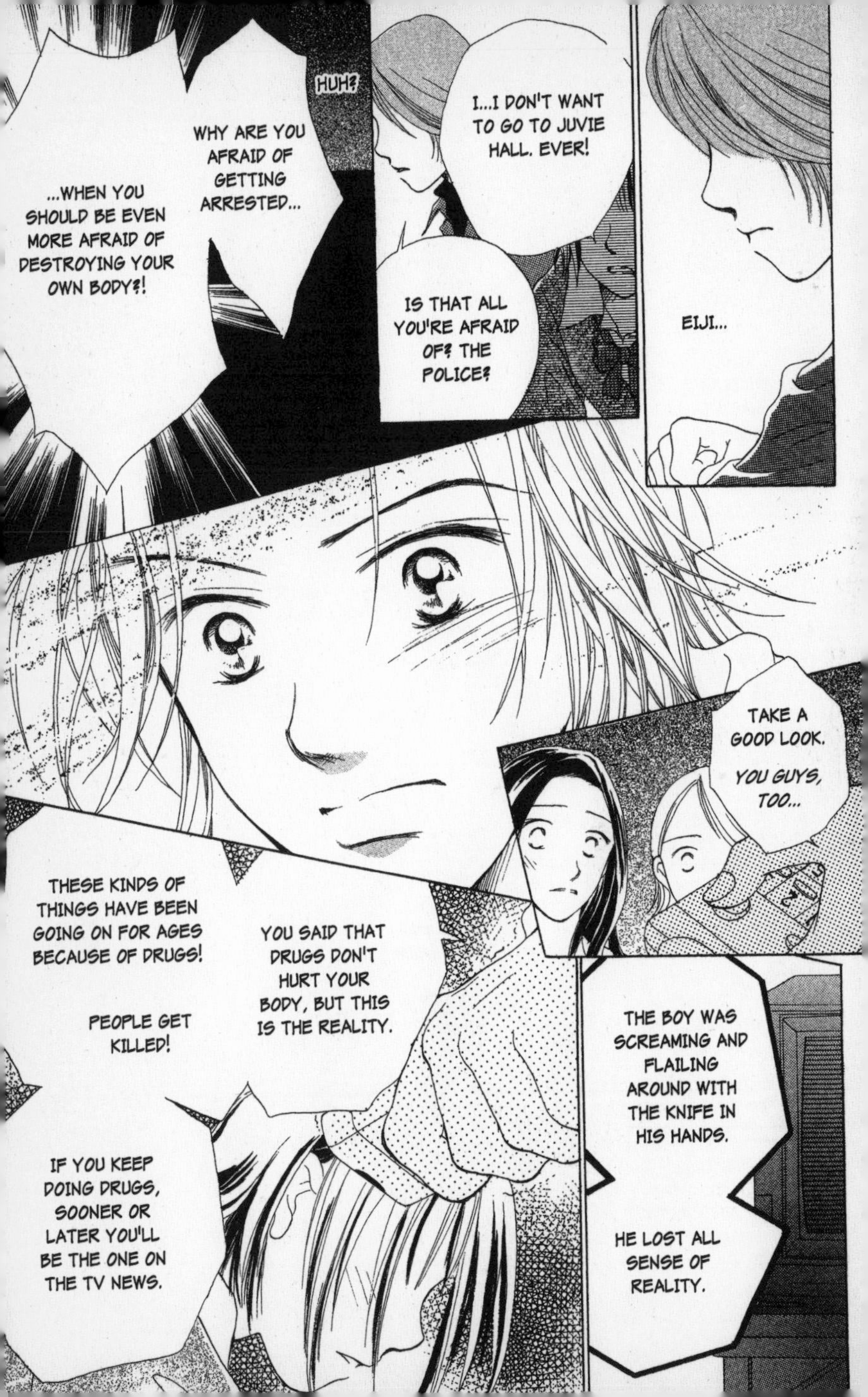
EIJI...
I...I DON'T WANT TO GO TO JUVIE HALL. EVER!
IS THAT ALL YOU'RE AFRAID OF? THE POLICE?
HUH?
WHY ARE YOU AFRAID OF GETTING ARRESTED...
...WHEN YOU SHOULD BE EVEN MORE AFRAID OF DESTROYING YOUR OWN BODY?!
TAKE A GOOD LOOK.
YOU GUYS, TOO...
THE BOY WAS SCREAMING AND FLAILING AROUND WITH THE KNIFE IN HIS HANDS.
HE LOST ALL SENSE OF REALITY.
YOU SAID THAT DRUGS DON'T HURT YOUR BODY, BUT THIS IS THE REALITY.
THESE KINDS OF THINGS HAVE BEEN GOING ON FOR AGES BECAUSE OF DRUGS!
PEOPLE GET KILLED!
IF YOU KEEP DOING DRUGS, SOONER OR LATER YOU'LL BE THE ONE ON THE TV NEWS.

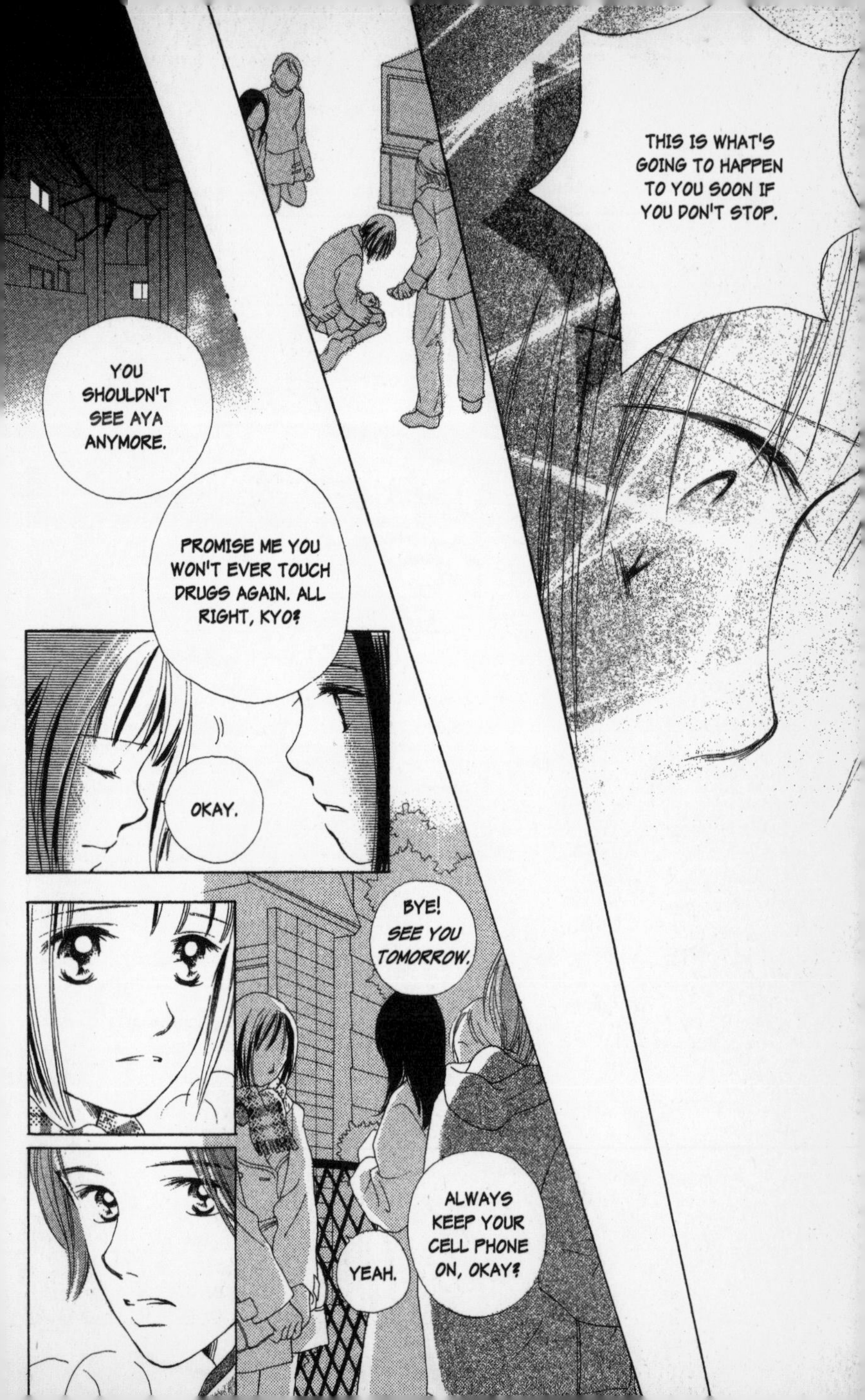
THIS IS WHAT'S GOING TO HAPPEN TO YOU SOON IF YOU DON'T STOP.
YOU SHOULDN'T SEE AYA ANYMORE.
PROMISE ME YOU WON'T EVER TOUCH DRUGS AGAIN. ALL RIGHT, KYO?
OKAY.
BYE! SEE YOU TOMORROW.
ALWAYS KEEP YOUR CELL PHONE ON, OKAY?
YEAH.

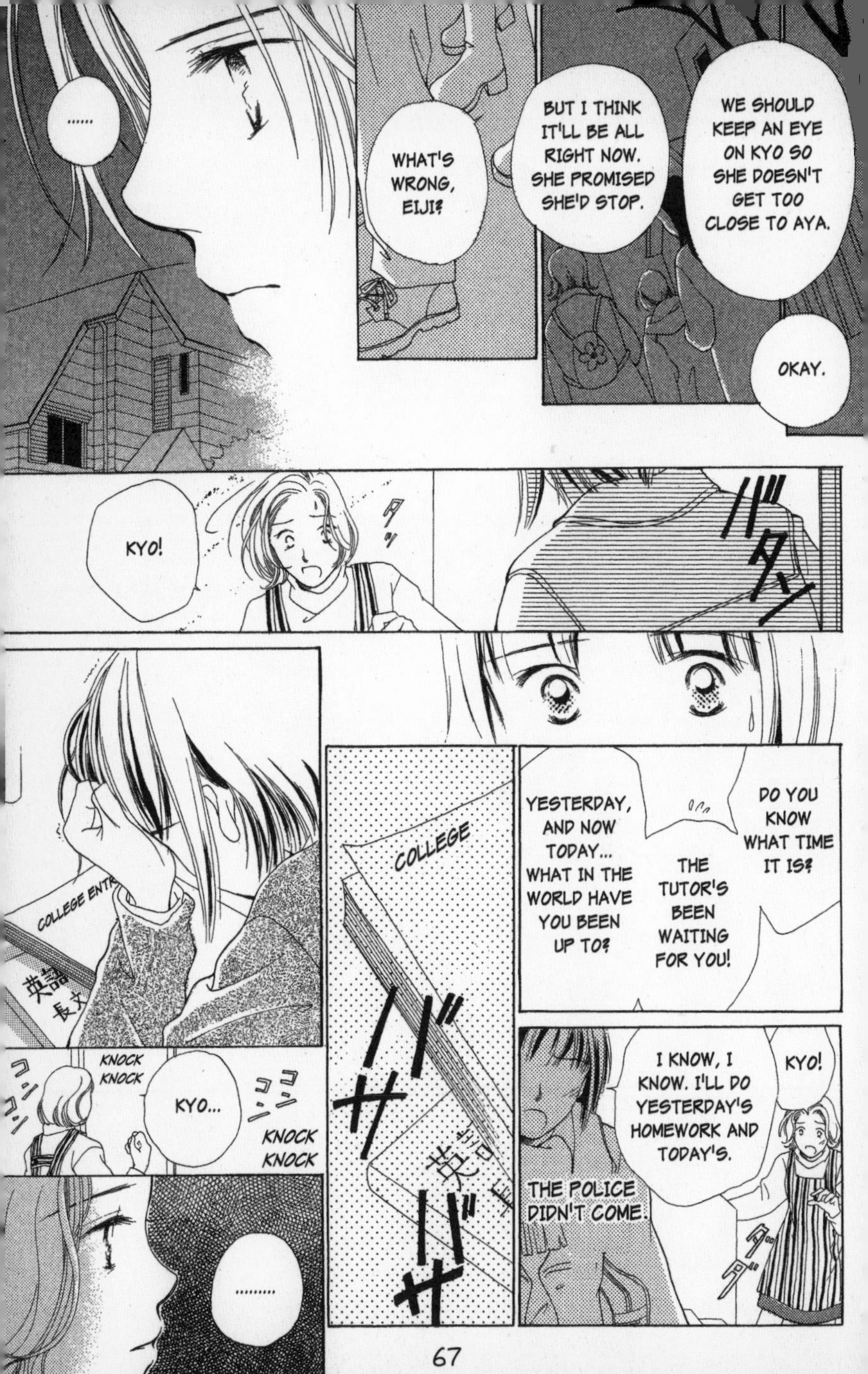
WE SHOULD KEEP AN EYE ON KYO SO SHE DOESN'T GET TOO CLOSE TO AYA.
BUT I THINK IT'LL BE ALL RIGHT NOW. SHE PROMISED SHE'D STOP.
OKAY.
WHAT'S WRONG, EIJI?
......
バタン
タッ
KYO!
DO YOU KNOW WHAT TIME IT IS?
THE TUTOR'S BEEN WAITING FOR YOU!
YESTERDAY, AND NOW TODAY... WHAT IN THE WORLD HAVE YOU BEEN UP TO?
KYO!
I KNOW, I KNOW. I'LL DO YESTERDAY'S HOMEWORK AND TODAY'S.
THE POLICE DIDN'T COME.
COLLEGE
バサ
バサ
COLLEGE ENTR
英語長文
KNOCK KNOCK
KYO...
KNOCK KNOCK
....

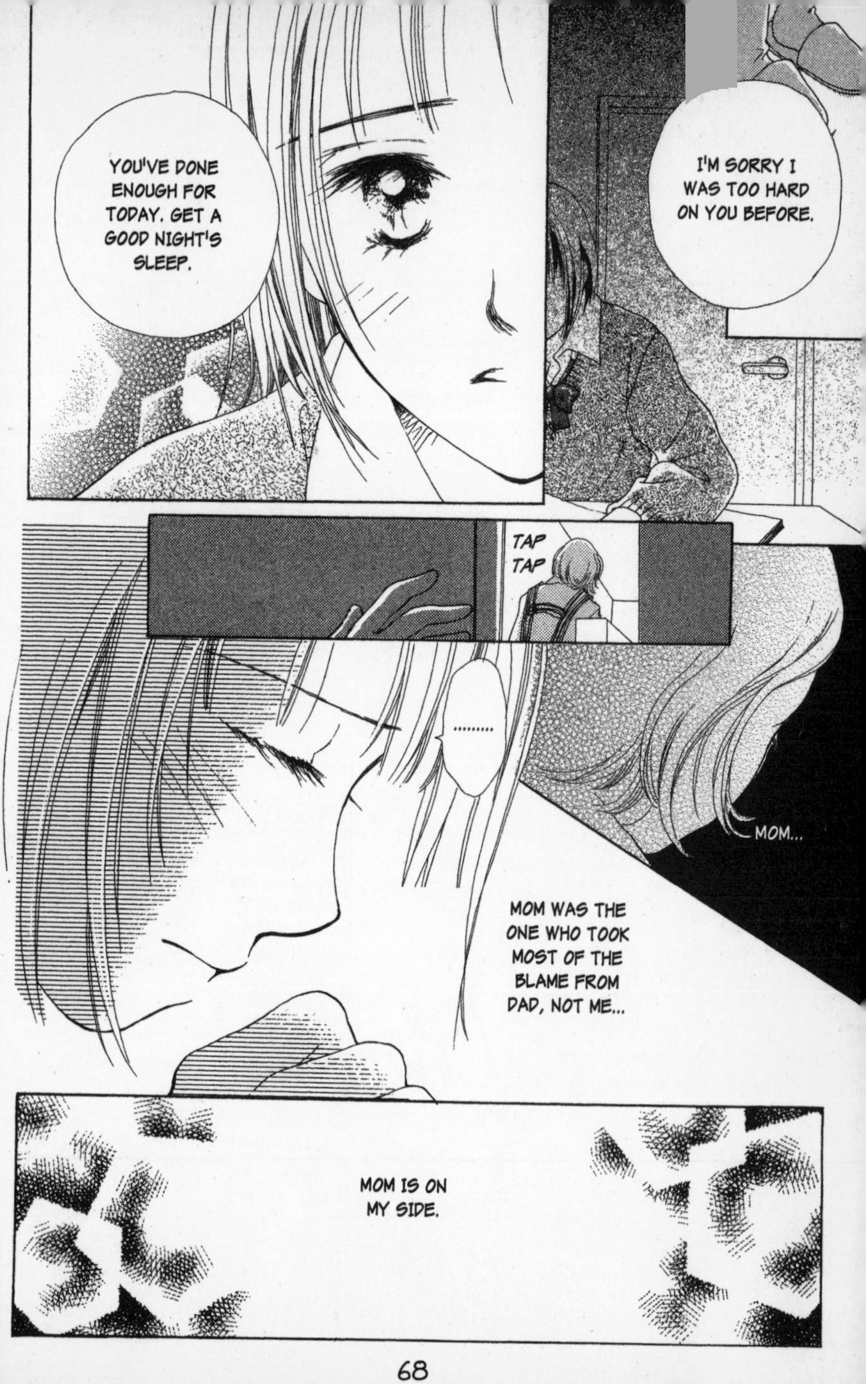
I'M SORRY I WAS TOO HARD ON YOU BEFORE.
YOU'VE DONE ENOUGH FOR TODAY. GET A GOOD NIGHT'S SLEEP.
TAP TAP
....
MOM...
MOM WAS THE ONE WHO TOOK MOST OF THE BLAME FROM DAD, NOT ME...
MOM IS ON MY SIDE.

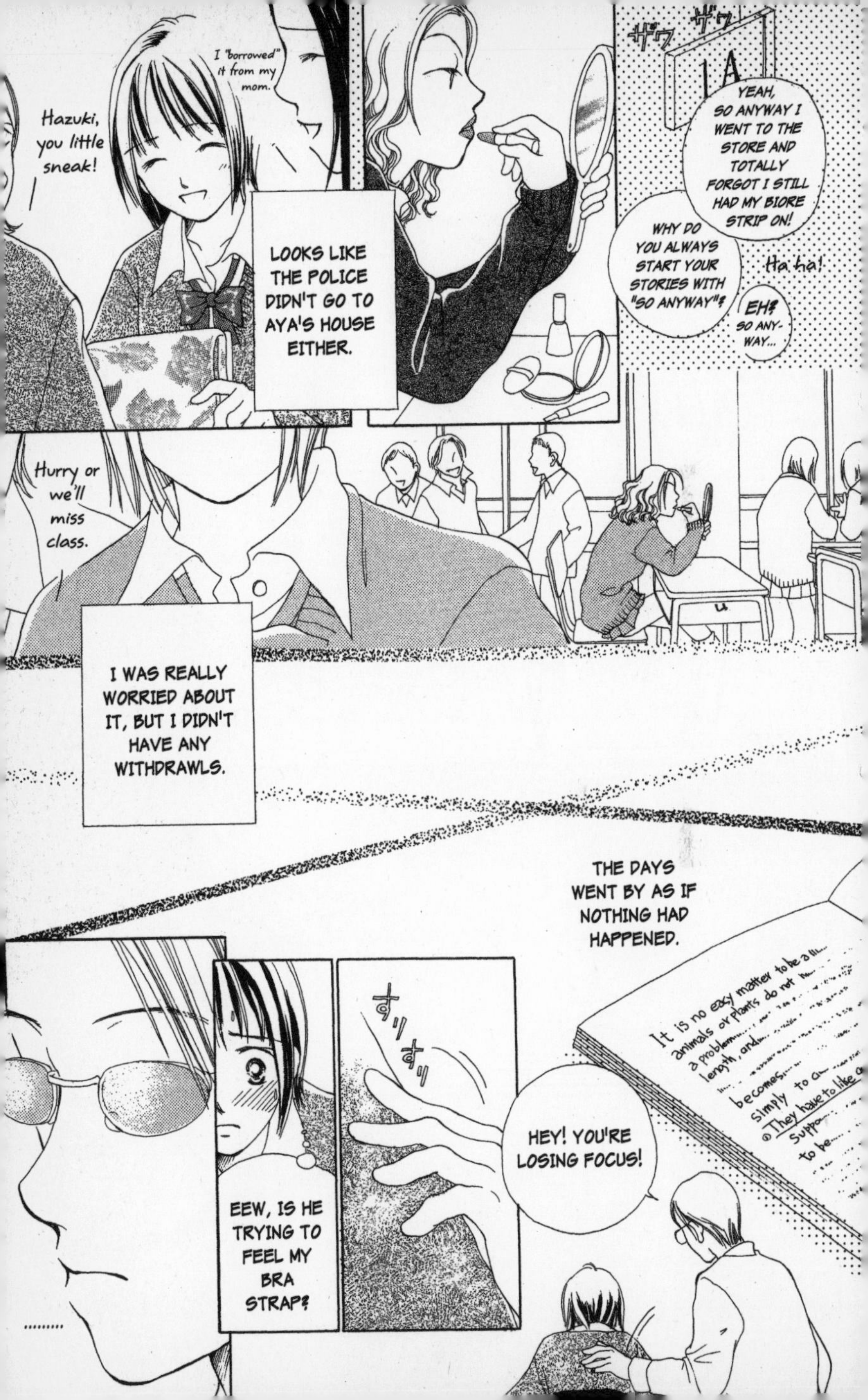
ザワ ザワッ
1A
YEAH, SO ANYWAY I WENT TO THE STORE AND TOTALLY FORGOT I STILL HAD MY BIORE STRIP ON!
WHY DO YOU ALWAYS START YOUR STORIES WITH "SO ANYWAY"?
Ha ha!
EH? SO ANYWAY...
LOOKS LIKE THE POLICE DIDN'T GO TO AYA'S HOUSE EITHER.
I "borrowed" it from my mom.
Hazuki, you little sneak!
Hurry or we'll miss class.
I WAS REALLY WORRIED ABOUT IT, BUT I DIDN'T HAVE ANY WITHDRAWLS.
THE DAYS WENT BY AS IF NOTHING HAD HAPPENED.
It is no easy matter to be a
animals or plants do not
a problem
length, and
becomes
simply to a
They have to like a
Supp
to be
HEY! YOU'RE LOSING FOCUS!
すりすり
EEW, IS HE TRYING TO FEEL MY BRA STRAP?
....

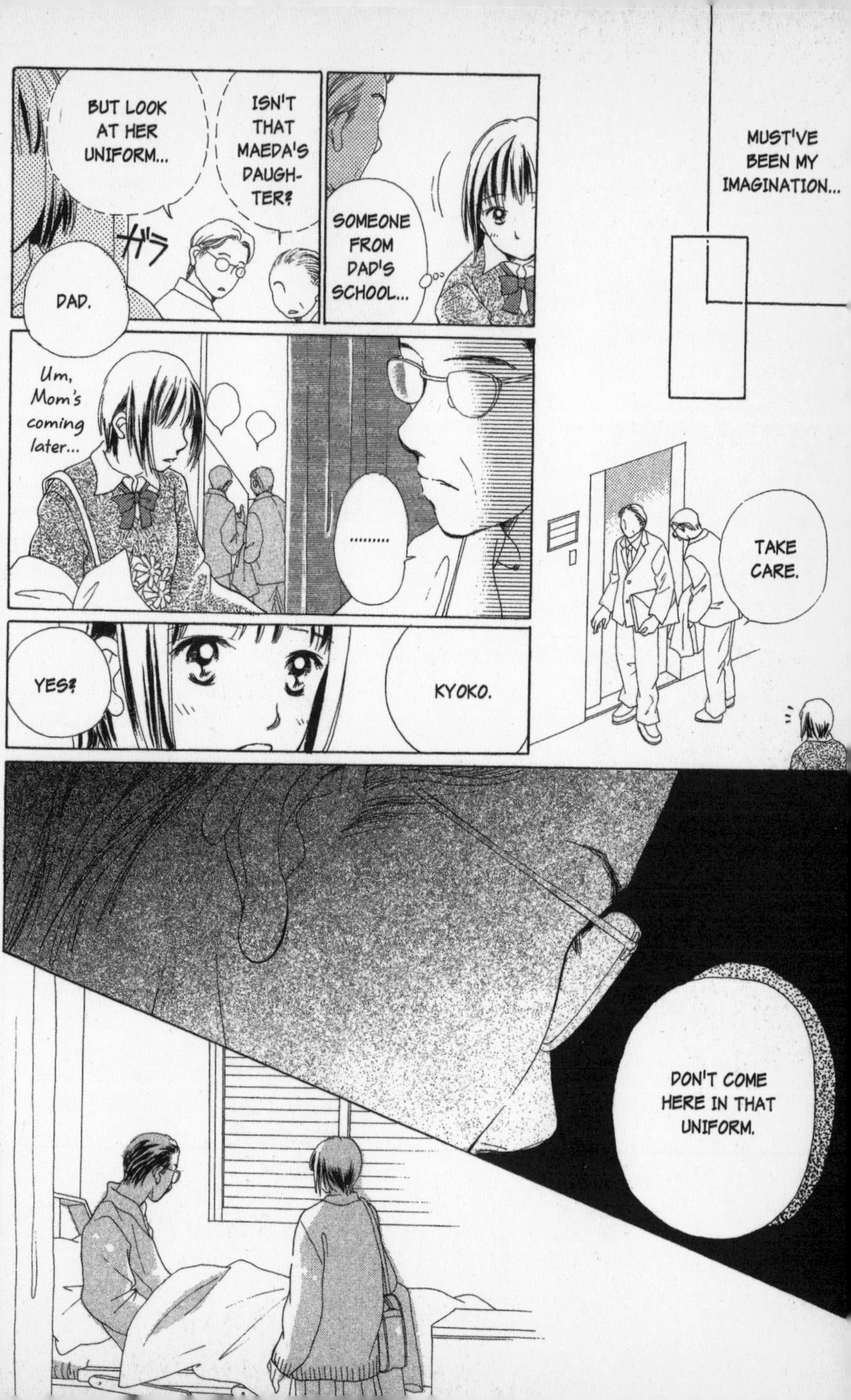
MUST'VE BEEN MY IMAGINATION...
TAKE CARE.
SOMEONE FROM DAD'S SCHOOL...
ISN'T THAT MAEDA'S DAUGHTER?
BUT LOOK AT HER UNIFORM...
ガラ
DAD.
....
Um, Mom's coming later...
KYOKO.
YES?
DON'T COME HERE IN THAT UNIFORM.

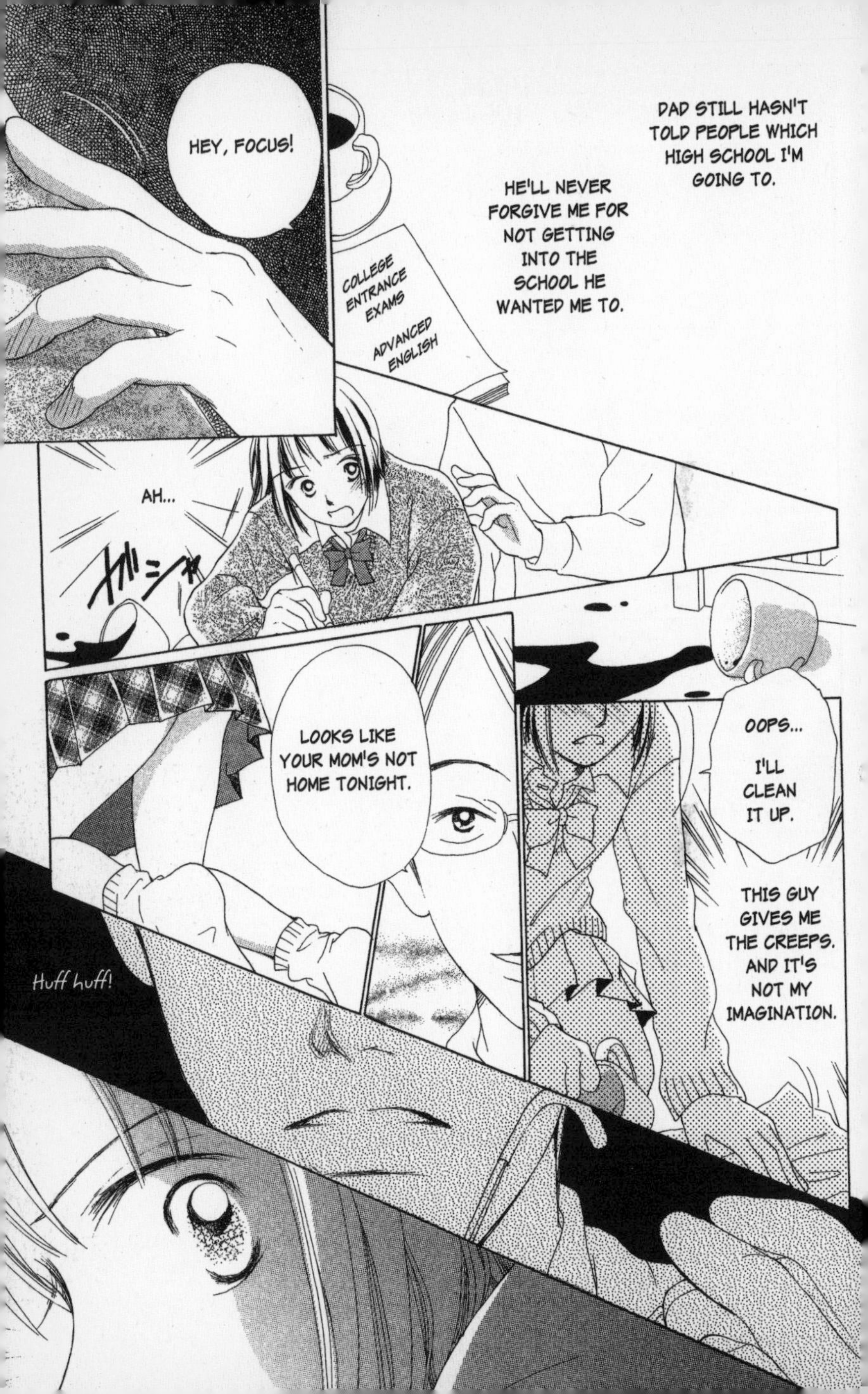
DAD STILL HASN'T TOLD PEOPLE WHICH HIGH SCHOOL I'M GOING TO.
HE'LL NEVER FORGIVE ME FOR NOT GETTING INTO THE SCHOOL HE WANTED ME TO.
COLLEGE ENTRANCE EXAMS
ADVANCED ENGLISH
HEY, FOCUS!
AH...
ガシャ
OOPS...
I'LL CLEAN IT UP.
THIS GUY GIVES ME THE CREEPS. AND IT'S NOT MY IMAGINATION.
LOOKS LIKE YOUR MOM'S NOT HOME TONIGHT.
Huff huff!

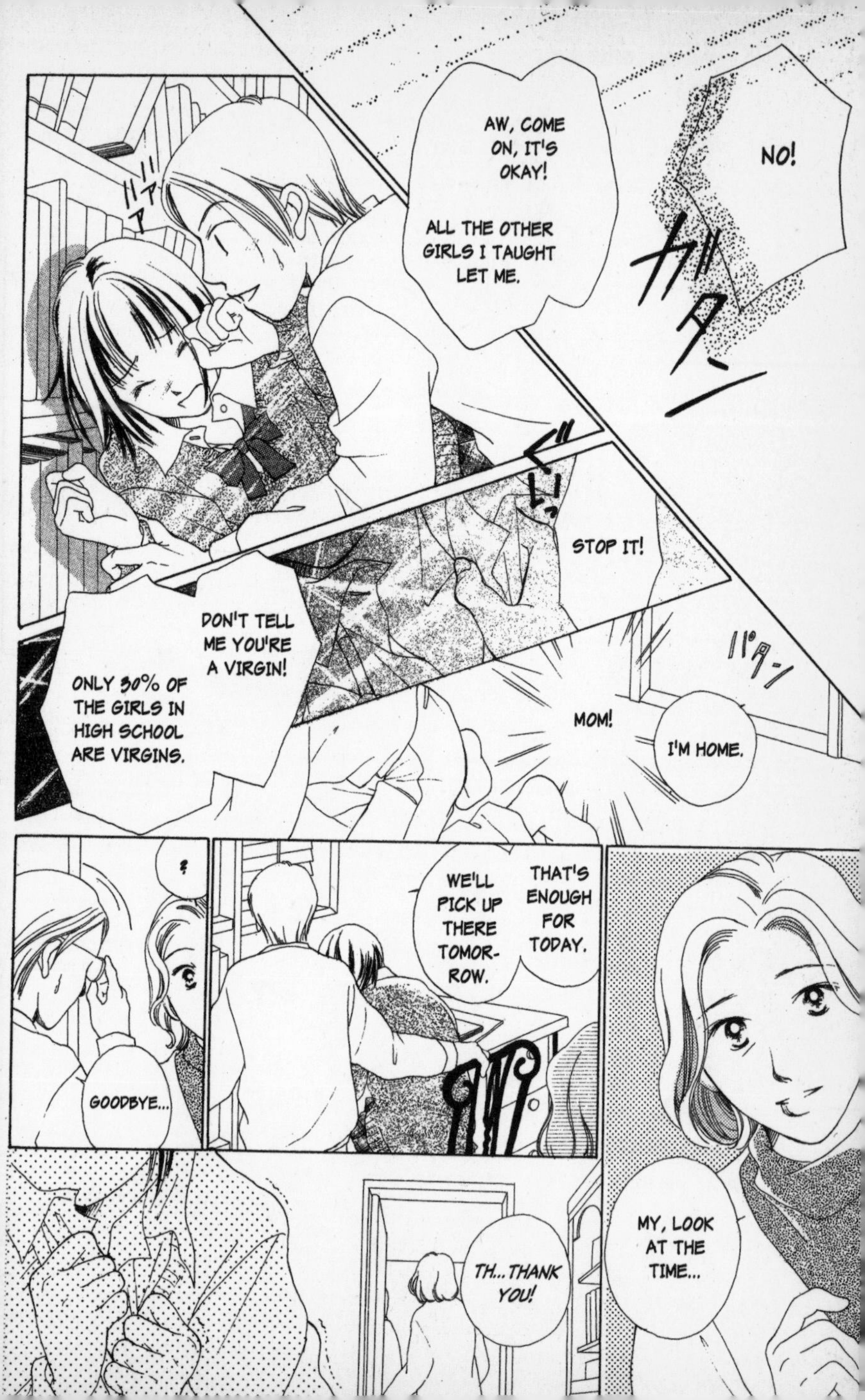

NO!
AW, COME ON, IT'S OKAY!
ALL THE OTHER GIRLS I TAUGHT LET ME.
STOP IT!
DON'T TELL ME YOU'RE A VIRGIN!
ONLY 30% OF THE GIRLS IN HIGH SCHOOL ARE VIRGINS.
I'M HOME.
MOM!
MY, LOOK AT THE TIME...
THAT'S ENOUGH FOR TODAY.
WE'LL PICK UP THERE TOMORROW.
?
GOODBYE...
TH...THANK YOU!

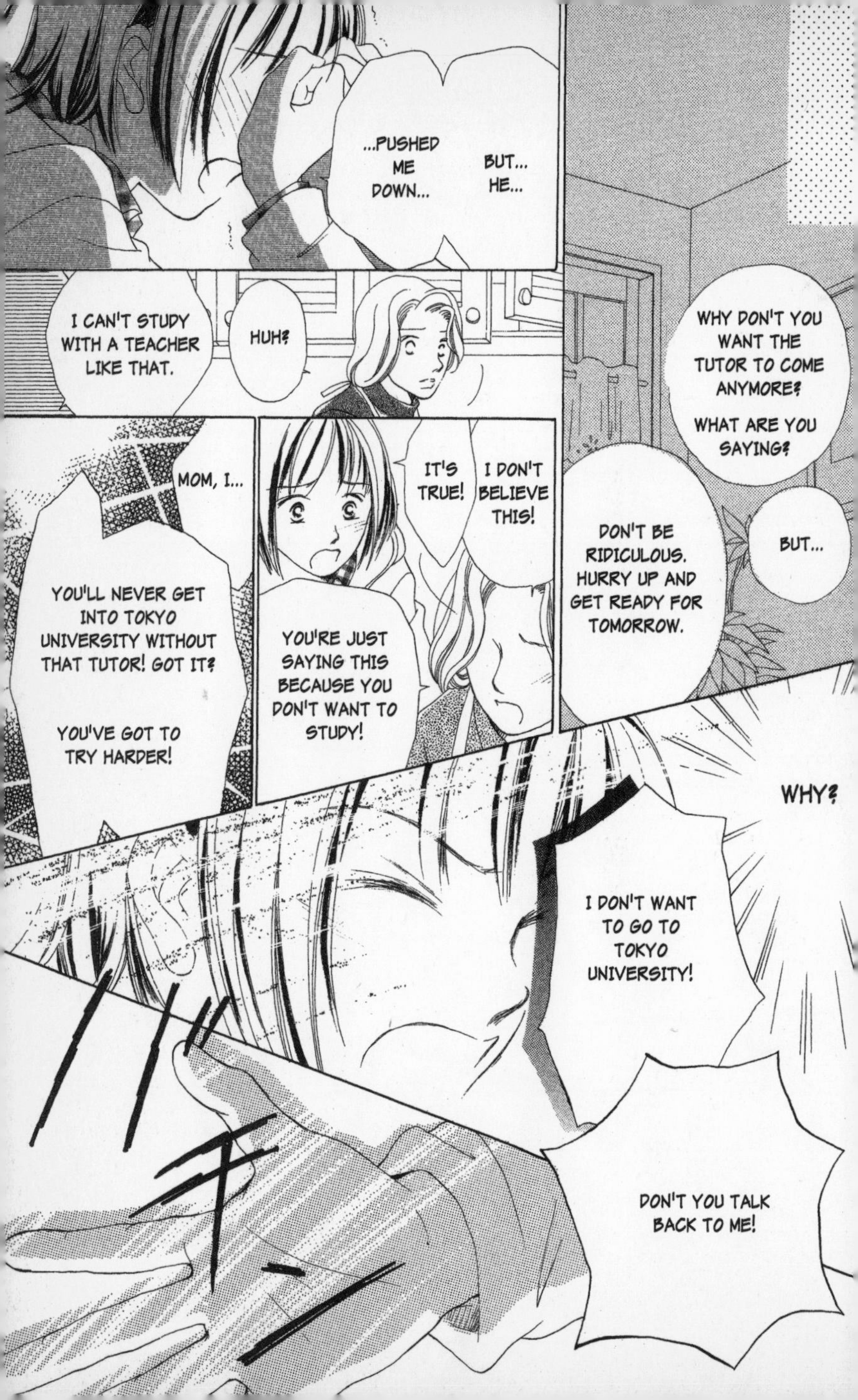
WHY DON'T YOU WANT THE TUTOR TO COME ANYMORE?
WHAT ARE YOU SAYING?
BUT...
DON'T BE RIDICULOUS. HURRY UP AND GET READY FOR TOMORROW.
BUT... HE...
...PUSHED ME DOWN...
HUH?
I CAN'T STUDY WITH A TEACHER LIKE THAT.
I DON'T BELIEVE THIS!
IT'S TRUE!
YOU'RE JUST SAYING THIS BECAUSE YOU DON'T WANT TO STUDY!
MOM, I...
YOU'LL NEVER GET INTO TOKYO UNIVERSITY WITHOUT THAT TUTOR! GOT IT?
YOU'VE GOT TO TRY HARDER!
WHY?
I DON'T WANT TO GO TO TOKYO UNIVERSITY!
DON'T YOU TALK BACK TO ME!

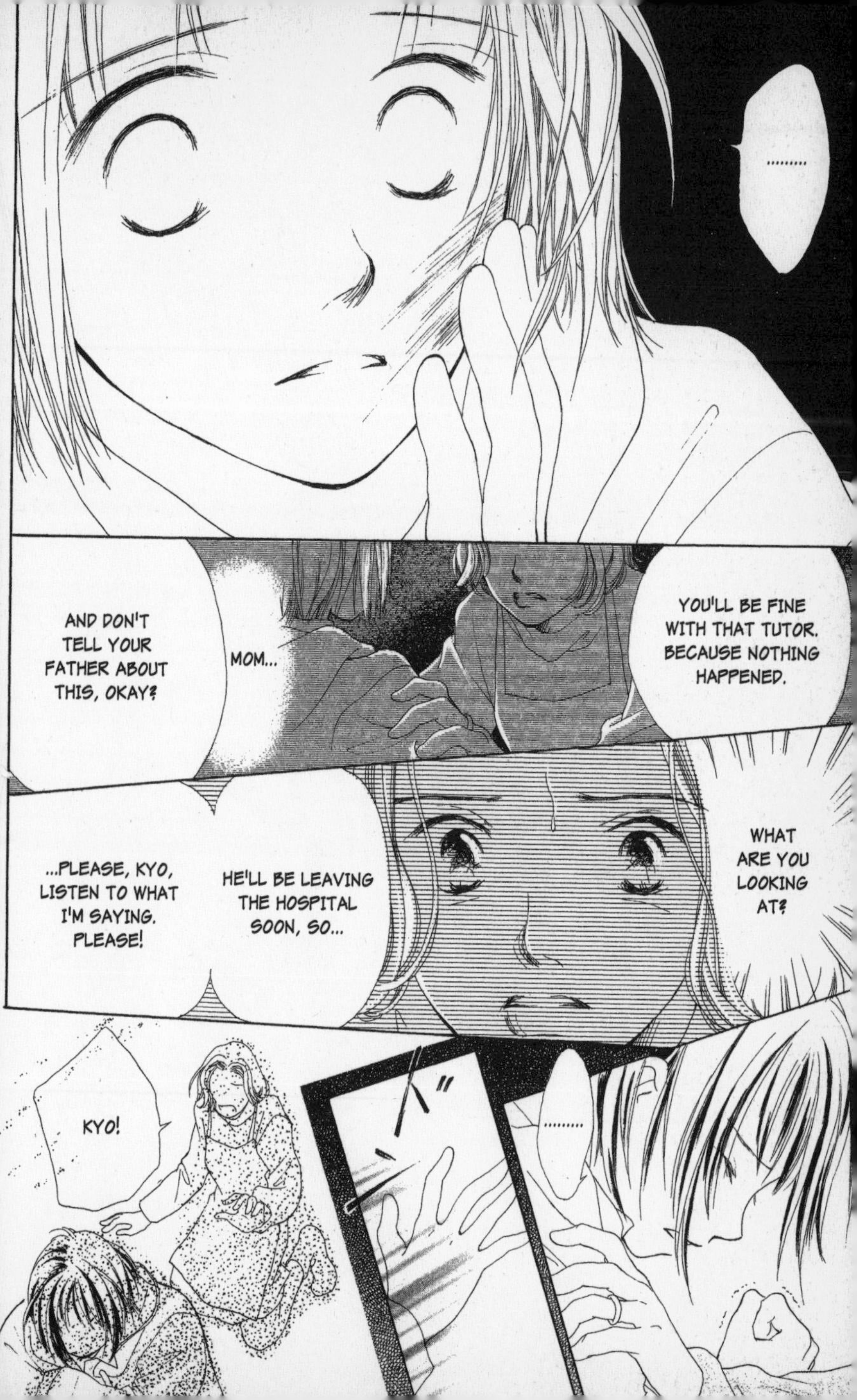

....
YOU'LL BE FINE WITH THAT TUTOR. BECAUSE NOTHING HAPPENED.
MOM...
AND DON'T TELL YOUR FATHER ABOUT THIS, OKAY?
WHAT ARE YOU LOOKING AT?
HE'LL BE LEAVING THE HOSPITAL SOON, SO...
...PLEASE, KYO, LISTEN TO WHAT I'M SAYING. PLEASE!
....
KYO!

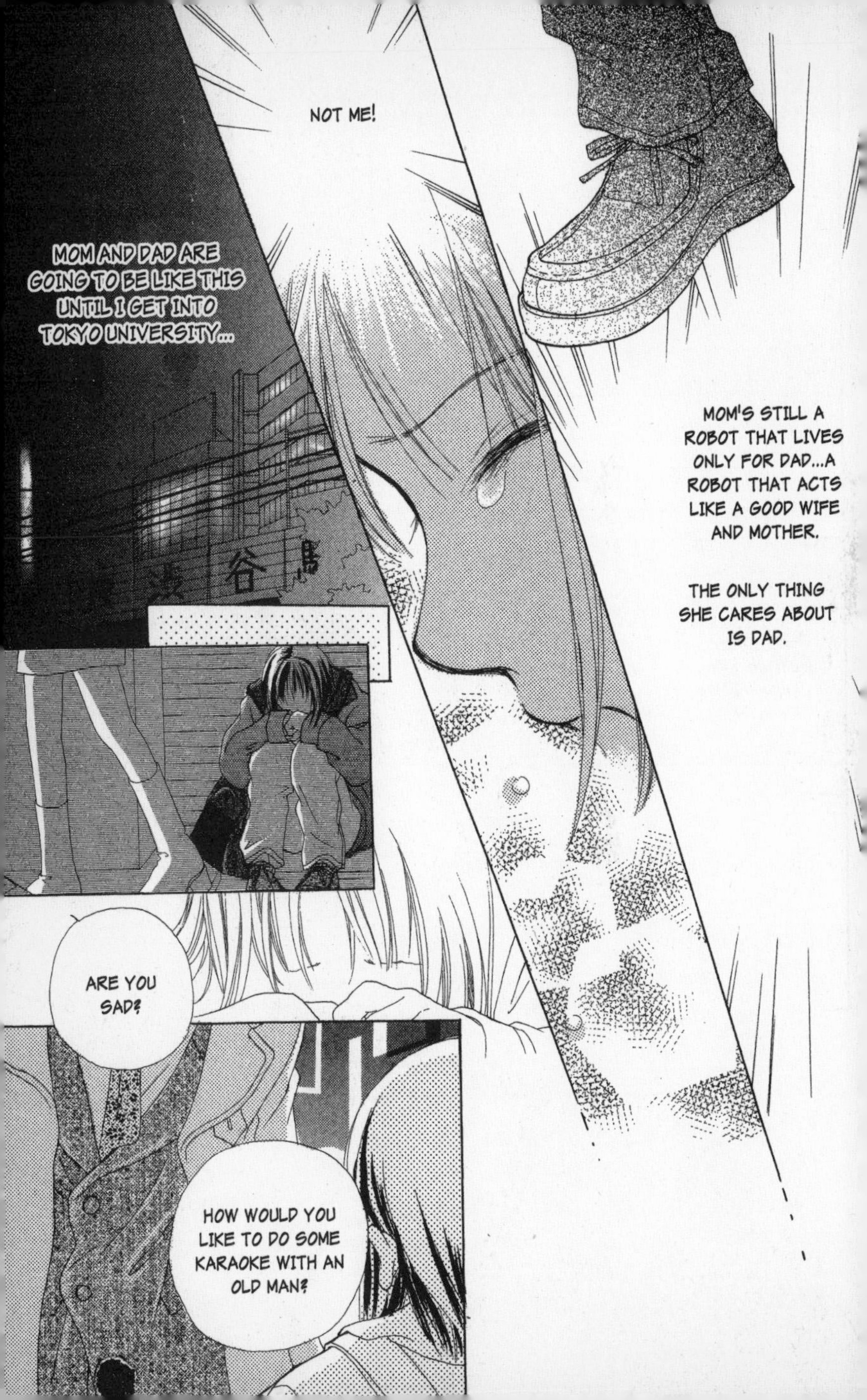
MOM'S STILL A ROBOT THAT LIVES ONLY FOR DAD...A ROBOT THAT ACTS LIKE A GOOD WIFE AND MOTHER.
THE ONLY THING SHE CARES ABOUT IS DAD.
NOT ME!
MOM AND DAD ARE GOING TO BE LIKE THIS UNTIL I GET INTO TOKYO UNIVERSITY...
渋谷 [illegible]
ARE YOU SAD?
HOW WOULD YOU LIKE TO DO SOME KARAOKE WITH AN OLD MAN?

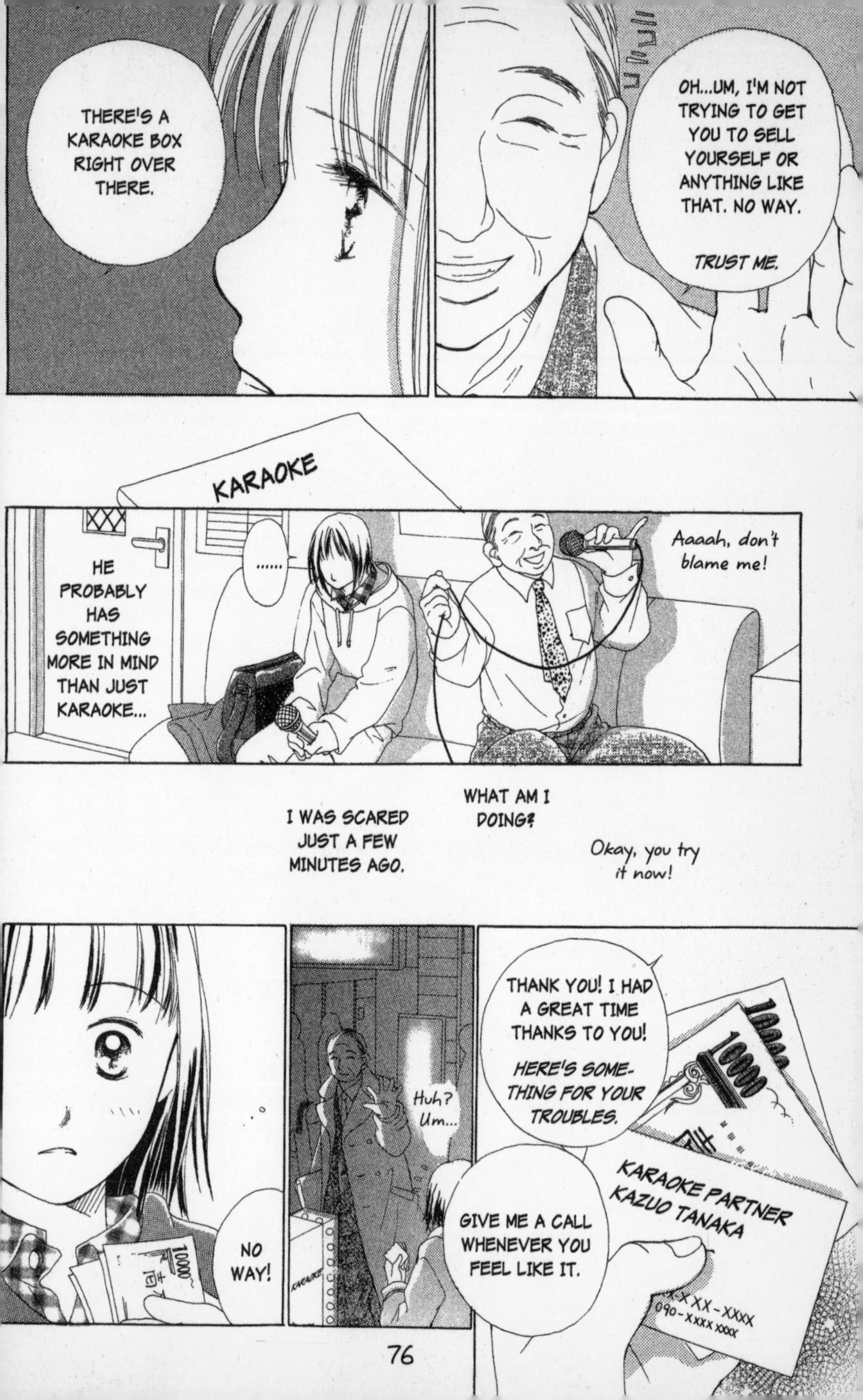
OH...UM, I'M NOT TRYING TO GET YOU TO SELL YOURSELF OR ANYTHING LIKE THAT. NO WAY.
TRUST ME.
THERE'S A KARAOKE BOX RIGHT OVER THERE.
KARAOKE
Aaaah, don't blame me!
......
HE PROBABLY HAS SOMETHING MORE IN MIND THAN JUST KARAOKE...
Okay, you try it now!
WHAT AM I DOING?
I WAS SCARED JUST A FEW MINUTES AGO.
THANK YOU! I HAD A GREAT TIME THANKS TO YOU!
HERE'S SOME-THING FOR YOUR TROUBLES.
GIVE ME A CALL WHENEVER YOU FEEL LIKE IT.
KARAOKE PARTNER
KAZUO TANAKA
XX-XXXX
090-XXXX XXXX
Huh? Um...
NO WAY!

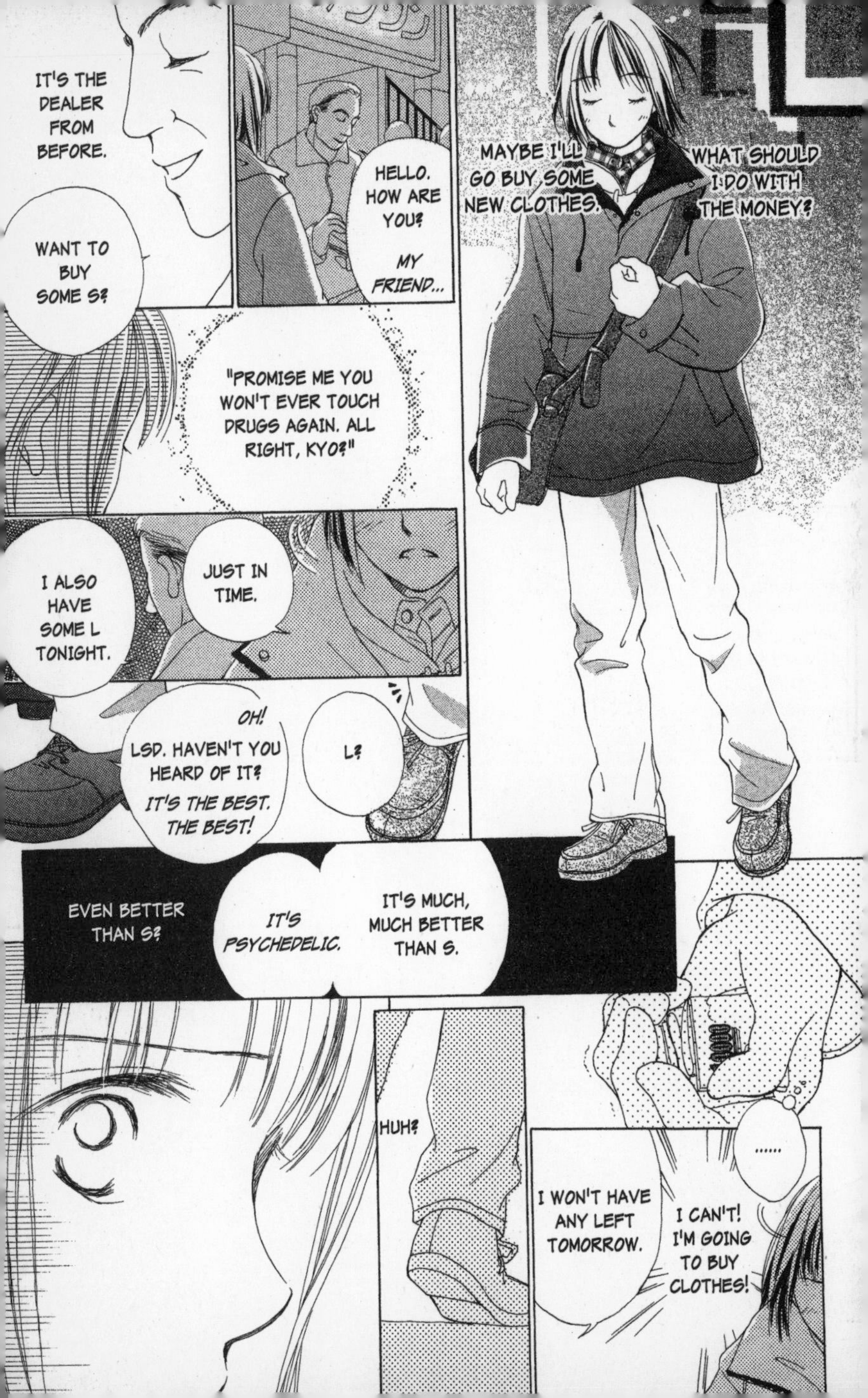
WHAT SHOULD I DO WITH THE MONEY?
MAYBE I'LL GO BUY SOME NEW CLOTHES.
HELLO. HOW ARE YOU?
MY FRIEND...
IT'S THE DEALER FROM BEFORE.
WANT TO BUY SOME S?
"PROMISE ME YOU WON'T EVER TOUCH DRUGS AGAIN. ALL RIGHT, KYO?"
JUST IN TIME.
I ALSO HAVE SOME L TONIGHT.
L?
OH!
LSD. HAVEN'T YOU HEARD OF IT?
IT'S THE BEST. THE BEST!
IT'S MUCH, MUCH BETTER THAN S.
IT'S PSYCHEDELIC.
EVEN BETTER THAN S?
......
I CAN'T! I'M GOING TO BUY CLOTHES!
I WON'T HAVE ANY LEFT TOMORROW.
HUH?

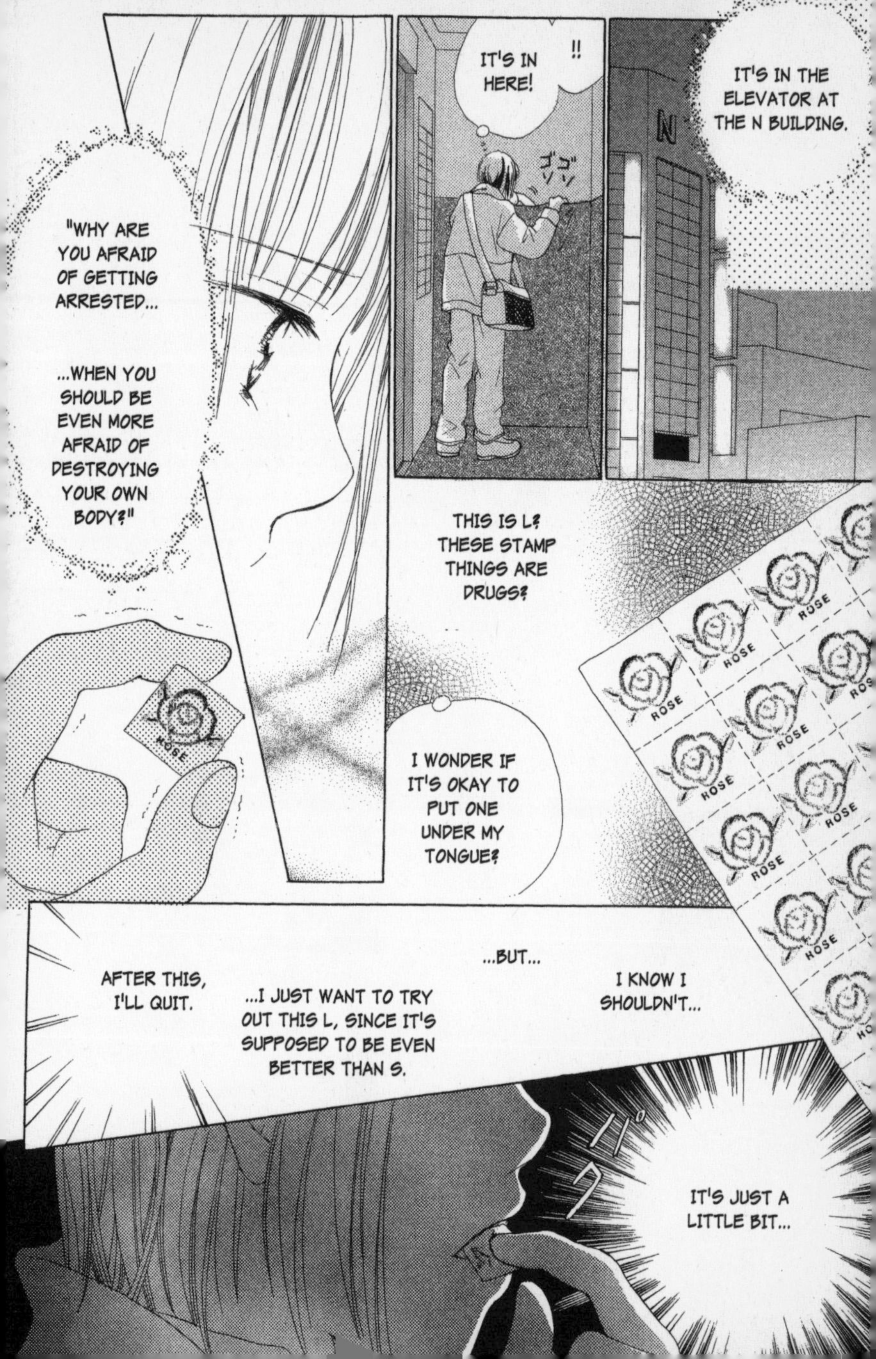
IT'S IN THE ELEVATOR AT THE N BUILDING.
IT'S IN HERE!
!!
THIS IS L? THESE STAMP THINGS ARE DRUGS?
I WONDER IF IT'S OKAY TO PUT ONE UNDER MY TONGUE?
"WHY ARE YOU AFRAID OF GETTING ARRESTED...
...WHEN YOU SHOULD BE EVEN MORE AFRAID OF DESTROYING YOUR OWN BODY?"
I KNOW I SHOULDN'T...
...BUT...
...I JUST WANT TO TRY OUT THIS L, SINCE IT'S SUPPOSED TO BE EVEN BETTER THAN S.
AFTER THIS, I'LL QUIT.
IT'S JUST A LITTLE BIT...

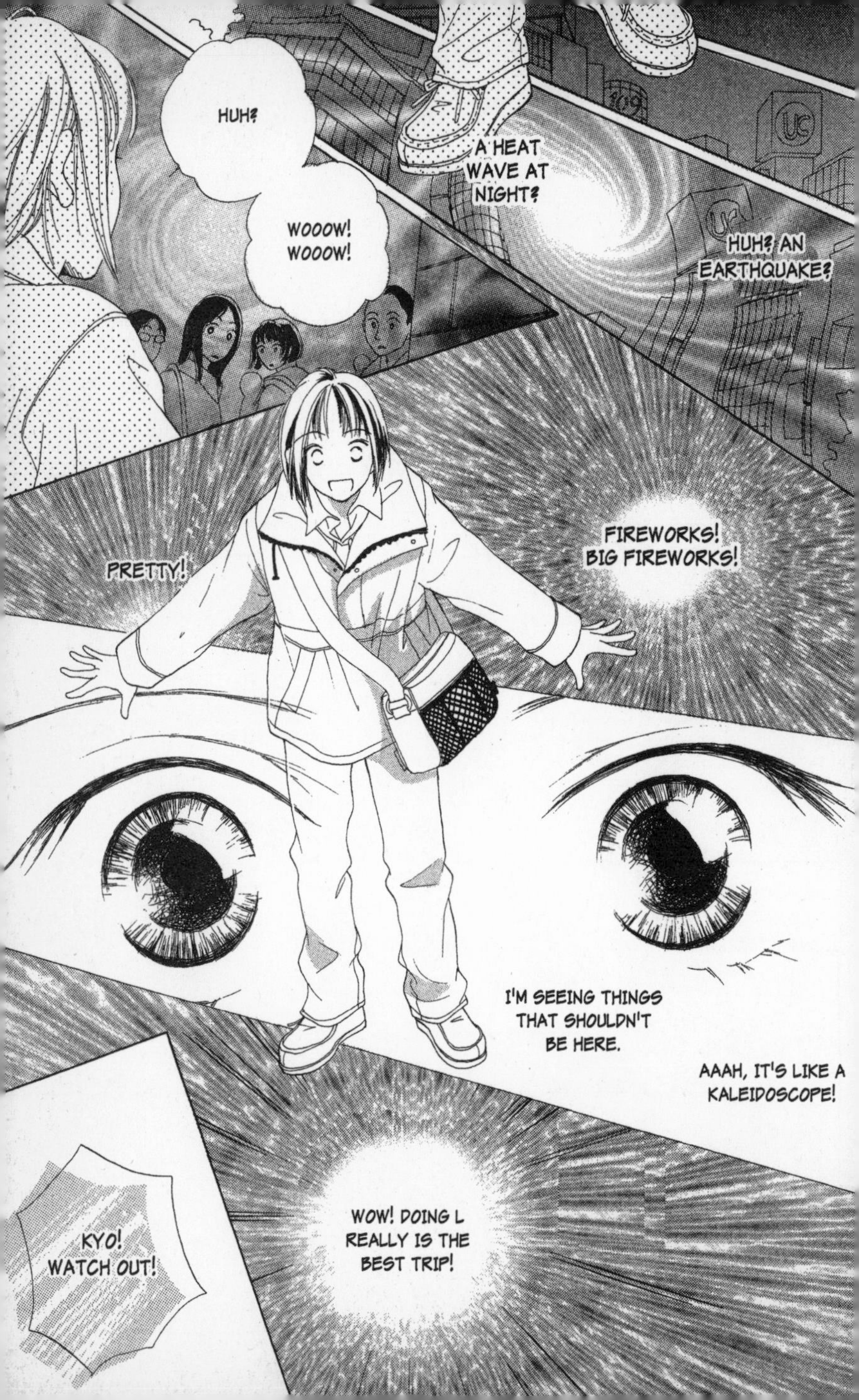
A HEAT WAVE AT NIGHT?
HUH? AN EARTHQUAKE?
HUH?
WOOOW! WOOOW!
FIREWORKS! BIG FIREWORKS!
PRETTY!
AAAH, IT'S LIKE A KALEIDOSCOPE!
I'M SEEING THINGS THAT SHOULDN'T BE HERE.
WOW! DOING L REALLY IS THE BEST TRIP!
KYO! WATCH OUT!

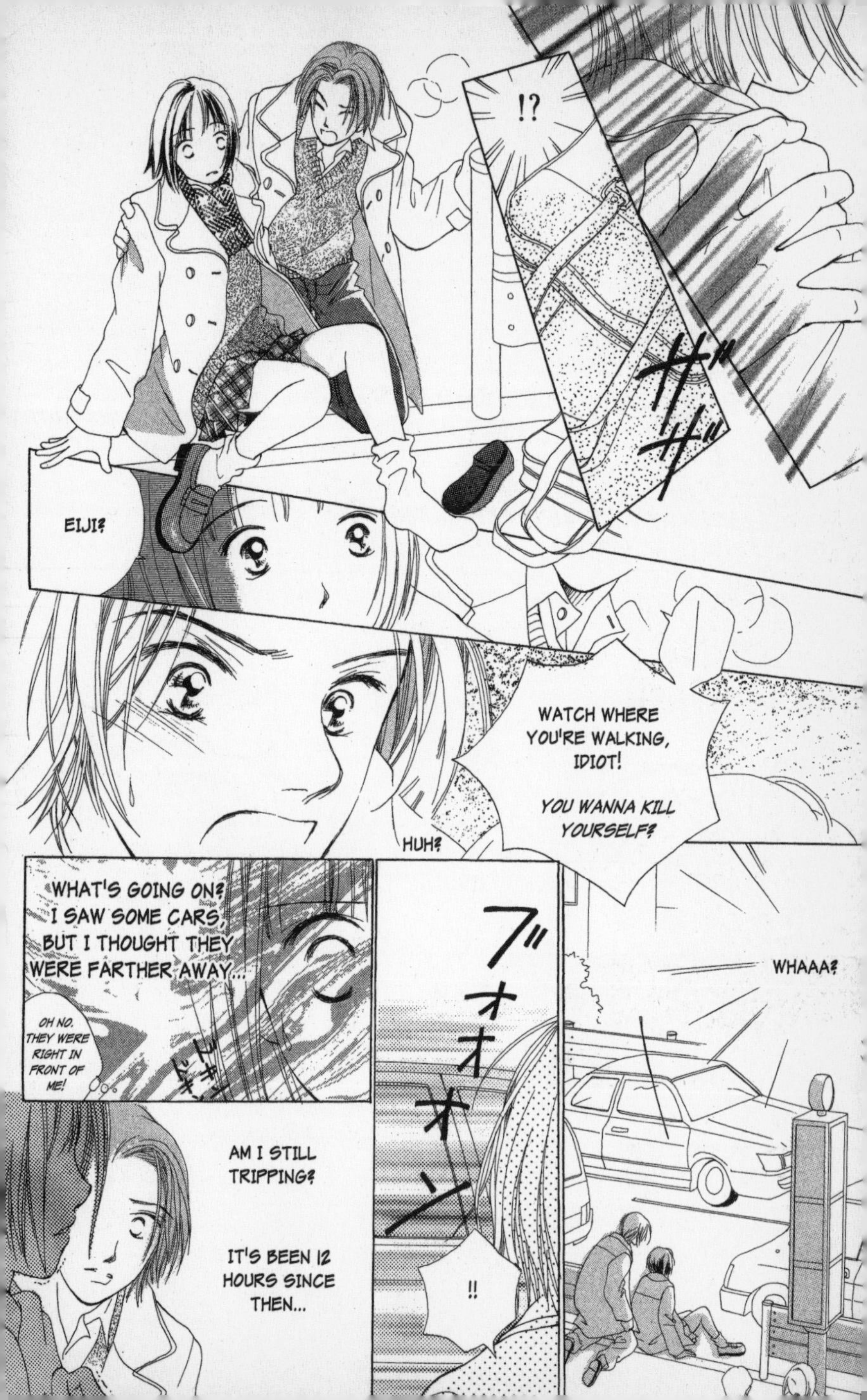
!?
EIJI?
WATCH WHERE YOU'RE WALKING, IDIOT!
YOU WANNA KILL YOURSELF?
HUH?
WHAAA?
ブオオン
!!
WHAT'S GOING ON? I SAW SOME CARS, BUT I THOUGHT THEY WERE FARTHER AWAY...
OH NO. THEY WERE RIGHT IN FRONT OF ME!
AM I STILL TRIPPING?
IT'S BEEN 12 HOURS SINCE THEN...

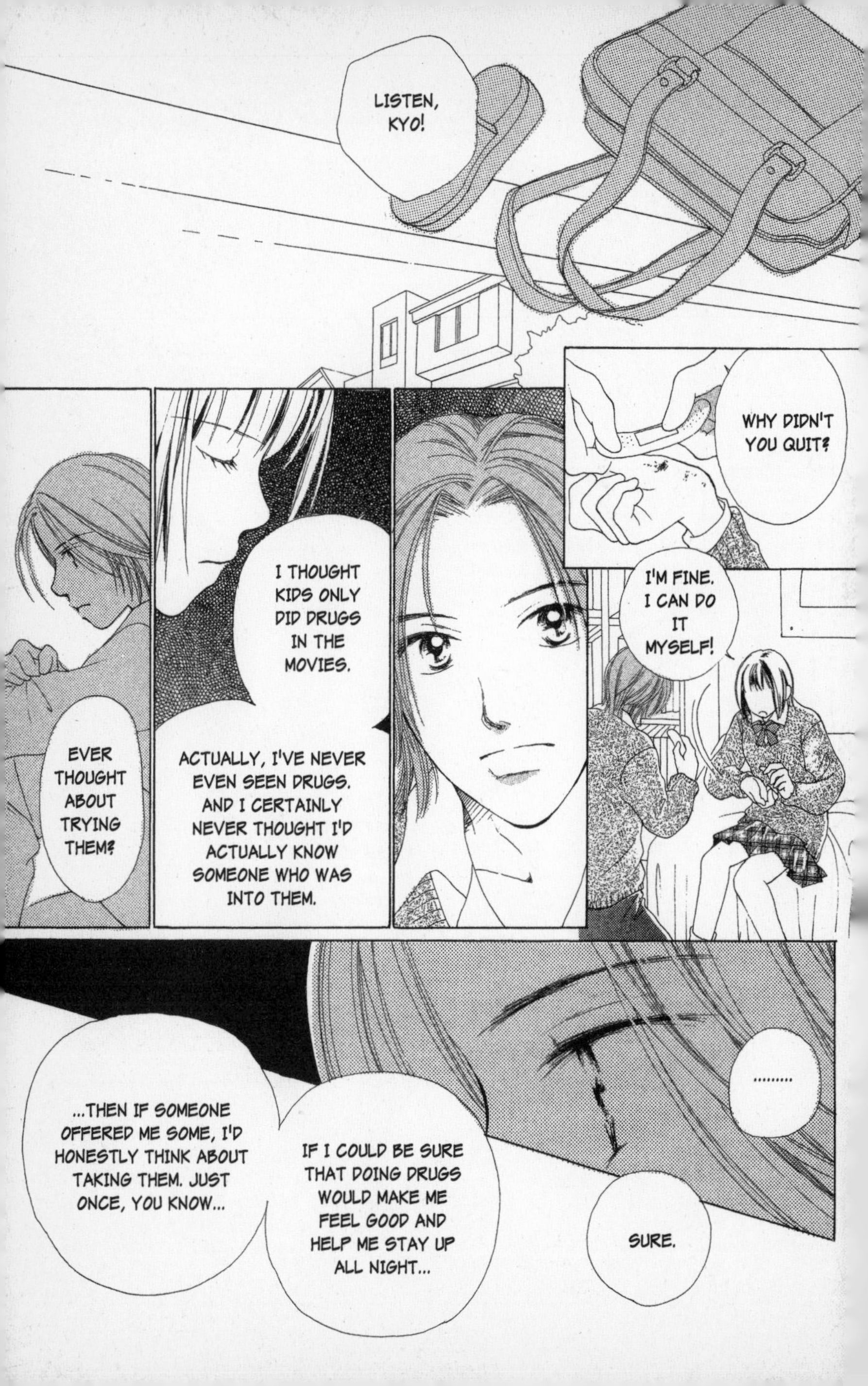
LISTEN, KYO!
WHY DIDN'T YOU QUIT?
I'M FINE. I CAN DO IT MYSELF!
I THOUGHT KIDS ONLY DID DRUGS IN THE MOVIES.
ACTUALLY, I'VE NEVER EVEN SEEN DRUGS. AND I CERTAINLY NEVER THOUGHT I'D ACTUALLY KNOW SOMEONE WHO WAS INTO THEM.
EVER THOUGHT ABOUT TRYING THEM?
....
SURE.
IF I COULD BE SURE THAT DOING DRUGS WOULD MAKE ME FEEL GOOD AND HELP ME STAY UP ALL NIGHT...
...THEN IF SOMEONE OFFERED ME SOME, I'D HONESTLY THINK ABOUT TAKING THEM. JUST ONCE, YOU KNOW...

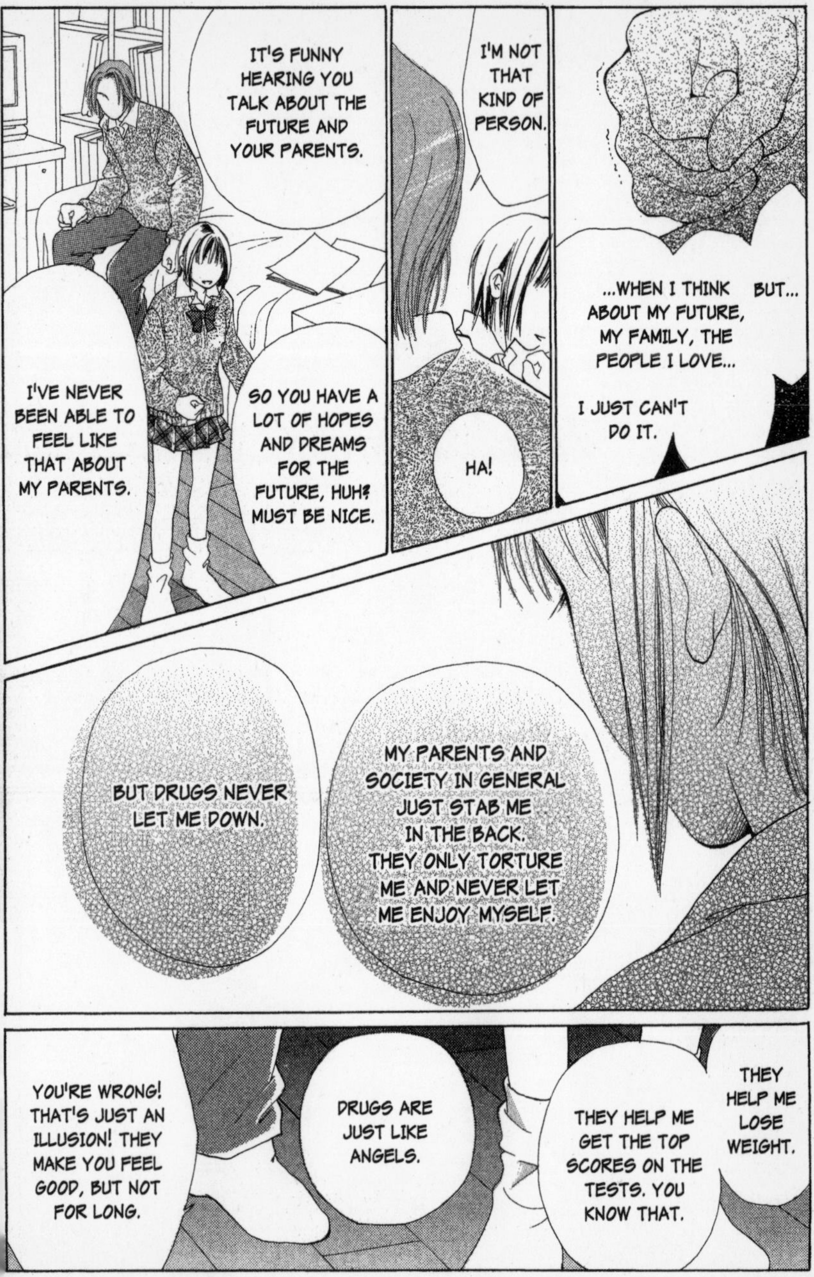
BUT...
...WHEN I THINK ABOUT MY FUTURE, MY FAMILY, THE PEOPLE I LOVE...
I JUST CAN'T DO IT.
I'M NOT THAT KIND OF PERSON.
HA!
IT'S FUNNY HEARING YOU TALK ABOUT THE FUTURE AND YOUR PARENTS.
SO YOU HAVE A LOT OF HOPES AND DREAMS FOR THE FUTURE, HUH? MUST BE NICE.
I'VE NEVER BEEN ABLE TO FEEL LIKE THAT ABOUT MY PARENTS.
MY PARENTS AND SOCIETY IN GENERAL JUST STAB ME IN THE BACK. THEY ONLY TORTURE ME AND NEVER LET ME ENJOY MYSELF.
BUT DRUGS NEVER LET ME DOWN.
THEY HELP ME LOSE WEIGHT.
THEY HELP ME GET THE TOP SCORES ON THE TESTS. YOU KNOW THAT.
DRUGS ARE JUST LIKE ANGELS.
YOU'RE WRONG! THAT'S JUST AN ILLUSION! THEY MAKE YOU FEEL GOOD, BUT NOT FOR LONG.

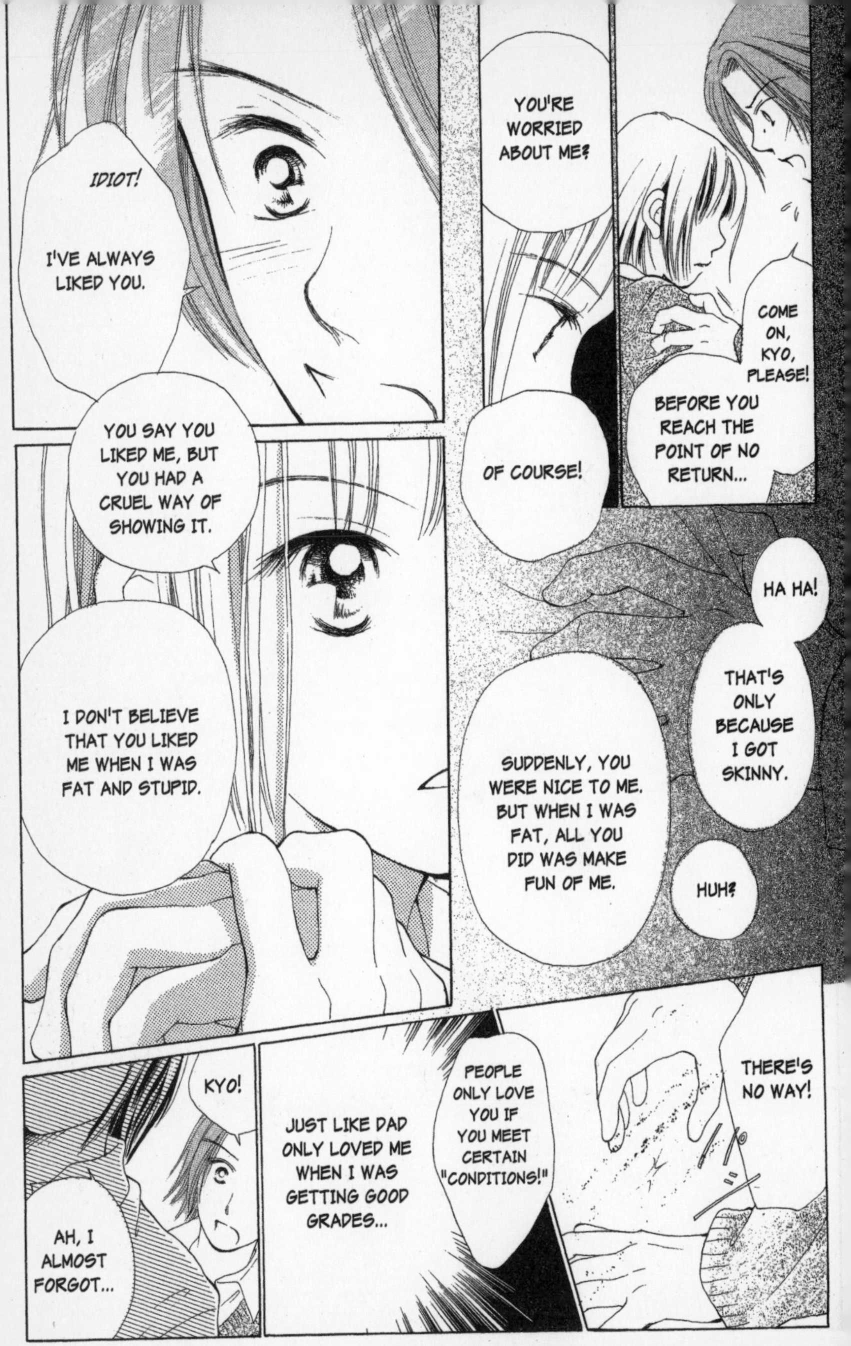
COME ON, KYO, PLEASE!
BEFORE YOU REACH THE POINT OF NO RETURN...
YOU'RE WORRIED ABOUT ME?
OF COURSE!
HA HA!
THAT'S ONLY BECAUSE I GOT SKINNY.
HUH?
SUDDENLY, YOU WERE NICE TO ME. BUT WHEN I WAS FAT, ALL YOU DID WAS MAKE FUN OF ME.
IDIOT!
I'VE ALWAYS LIKED YOU.
YOU SAY YOU LIKED ME, BUT YOU HAD A CRUEL WAY OF SHOWING IT.
I DON'T BELIEVE THAT YOU LIKED ME WHEN I WAS FAT AND STUPID.
THERE'S NO WAY!
PEOPLE ONLY LOVE YOU IF YOU MEET CERTAIN "CONDITIONS!"
JUST LIKE DAD ONLY LOVED ME WHEN I WAS GETTING GOOD GRADES...
KYO!
AH, I ALMOST FORGOT...

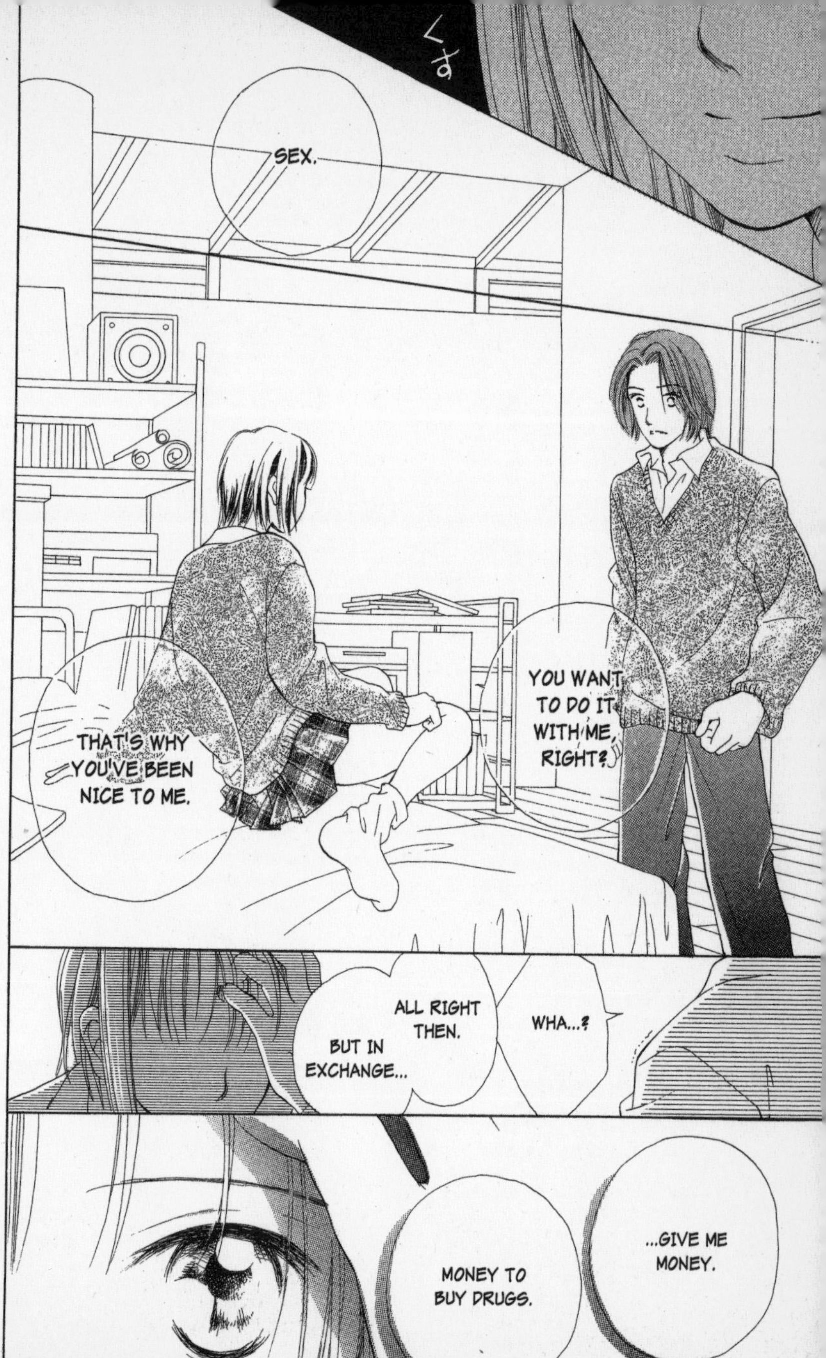
くす
SEX.
YOU WANT TO DO IT WITH ME, RIGHT?
THAT'S WHY YOU'VE BEEN NICE TO ME.
WHA...?
ALL RIGHT THEN.
BUT IN EXCHANGE...
...GIVE ME MONEY.
MONEY TO BUY DRUGS.

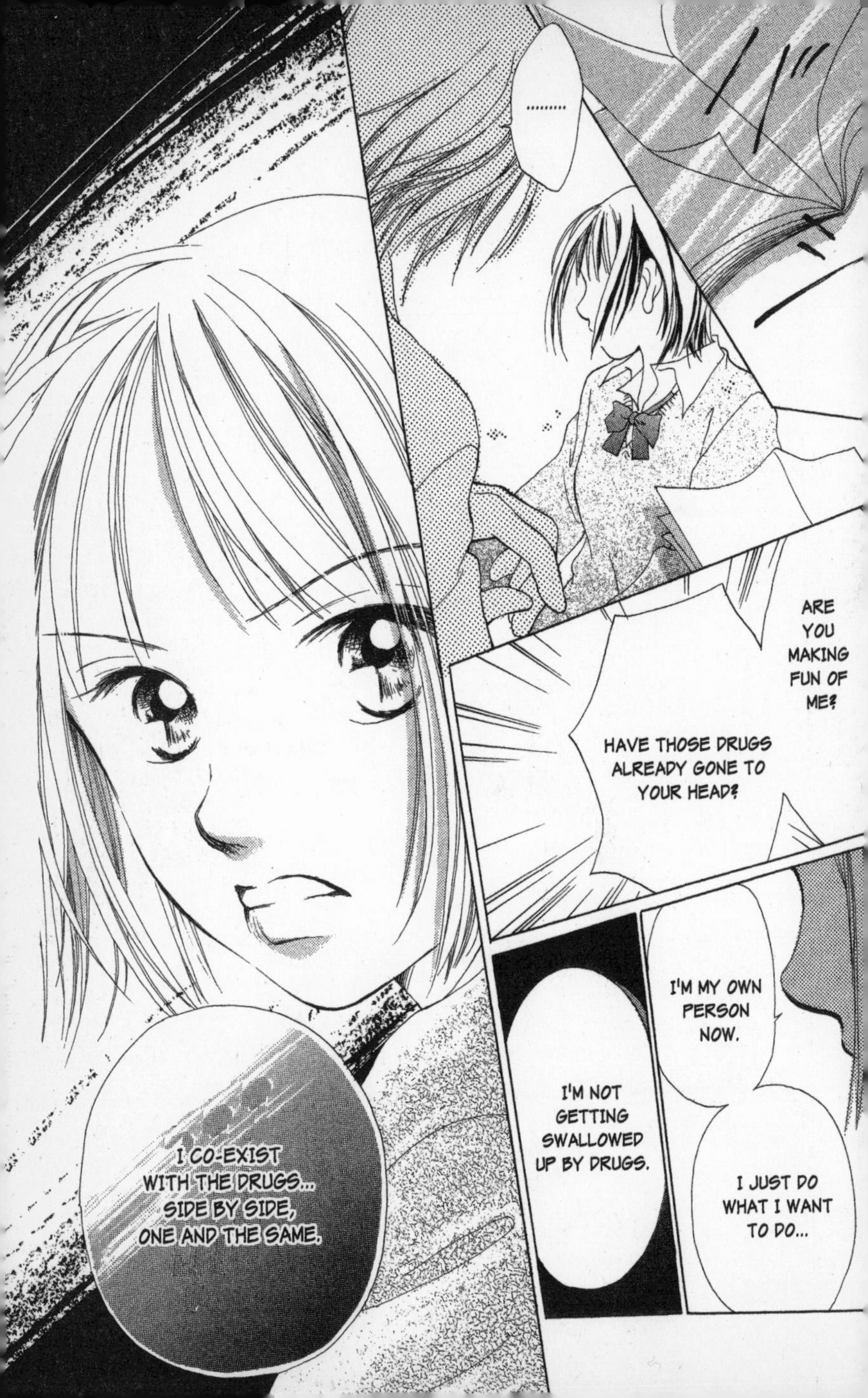
....
ARE YOU MAKING FUN OF ME?
HAVE THOSE DRUGS ALREADY GONE TO YOUR HEAD?
I'M MY OWN PERSON NOW.
I JUST DO WHAT I WANT TO DO...
I'M NOT GETTING SWALLOWED UP BY DRUGS.
I CO-EXIST WITH THE DRUGS... SIDE BY SIDE, ONE AND THE SAME.

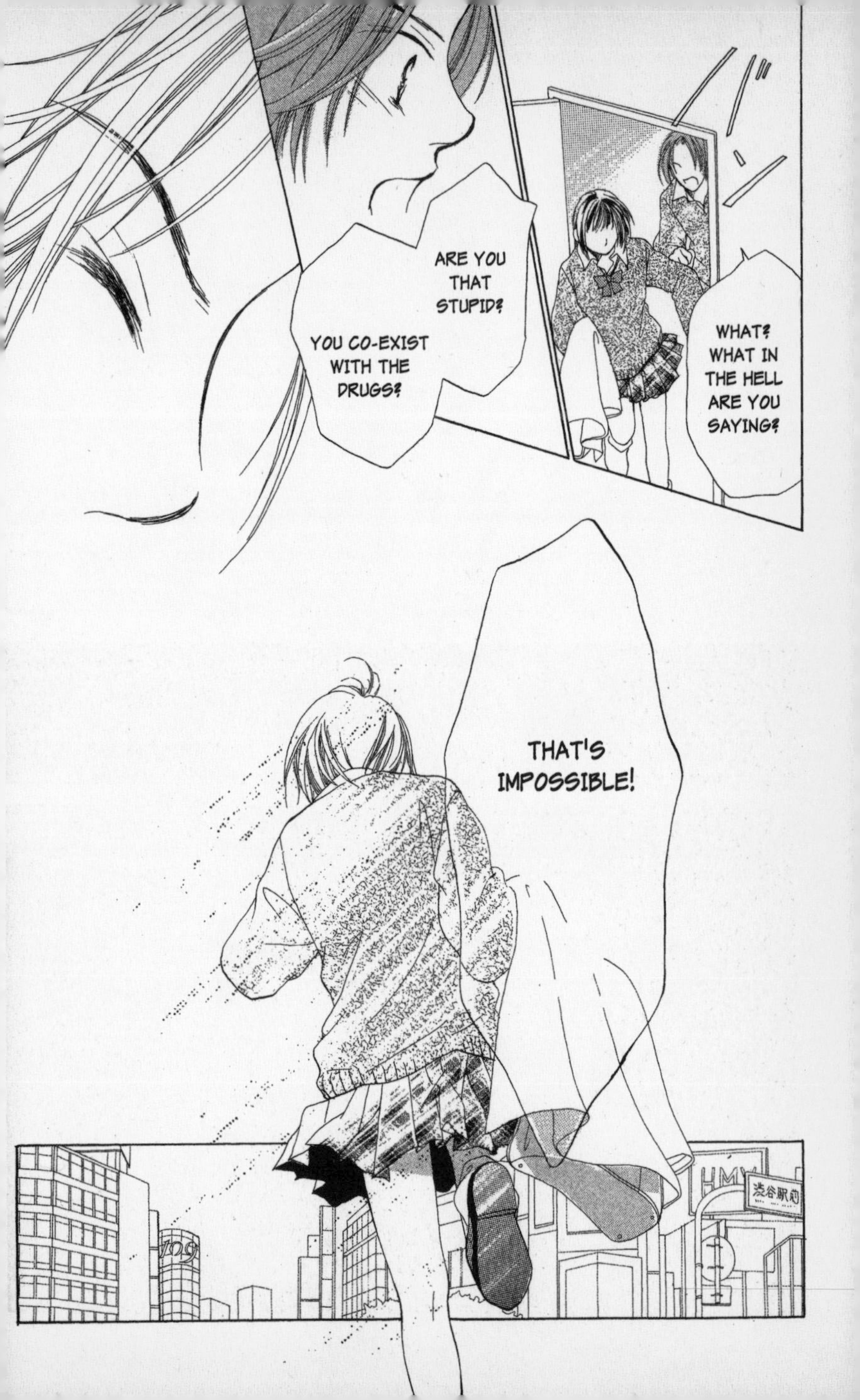
WHAT? WHAT IN THE HELL ARE YOU SAYING?
ARE YOU THAT STUPID?
YOU CO-EXIST WITH THE DRUGS?
THAT'S IMPOSSIBLE!

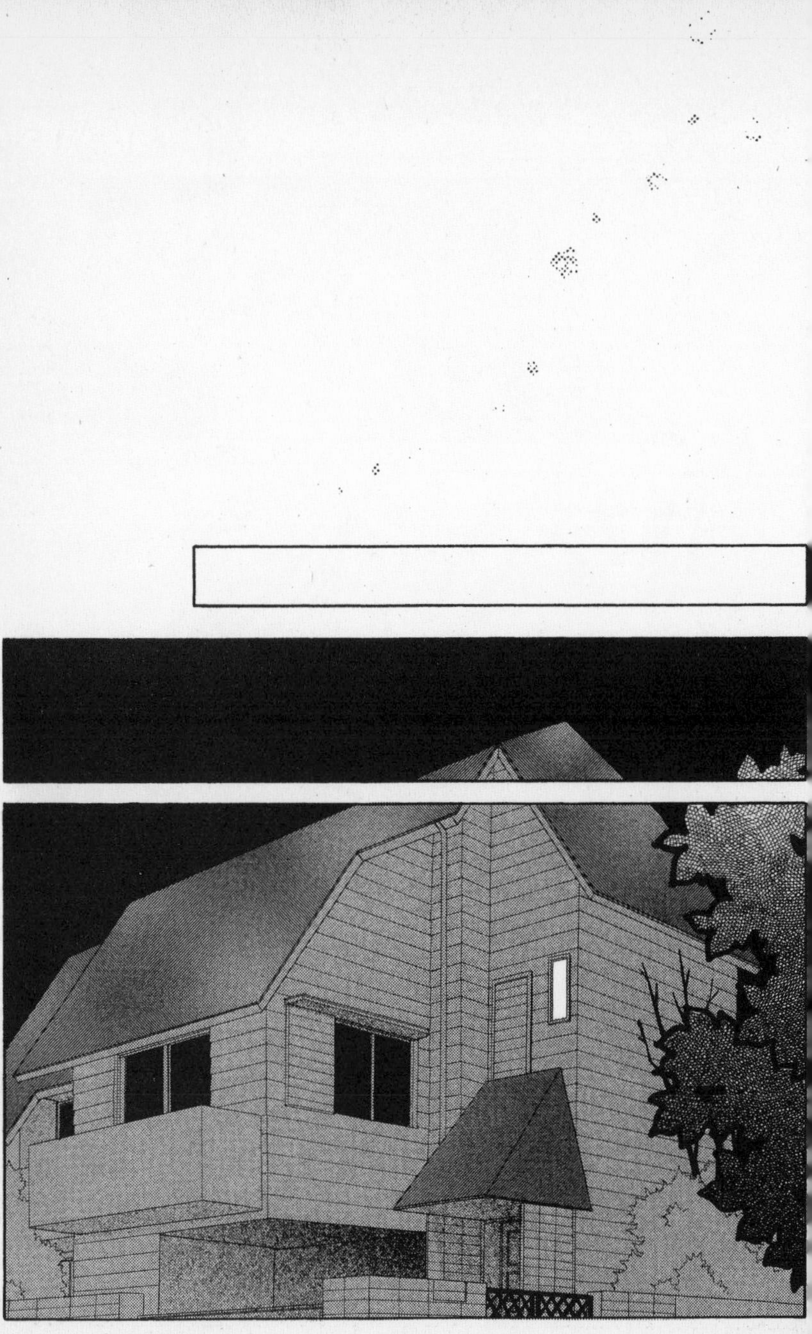

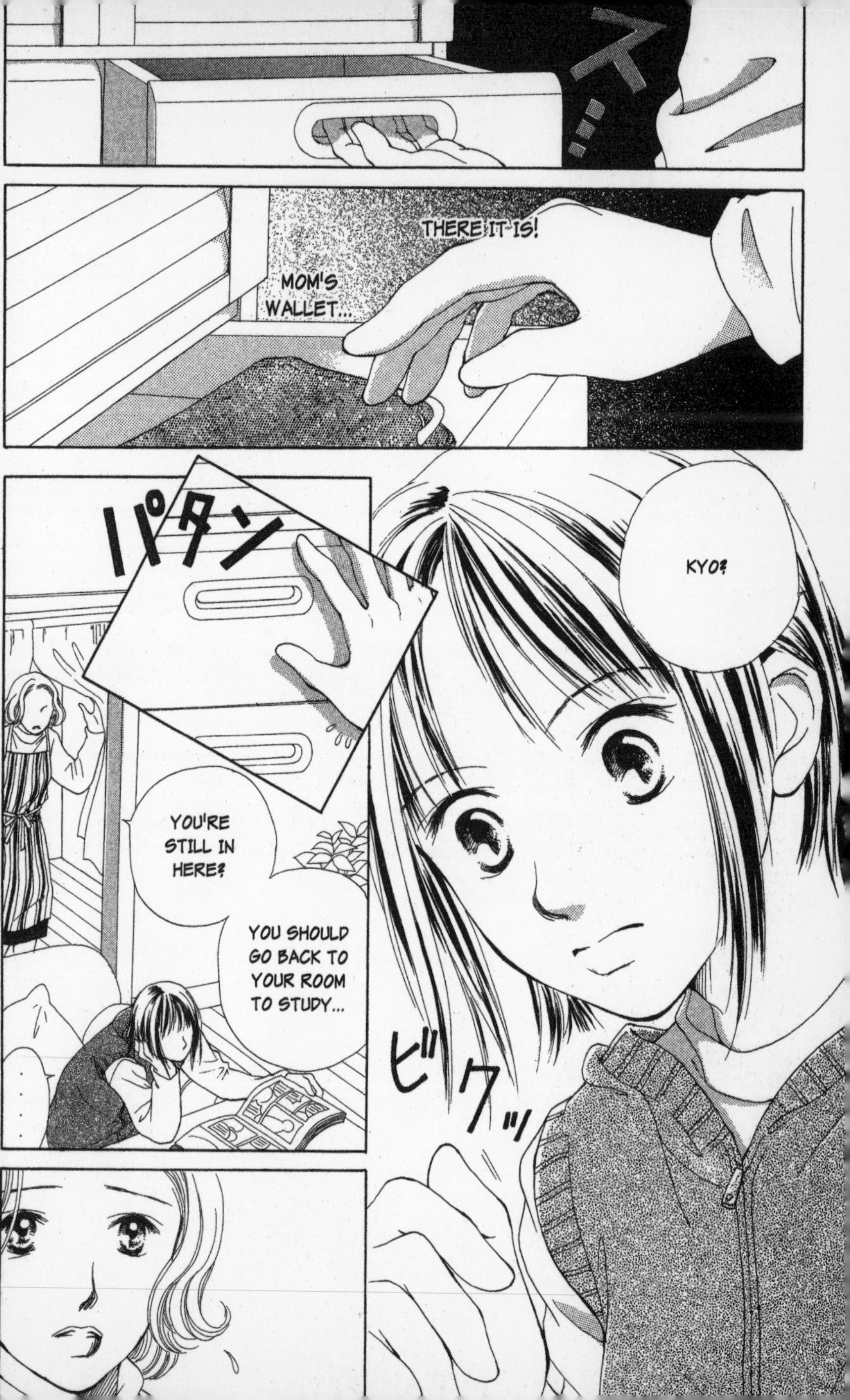

ス…
THERE IT IS!
MOM'S WALLET...
KYO?
ビクッ
パタン
YOU'RE STILL IN HERE?
YOU SHOULD GO BACK TO YOUR ROOM TO STUDY...

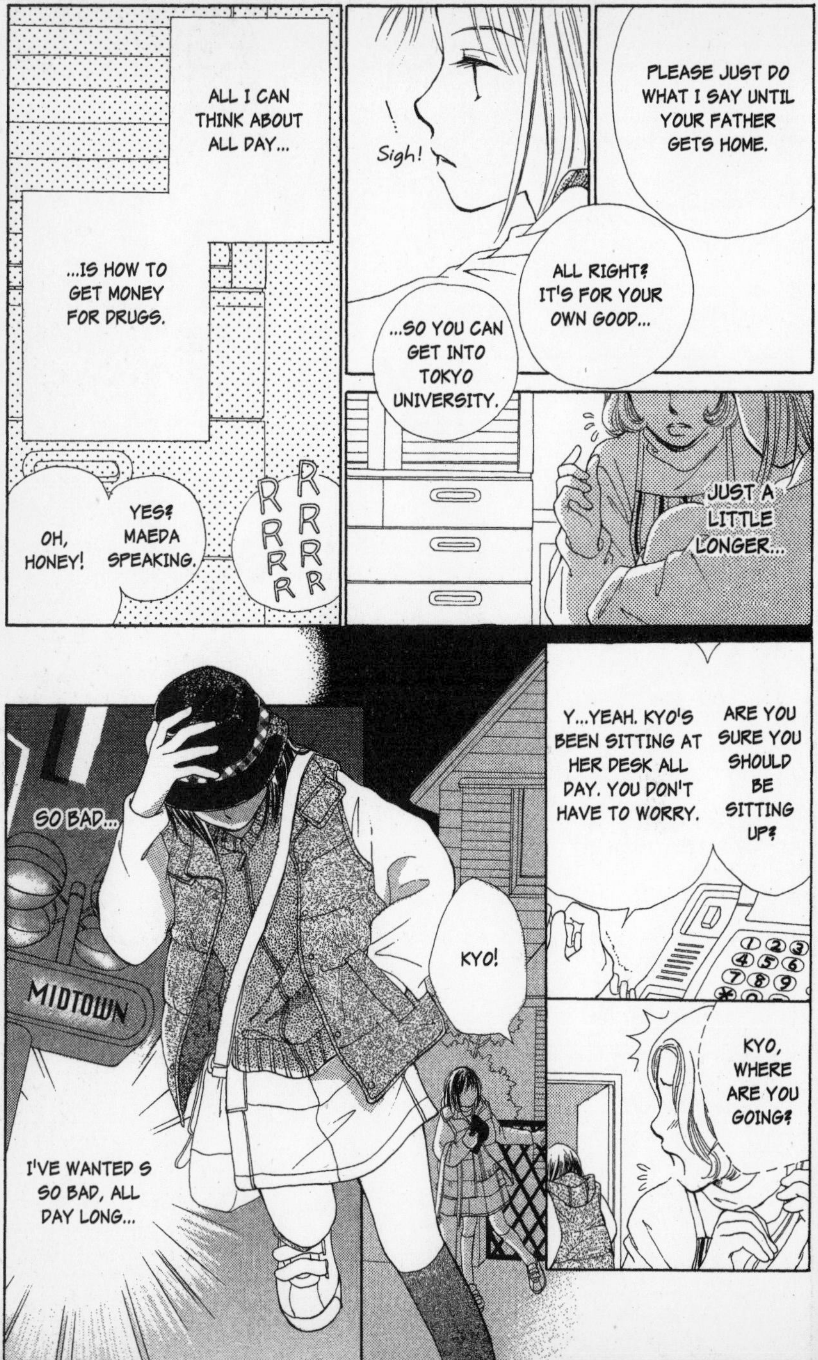
PLEASE JUST DO WHAT I SAY UNTIL YOUR FATHER GETS HOME.
Sigh!
ALL RIGHT? IT'S FOR YOUR OWN GOOD...
...SO YOU CAN GET INTO TOKYO UNIVERSITY.
JUST A LITTLE LONGER...
ALL I CAN THINK ABOUT ALL DAY...
...IS HOW TO GET MONEY FOR DRUGS.
RRRR RRRR
YES? MAEDA SPEAKING.
OH, HONEY!
ARE YOU SURE YOU SHOULD BE SITTING UP?
Y...YEAH. KYO'S BEEN SITTING AT HER DESK ALL DAY. YOU DON'T HAVE TO WORRY.
KYO, WHERE ARE YOU GOING?
KYO!
SO BAD...
MIDTOWN
I'VE WANTED S SO BAD, ALL DAY LONG...

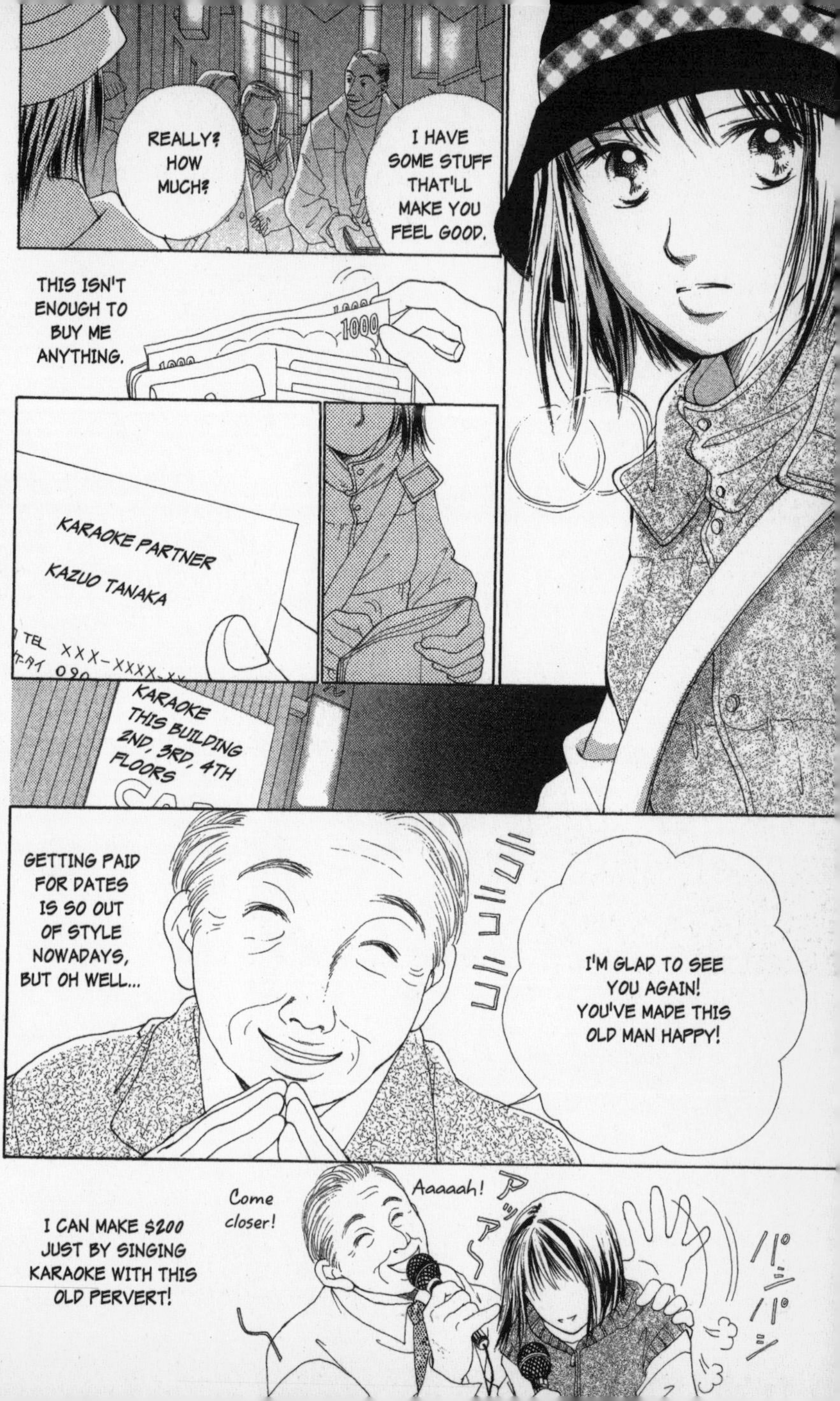
I HAVE SOME STUFF THAT'LL MAKE YOU FEEL GOOD.
REALLY? HOW MUCH?
THIS ISN'T ENOUGH TO BUY ME ANYTHING.
1000
KARAOKE PARTNER
KAZUO TANAKA
TEL XXX-XXXX-XX
KARAOKE THIS BUILDING 2ND, 3RD, 4TH FLOORS
ニコニコ
I'M GLAD TO SEE YOU AGAIN! YOU'VE MADE THIS OLD MAN HAPPY!
GETTING PAID FOR DATES IS SO OUT OF STYLE NOWADAYS, BUT OH WELL...
パンパン
アッア～
Aaaaah!
Come closer!
I CAN MAKE $200 JUST BY SINGING KARAOKE WITH THIS OLD PERVERT!

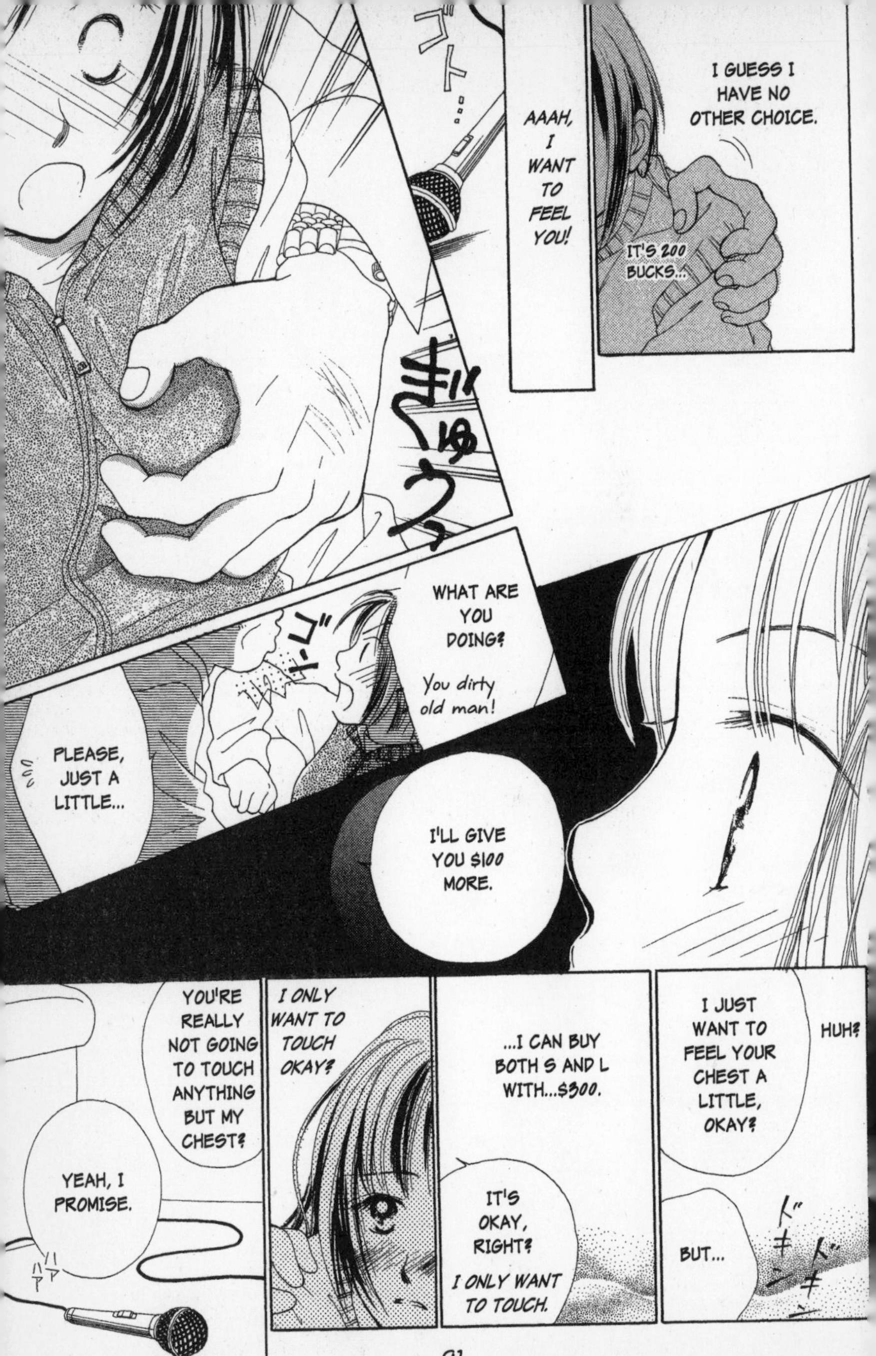

I GUESS I HAVE NO OTHER CHOICE.
IT'S 200 BUCKS...
AAAH, I WANT TO FEEL YOU!
ゴト…
WHAT ARE YOU DOING?
You dirty old man!
ゴン
PLEASE, JUST A LITTLE...
I'LL GIVE YOU $100 MORE.
HUH?
I JUST WANT TO FEEL YOUR CHEST A LITTLE, OKAY?
BUT...
...I CAN BUY BOTH S AND L WITH...$300.
IT'S OKAY, RIGHT?
I ONLY WANT TO TOUCH.
I ONLY WANT TO TOUCH OKAY?
YOU'RE REALLY NOT GOING TO TOUCH ANYTHING BUT MY CHEST?
YEAH, I PROMISE.
ハァ ハァ

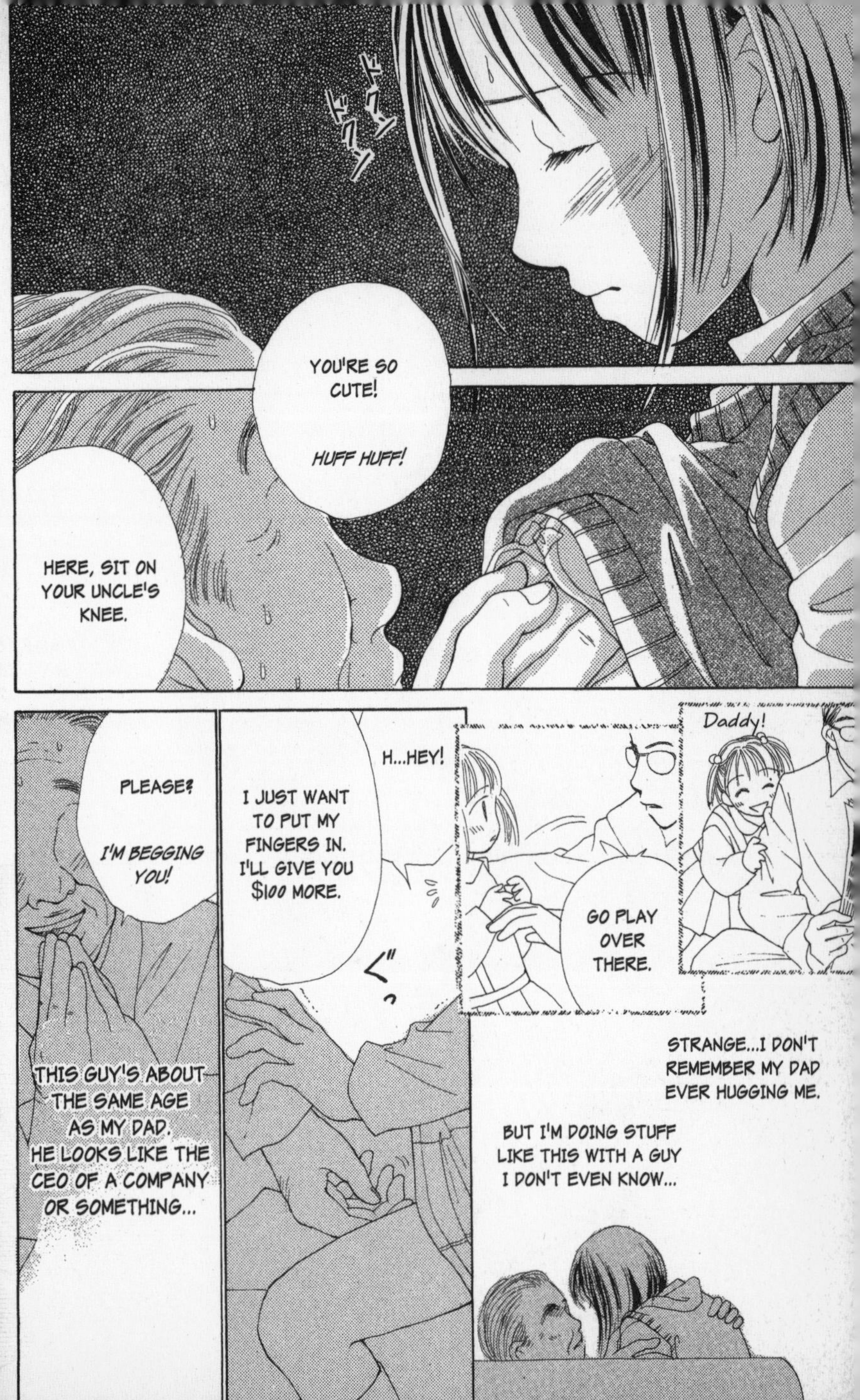
YOU'RE SO CUTE!
HUFF HUFF!
HERE, SIT ON YOUR UNCLE'S KNEE.
Daddy!
GO PLAY OVER THERE.
STRANGE...I DON'T REMEMBER MY DAD EVER HUGGING ME.
BUT I'M DOING STUFF LIKE THIS WITH A GUY I DON'T EVEN KNOW...
H...HEY!
I JUST WANT TO PUT MY FINGERS IN. I'LL GIVE YOU $100 MORE.
PLEASE?
I'M BEGGING YOU!
THIS GUY'S ABOUT THE SAME AGE AS MY DAD. HE LOOKS LIKE THE CEO OF A COMPANY OR SOMETHING...

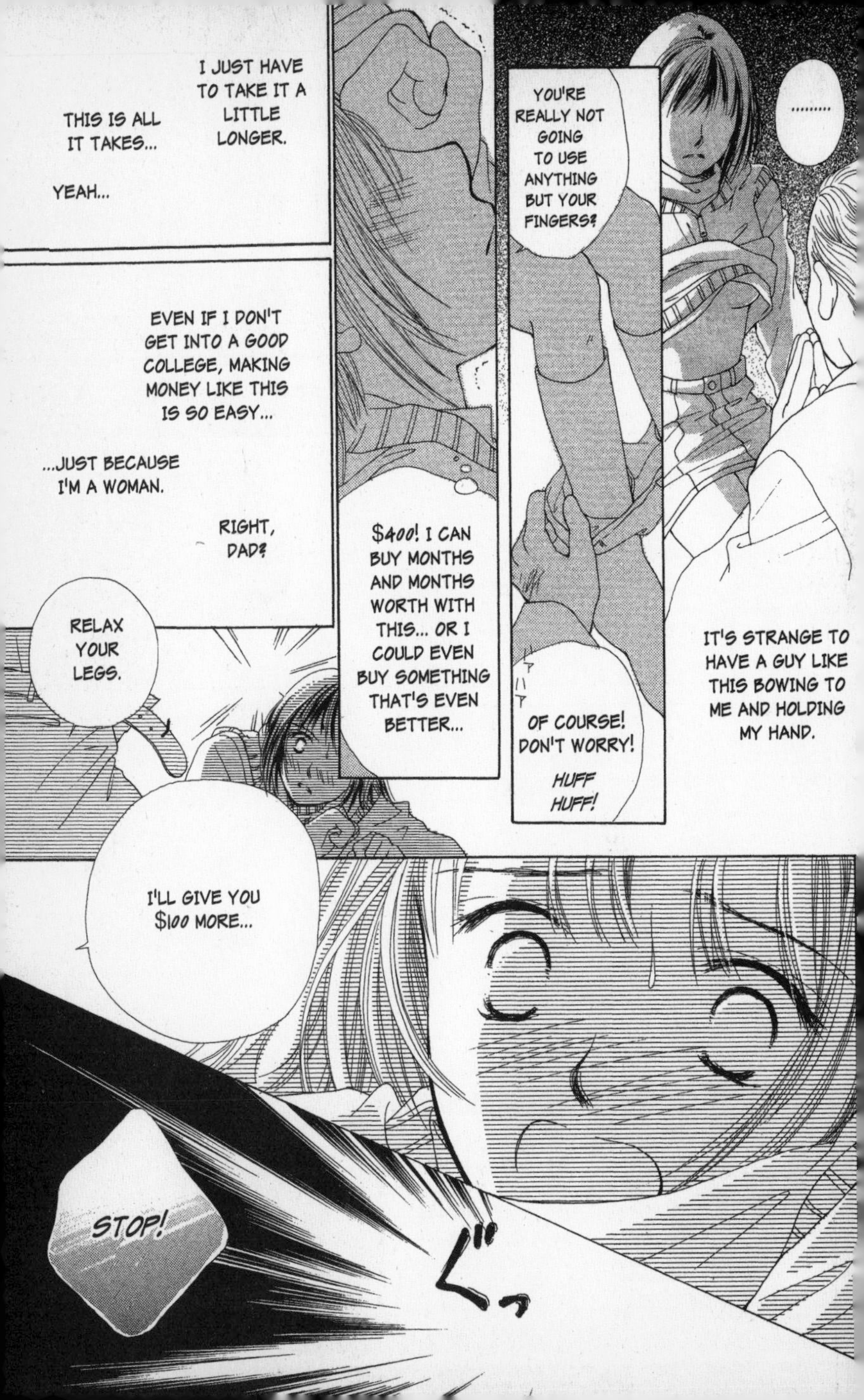

....
YOU'RE REALLY NOT GOING TO USE ANYTHING BUT YOUR FINGERS?
IT'S STRANGE TO HAVE A GUY LIKE THIS BOWING TO ME AND HOLDING MY HAND.
OF COURSE! DON'T WORRY!
HUFF HUFF!
$400! I CAN BUY MONTHS AND MONTHS WORTH WITH THIS... OR I COULD EVEN BUY SOMETHING THAT'S EVEN BETTER...
I JUST HAVE TO TAKE IT A LITTLE LONGER.
THIS IS ALL IT TAKES...
YEAH...
EVEN IF I DON'T GET INTO A GOOD COLLEGE, MAKING MONEY LIKE THIS IS SO EASY...
...JUST BECAUSE I'M A WOMAN.
RIGHT, DAD?
RELAX YOUR LEGS.
I'LL GIVE YOU $100 MORE...
STOP!

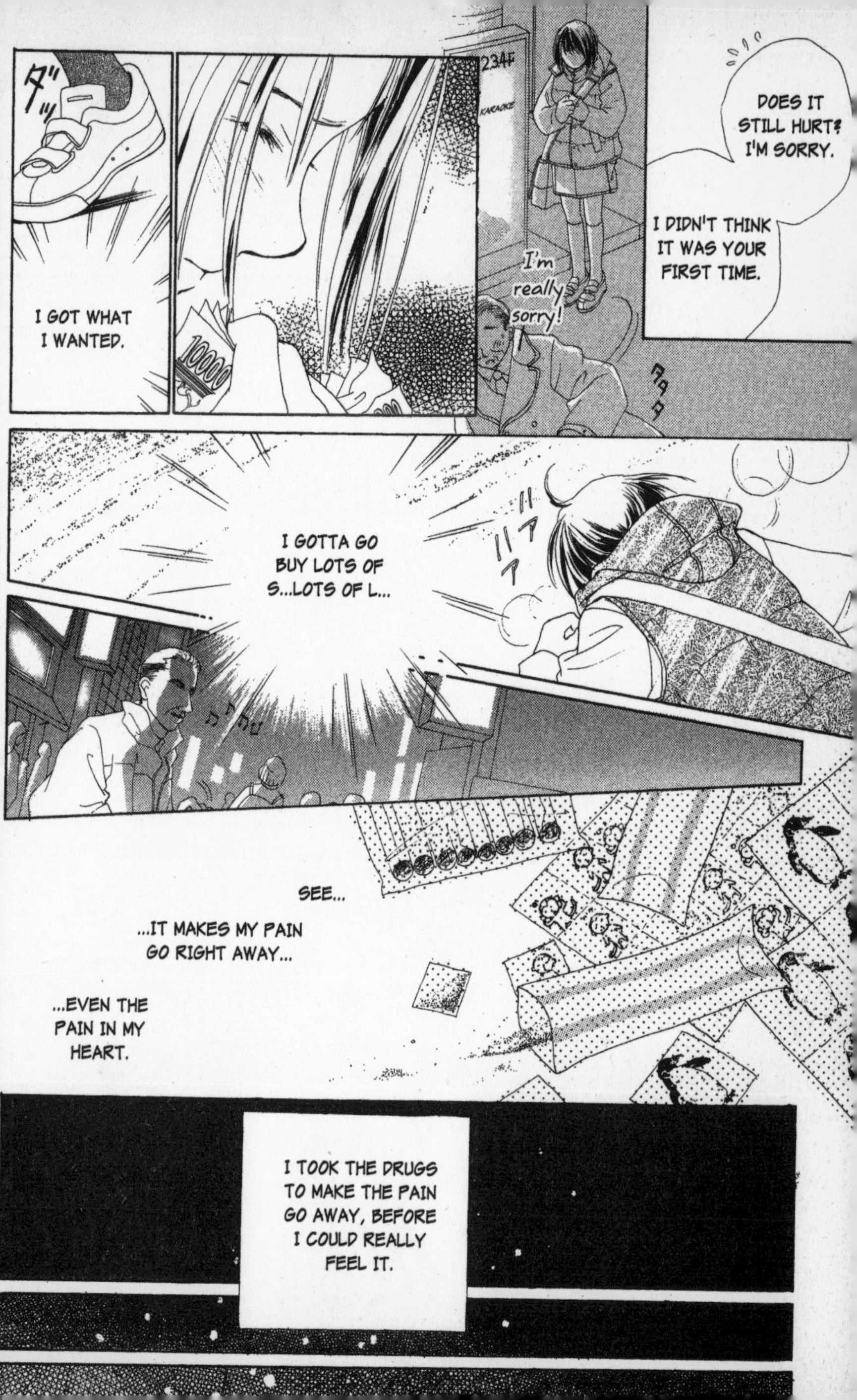
DOES IT STILL HURT? I'M SORRY.
I DIDN'T THINK IT WAS YOUR FIRST TIME.
I'm really sorry!
I GOT WHAT I WANTED.
I GOTTA GO BUY LOTS OF S...LOTS OF L...
SEE...
...IT MAKES MY PAIN GO RIGHT AWAY...
...EVEN THE PAIN IN MY HEART.
I TOOK THE DRUGS TO MAKE THE PAIN GO AWAY, BEFORE I COULD REALLY FEEL IT.

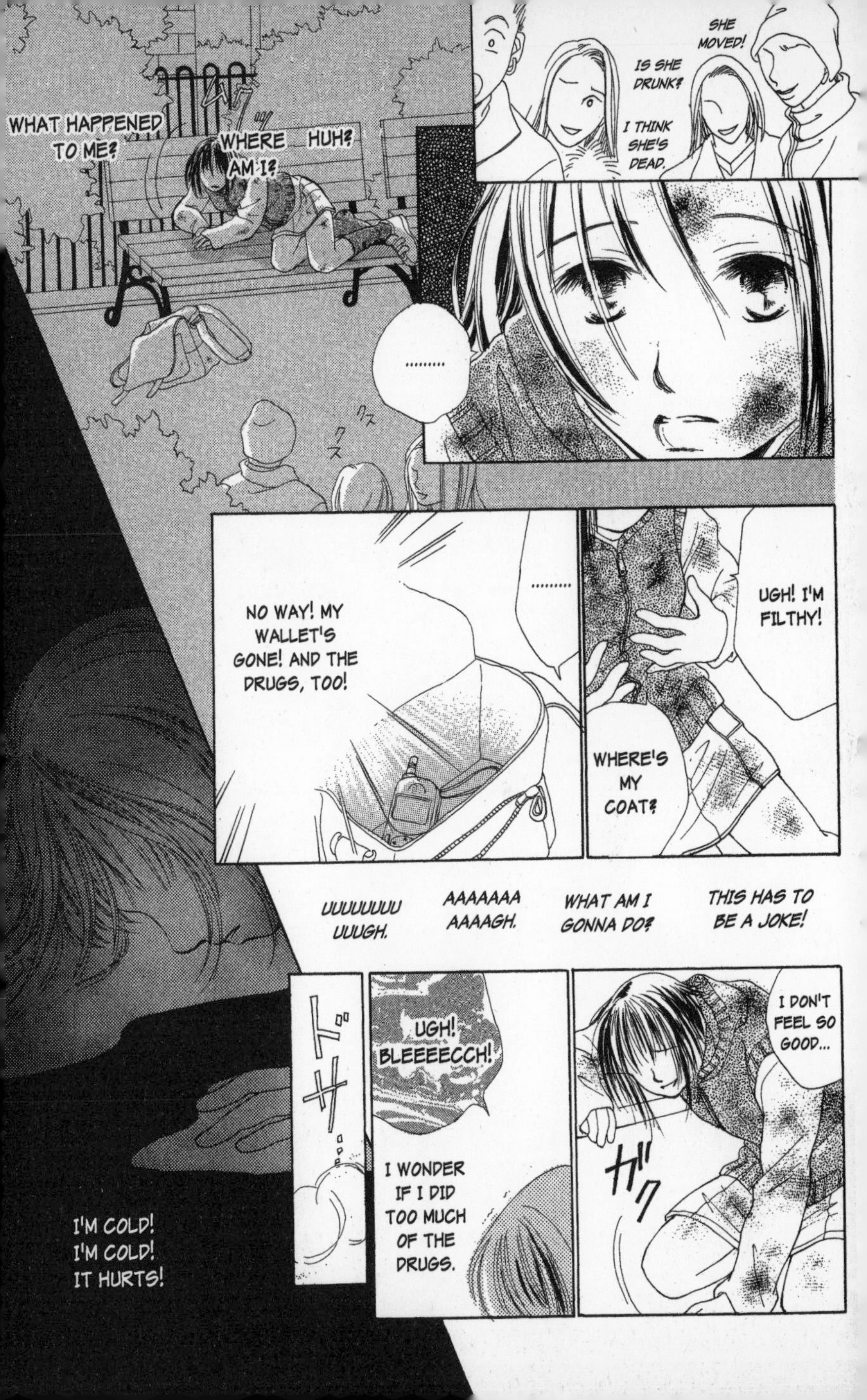
SHE MOVED!
IS SHE DRUNK?
I THINK SHE'S DEAD.
....
HUH?
WHERE AM I?
WHAT HAPPENED TO ME?
UGH! I'M FILTHY!
WHERE'S MY COAT?
....
NO WAY! MY WALLET'S GONE! AND THE DRUGS, TOO!
THIS HAS TO BE A JOKE!
WHAT AM I GONNA DO?
AAAAAAA AAAAGH.
UUUUUUUU UUUGH.
I DON'T FEEL SO GOOD...
UGH! BLEEEECCH!
I WONDER IF I DID TOO MUCH OF THE DRUGS.
I'M COLD! I'M COLD! IT HURTS!

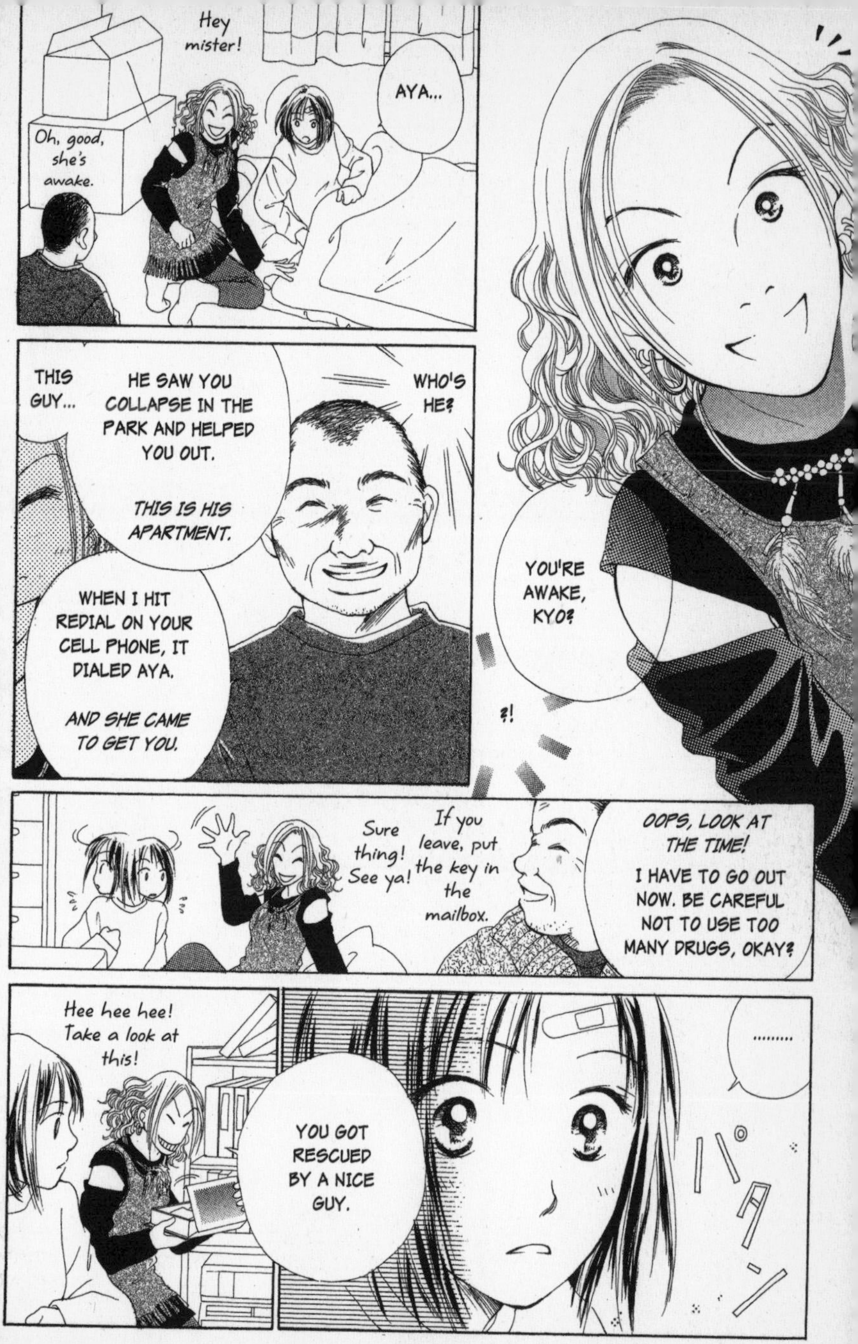
YOU'RE AWAKE, KYO?
?!
AYA...
Hey mister!
Oh, good, she's awake.
WHO'S HE?
THIS GUY... HE SAW YOU COLLAPSE IN THE PARK AND HELPED YOU OUT. THIS IS HIS APARTMENT.
WHEN I HIT REDIAL ON YOUR CELL PHONE, IT DIALED AYA. AND SHE CAME TO GET YOU.
OOPS, LOOK AT THE TIME! I HAVE TO GO OUT NOW. BE CAREFUL NOT TO USE TOO MANY DRUGS, OKAY?
If you leave, put the key in the mailbox.
Sure thing! See ya!
....
パタン
Hee hee hee! Take a look at this!
YOU GOT RESCUED BY A NICE GUY.

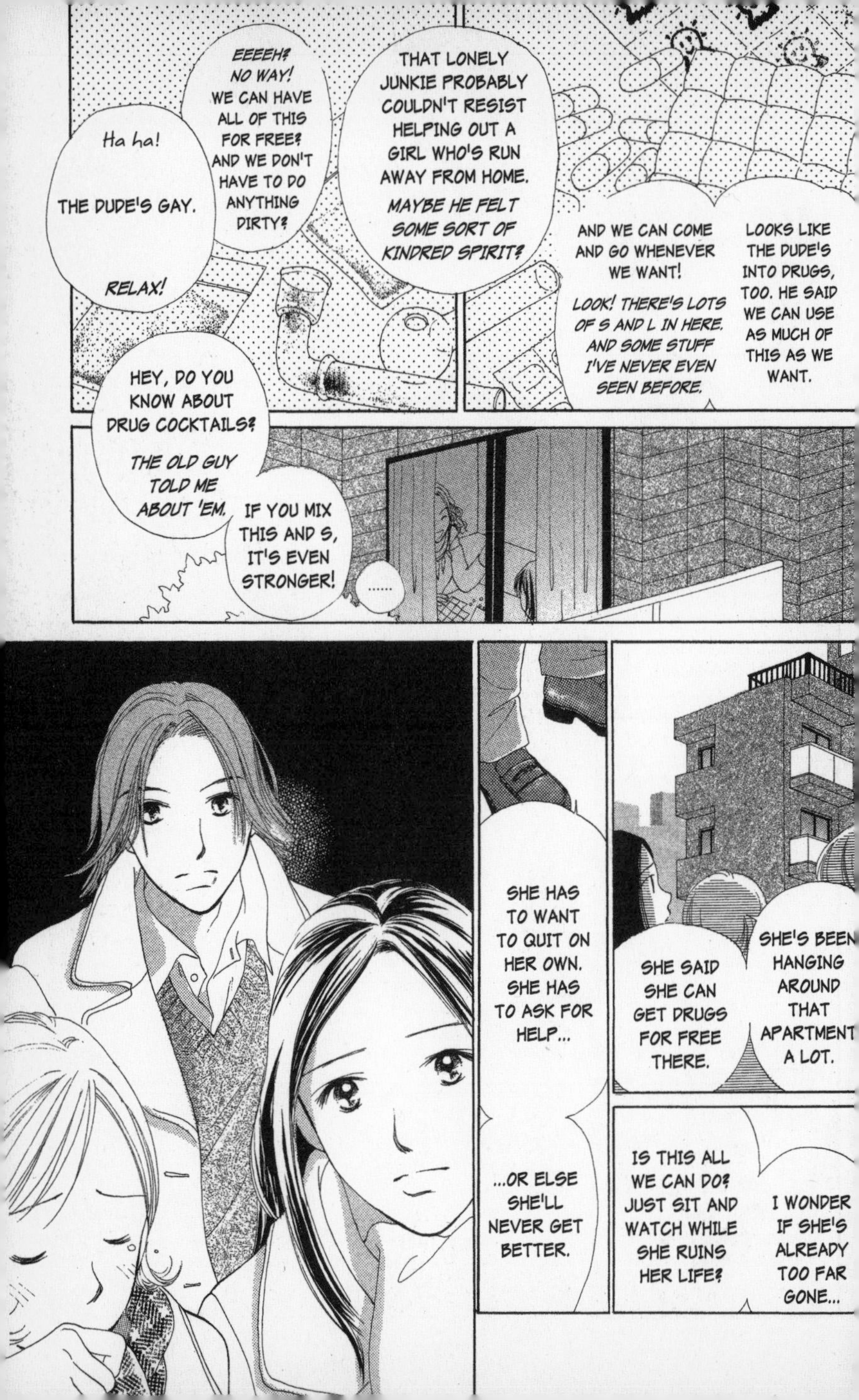
LOOKS LIKE THE DUDE'S INTO DRUGS, TOO. HE SAID WE CAN USE AS MUCH OF THIS AS WE WANT.
AND WE CAN COME AND GO WHENEVER WE WANT! LOOK! THERE'S LOTS OF S AND L IN HERE. AND SOME STUFF I'VE NEVER EVEN SEEN BEFORE.
THAT LONELY JUNKIE PROBABLY COULDN'T RESIST HELPING OUT A GIRL WHO'S RUN AWAY FROM HOME. MAYBE HE FELT SOME SORT OF KINDRED SPIRIT?
EEEEH? NO WAY! WE CAN HAVE ALL OF THIS FOR FREE? AND WE DON'T HAVE TO DO ANYTHING DIRTY?
Ha ha! THE DUDE'S GAY. RELAX!
HEY, DO YOU KNOW ABOUT DRUG COCKTAILS? THE OLD GUY TOLD ME ABOUT 'EM.
IF YOU MIX THIS AND S, IT'S EVEN STRONGER!
......
SHE'S BEEN HANGING AROUND THAT APARTMENT A LOT.
SHE SAID SHE CAN GET DRUGS FOR FREE THERE.
I WONDER IF SHE'S ALREADY TOO FAR GONE...
IS THIS ALL WE CAN DO? JUST SIT AND WATCH WHILE SHE RUINS HER LIFE?
SHE HAS TO WANT TO QUIT ON HER OWN. SHE HAS TO ASK FOR HELP...
...OR ELSE SHE'LL NEVER GET BETTER.

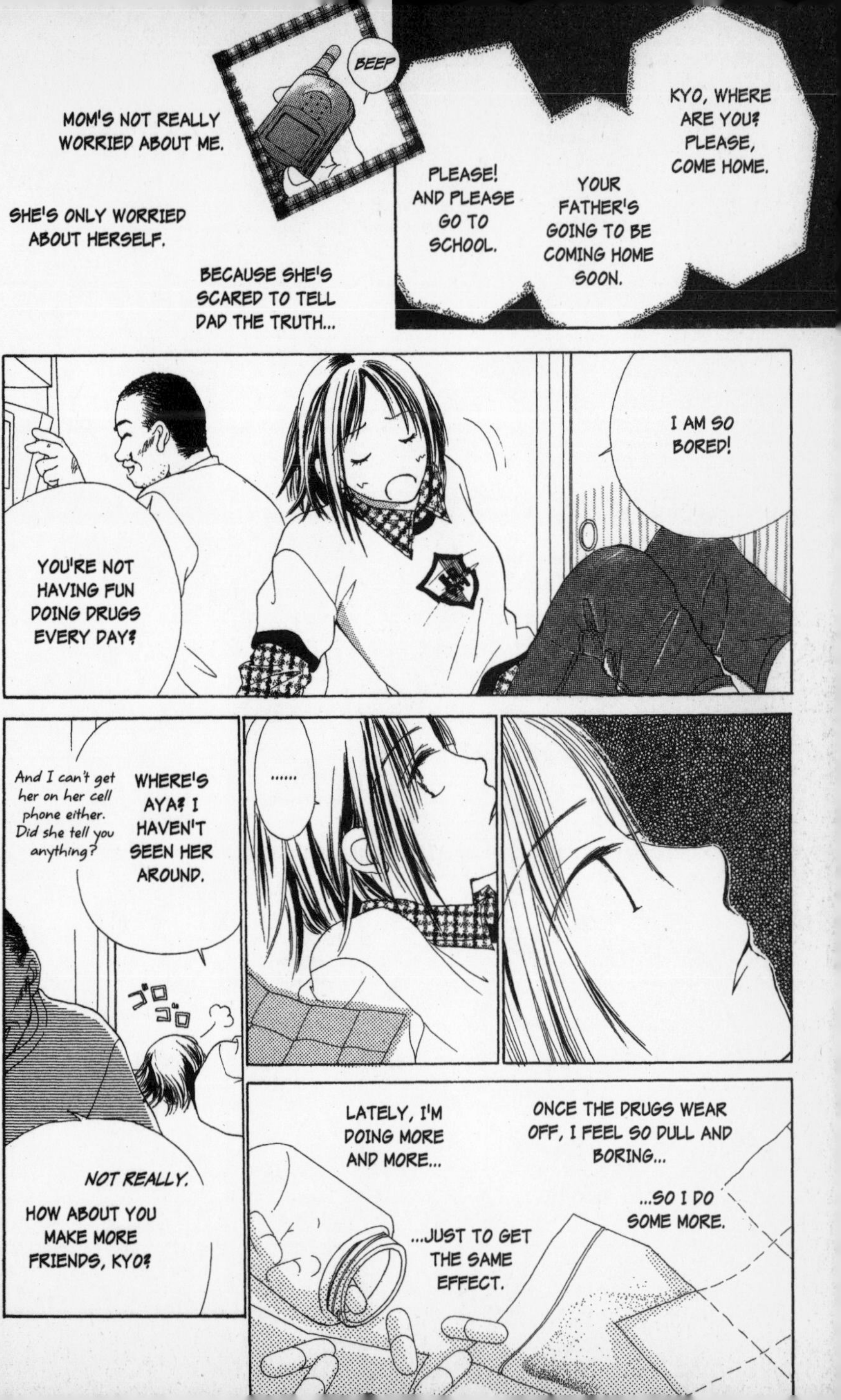
KYO, WHERE ARE YOU? PLEASE, COME HOME.
YOUR FATHER'S GOING TO BE COMING HOME SOON.
PLEASE! AND PLEASE GO TO SCHOOL.
BEEP
MOM'S NOT REALLY WORRIED ABOUT ME.
SHE'S ONLY WORRIED ABOUT HERSELF.
BECAUSE SHE'S SCARED TO TELL DAD THE TRUTH...
I AM SO BORED!
YOU'RE NOT HAVING FUN DOING DRUGS EVERY DAY?
......
WHERE'S AYA? I HAVEN'T SEEN HER AROUND.
And I can't get her on her cell phone either. Did she tell you anything?
ゴロゴロ
NOT REALLY.
HOW ABOUT YOU MAKE MORE FRIENDS, KYO?
ONCE THE DRUGS WEAR OFF, I FEEL SO DULL AND BORING...
...SO I DO SOME MORE.
LATELY, I'M DOING MORE AND MORE...
...JUST TO GET THE SAME EFFECT.

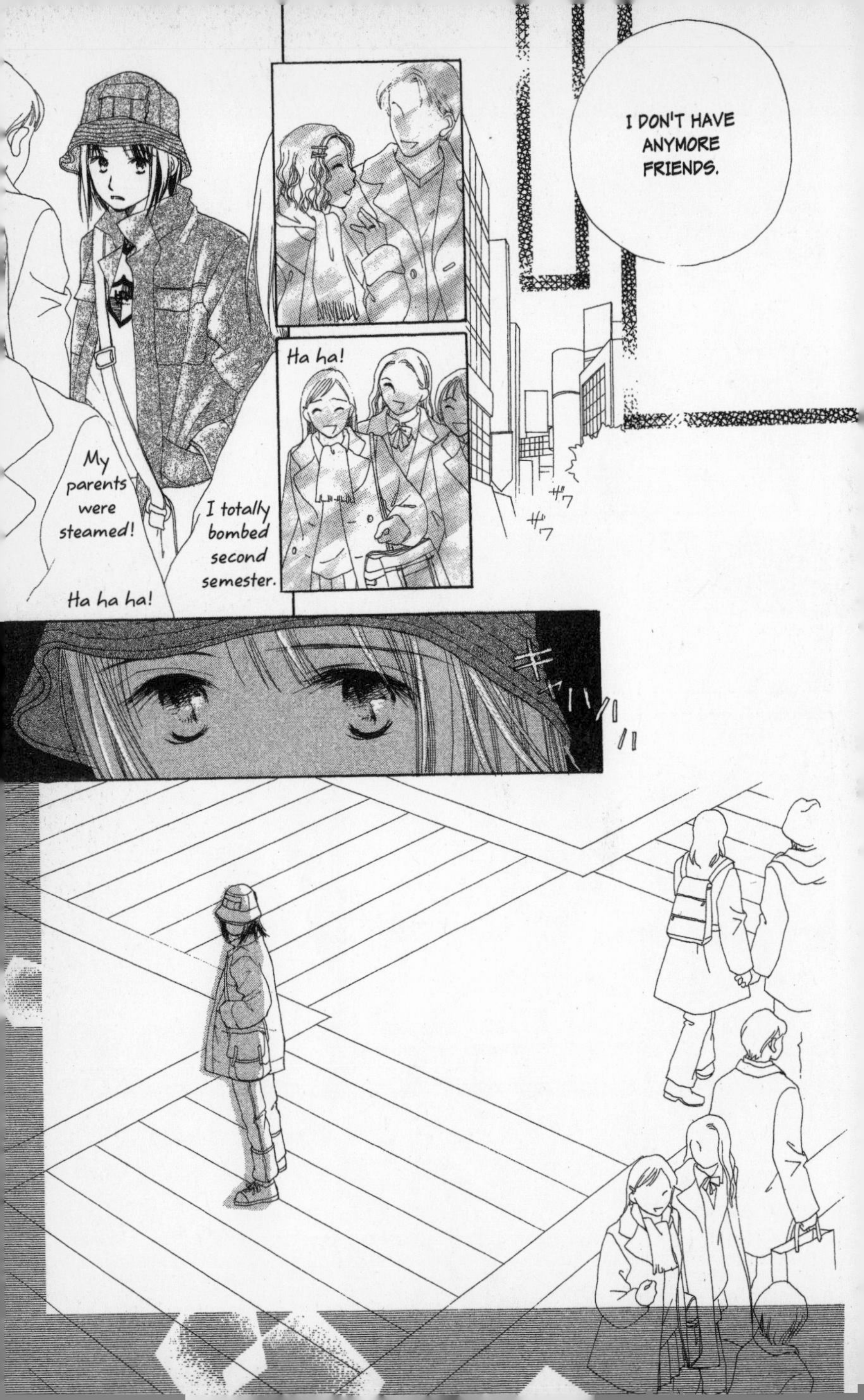
I DON'T HAVE ANYMORE FRIENDS.
ザワ
ザワ
Ha ha!
I totally bombed second semester.
My parents were steamed!
Ha ha ha!
ギャハハハ

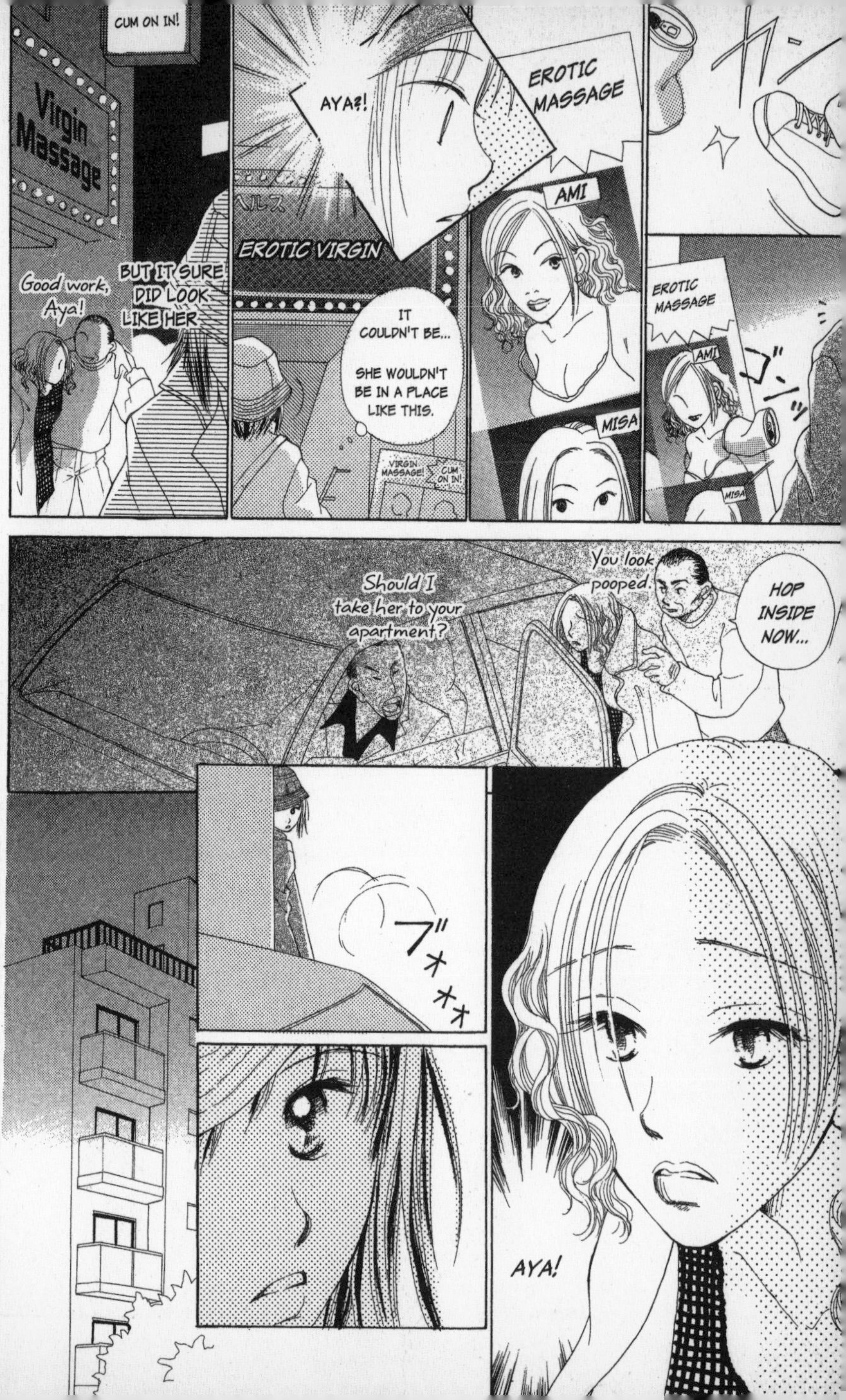
EROTIC MASSAGE
AMI
MISA
EROTIC MASSAGE
AMI
MISA
AYA?!
ヘルス
EROTIC VIRGIN
IT COULDN'T BE...
SHE WOULDN'T BE IN A PLACE LIKE THIS.
VIRGIN MASSAGE!
CUM ON IN!
CUM ON IN!
Virgin Massage
BUT IT SURE DID LOOK LIKE HER
Good work, Aya!
HOP INSIDE NOW...
You look pooped.
Should I take her to your apartment?
AYA!
ブォォォ

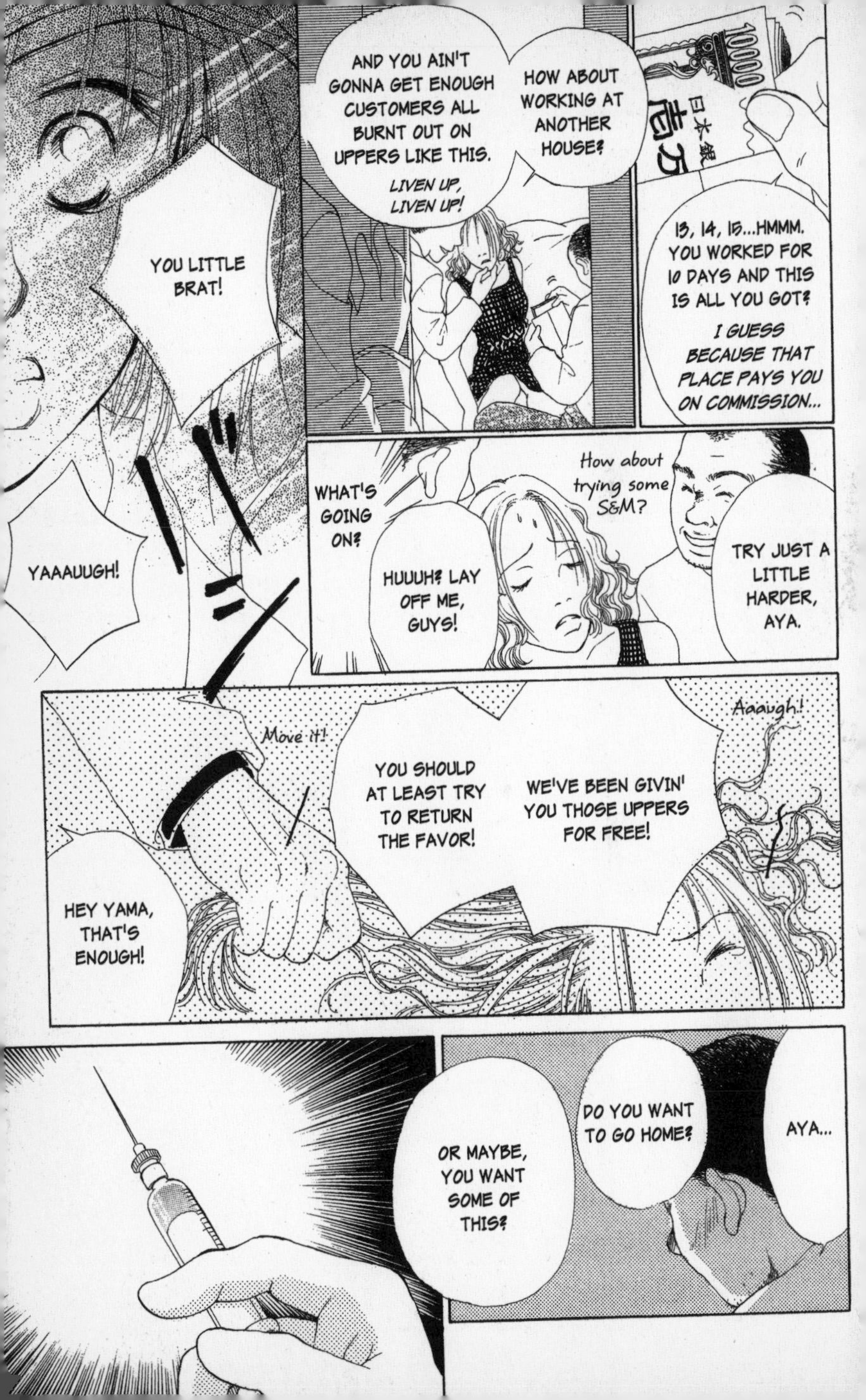
13, 14, 15...HMMM. YOU WORKED FOR 10 DAYS AND THIS IS ALL YOU GOT?
I GUESS BECAUSE THAT PLACE PAYS YOU ON COMMISSION...
HOW ABOUT WORKING AT ANOTHER HOUSE?
AND YOU AIN'T GONNA GET ENOUGH CUSTOMERS ALL BURNT OUT ON UPPERS LIKE THIS.
LIVEN UP, LIVEN UP!
TRY JUST A LITTLE HARDER, AYA.
How about trying some S&M?
HUUUH? LAY OFF ME, GUYS!
WHAT'S GOING ON?
YOU LITTLE BRAT!
YAAAUUGH!
Aaaugh!
WE'VE BEEN GIVIN' YOU THOSE UPPERS FOR FREE!
YOU SHOULD AT LEAST TRY TO RETURN THE FAVOR!
Move it!
HEY YAMA, THAT'S ENOUGH!
AYA...
DO YOU WANT TO GO HOME?
OR MAYBE, YOU WANT SOME OF THIS?

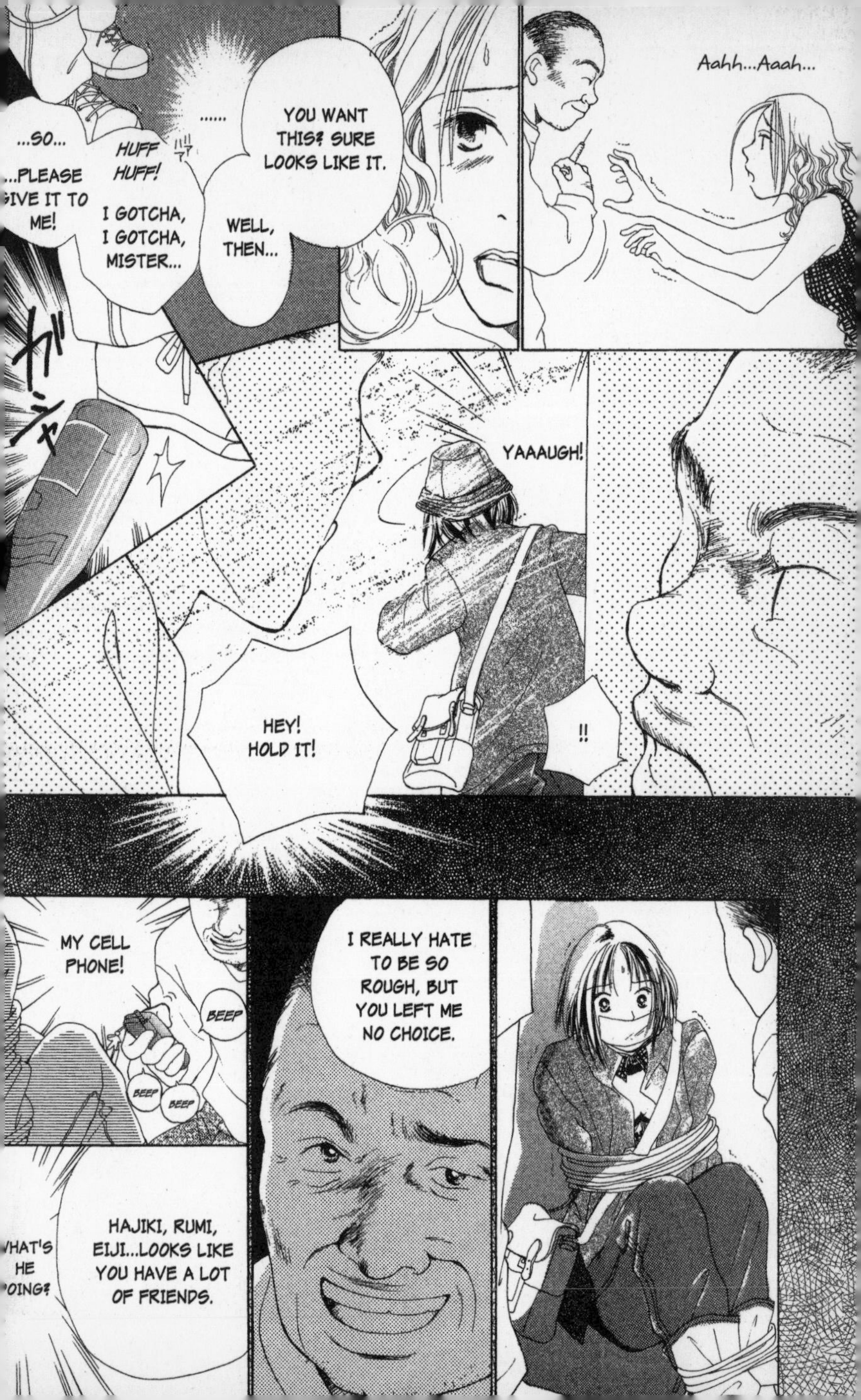

Aahh...Aaah...
YOU WANT THIS? SURE LOOKS LIKE IT.
......
WELL, THEN...
HUFF HUFF!
...SO...
...PLEASE GIVE IT TO ME!
I GOTCHA, I GOTCHA, MISTER...
!!
YAAAUGH!
HEY! HOLD IT!
I REALLY HATE TO BE SO ROUGH, BUT YOU LEFT ME NO CHOICE.
MY CELL PHONE!
BEEP
BEEP
BEEP
HAJIKI, RUMI, EIJI...LOOKS LIKE YOU HAVE A LOT OF FRIENDS.
HAT'S HE OING?

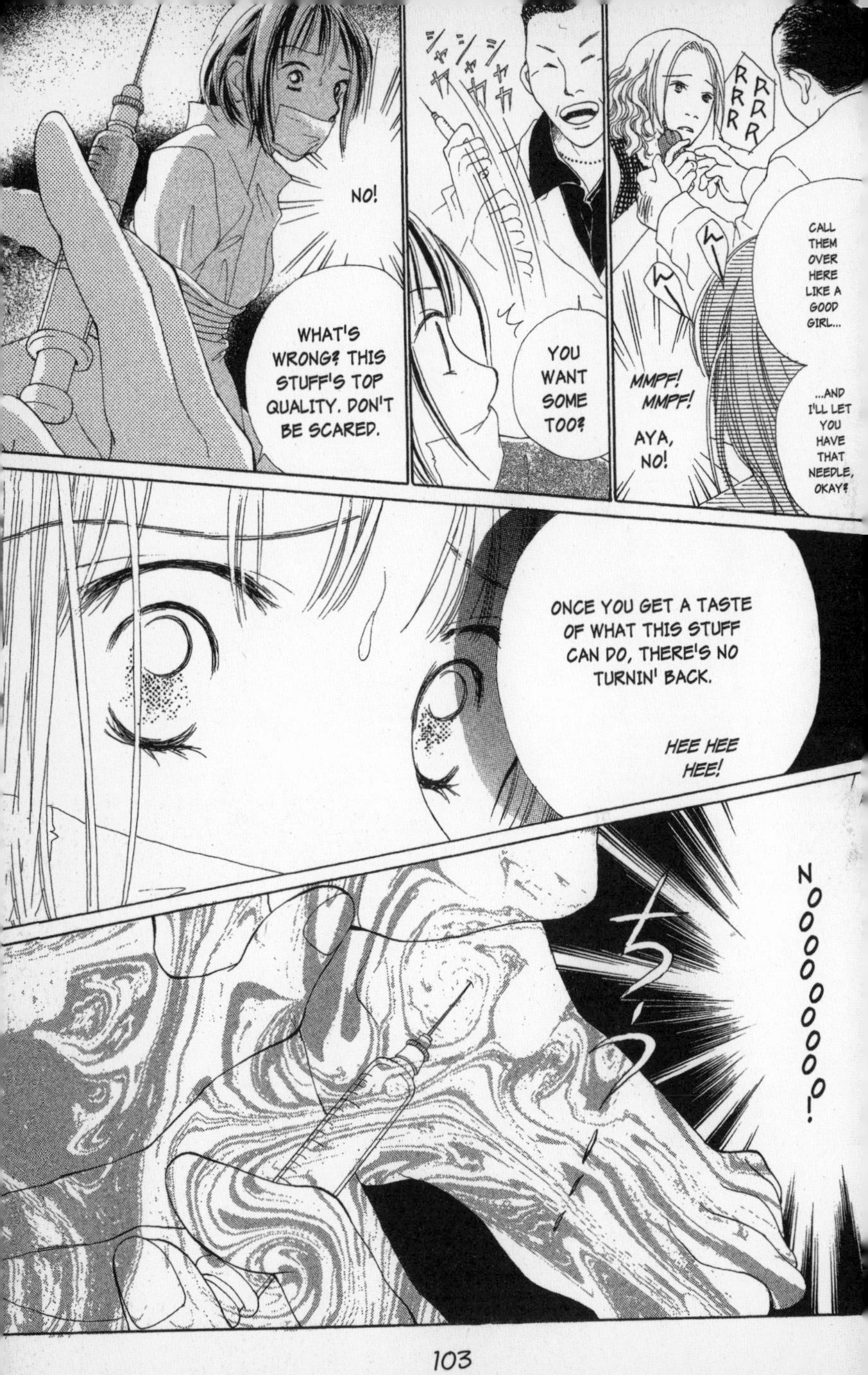
CALL THEM OVER HERE LIKE A GOOD GIRL...
RRR RRR
...AND I'LL LET YOU HAVE THAT NEEDLE, OKAY?
MMPF! MMPF!
AYA, NO!
YOU WANT SOME TOO?
NO!
WHAT'S WRONG? THIS STUFF'S TOP QUALITY. DON'T BE SCARED.
ONCE YOU GET A TASTE OF WHAT THIS STUFF CAN DO, THERE'S NO TURNIN' BACK.
HEE HEE HEE!
NOOOOOOOOO!

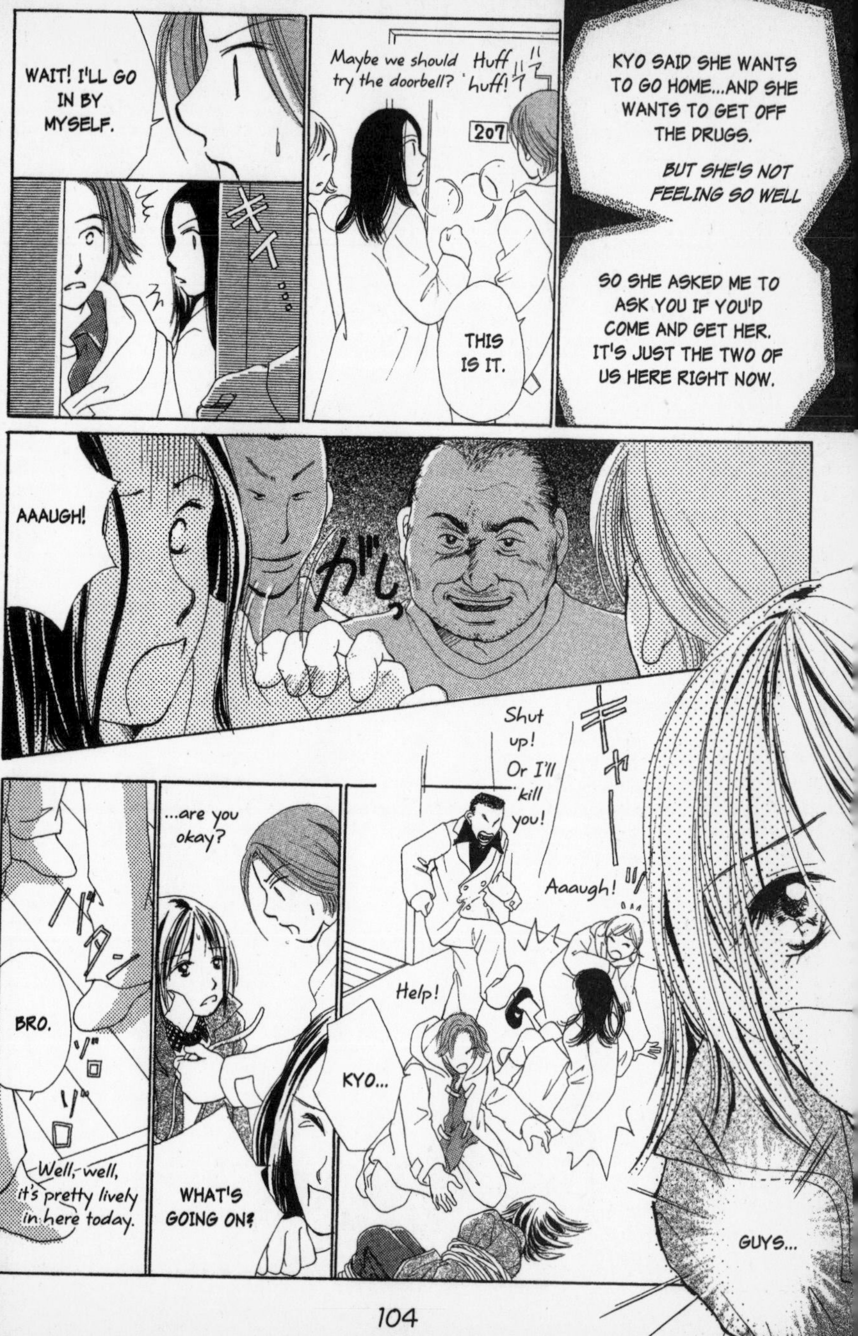

KYO SAID SHE WANTS TO GO HOME...AND SHE WANTS TO GET OFF THE DRUGS.
BUT SHE'S NOT FEELING SO WELL
SO SHE ASKED ME TO ASK YOU IF YOU'D COME AND GET HER. IT'S JUST THE TWO OF US HERE RIGHT NOW.
Huff huff!
Maybe we should try the doorbell?
207
THIS IS IT.
WAIT! I'LL GO IN BY MYSELF.
キイ…
AAAUGH!
がし
GUYS...
キャー
Shut up! Or I'll kill you!
Aaaugh!
Help!
KYO...
...are you okay?
WHAT'S GOING ON?
バタン
BRO.
Well, well, it's pretty lively in here today.

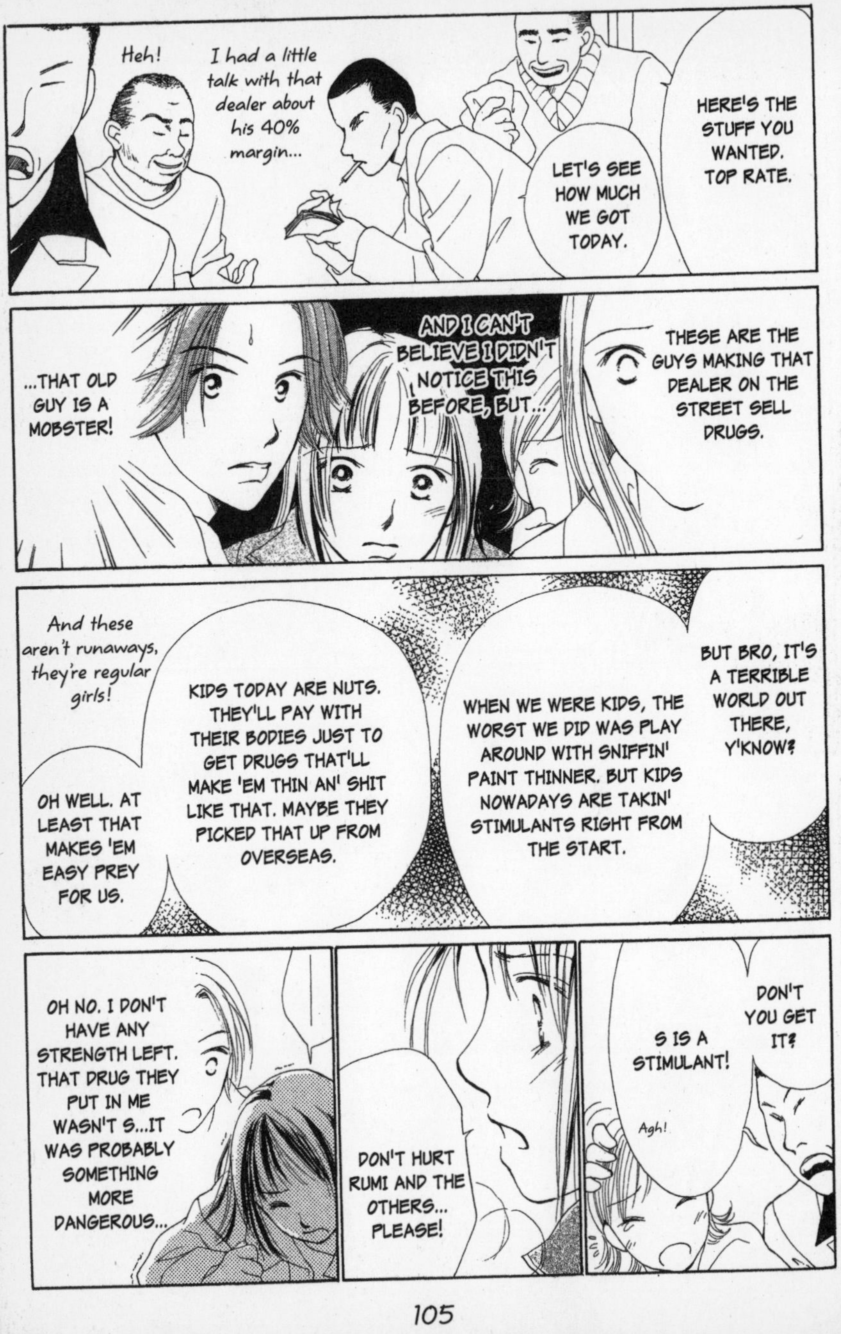
HERE'S THE STUFF YOU WANTED. TOP RATE.
LET'S SEE HOW MUCH WE GOT TODAY.
I had a little talk with that dealer about his 40% margin...
Heh!
THESE ARE THE GUYS MAKING THAT DEALER ON THE STREET SELL DRUGS.
AND I CAN'T BELIEVE I DIDN'T NOTICE THIS BEFORE, BUT...
...THAT OLD GUY IS A MOBSTER!
BUT BRO, IT'S A TERRIBLE WORLD OUT THERE, Y'KNOW?
WHEN WE WERE KIDS, THE WORST WE DID WAS PLAY AROUND WITH SNIFFIN' PAINT THINNER. BUT KIDS NOWADAYS ARE TAKIN' STIMULANTS RIGHT FROM THE START.
KIDS TODAY ARE NUTS. THEY'LL PAY WITH THEIR BODIES JUST TO GET DRUGS THAT'LL MAKE 'EM THIN AN' SHIT LIKE THAT. MAYBE THEY PICKED THAT UP FROM OVERSEAS.
And these aren't runaways, they're regular girls!
OH WELL. AT LEAST THAT MAKES 'EM EASY PREY FOR US.
DON'T YOU GET IT?
S IS A STIMULANT!
Agh!
DON'T HURT RUMI AND THE OTHERS... PLEASE!
OH NO. I DON'T HAVE ANY STRENGTH LEFT. THAT DRUG THEY PUT IN ME WASN'T S...IT WAS PROBABLY SOMETHING MORE DANGEROUS...

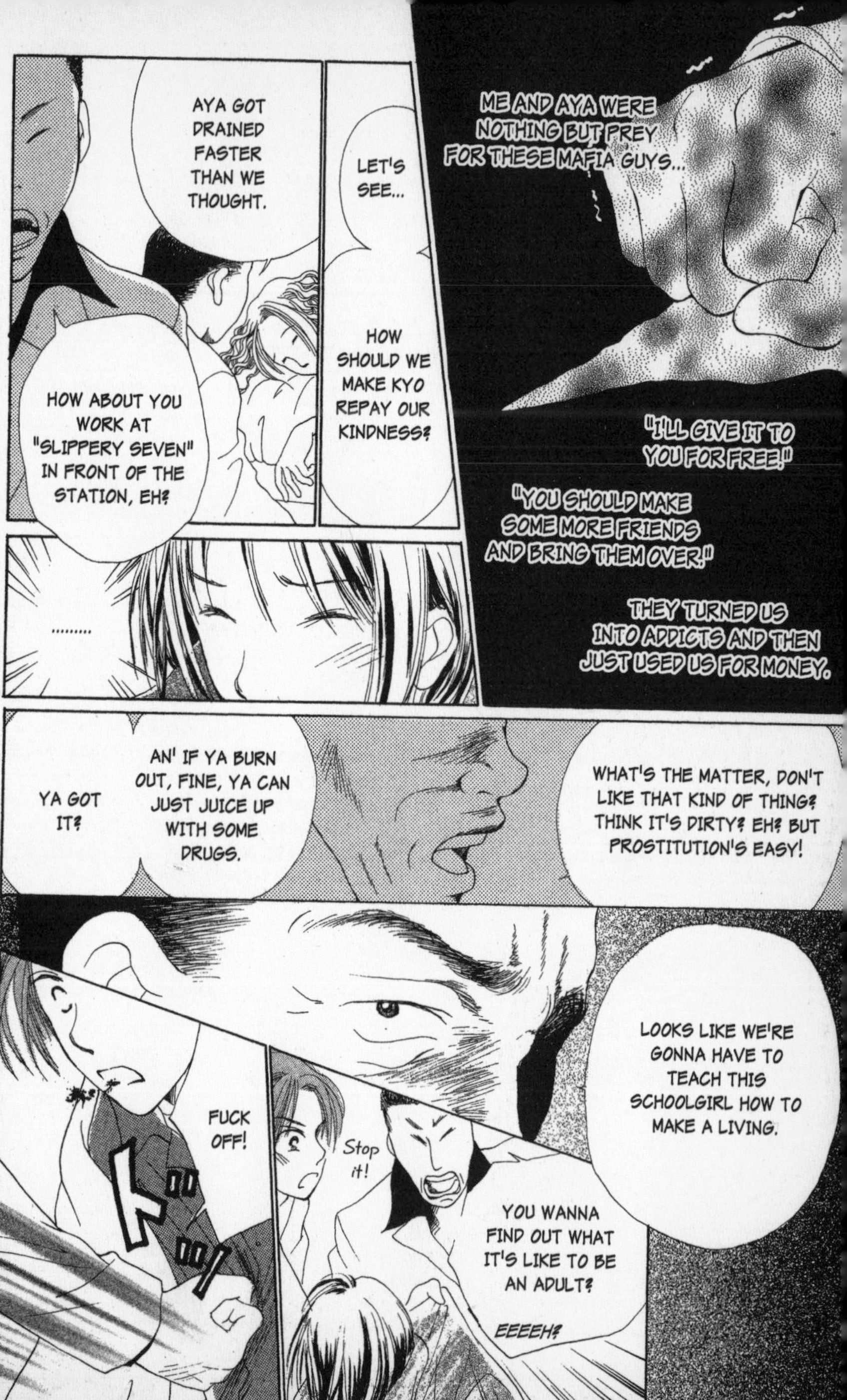

ME AND AYA WERE NOTHING BUT PREY FOR THESE MAFIA GUYS...
"I'LL GIVE IT TO YOU FOR FREE!"
"YOU SHOULD MAKE SOME MORE FRIENDS AND BRING THEM OVER!"
THEY TURNED US INTO ADDICTS AND THEN JUST USED US FOR MONEY.
LET'S SEE...
HOW SHOULD WE MAKE KYO REPAY OUR KINDNESS?
AYA GOT DRAINED FASTER THAN WE THOUGHT.
HOW ABOUT YOU WORK AT "SLIPPERY SEVEN" IN FRONT OF THE STATION, EH?
....
WHAT'S THE MATTER, DON'T LIKE THAT KIND OF THING? THINK IT'S DIRTY? EH? BUT PROSTITUTION'S EASY!
AN' IF YA BURN OUT, FINE, YA CAN JUST JUICE UP WITH SOME DRUGS.
YA GOT IT?
LOOKS LIKE WE'RE GONNA HAVE TO TEACH THIS SCHOOLGIRL HOW TO MAKE A LIVING.
YOU WANNA FIND OUT WHAT IT'S LIKE TO BE AN ADULT?
EEEEH?
Stop it!
FUCK OFF!

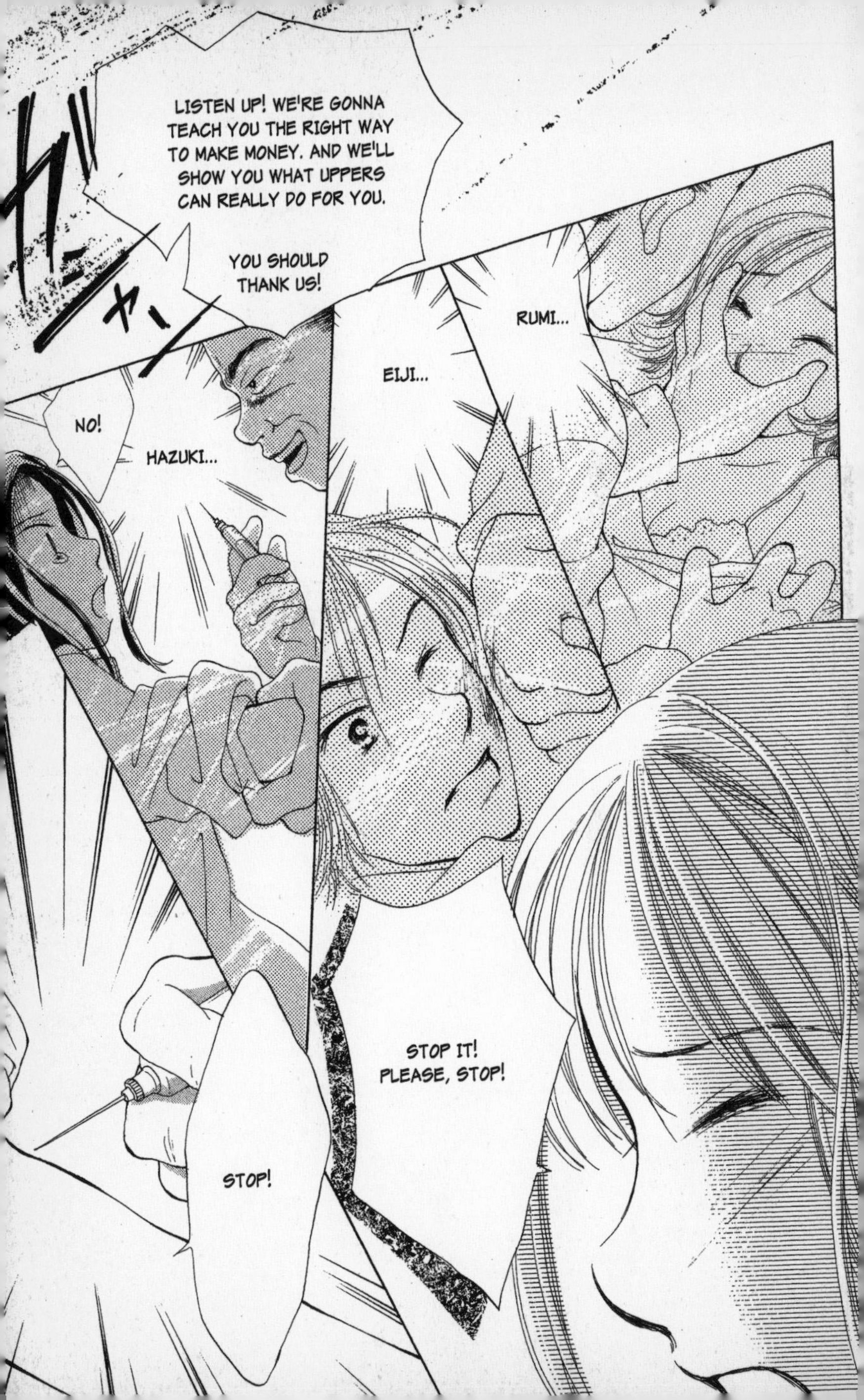
LISTEN UP! WE'RE GONNA TEACH YOU THE RIGHT WAY TO MAKE MONEY. AND WE'LL SHOW YOU WHAT UPPERS CAN REALLY DO FOR YOU.
YOU SHOULD THANK US!
RUMI...
EIJI...
HAZUKI...
NO!
STOP IT! PLEASE, STOP!
STOP!

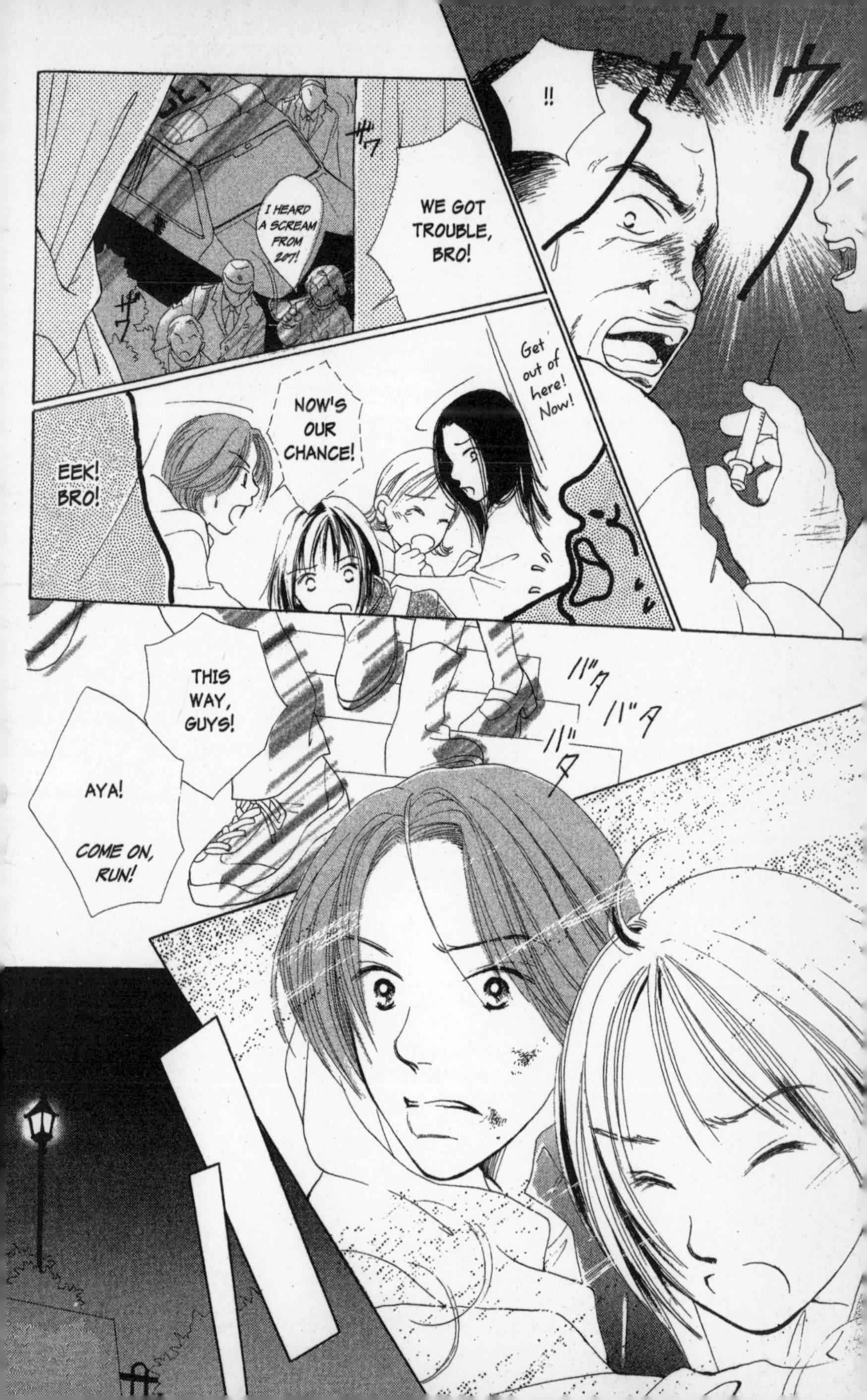
!!
WE GOT TROUBLE, BRO!
I HEARD A SCREAM FROM 207!
Get out of here! Now!
NOW'S OUR CHANCE!
EEK! BRO!
THIS WAY, GUYS!
AYA!
COME ON, RUN!

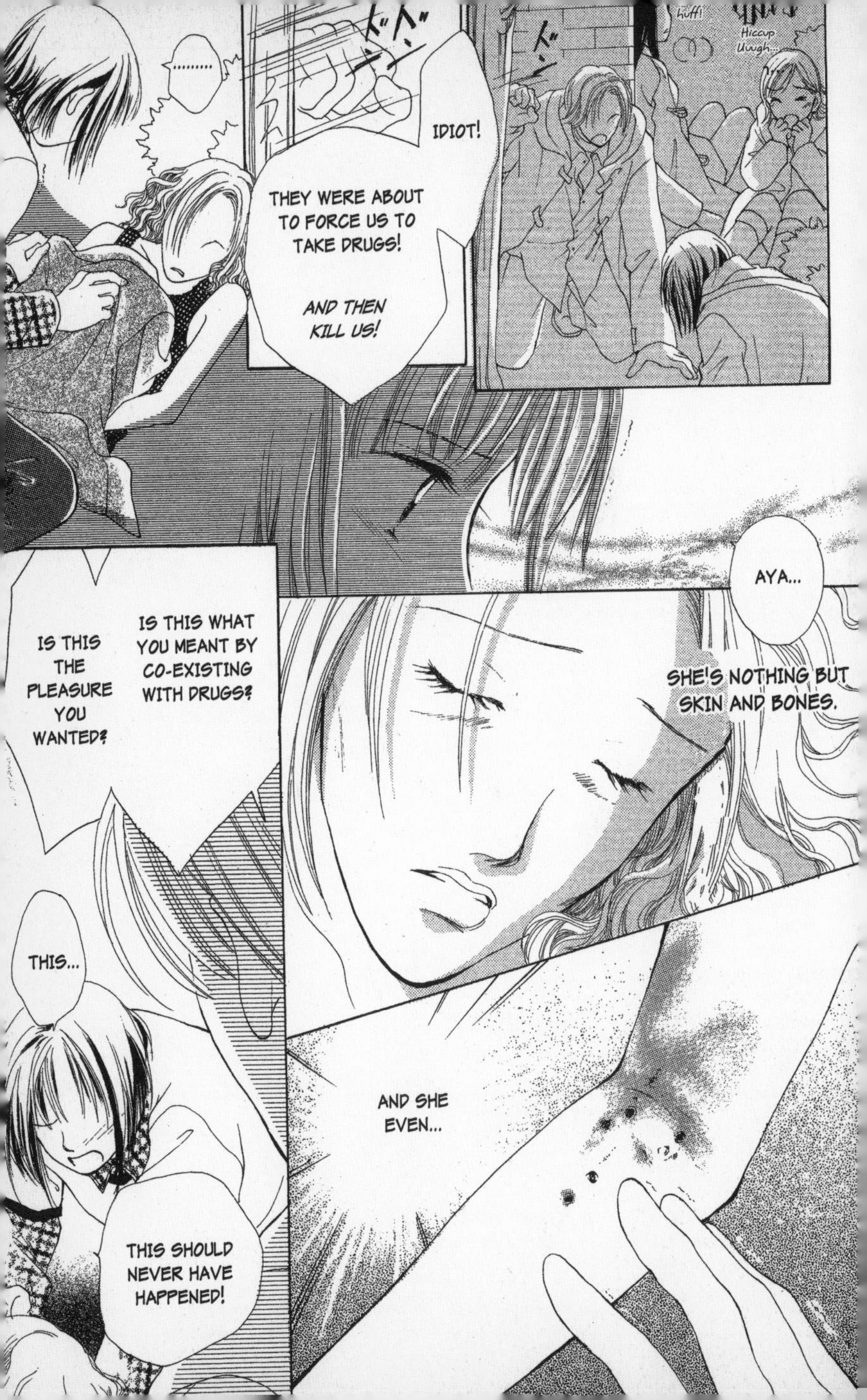
huff!
Hiccup
Uuugh...
IDIOT!
THEY WERE ABOUT TO FORCE US TO TAKE DRUGS!
AND THEN KILL US!
....
AYA...
SHE'S NOTHING BUT SKIN AND BONES.
AND SHE EVEN...
IS THIS WHAT YOU MEANT BY CO-EXISTING WITH DRUGS?
IS THIS THE PLEASURE YOU WANTED?
THIS...
THIS SHOULD NEVER HAVE HAPPENED!

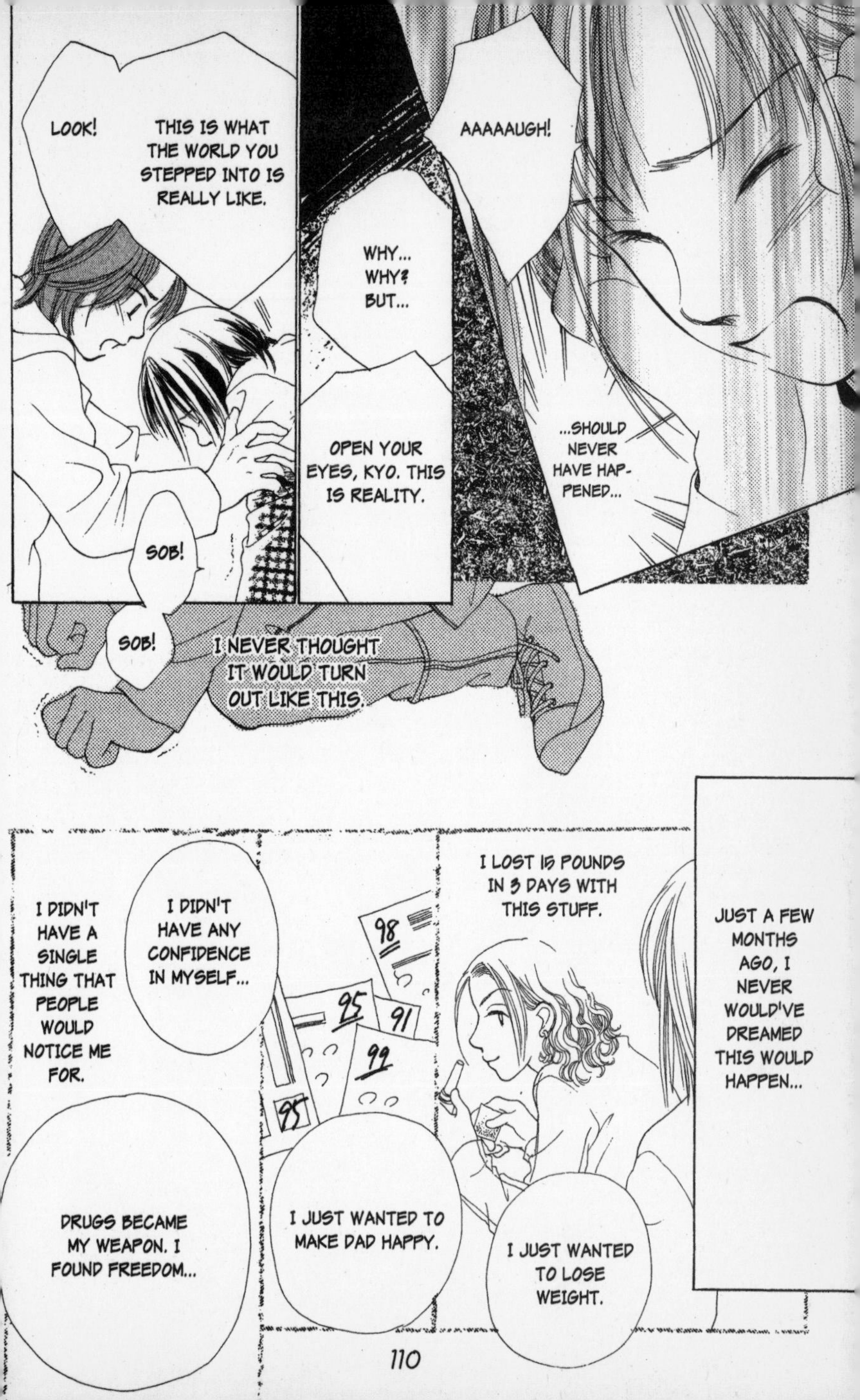
AAAAAUGH!
...SHOULD NEVER HAVE HAP-PENED...
WHY... WHY? BUT...
OPEN YOUR EYES, KYO. THIS IS REALITY.
LOOK! THIS IS WHAT THE WORLD YOU STEPPED INTO IS REALLY LIKE.
SOB!
SOB!
I NEVER THOUGHT IT WOULD TURN OUT LIKE THIS.
JUST A FEW MONTHS AGO, I NEVER WOULD'VE DREAMED THIS WOULD HAPPEN...
I LOST 15 POUNDS IN 3 DAYS WITH THIS STUFF.
I JUST WANTED TO LOSE WEIGHT.
98
95
91
99
95
I JUST WANTED TO MAKE DAD HAPPY.
I DIDN'T HAVE ANY CONFIDENCE IN MYSELF...
I DIDN'T HAVE A SINGLE THING THAT PEOPLE WOULD NOTICE ME FOR.
DRUGS BECAME MY WEAPON. I FOUND FREEDOM...

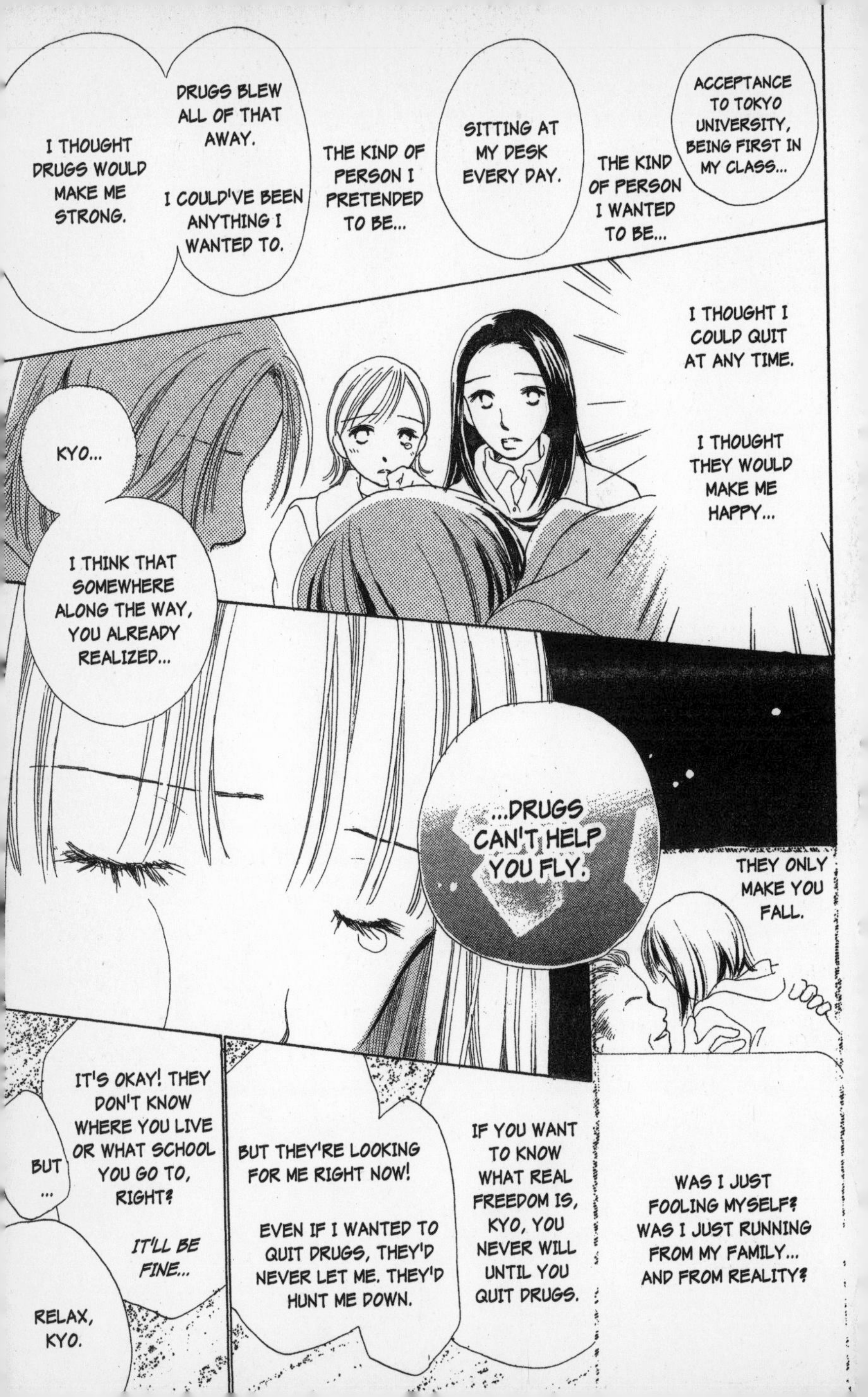
ACCEPTANCE TO TOKYO UNIVERSITY, BEING FIRST IN MY CLASS...
THE KIND OF PERSON I WANTED TO BE...
SITTING AT MY DESK EVERY DAY.
THE KIND OF PERSON I PRETENDED TO BE...
DRUGS BLEW ALL OF THAT AWAY.
I COULD'VE BEEN ANYTHING I WANTED TO.
I THOUGHT DRUGS WOULD MAKE ME STRONG.
I THOUGHT I COULD QUIT AT ANY TIME.
I THOUGHT THEY WOULD MAKE ME HAPPY...
KYO...
I THINK THAT SOMEWHERE ALONG THE WAY, YOU ALREADY REALIZED...
...DRUGS CAN'T HELP YOU FLY.
THEY ONLY MAKE YOU FALL.
WAS I JUST FOOLING MYSELF? WAS I JUST RUNNING FROM MY FAMILY... AND FROM REALITY?
IF YOU WANT TO KNOW WHAT REAL FREEDOM IS, KYO, YOU NEVER WILL UNTIL YOU QUIT DRUGS.
BUT THEY'RE LOOKING FOR ME RIGHT NOW!
EVEN IF I WANTED TO QUIT DRUGS, THEY'D NEVER LET ME. THEY'D HUNT ME DOWN.
IT'S OKAY! THEY DON'T KNOW WHERE YOU LIVE OR WHAT SCHOOL YOU GO TO, RIGHT?
BUT...
IT'LL BE FINE...
RELAX, KYO.

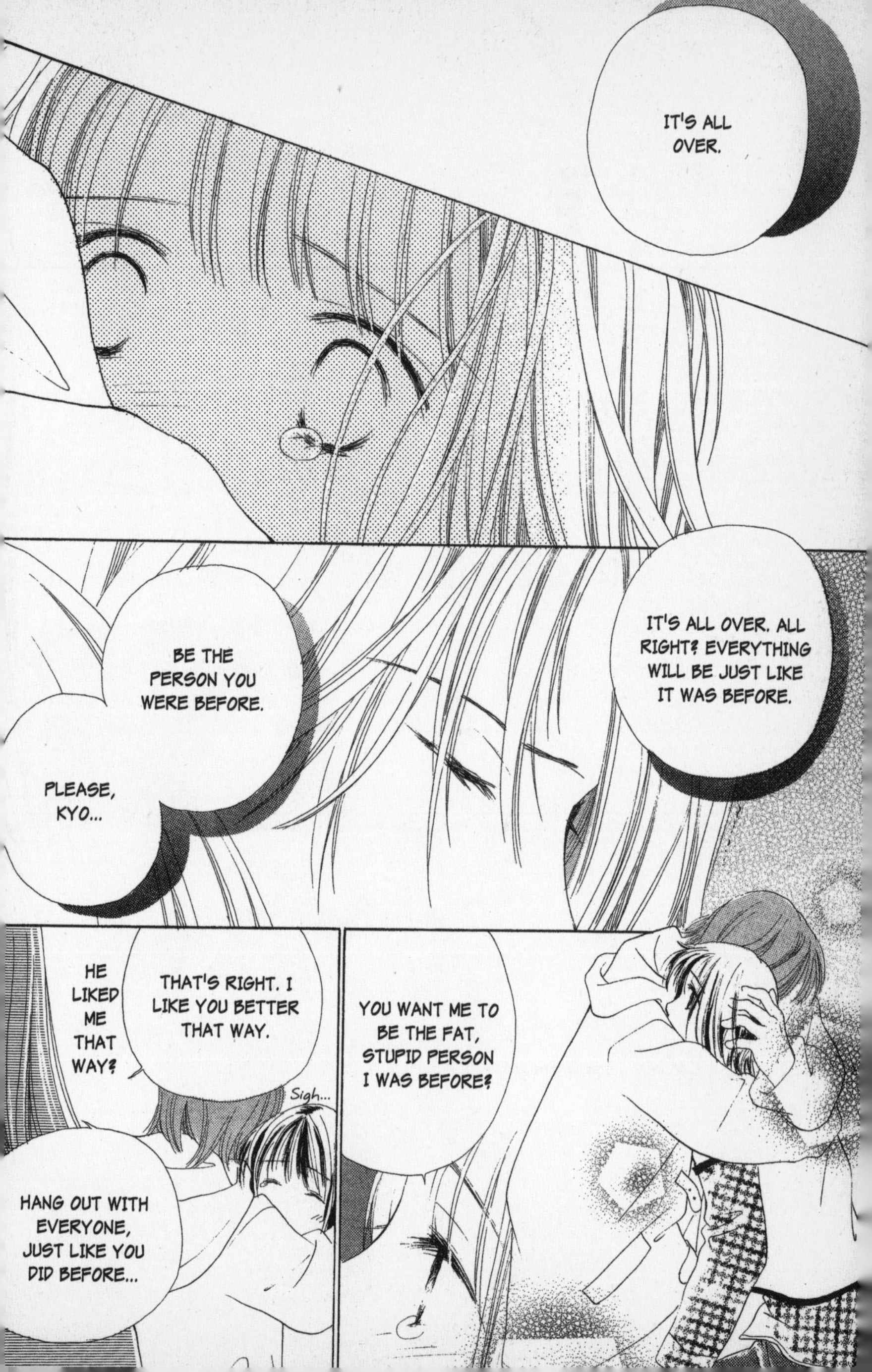
IT'S ALL OVER.
IT'S ALL OVER. ALL RIGHT? EVERYTHING WILL BE JUST LIKE IT WAS BEFORE.
BE THE PERSON YOU WERE BEFORE.
PLEASE, KYO...
YOU WANT ME TO BE THE FAT, STUPID PERSON I WAS BEFORE?
THAT'S RIGHT. I LIKE YOU BETTER THAT WAY.
HE LIKED ME THAT WAY?
Sigh...
HANG OUT WITH EVERYONE, JUST LIKE YOU DID BEFORE...

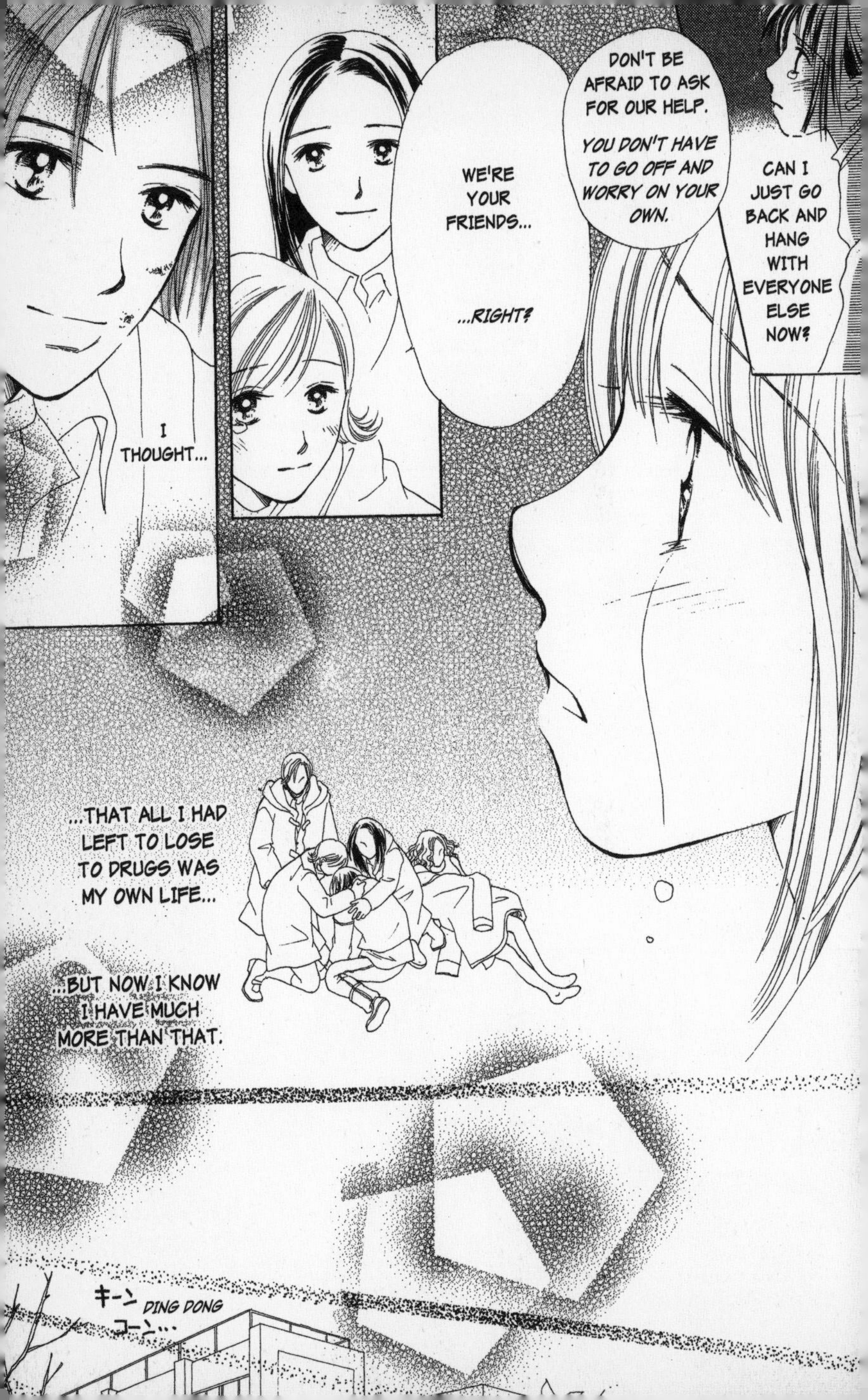
CAN I JUST GO BACK AND HANG WITH EVERYONE ELSE NOW?
DON'T BE AFRAID TO ASK FOR OUR HELP.
YOU DON'T HAVE TO GO OFF AND WORRY ON YOUR OWN.
WE'RE YOUR FRIENDS...
...RIGHT?
I THOUGHT...
...THAT ALL I HAD LEFT TO LOSE TO DRUGS WAS MY OWN LIFE...
...BUT NOW I KNOW I HAVE MUCH MORE THAN THAT.
キーン DING DONG
コーン…

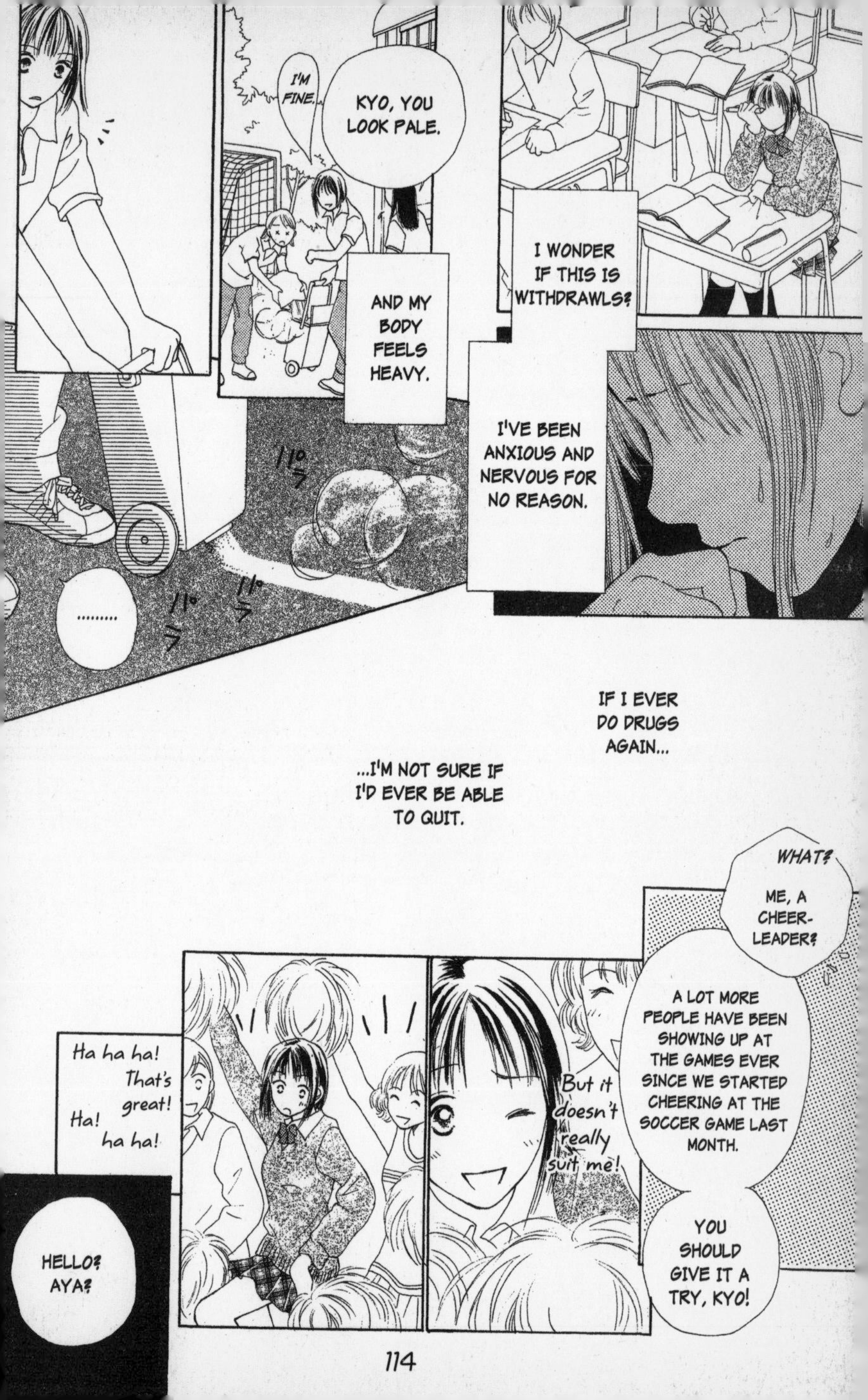
I WONDER IF THIS IS WITHDRAWLS?
I'VE BEEN ANXIOUS AND NERVOUS FOR NO REASON.
AND MY BODY FEELS HEAVY.
KYO, YOU LOOK PALE.
I'M FINE.
....
IF I EVER DO DRUGS AGAIN...
...I'M NOT SURE IF I'D EVER BE ABLE TO QUIT.
WHAT?
ME, A CHEER-LEADER?
A LOT MORE PEOPLE HAVE BEEN SHOWING UP AT THE GAMES EVER SINCE WE STARTED CHEERING AT THE SOCCER GAME LAST MONTH.
YOU SHOULD GIVE IT A TRY, KYO!
But it doesn't really suit me!
Ha ha ha! That's great! Ha! ha ha!
HELLO? AYA?

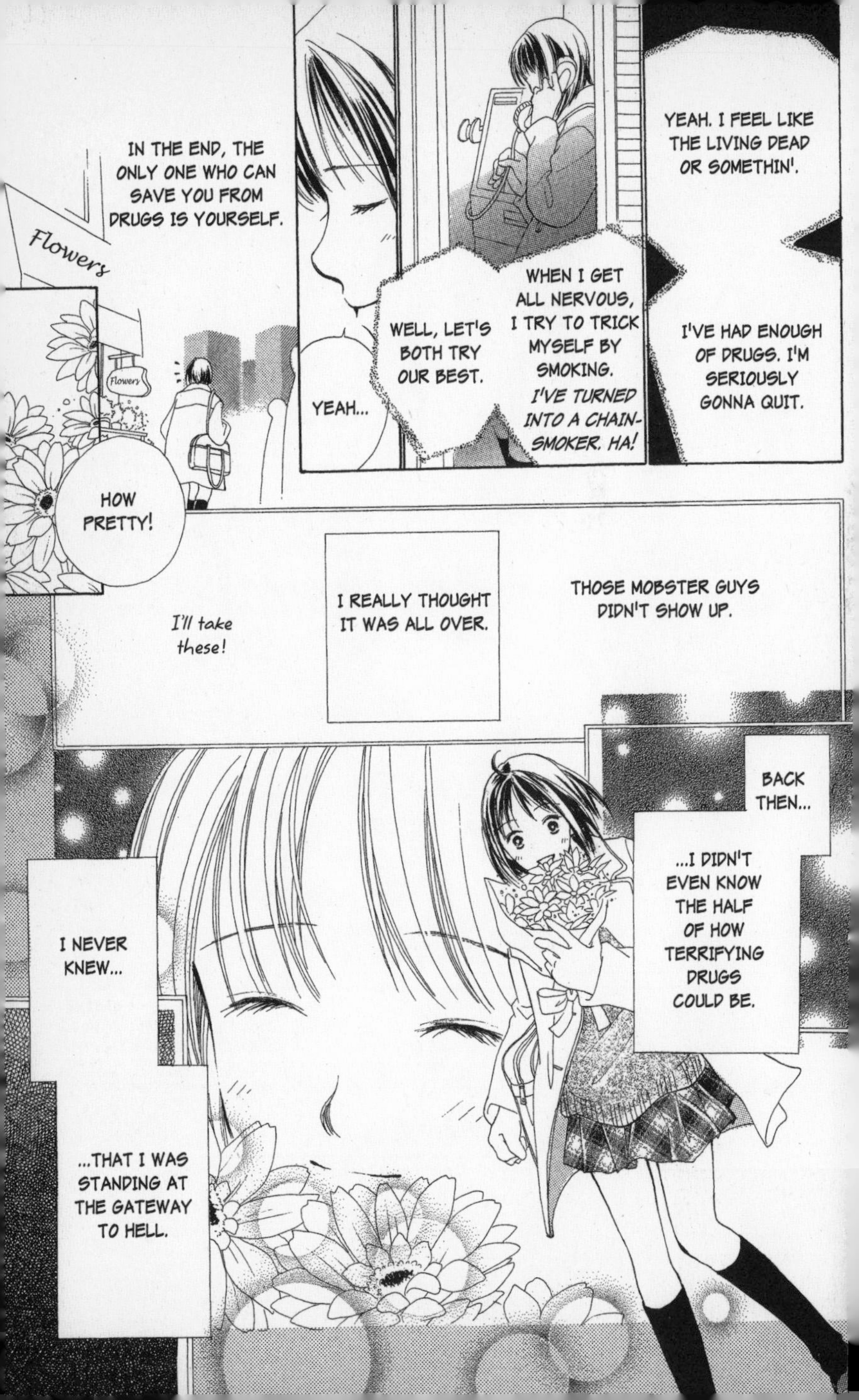
YEAH. I FEEL LIKE THE LIVING DEAD OR SOMETHIN'.
I'VE HAD ENOUGH OF DRUGS. I'M SERIOUSLY GONNA QUIT.
WHEN I GET ALL NERVOUS, I TRY TO TRICK MYSELF BY SMOKING. *I'VE TURNED INTO A CHAIN-SMOKER. HA!*
WELL, LET'S BOTH TRY OUR BEST.
YEAH...
IN THE END, THE ONLY ONE WHO CAN SAVE YOU FROM DRUGS IS YOURSELF.
Flowers
Flowers
HOW PRETTY!
THOSE MOBSTER GUYS DIDN'T SHOW UP.
I REALLY THOUGHT IT WAS ALL OVER.
I'll take these!
BACK THEN...
...I DIDN'T EVEN KNOW THE HALF OF HOW TERRIFYING DRUGS COULD BE.
I NEVER KNEW...
...THAT I WAS STANDING AT THE GATEWAY TO HELL.

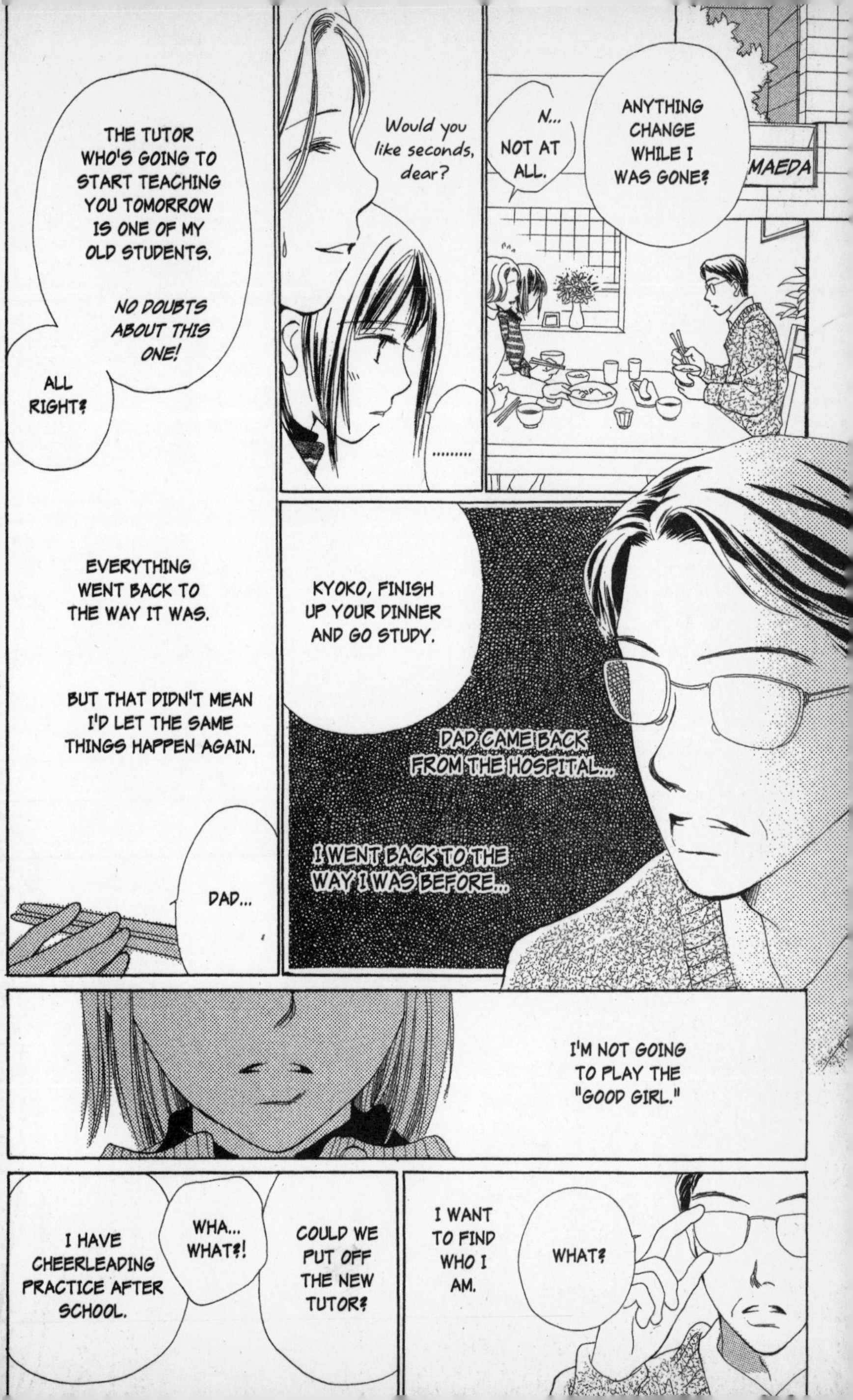
MAEDA
ANYTHING CHANGE WHILE I WAS GONE?
N... NOT AT ALL.
Would you like seconds, dear?
....
DAD CAME BACK FROM THE HOSPITAL...
I WENT BACK TO THE WAY I WAS BEFORE...
KYOKO, FINISH UP YOUR DINNER AND GO STUDY.
THE TUTOR WHO'S GOING TO START TEACHING YOU TOMORROW IS ONE OF MY OLD STUDENTS.
NO DOUBTS ABOUT THIS ONE!
ALL RIGHT?
EVERYTHING WENT BACK TO THE WAY IT WAS.
BUT THAT DIDN'T MEAN I'D LET THE SAME THINGS HAPPEN AGAIN.
DAD...
I'M NOT GOING TO PLAY THE "GOOD GIRL."
WHAT?
I WANT TO FIND WHO I AM.
COULD WE PUT OFF THE NEW TUTOR?
WHA... WHAT?!
I HAVE CHEERLEADING PRACTICE AFTER SCHOOL.

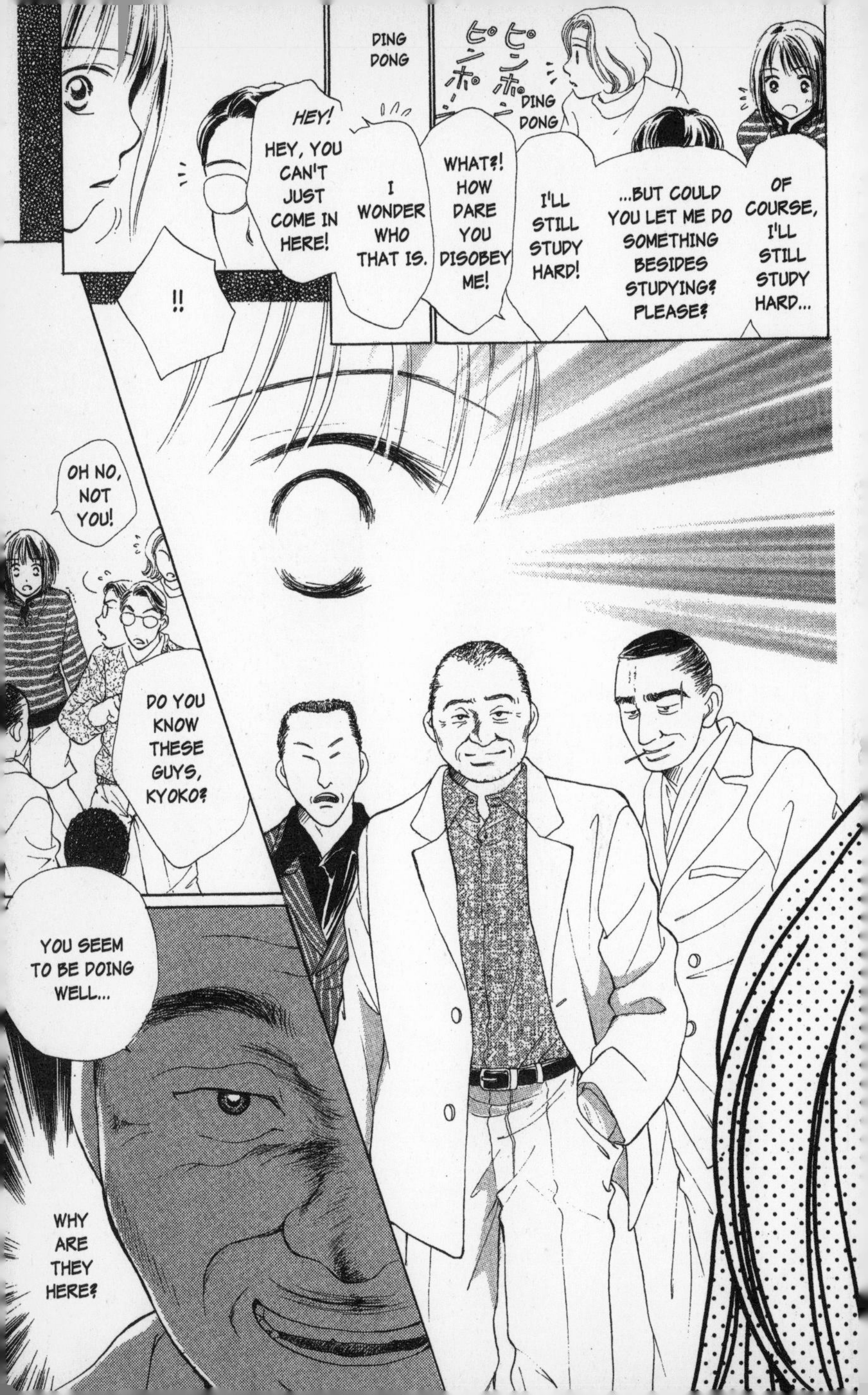

OF COURSE, I'LL STILL STUDY HARD...
...BUT COULD YOU LET ME DO SOMETHING BESIDES STUDYING? PLEASE?
I'LL STILL STUDY HARD!
ピンポン ピンポン
DING DONG
WHAT?! HOW DARE YOU DISOBEY ME!
DING DONG
I WONDER WHO THAT IS.
HEY! HEY, YOU CAN'T JUST COME IN HERE!
!!
OH NO, NOT YOU!
DO YOU KNOW THESE GUYS, KYOKO?
YOU SEEM TO BE DOING WELL...
WHY ARE THEY HERE?

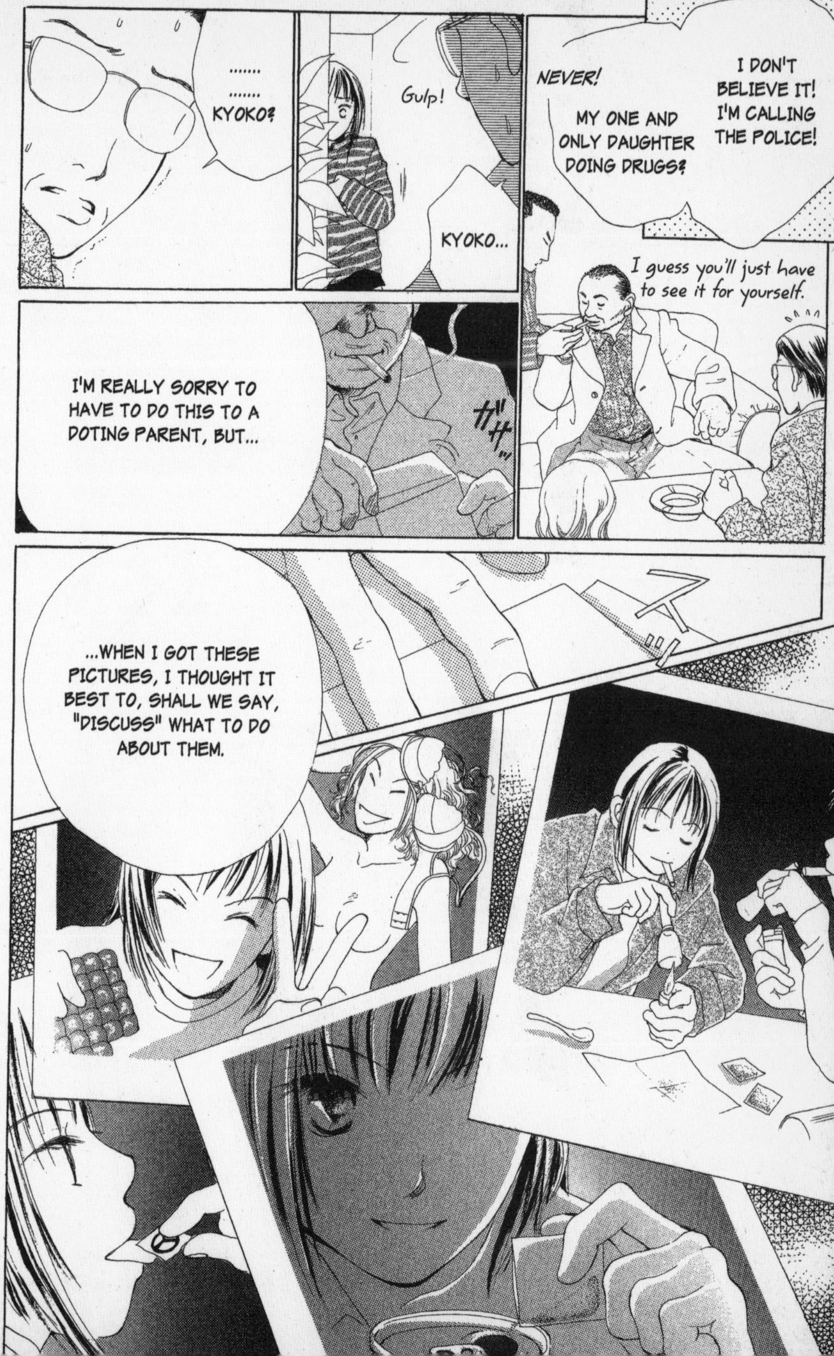
I DON'T BELIEVE IT! I'M CALLING THE POLICE!
NEVER!
MY ONE AND ONLY DAUGHTER DOING DRUGS?
Gulp!
KYOKO...
....
....
KYOKO?
I guess you'll just have to see it for yourself.
I'M REALLY SORRY TO HAVE TO DO THIS TO A DOTING PARENT, BUT...
...WHEN I GOT THESE PICTURES, I THOUGHT IT BEST TO, SHALL WE SAY, "DISCUSS" WHAT TO DO ABOUT THEM.

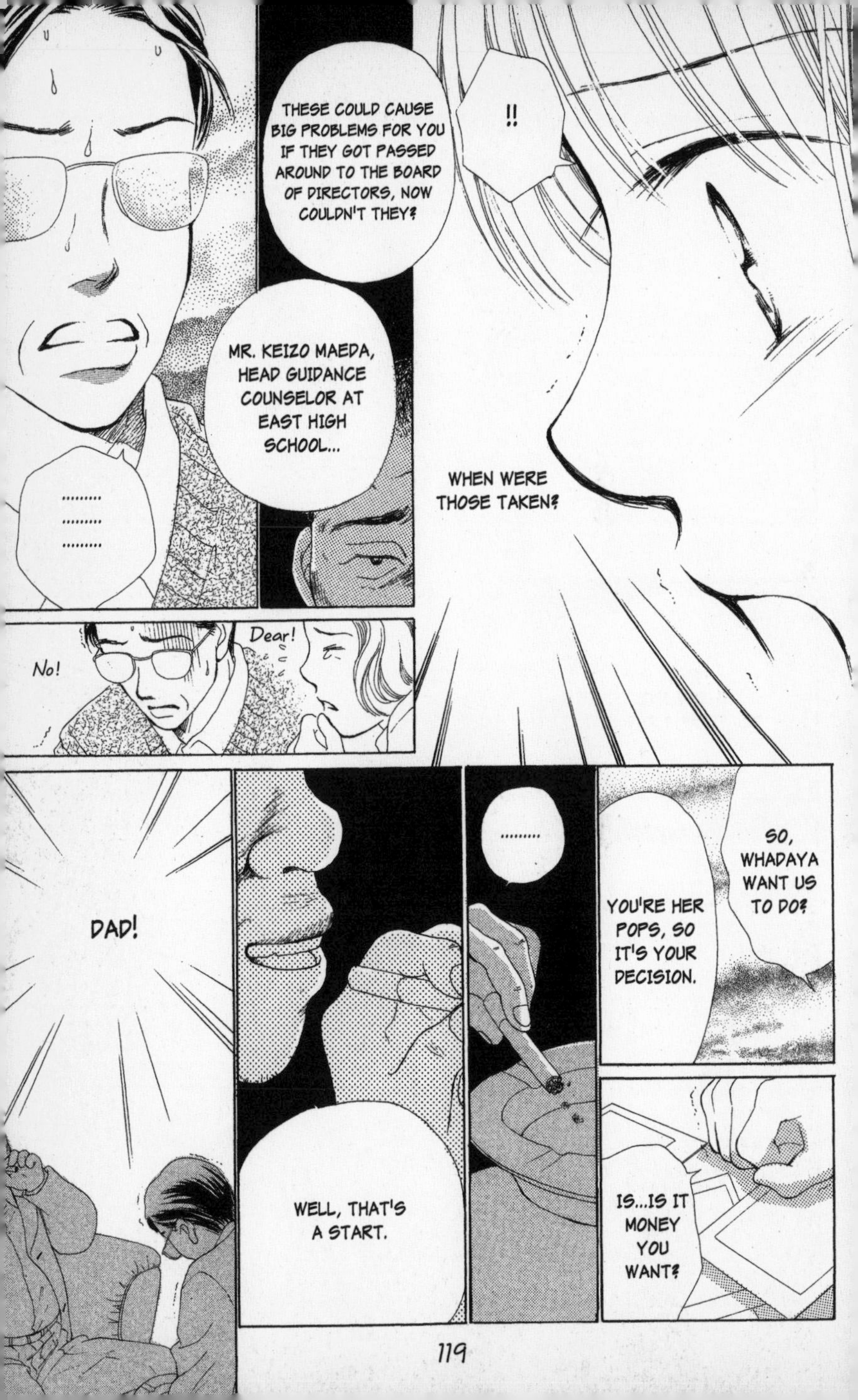
!!
WHEN WERE THOSE TAKEN?
THESE COULD CAUSE BIG PROBLEMS FOR YOU IF THEY GOT PASSED AROUND TO THE BOARD OF DIRECTORS, NOW COULDN'T THEY?
MR. KEIZO MAEDA, HEAD GUIDANCE COUNSELOR AT EAST HIGH SCHOOL...
....
....
....
Dear!
No!
SO, WHADAYA WANT US TO DO?
YOU'RE HER POPS, SO IT'S YOUR DECISION.
IS...IS IT MONEY YOU WANT?
....
WELL, THAT'S A START.
DAD!

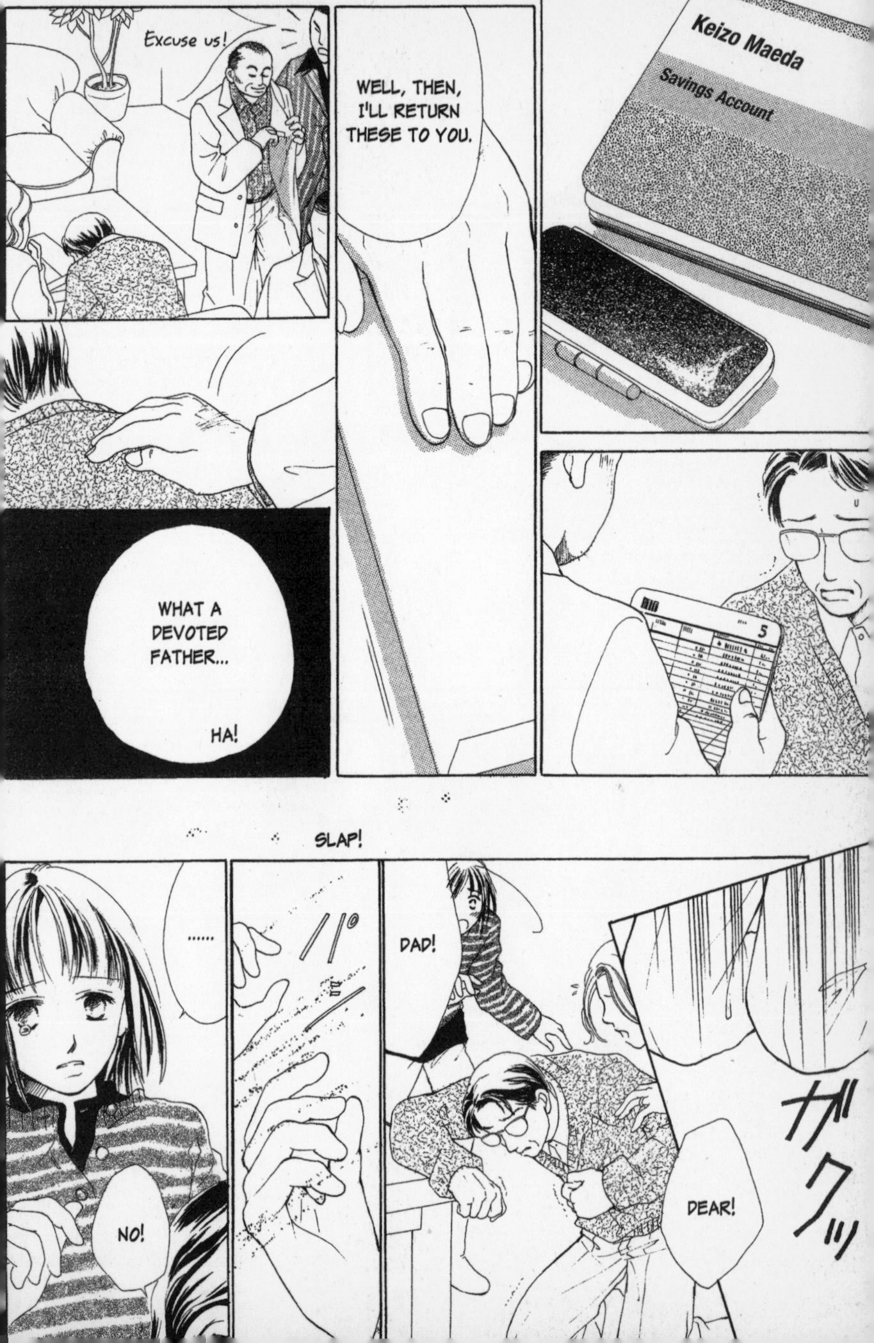

Keizo Maeda
Savings Account
WELL, THEN, I'LL RETURN THESE TO YOU.
Excuse us!
WHAT A DEVOTED FATHER...
HA!
SLAP!
ガクッ
DEAR!
DAD!
......
NO!

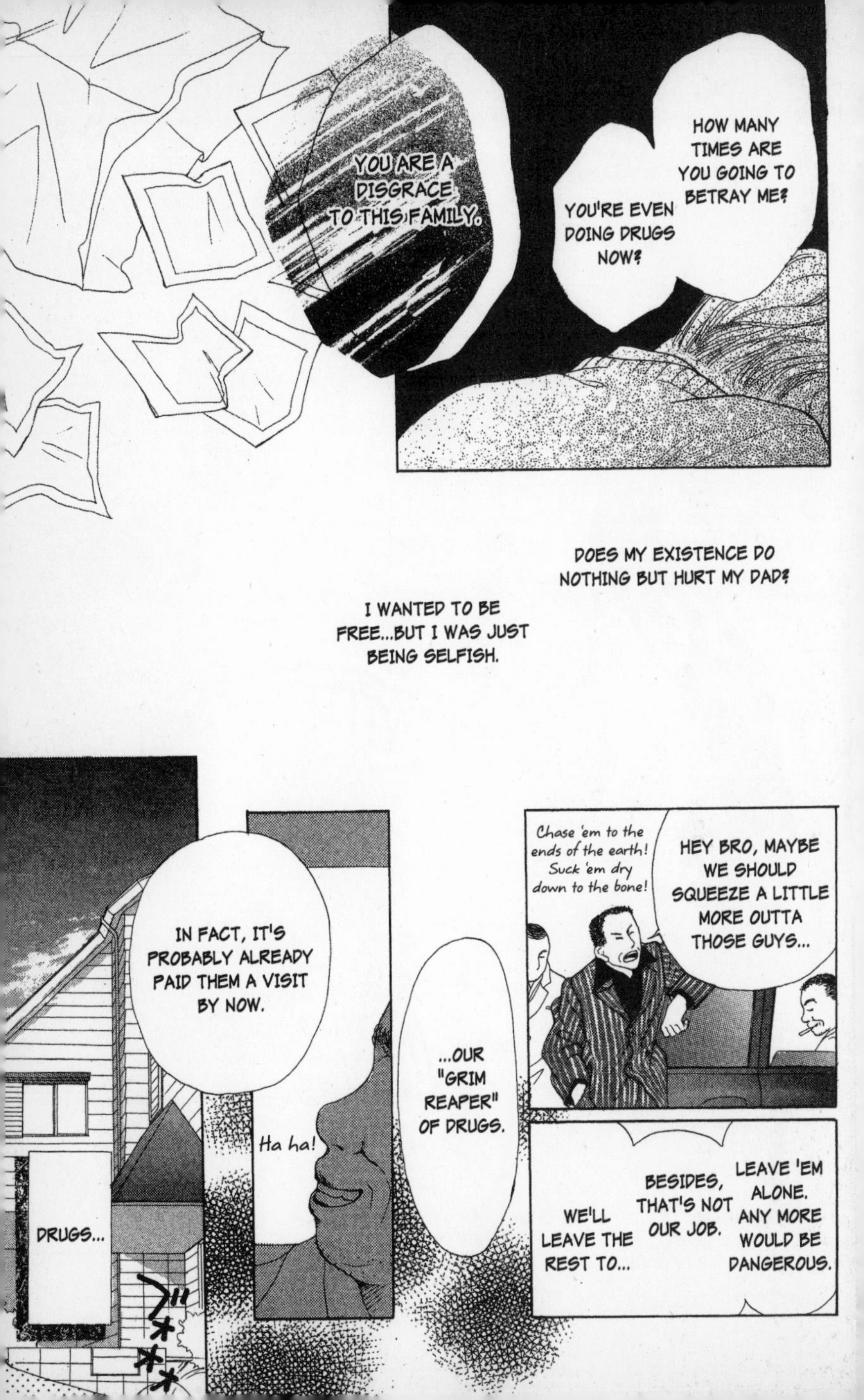
HOW MANY TIMES ARE YOU GOING TO BETRAY ME?
YOU'RE EVEN DOING DRUGS NOW?
YOU ARE A DISGRACE TO THIS FAMILY.
DOES MY EXISTENCE DO NOTHING BUT HURT MY DAD?
I WANTED TO BE FREE...BUT I WAS JUST BEING SELFISH.
HEY BRO, MAYBE WE SHOULD SQUEEZE A LITTLE MORE OUTTA THOSE GUYS...
Chase 'em to the ends of the earth! Suck 'em dry down to the bone!
LEAVE 'EM ALONE. ANY MORE WOULD BE DANGEROUS.
BESIDES, THAT'S NOT OUR JOB.
WE'LL LEAVE THE REST TO...
...OUR "GRIM REAPER" OF DRUGS.
Ha ha!
IN FACT, IT'S PROBABLY ALREADY PAID THEM A VISIT BY NOW.
DRUGS...

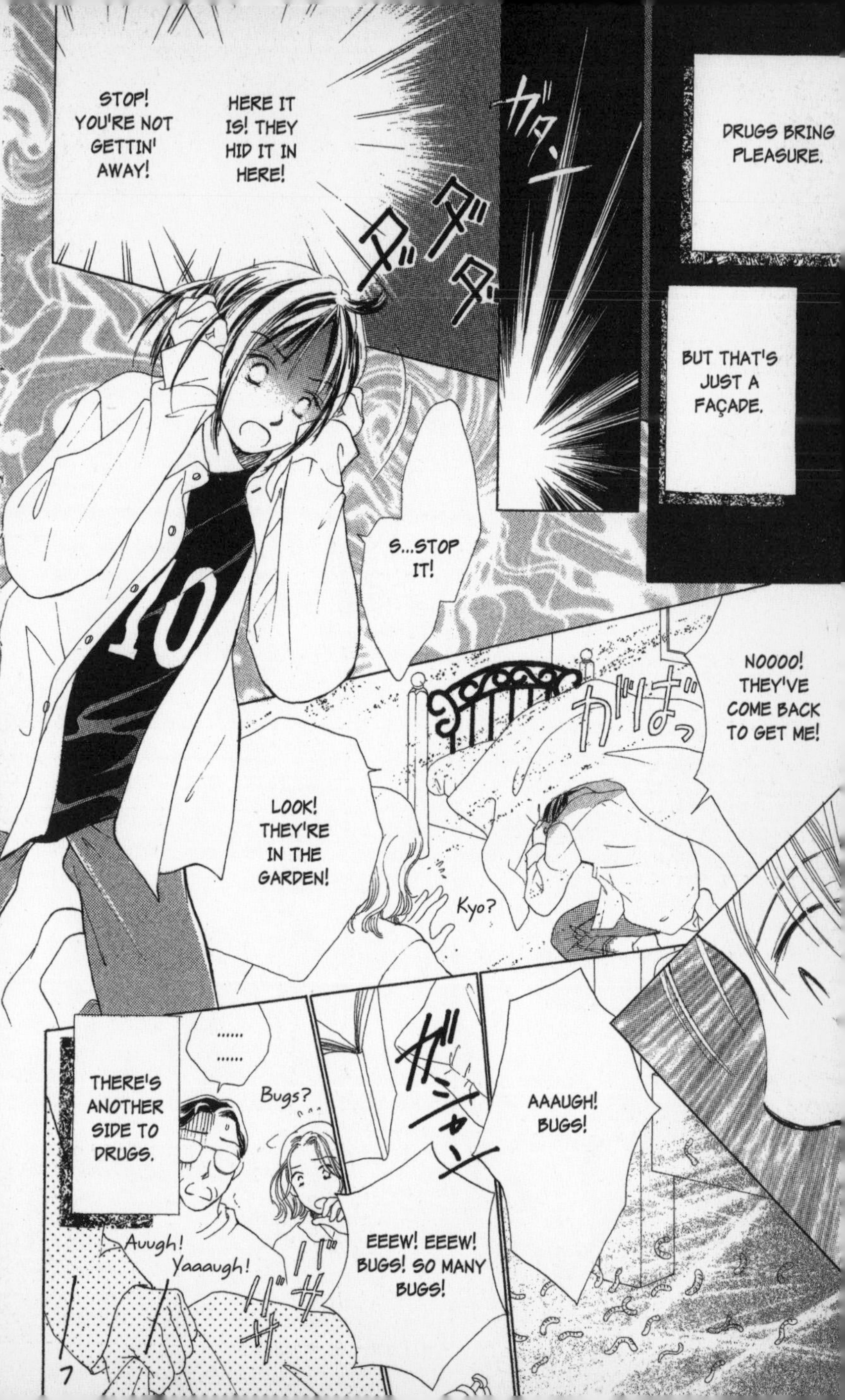
DRUGS BRING PLEASURE.
BUT THAT'S JUST A FAÇADE.
ガタン
ダダダ
HERE IT IS! THEY HID IT IN HERE!
STOP! YOU'RE NOT GETTIN' AWAY!
S...STOP IT!
NOOOO! THEY'VE COME BACK TO GET ME!
がばっ
Kyo?
LOOK! THEY'RE IN THE GARDEN!
AAAUGH! BUGS!
ガシャーン
EEEW! EEEW! BUGS! SO MANY BUGS!
Bugs?
......
......
THERE'S ANOTHER SIDE TO DRUGS.
Auugh!
Yaaaugh!
ガサガサ

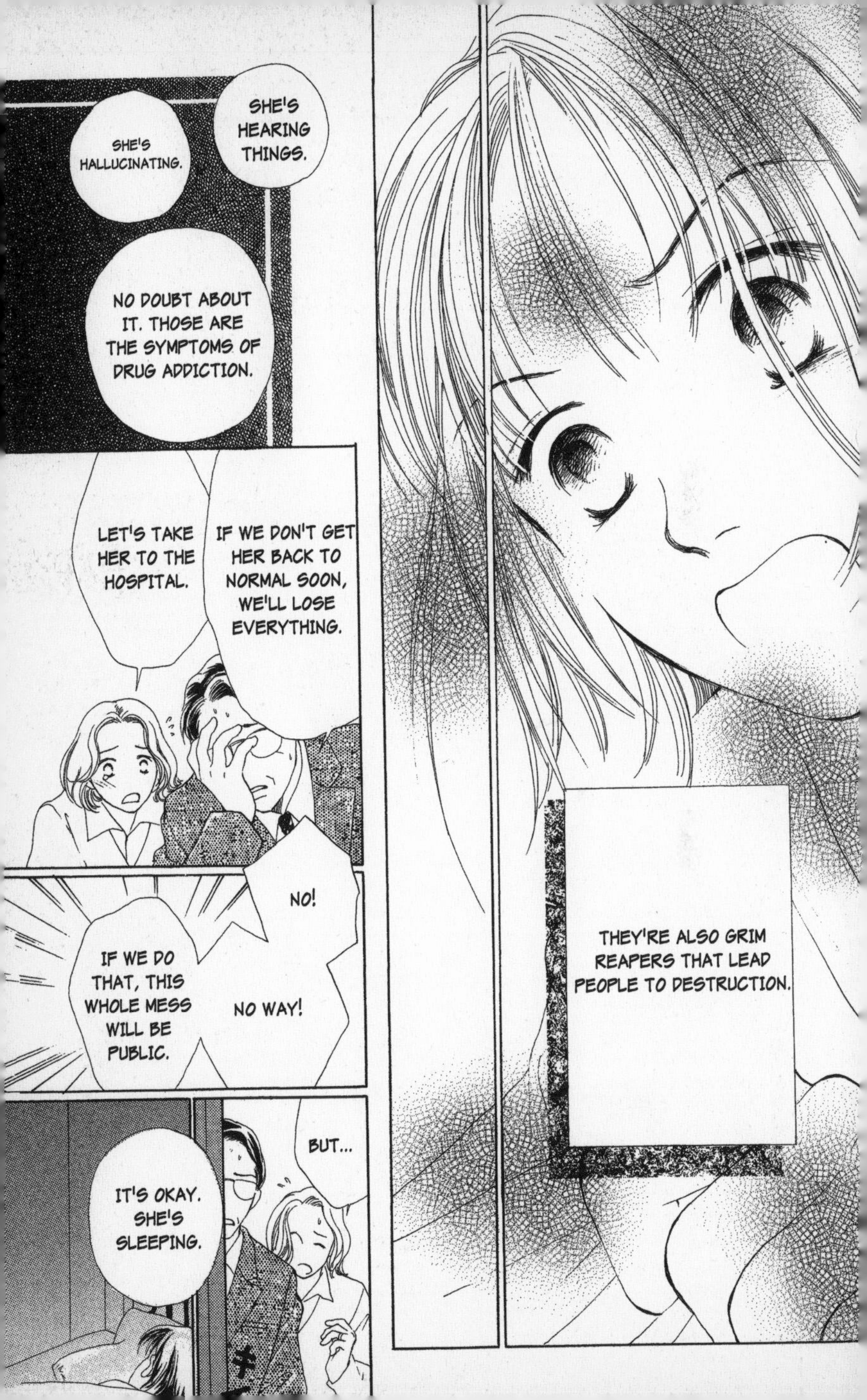
THEY'RE ALSO GRIM REAPERS THAT LEAD PEOPLE TO DESTRUCTION.
SHE'S HEARING THINGS.
SHE'S HALLUCINATING.
NO DOUBT ABOUT IT. THOSE ARE THE SYMPTOMS OF DRUG ADDICTION.
IF WE DON'T GET HER BACK TO NORMAL SOON, WE'LL LOSE EVERYTHING.
LET'S TAKE HER TO THE HOSPITAL.
NO!
NO WAY!
IF WE DO THAT, THIS WHOLE MESS WILL BE PUBLIC.
BUT...
IT'S OKAY. SHE'S SLEEPING.

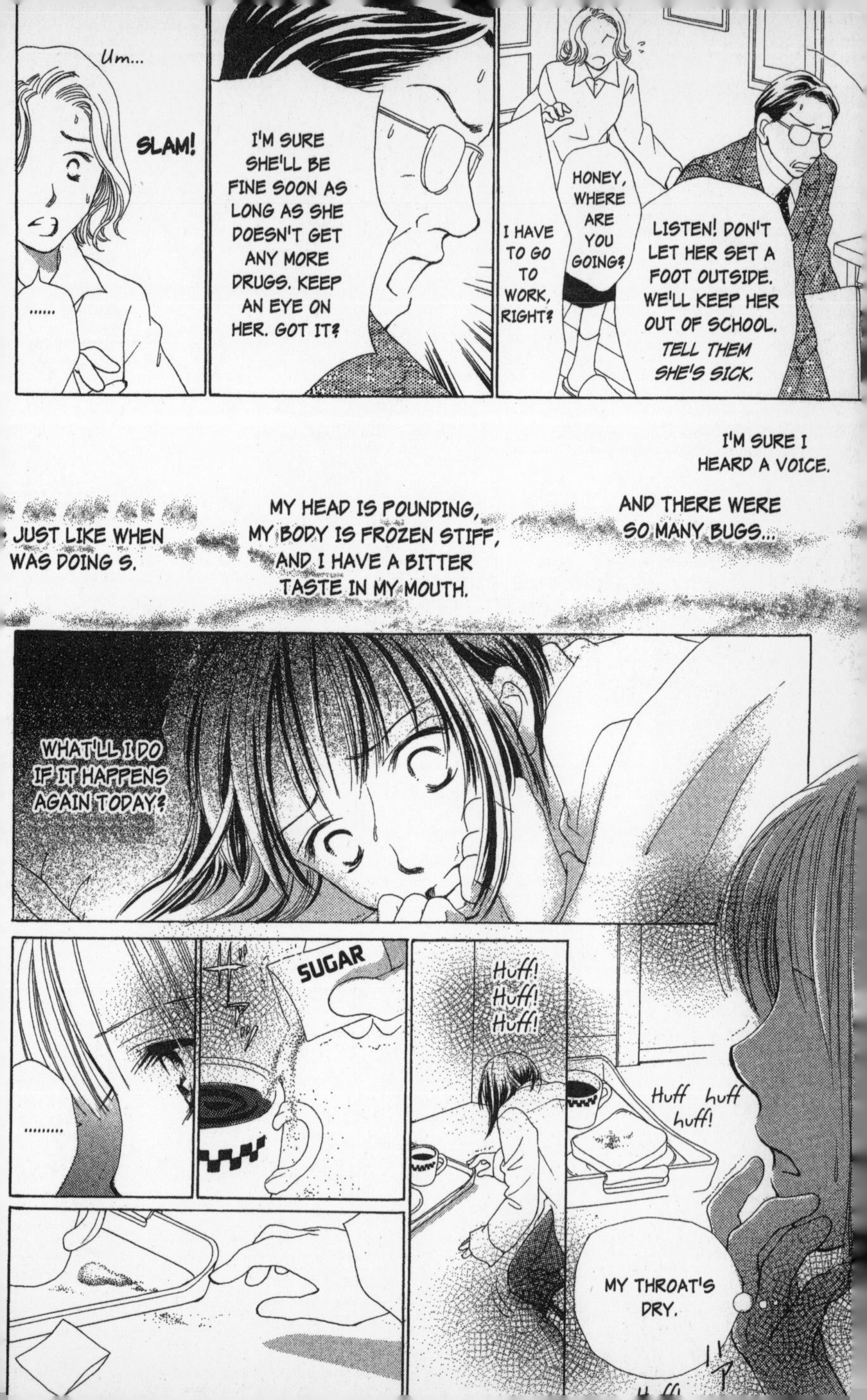
HONEY, WHERE ARE YOU GOING?
I HAVE TO GO TO WORK, RIGHT?
LISTEN! DON'T LET HER SET A FOOT OUTSIDE. WE'LL KEEP HER OUT OF SCHOOL. TELL THEM SHE'S SICK.
I'M SURE SHE'LL BE FINE SOON AS LONG AS SHE DOESN'T GET ANY MORE DRUGS. KEEP AN EYE ON HER. GOT IT?
Um...
SLAM!
......
I'M SURE I HEARD A VOICE.
AND THERE WERE SO MANY BUGS...
MY HEAD IS POUNDING, MY BODY IS FROZEN STIFF, AND I HAVE A BITTER TASTE IN MY MOUTH.
JUST LIKE WHEN
WAS DOING S.
WHAT'LL I DO IF IT HAPPENS AGAIN TODAY?
Huff huff huff!
MY THROAT'S DRY.
Huff! Huff! Huff!
SUGAR
....

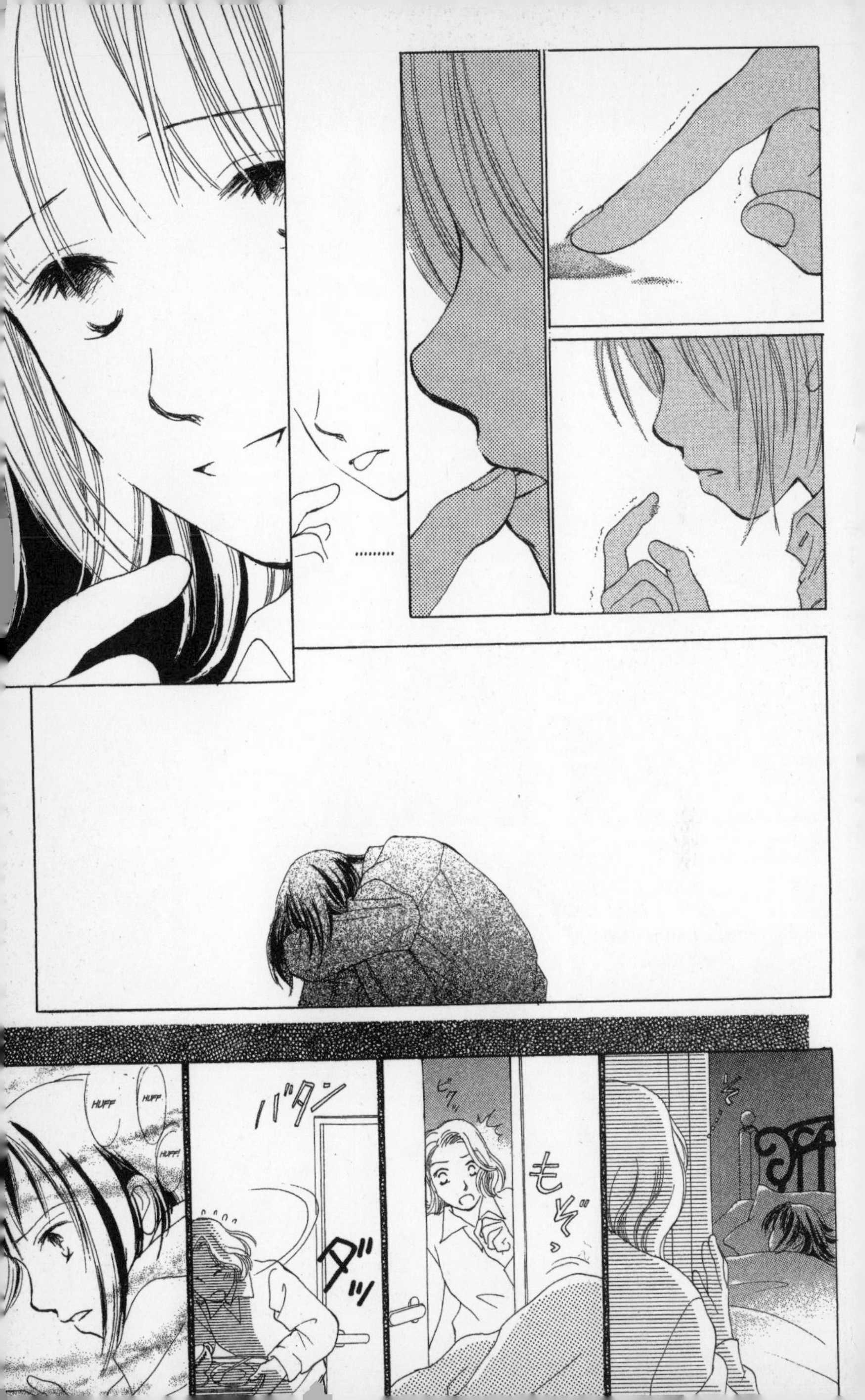
....
ビクッ
もぞっ
バタン
ダッ
HUFF
HUFF
HUFF!

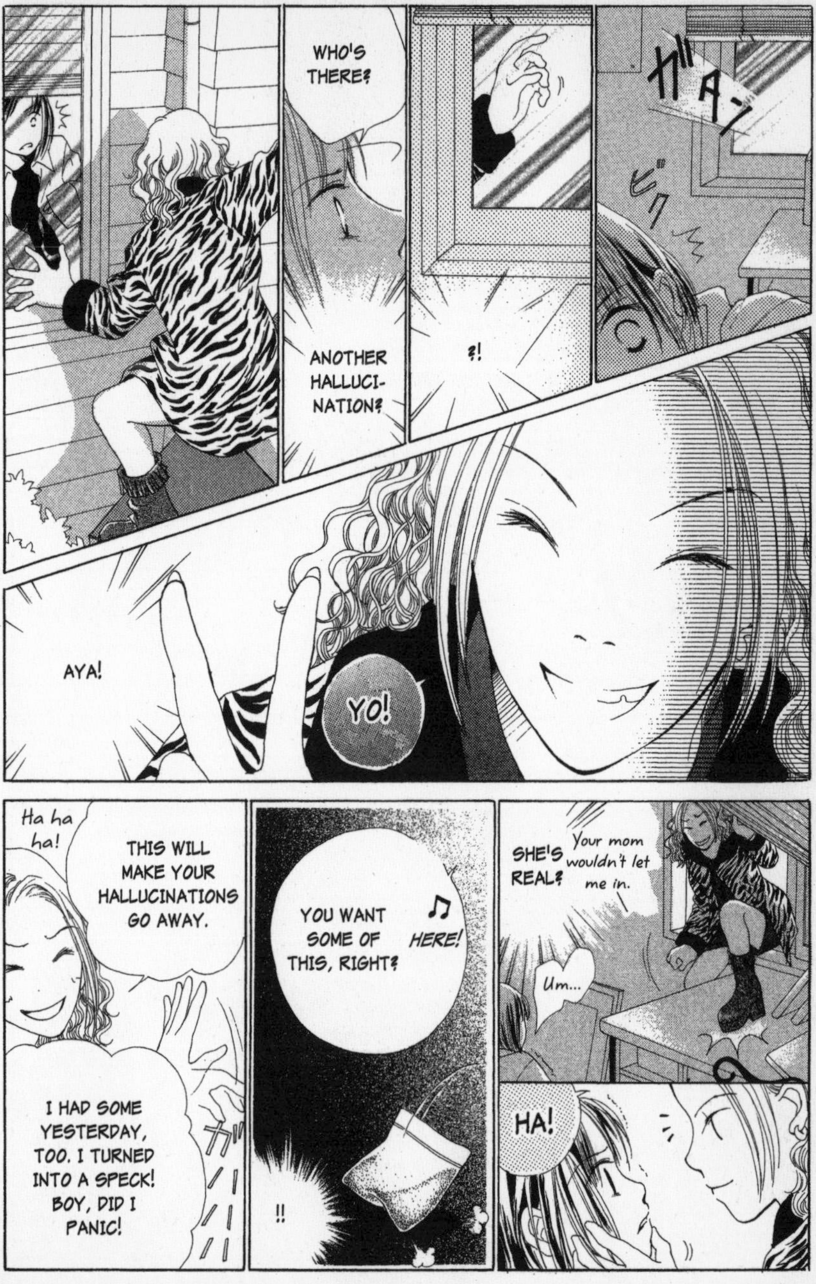
ガタン
ビク
?!
WHO'S THERE?
ANOTHER HALLUCI-NATION?
YO!
AYA!
Your mom wouldn't let me in.
SHE'S REAL?
Um...
HA!
♪ HERE!
YOU WANT SOME OF THIS, RIGHT?
!!
THIS WILL MAKE YOUR HALLUCINATIONS GO AWAY.
Ha ha ha!
I HAD SOME YESTERDAY, TOO. I TURNED INTO A SPECK! BOY, DID I PANIC!

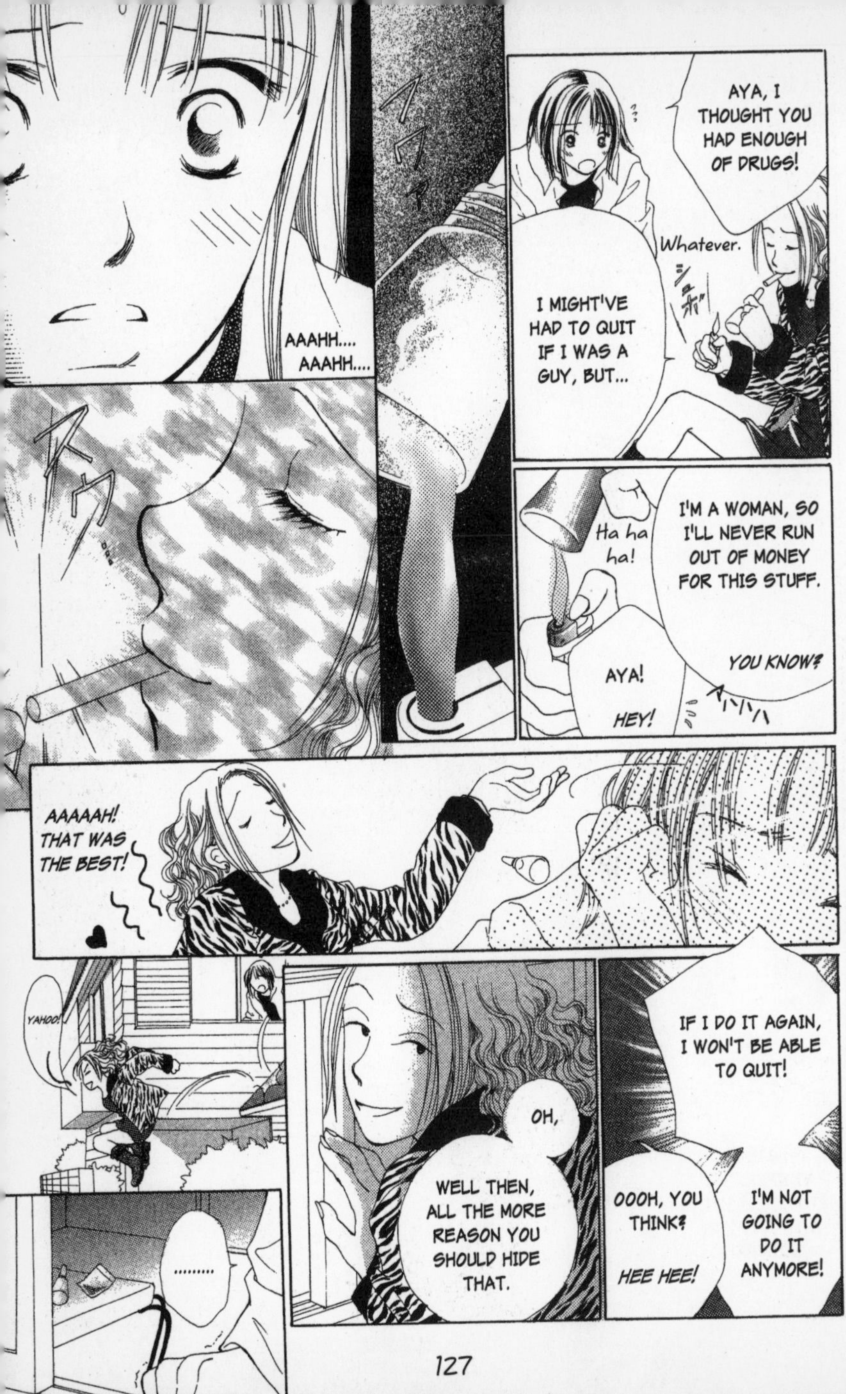
AYA, I THOUGHT YOU HAD ENOUGH OF DRUGS!
Whatever.
I MIGHT'VE HAD TO QUIT IF I WAS A GUY, BUT...
I'M A WOMAN, SO I'LL NEVER RUN OUT OF MONEY FOR THIS STUFF.
Ha ha ha!
YOU KNOW?
AYA!
HEY!
AAAHH.... AAAHH....
AAAAAH! THAT WAS THE BEST!
IF I DO IT AGAIN, I WON'T BE ABLE TO QUIT!
I'M NOT GOING TO DO IT ANYMORE!
OOOH, YOU THINK?
HEE HEE!
OH,
WELL THEN, ALL THE MORE REASON YOU SHOULD HIDE THAT.
YAHOO!
....

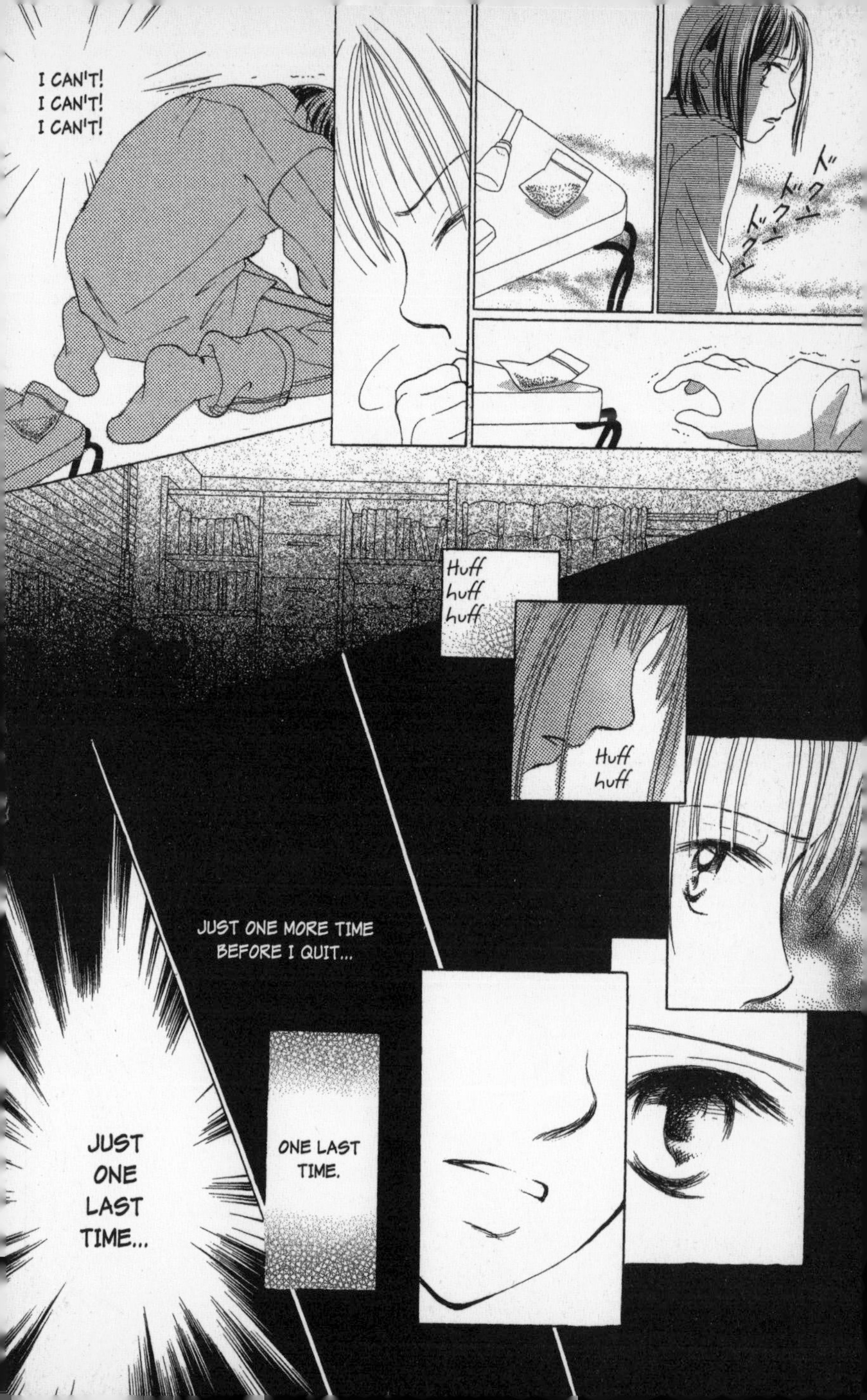
ドクン
ドクン
ドクン
I CAN'T!
I CAN'T!
I CAN'T!
Huff
huff
huff
Huff
huff
JUST ONE MORE TIME
BEFORE I QUIT...
ONE LAST
TIME.
JUST
ONE
LAST
TIME...

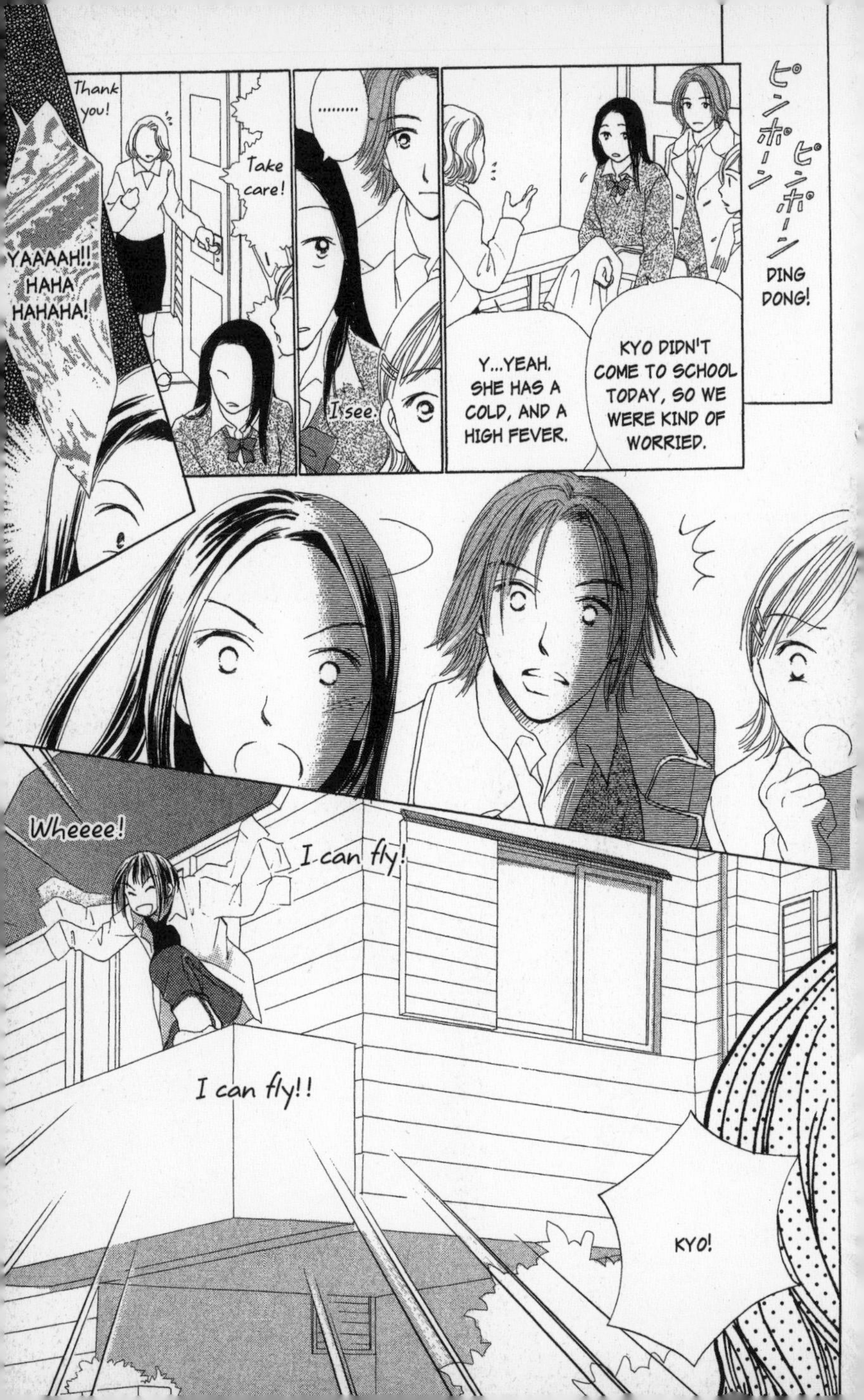
ピンポーン
ピンポーン
DING DONG!
KYO DIDN'T COME TO SCHOOL TODAY, SO WE WERE KIND OF WORRIED.
Y...YEAH. SHE HAS A COLD, AND A HIGH FEVER.
....
I see.
Take care!
Thank you!
YAAAAH!! HAHA HAHAHA!
Wheeee!
I can fly!
I can fly!!
KYO!

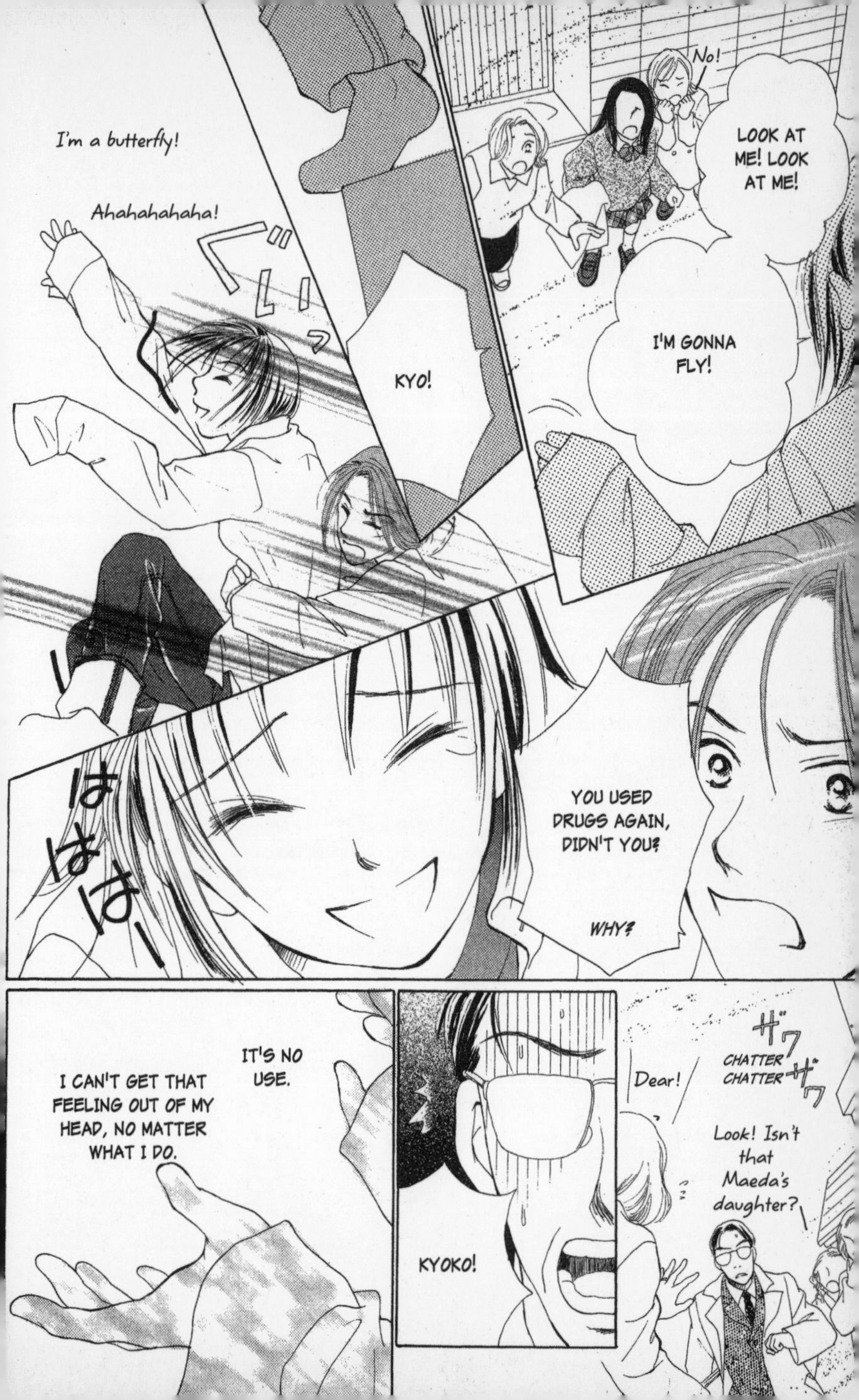
No!
LOOK AT ME! LOOK AT ME!
I'M GONNA FLY!
KYO!
I'm a butterfly!
Ahahahahaha!
YOU USED DRUGS AGAIN, DIDN'T YOU?
WHY?
ははは
ザワ
CHATTER CHATTER
ザワ
Look! Isn't that Maeda's daughter?
Dear!
KYOKO!
IT'S NO USE.
I CAN'T GET THAT FEELING OUT OF MY HEAD, NO MATTER WHAT I DO.

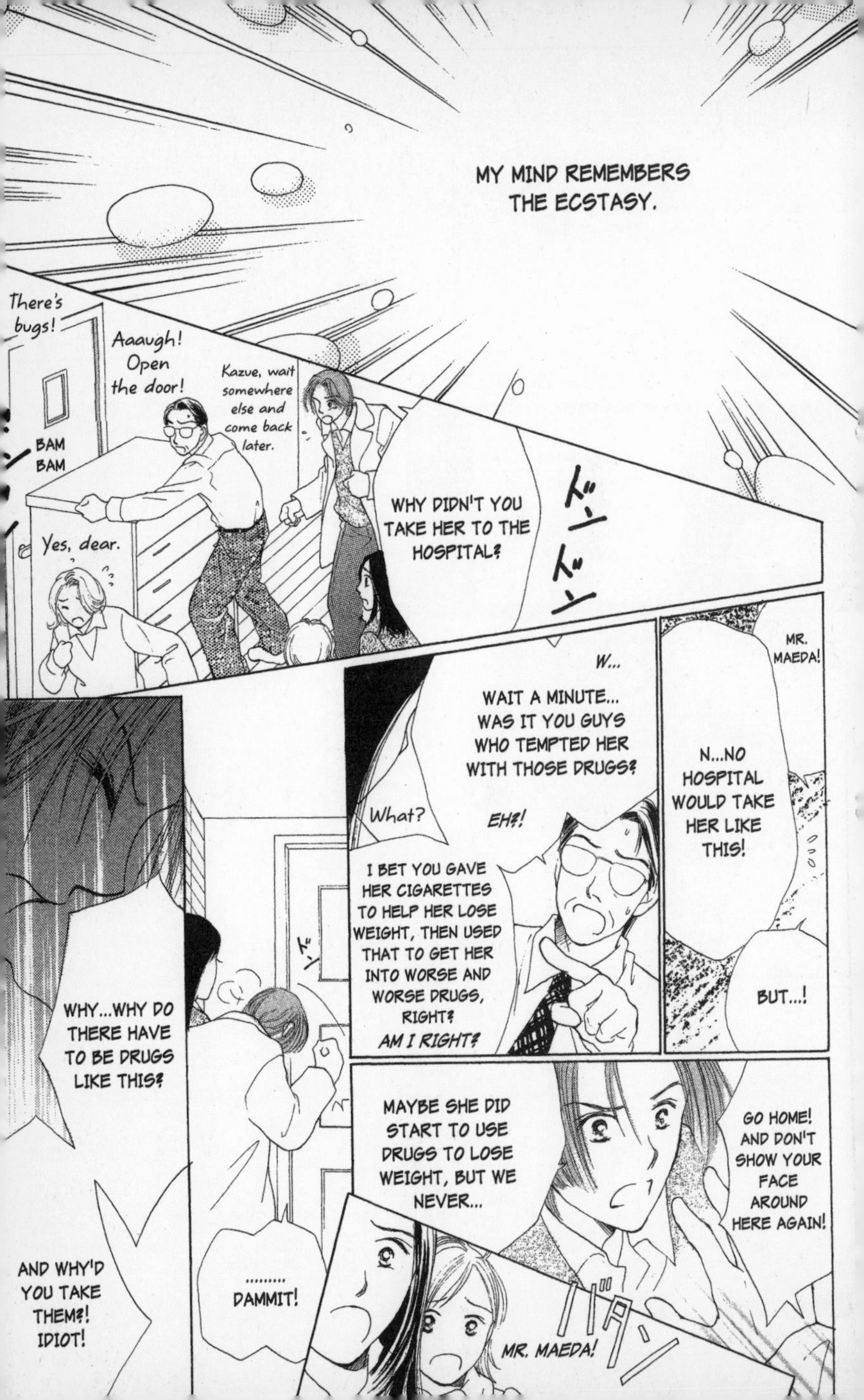
MY MIND REMEMBERS THE ECSTASY.
ドン ドン
WHY DIDN'T YOU TAKE HER TO THE HOSPITAL?
Kazue, wait somewhere else and come back later.
Aaaugh! Open the door!
There's bugs!
BAM BAM
Yes, dear.
MR. MAEDA!
N...NO HOSPITAL WOULD TAKE HER LIKE THIS!
BUT...!
W...
WAIT A MINUTE... WAS IT YOU GUYS WHO TEMPTED HER WITH THOSE DRUGS?
EH?!
What?
I BET YOU GAVE HER CIGARETTES TO HELP HER LOSE WEIGHT, THEN USED THAT TO GET HER INTO WORSE AND WORSE DRUGS, RIGHT? AM I RIGHT?
GO HOME! AND DON'T SHOW YOUR FACE AROUND HERE AGAIN!
MAYBE SHE DID START TO USE DRUGS TO LOSE WEIGHT, BUT WE NEVER...
バタン
MR. MAEDA!
WHY...WHY DO THERE HAVE TO BE DRUGS LIKE THIS?
.... DAMMIT!
AND WHY'D YOU TAKE THEM?! IDIOT!

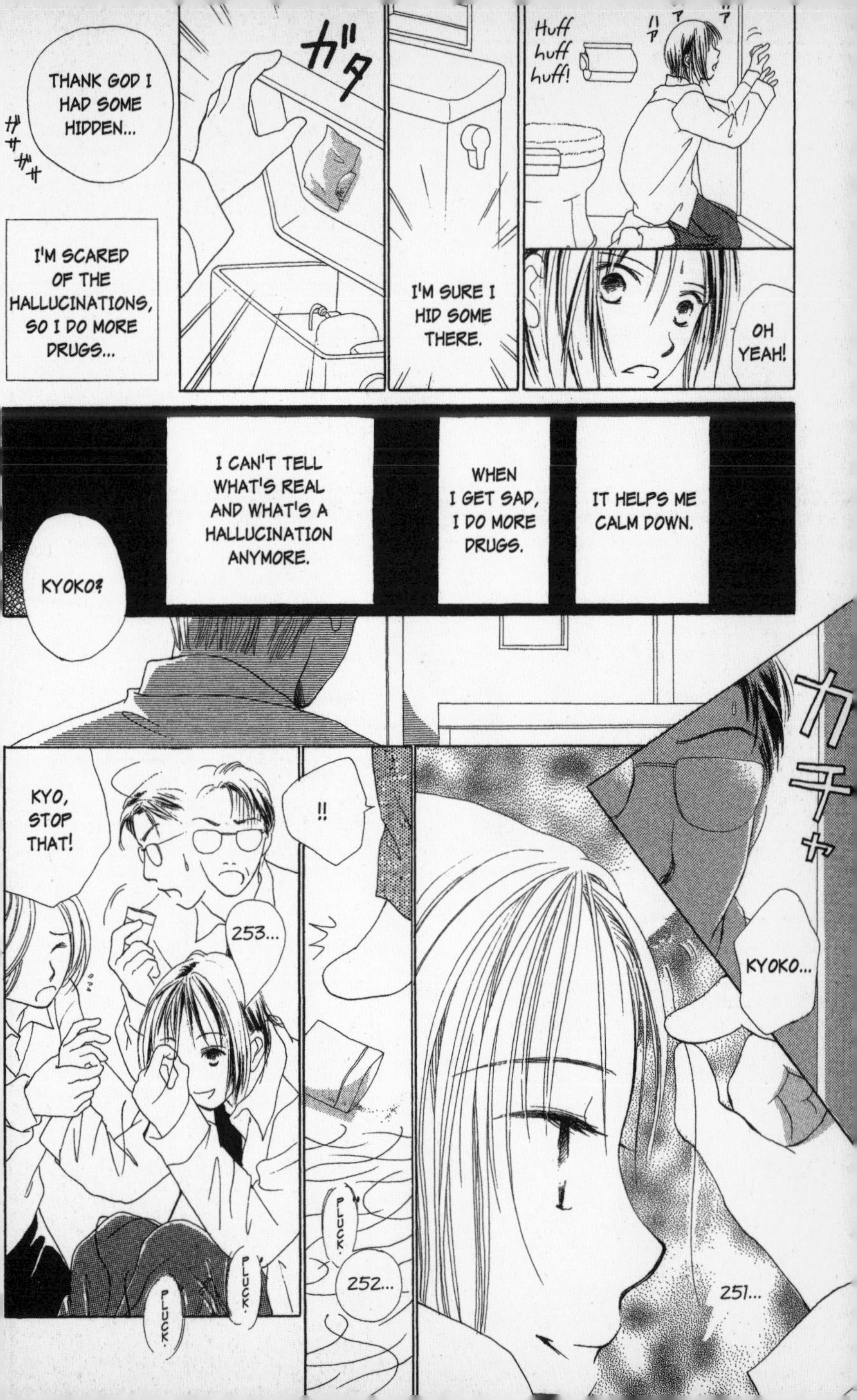

ハァ ハァ
Huff huff huff!
OH YEAH!
I'M SURE I HID SOME THERE.
ガタ
THANK GOD I HAD SOME HIDDEN...
ガサガサ
I'M SCARED OF THE HALLUCINATIONS, SO I DO MORE DRUGS...
IT HELPS ME CALM DOWN.
WHEN I GET SAD, I DO MORE DRUGS.
I CAN'T TELL WHAT'S REAL AND WHAT'S A HALLUCINATION ANYMORE.
KYOKO?
カチャ
KYOKO...
251...
!!
PLUCK.
252...
KYO, STOP THAT!
253...
PLUCK.
PLUCK.

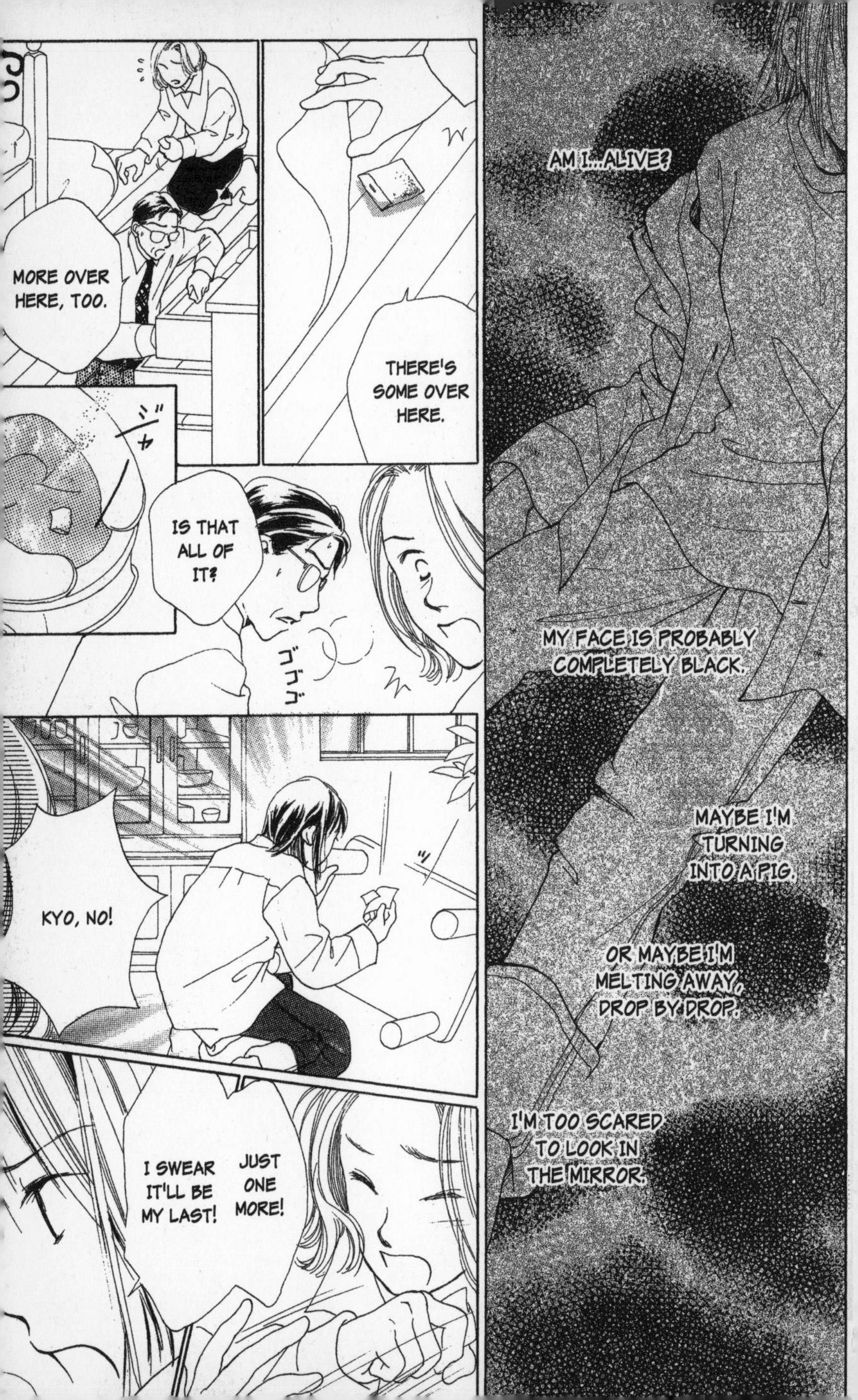
AM I...ALIVE?
MY FACE IS PROBABLY COMPLETELY BLACK.
MAYBE I'M TURNING INTO A PIG.
OR MAYBE I'M MELTING AWAY, DROP BY DROP.
I'M TOO SCARED TO LOOK IN THE MIRROR.
THERE'S SOME OVER HERE.
MORE OVER HERE, TOO.
IS THAT ALL OF IT?
ゴゴゴ
KYO, NO!
JUST ONE MORE!
I SWEAR IT'LL BE MY LAST!

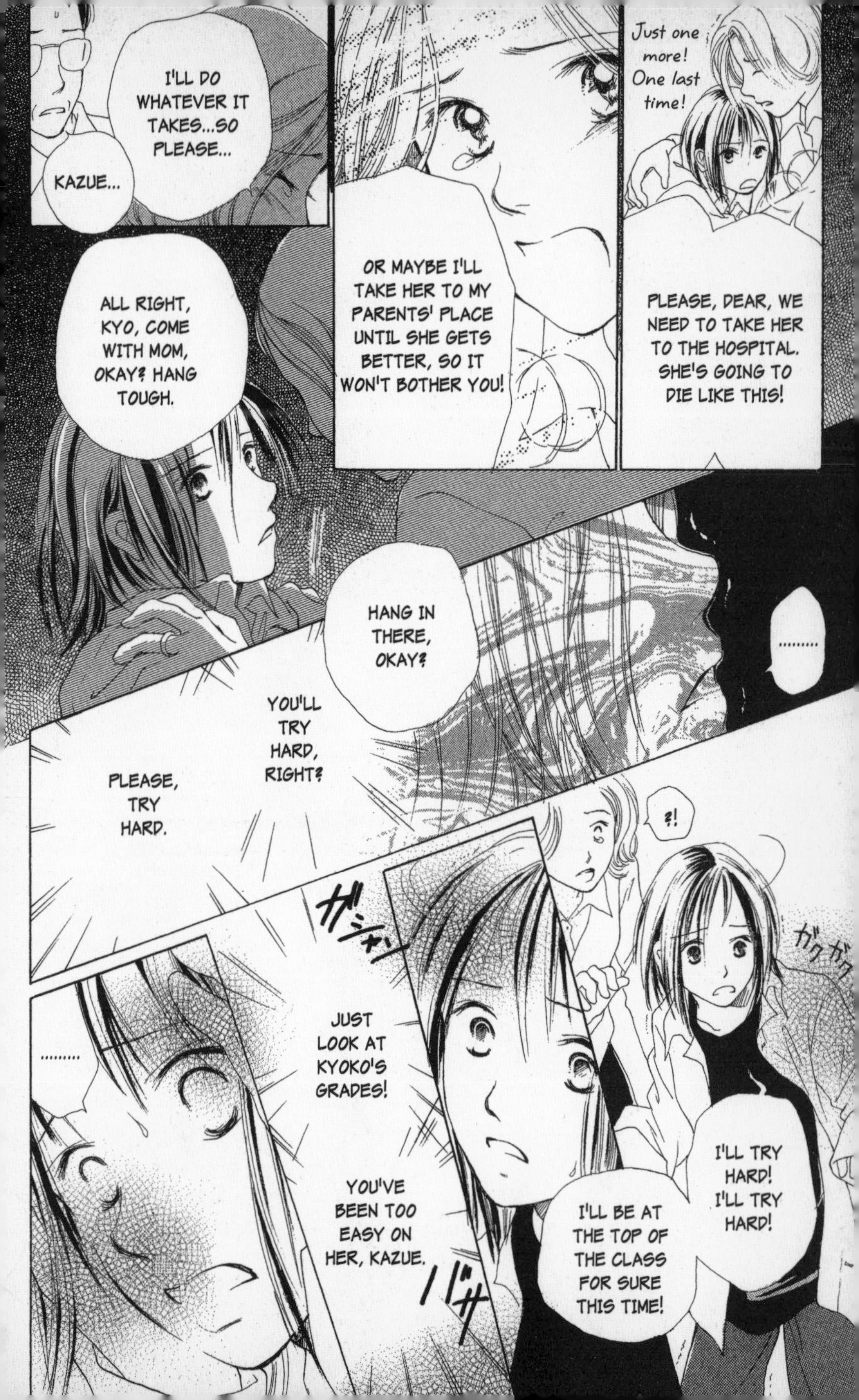
Just one more! One last time!
PLEASE, DEAR, WE NEED TO TAKE HER TO THE HOSPITAL. SHE'S GOING TO DIE LIKE THIS!
OR MAYBE I'LL TAKE HER TO MY PARENTS' PLACE UNTIL SHE GETS BETTER, SO IT WON'T BOTHER YOU!
I'LL DO WHATEVER IT TAKES...SO PLEASE...
KAZUE...
ALL RIGHT, KYO, COME WITH MOM, OKAY? HANG TOUGH.
....
HANG IN THERE, OKAY?
YOU'LL TRY HARD, RIGHT?
PLEASE, TRY HARD.
?!
I'LL TRY HARD! I'LL TRY HARD!
I'LL BE AT THE TOP OF THE CLASS FOR SURE THIS TIME!
JUST LOOK AT KYOKO'S GRADES!
YOU'VE BEEN TOO EASY ON HER, KAZUE.
....

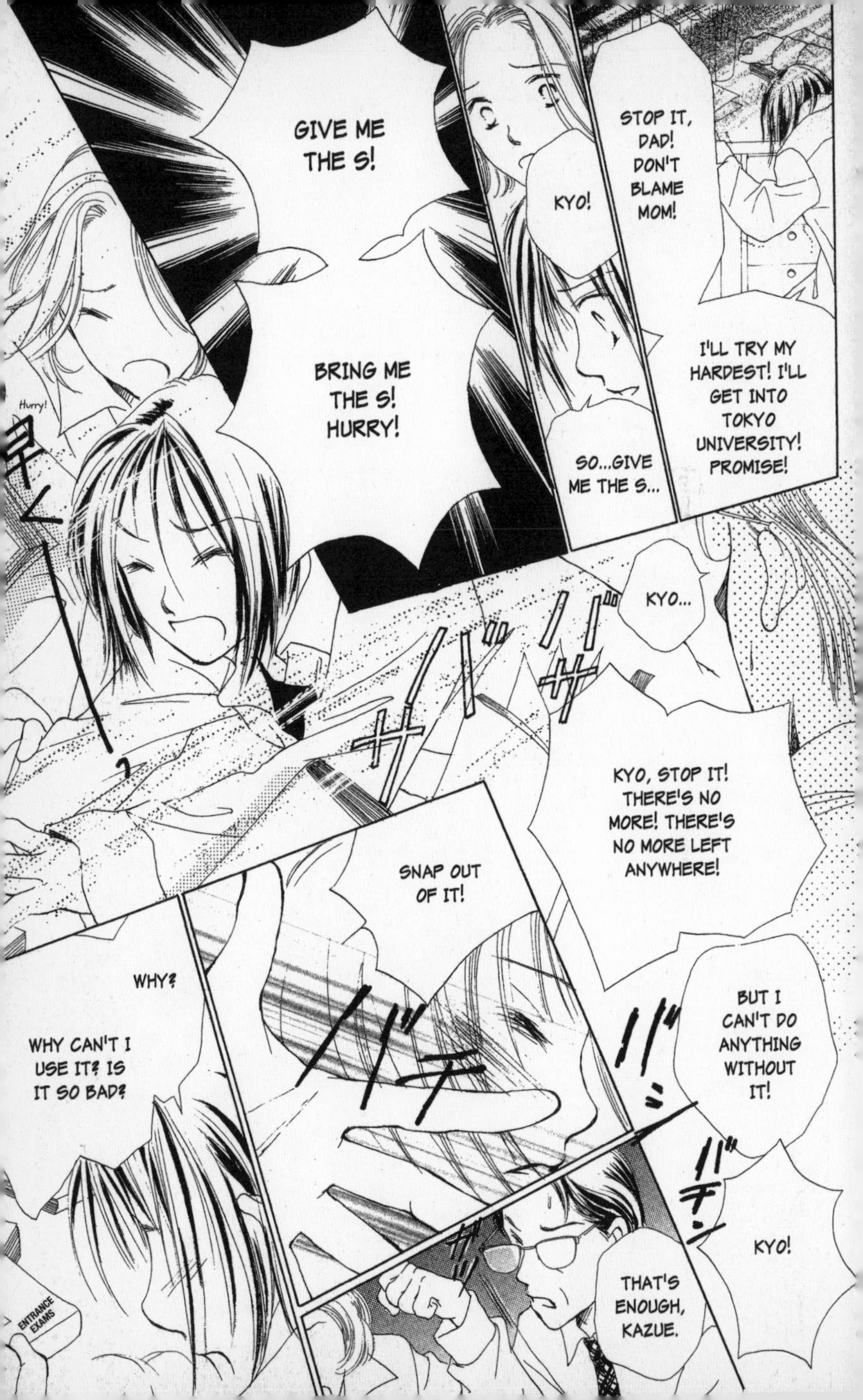

STOP IT, DAD! DON'T BLAME MOM!
KYO!
I'LL TRY MY HARDEST! I'LL GET INTO TOKYO UNIVERSITY! PROMISE!
SO...GIVE ME THE S...
GIVE ME THE S!
BRING ME THE S! HURRY!
Hurry!
KYO...
KYO, STOP IT! THERE'S NO MORE! THERE'S NO MORE LEFT ANYWHERE!
SNAP OUT OF IT!
BUT I CAN'T DO ANYTHING WITHOUT IT!
KYO!
THAT'S ENOUGH, KAZUE.
WHY?
WHY CAN'T I USE IT? IS IT SO BAD?
ENTRANCE EXAMS

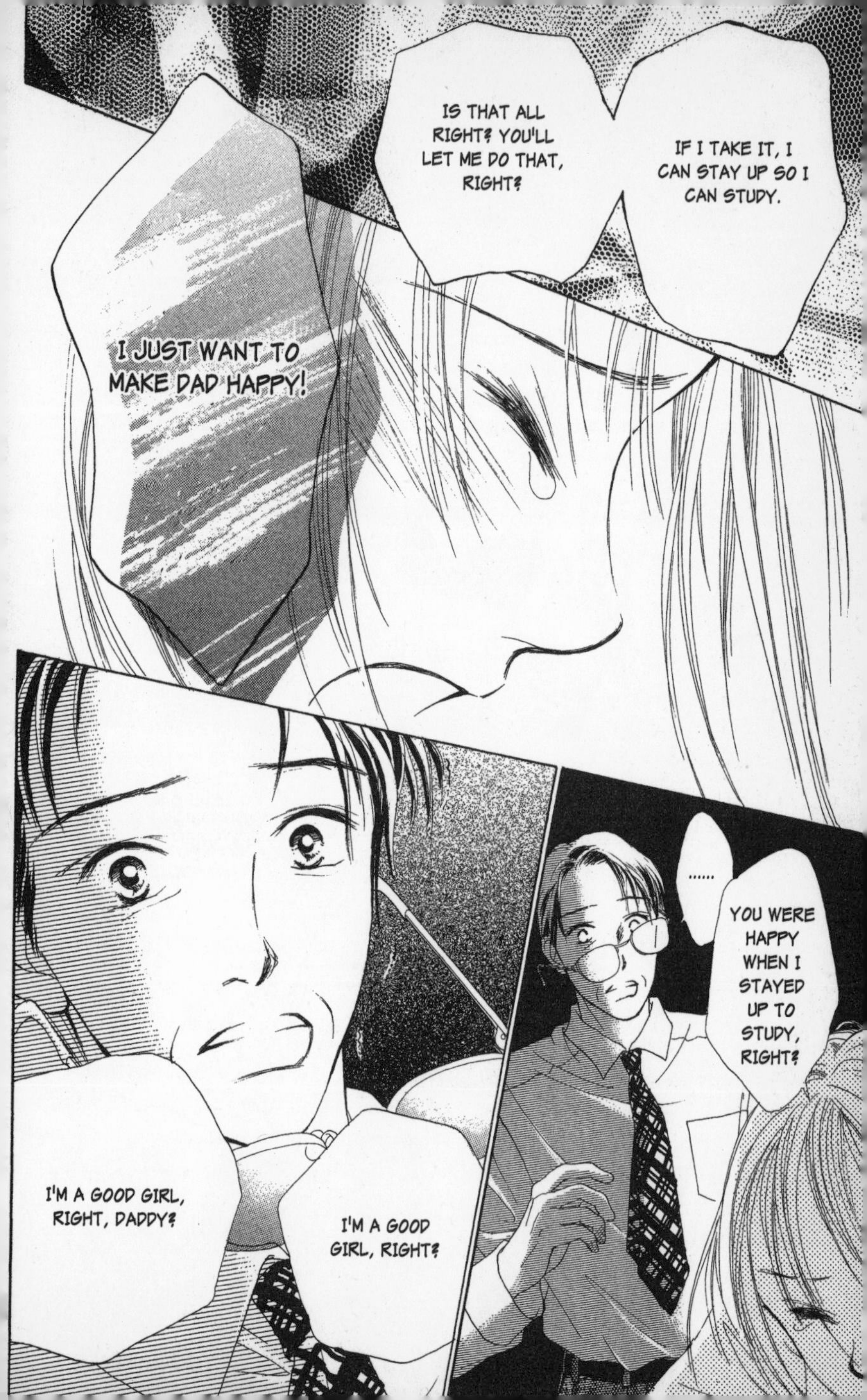
IF I TAKE IT, I CAN STAY UP SO I CAN STUDY.
IS THAT ALL RIGHT? YOU'LL LET ME DO THAT, RIGHT?
I JUST WANT TO MAKE DAD HAPPY!
......
YOU WERE HAPPY WHEN I STAYED UP TO STUDY, RIGHT?
I'M A GOOD GIRL, RIGHT?
I'M A GOOD GIRL, RIGHT, DADDY?

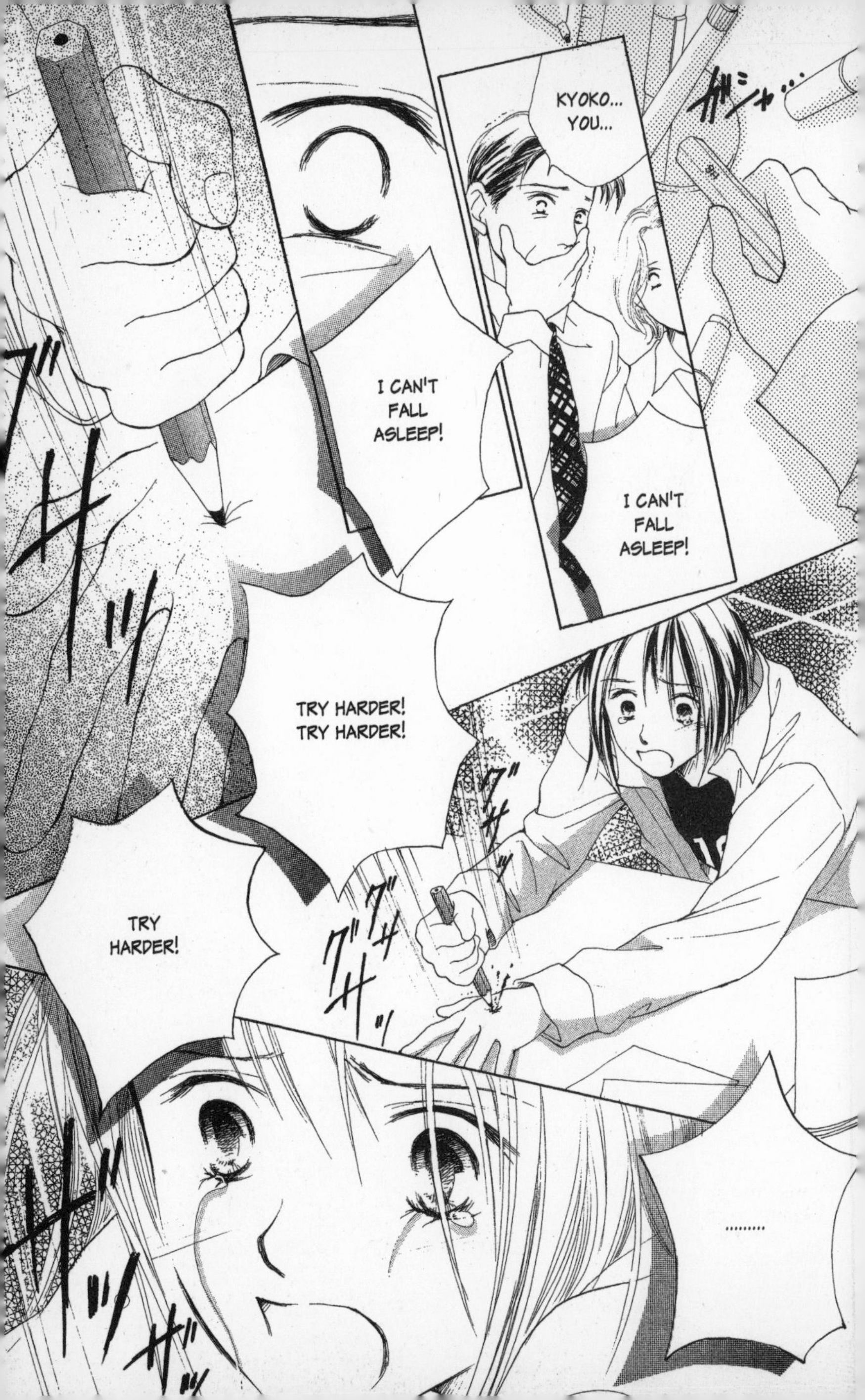
KYOKO... YOU...
I CAN'T FALL ASLEEP!
I CAN'T FALL ASLEEP!
TRY HARDER! TRY HARDER!
TRY HARDER!
....

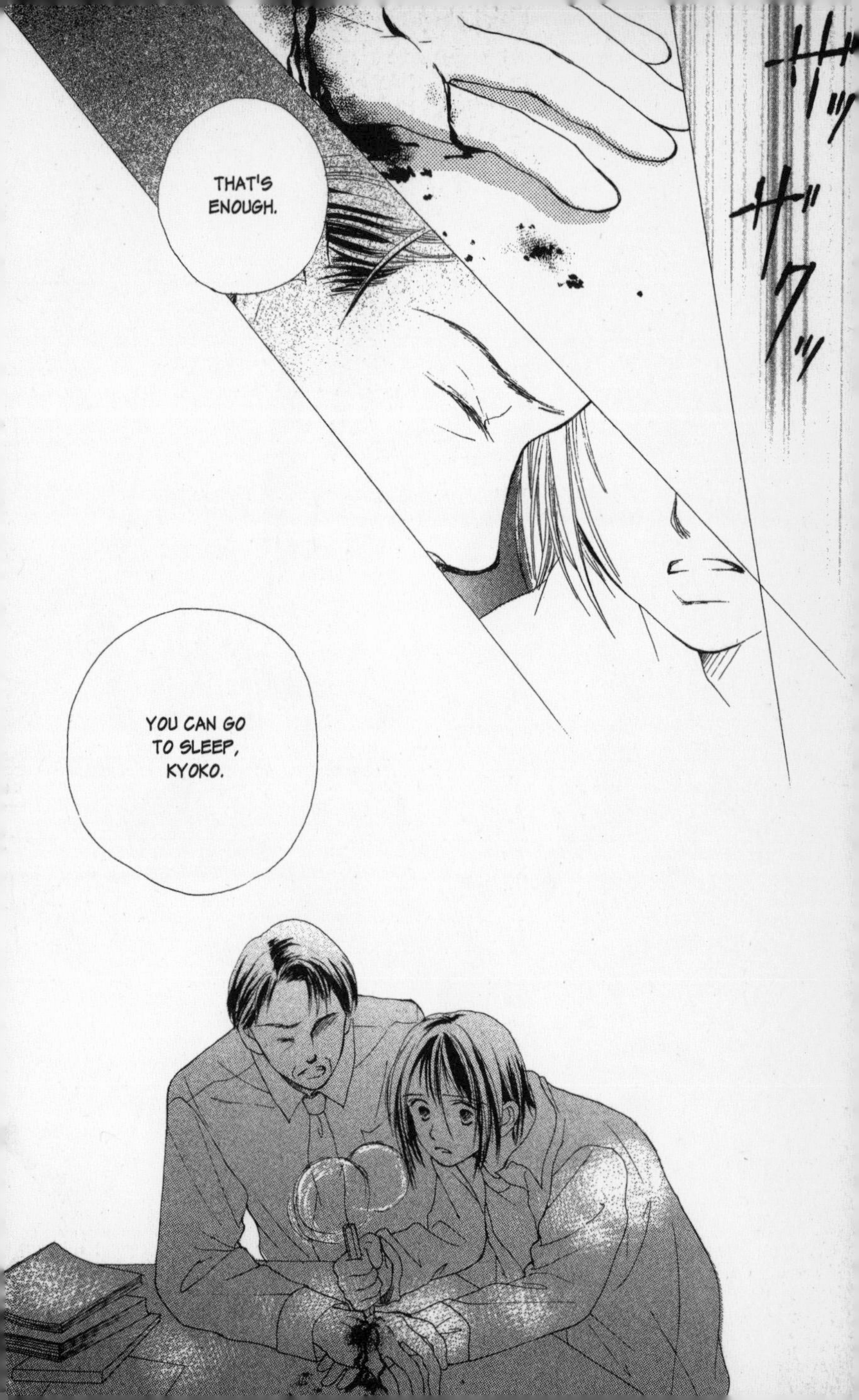
ザッ
ザクッ
THAT'S ENOUGH.
YOU CAN GO TO SLEEP, KYOKO.

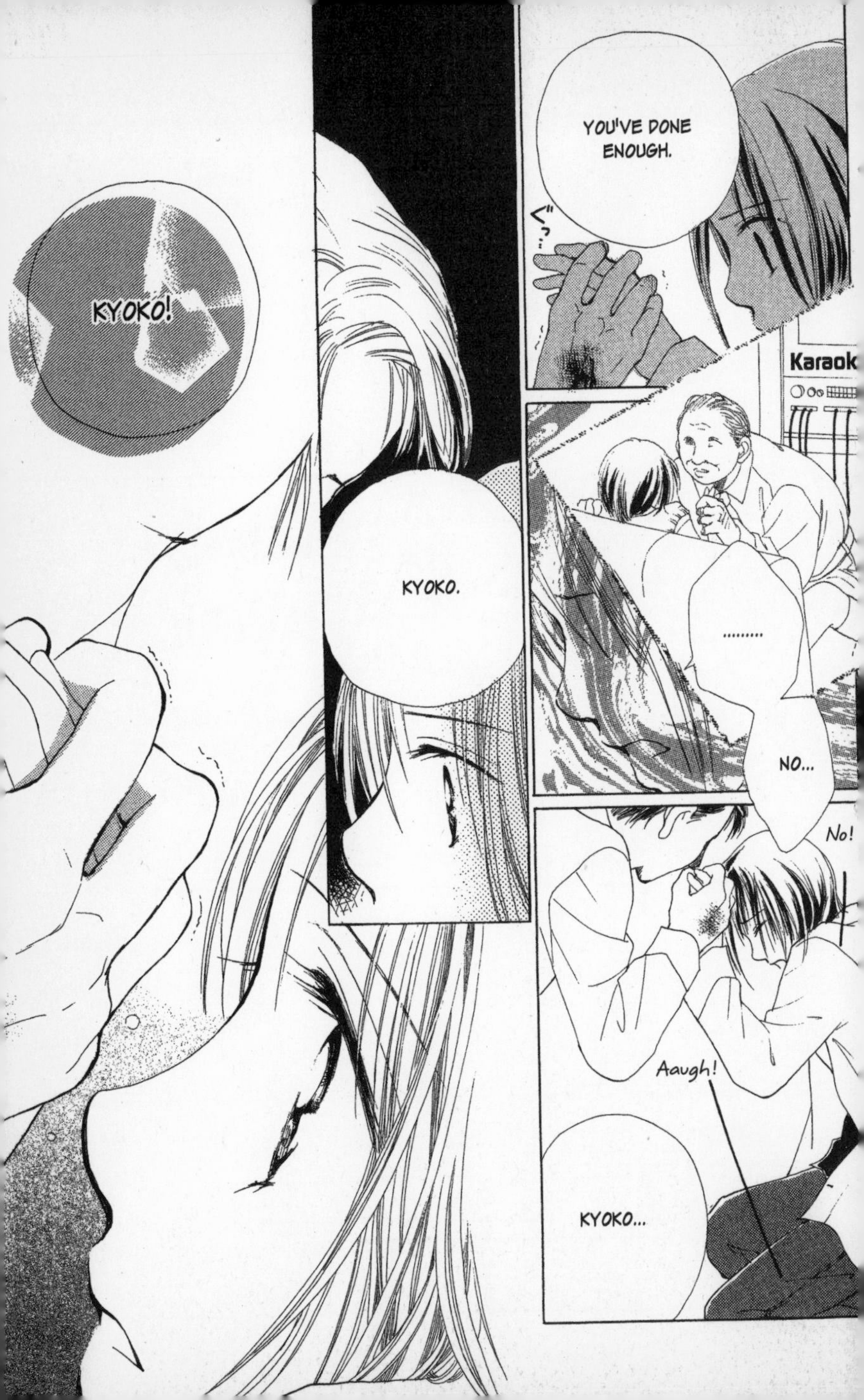
YOU'VE DONE ENOUGH.
Karaok
....
NO...
No!
Aaugh!
KYOKO...
KYOKO.
KYOKO!

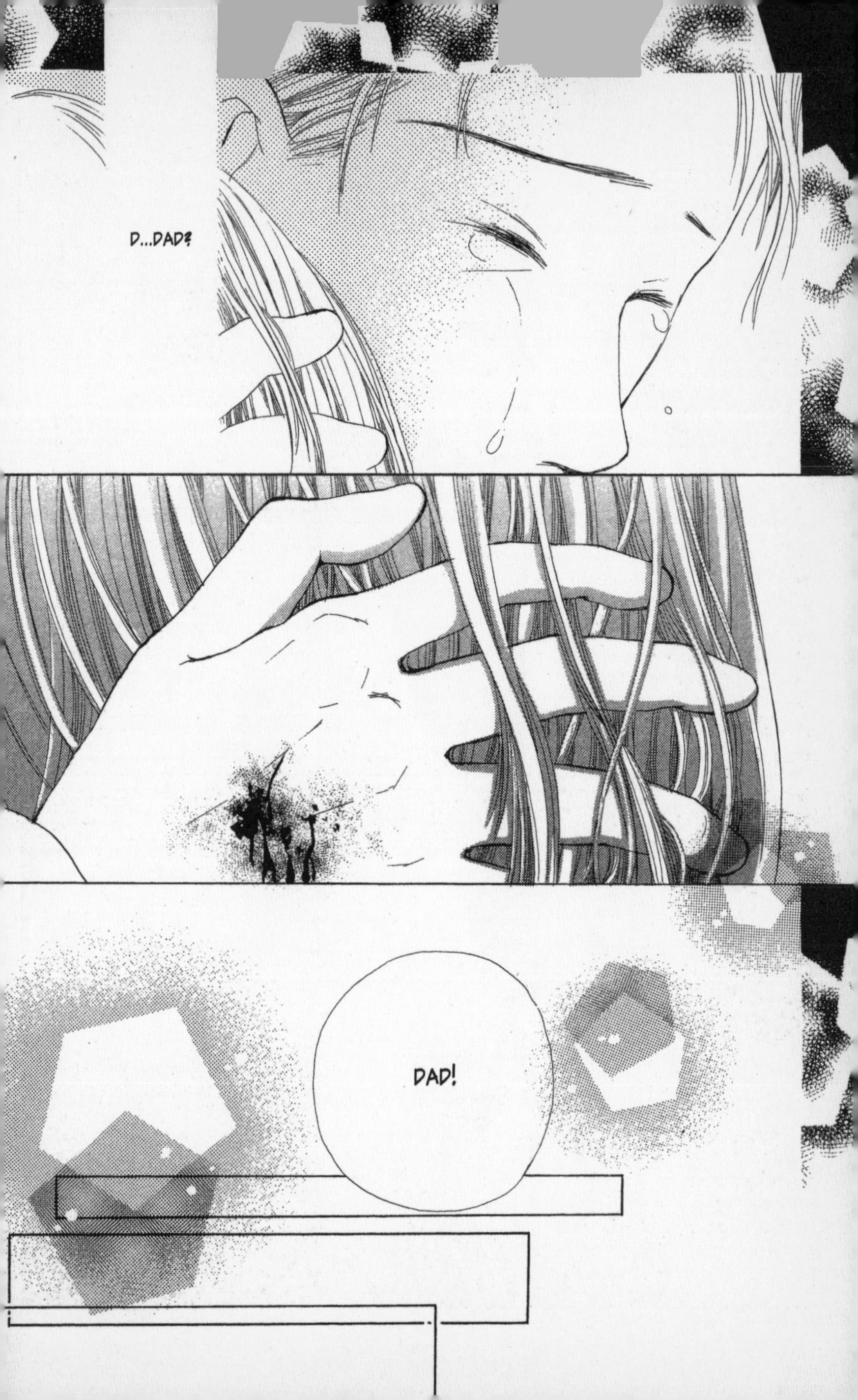
D...DAD?
DAD!

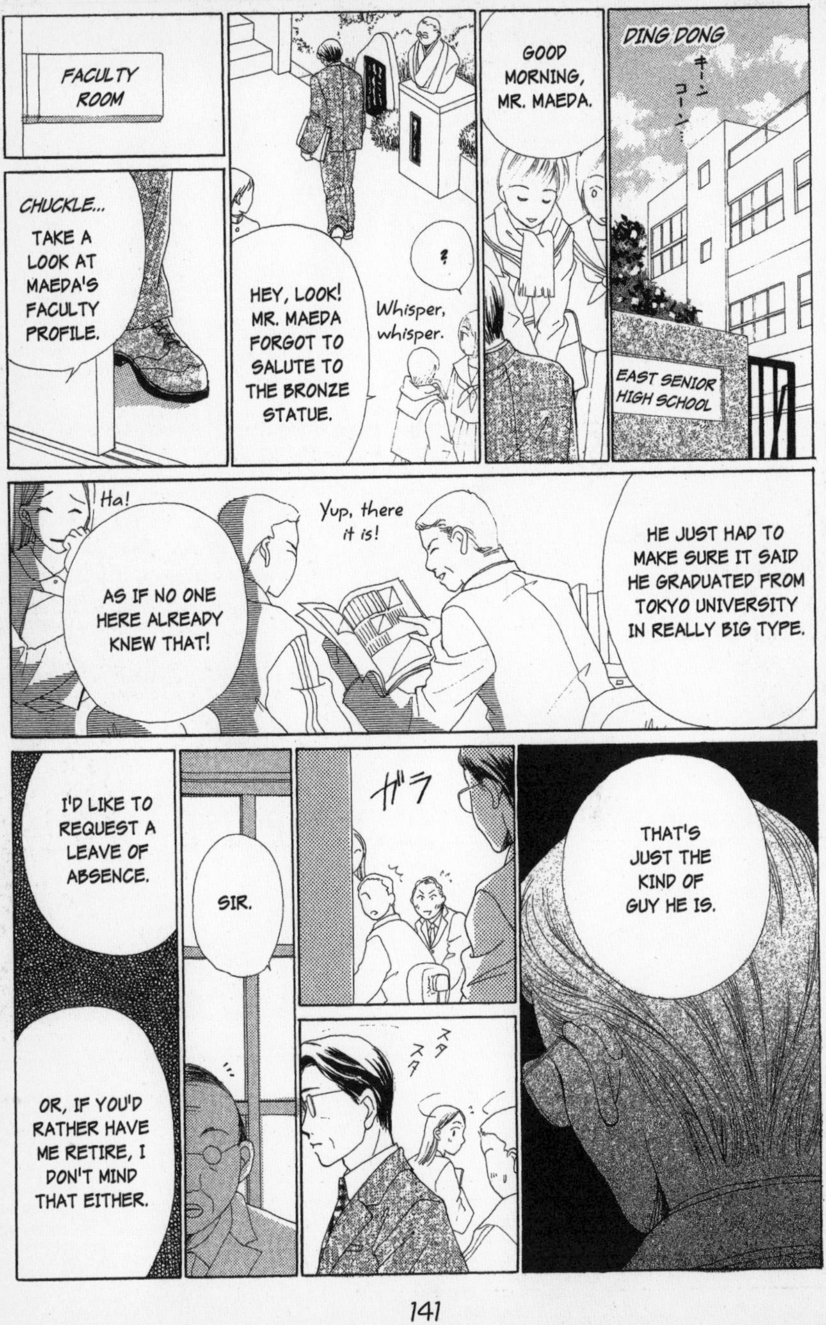
DING DONG
キーンコーン
EAST SENIOR HIGH SCHOOL
GOOD MORNING, MR. MAEDA.
?
Whisper, whisper.
HEY, LOOK! MR. MAEDA FORGOT TO SALUTE TO THE BRONZE STATUE.
FACULTY ROOM
CHUCKLE...
TAKE A LOOK AT MAEDA'S FACULTY PROFILE.
HE JUST HAD TO MAKE SURE IT SAID HE GRADUATED FROM TOKYO UNIVERSITY IN REALLY BIG TYPE.
Yup, there it is!
Ha!
AS IF NO ONE HERE ALREADY KNEW THAT!
THAT'S JUST THE KIND OF GUY HE IS.
ガラ
スタスタ
SIR.
I'D LIKE TO REQUEST A LEAVE OF ABSENCE.
OR, IF YOU'D RATHER HAVE ME RETIRE, I DON'T MIND THAT EITHER.

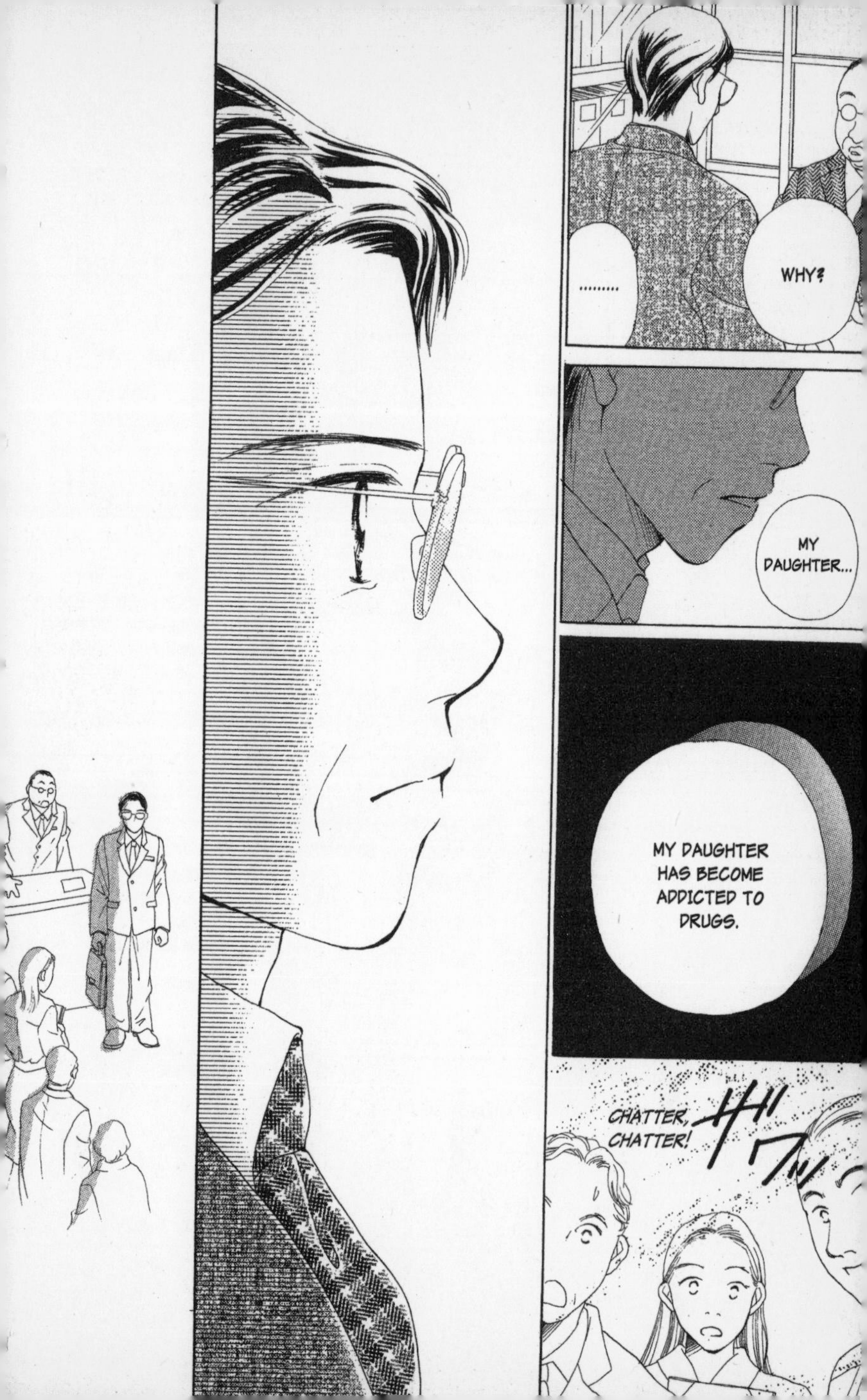
WHY?
....
MY DAUGHTER...
MY DAUGHTER HAS BECOME ADDICTED TO DRUGS.
CHATTER, CHATTER!

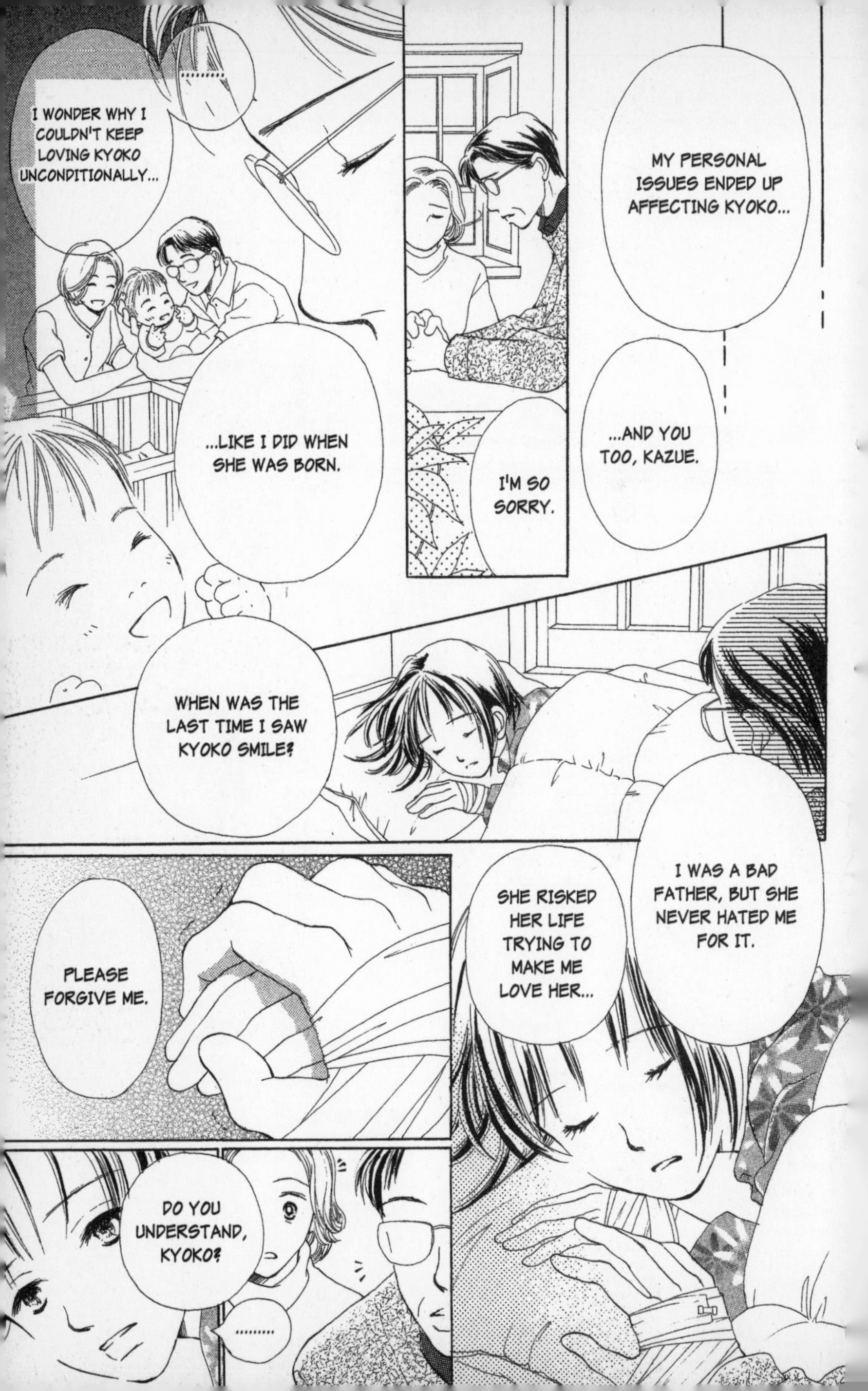
MY PERSONAL ISSUES ENDED UP AFFECTING KYOKO...
...AND YOU TOO, KAZUE.
I'M SO SORRY.
....
I WONDER WHY I COULDN'T KEEP LOVING KYOKO UNCONDITIONALLY...
...LIKE I DID WHEN SHE WAS BORN.
WHEN WAS THE LAST TIME I SAW KYOKO SMILE?
I WAS A BAD FATHER, BUT SHE NEVER HATED ME FOR IT.
SHE RISKED HER LIFE TRYING TO MAKE ME LOVE HER...
PLEASE FORGIVE ME.
DO YOU UNDERSTAND, KYOKO?
....

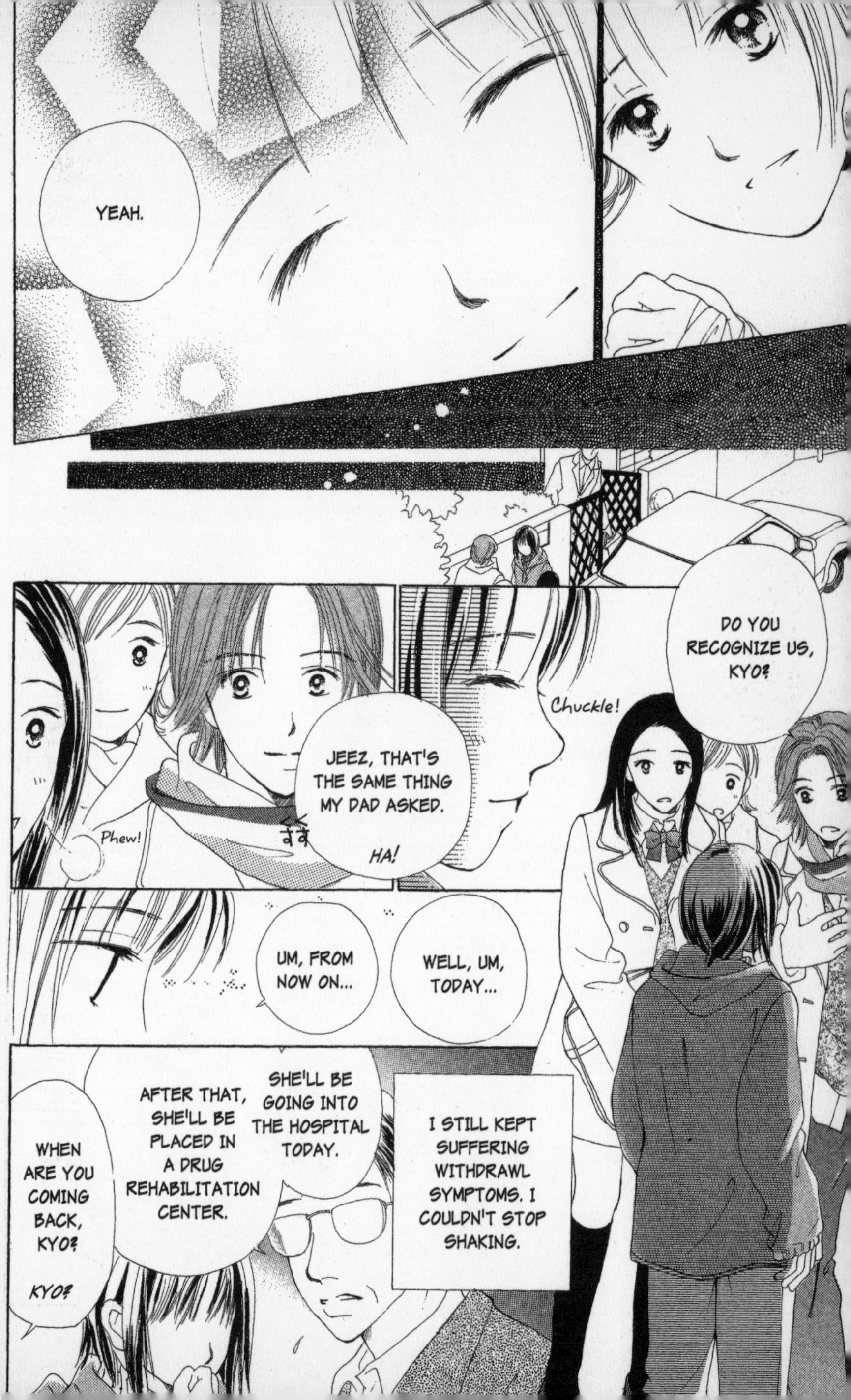
YEAH.
DO YOU RECOGNIZE US, KYO?
Chuckle!
JEEZ, THAT'S THE SAME THING MY DAD ASKED.
HA!
Phew!
WELL, UM, TODAY...
UM, FROM NOW ON...
I STILL KEPT SUFFERING WITHDRAWL SYMPTOMS. I COULDN'T STOP SHAKING.
SHE'LL BE GOING INTO THE HOSPITAL TODAY.
AFTER THAT, SHE'LL BE PLACED IN A DRUG REHABILITATION CENTER.
WHEN ARE YOU COMING BACK, KYO?
KYO?

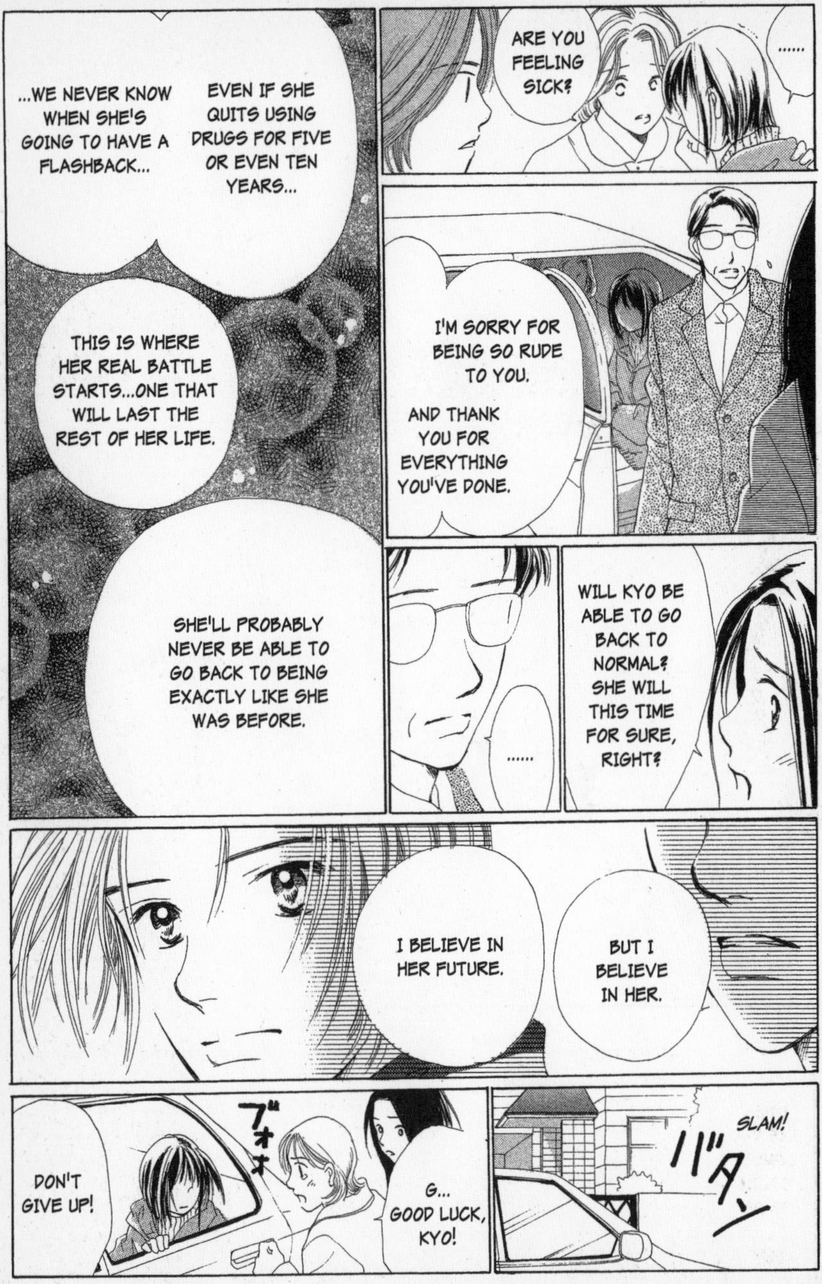

......
ARE YOU FEELING SICK?
I'M SORRY FOR BEING SO RUDE TO YOU.
AND THANK YOU FOR EVERYTHING YOU'VE DONE.
WILL KYO BE ABLE TO GO BACK TO NORMAL? SHE WILL THIS TIME FOR SURE, RIGHT?
......
EVEN IF SHE QUITS USING DRUGS FOR FIVE OR EVEN TEN YEARS...
...WE NEVER KNOW WHEN SHE'S GOING TO HAVE A FLASHBACK...
THIS IS WHERE HER REAL BATTLE STARTS...ONE THAT WILL LAST THE REST OF HER LIFE.
SHE'LL PROBABLY NEVER BE ABLE TO GO BACK TO BEING EXACTLY LIKE SHE WAS BEFORE.
BUT I BELIEVE IN HER.
I BELIEVE IN HER FUTURE.
SLAM!
バタン
ブォォ
G... GOOD LUCK, KYO!
DON'T GIVE UP!

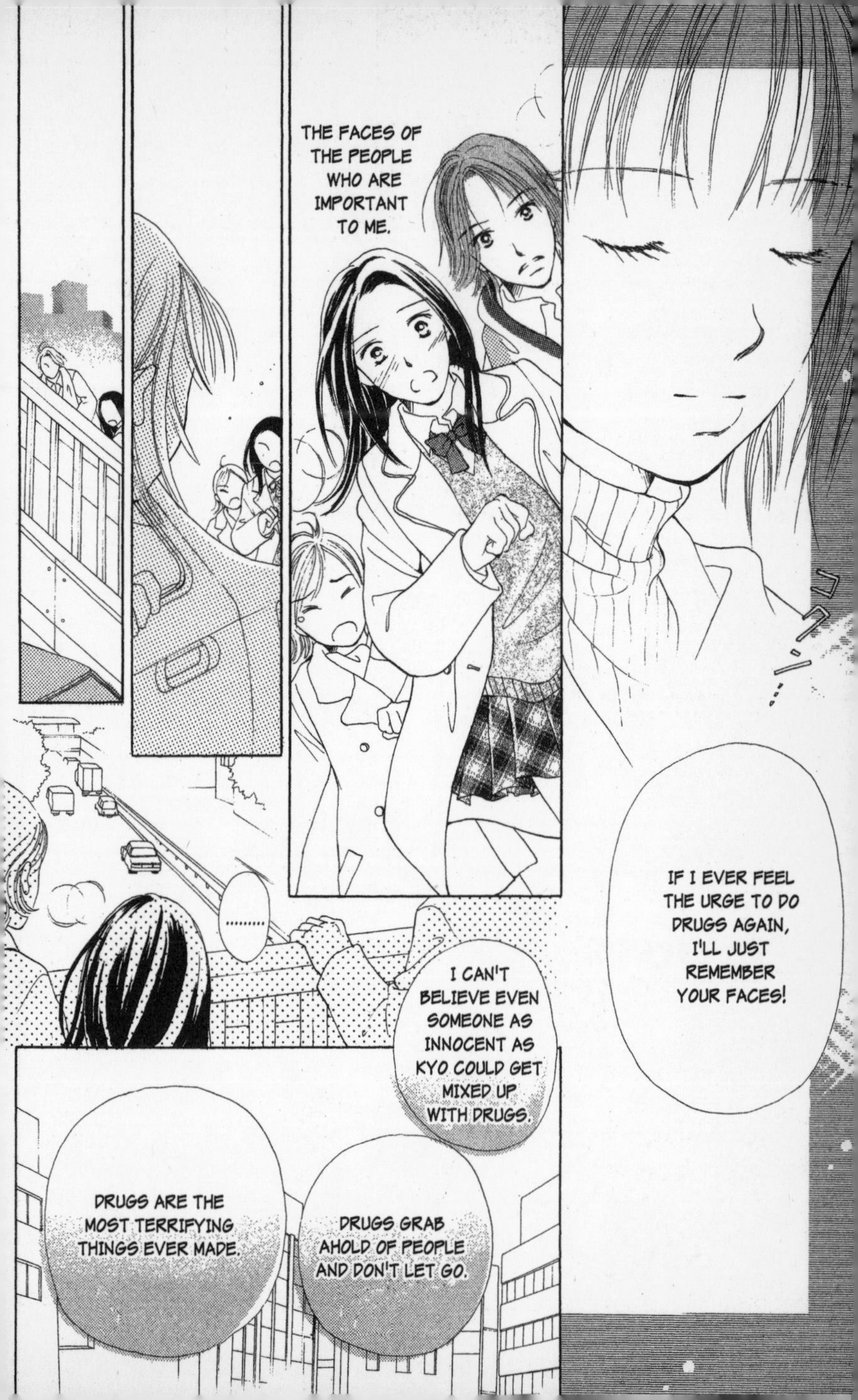
IF I EVER FEEL THE URGE TO DO DRUGS AGAIN, I'LL JUST REMEMBER YOUR FACES!
THE FACES OF THE PEOPLE WHO ARE IMPORTANT TO ME.
....
I CAN'T BELIEVE EVEN SOMEONE AS INNOCENT AS KYO COULD GET MIXED UP WITH DRUGS.
DRUGS GRAB AHOLD OF PEOPLE AND DON'T LET GO.
DRUGS ARE THE MOST TERRIFYING THINGS EVER MADE.

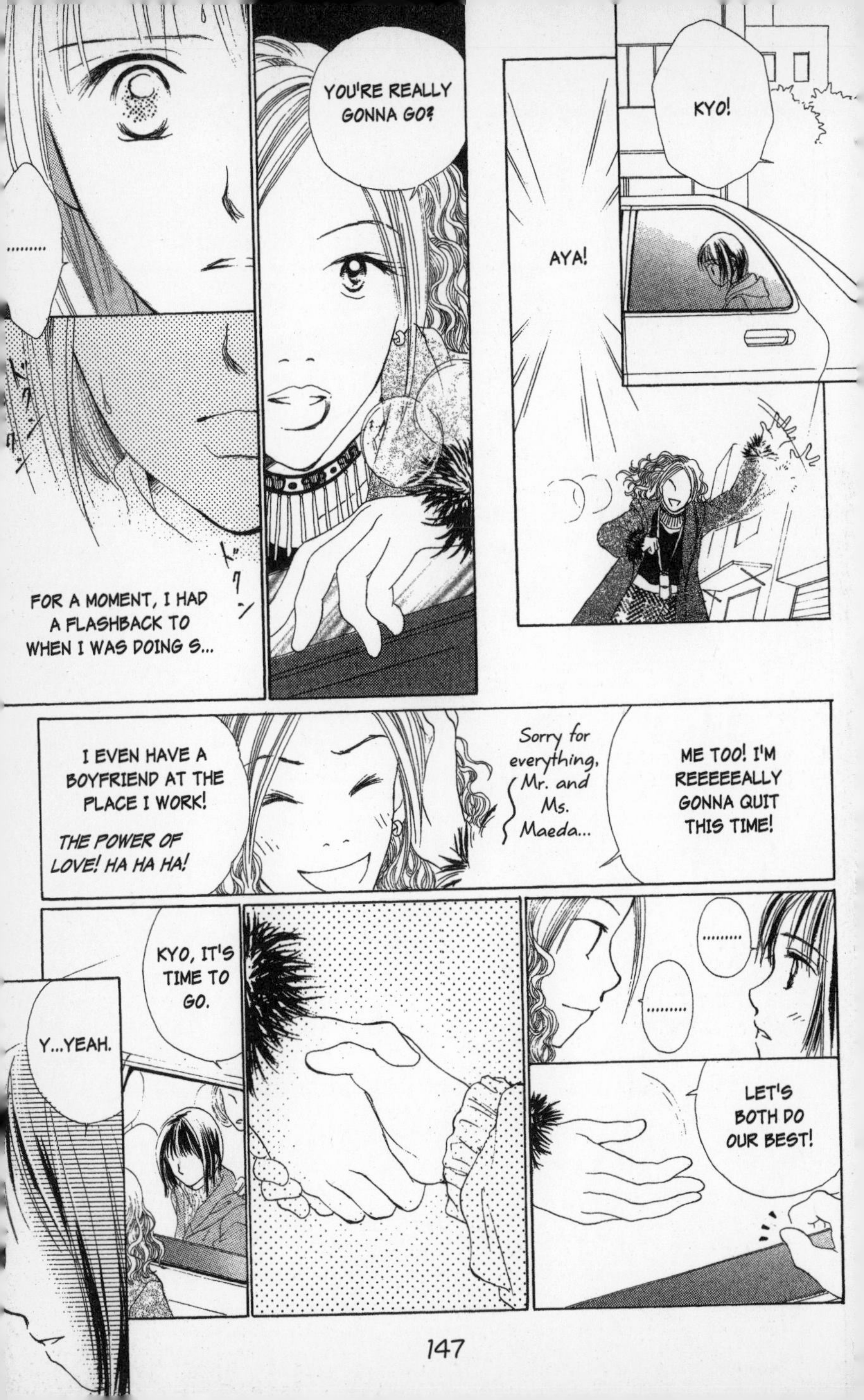
KYO!
AYA!
YOU'RE REALLY GONNA GO?
....
FOR A MOMENT, I HAD A FLASHBACK TO WHEN I WAS DOING S...
ME TOO! I'M REEEEEALLY GONNA QUIT THIS TIME!
Sorry for everything, Mr. and Ms. Maeda...
I EVEN HAVE A BOYFRIEND AT THE PLACE I WORK!
THE POWER OF LOVE! HA HA HA!
....
....
LET'S BOTH DO OUR BEST!
KYO, IT'S TIME TO GO.
Y...YEAH.

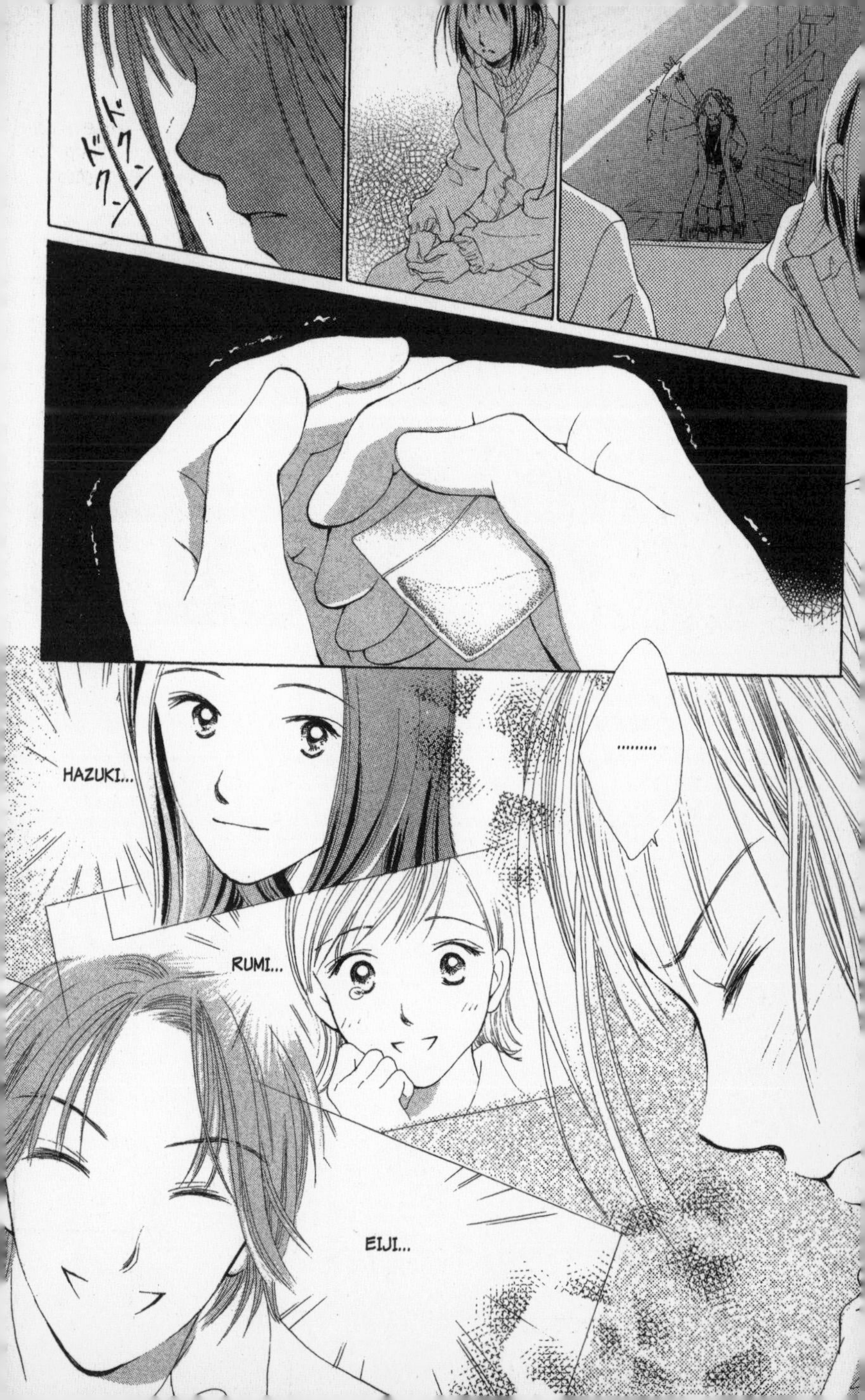
ドクン
ドクン
....
HAZUKI...
RUMI...
EIJI...

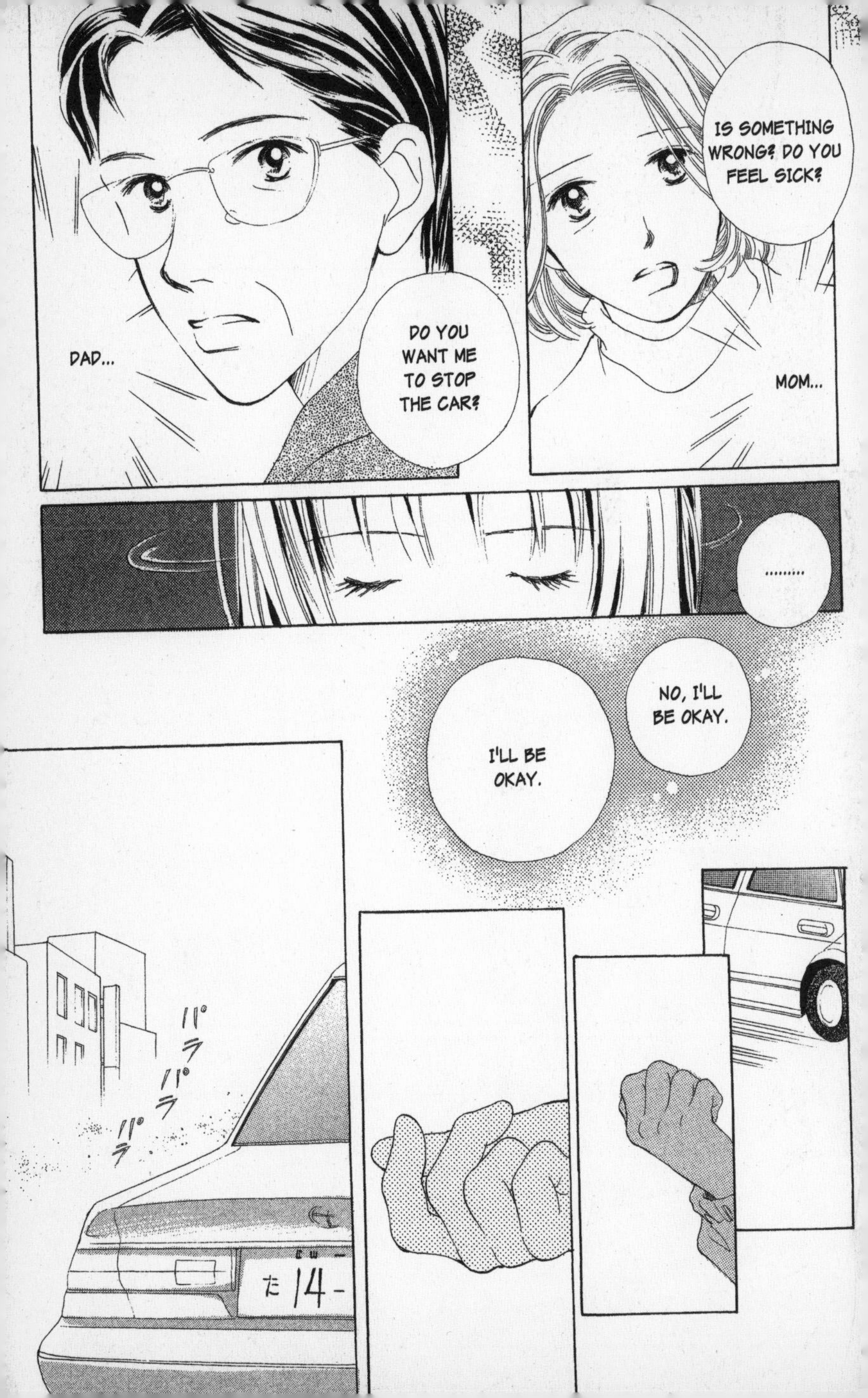
IS SOMETHING WRONG? DO YOU FEEL SICK?
MOM...
DO YOU WANT ME TO STOP THE CAR?
DAD...
....
NO, I'LL BE OKAY.
I'LL BE OKAY.
パラパラパラ

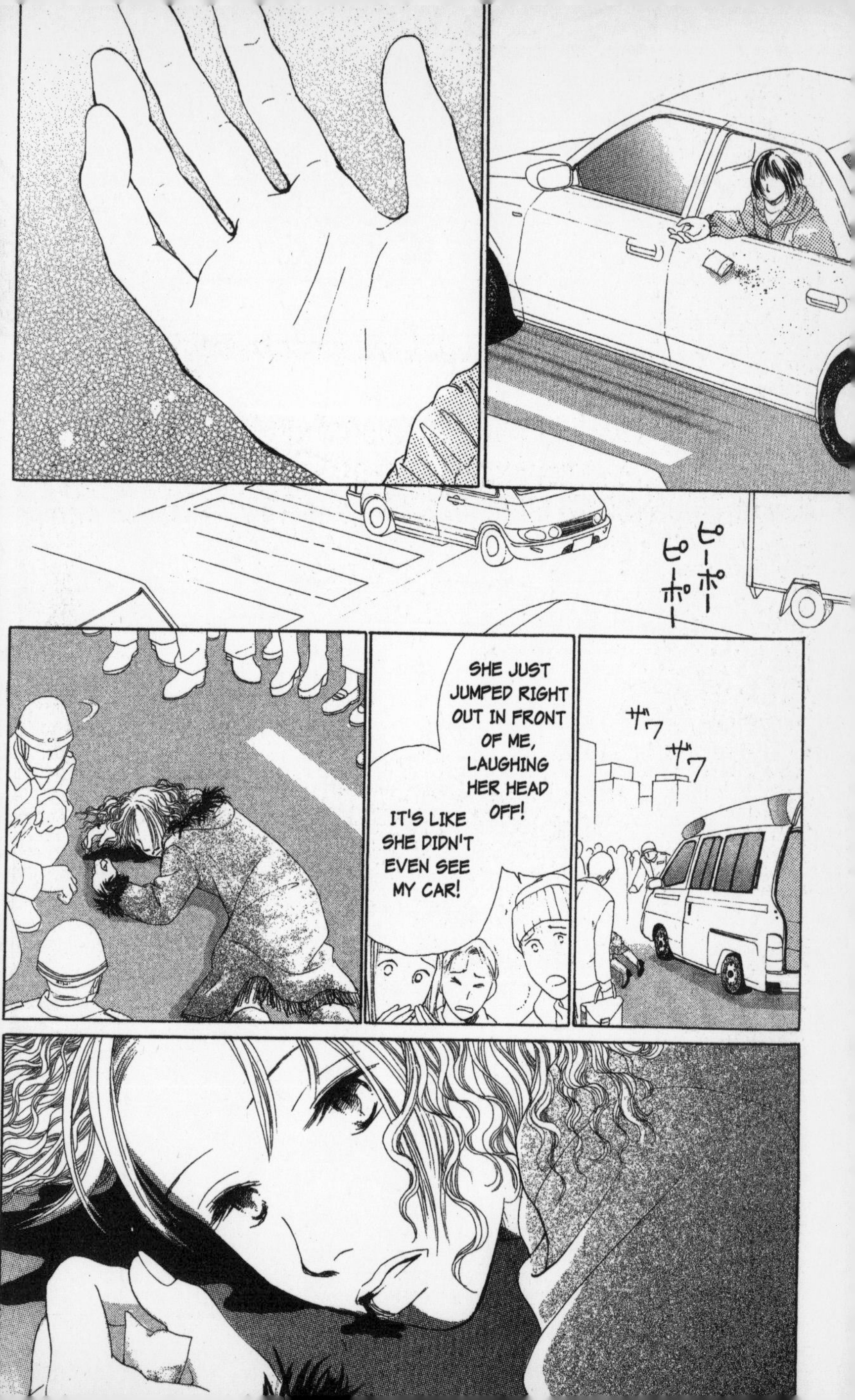
ピーポーピーポー
ザワ ザワ
SHE JUST JUMPED RIGHT OUT IN FRONT OF ME, LAUGHING HER HEAD OFF!
IT'S LIKE SHE DIDN'T EVEN SEE MY CAR!

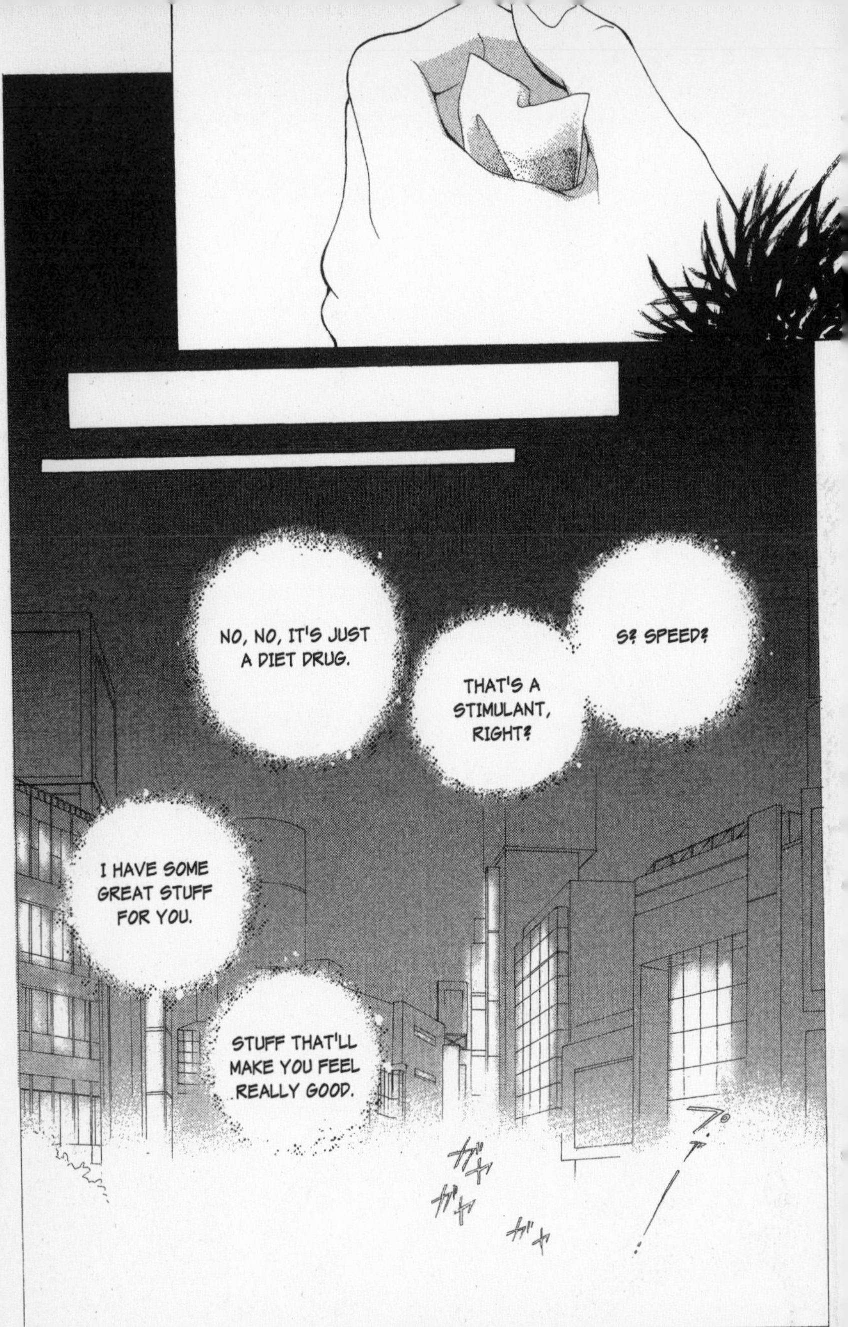
S? SPEED?
THAT'S A STIMULANT, RIGHT?
NO, NO, IT'S JUST A DIET DRUG.
I HAVE SOME GREAT STUFF FOR YOU.
STUFF THAT'LL MAKE YOU FEEL REALLY GOOD.

THE END

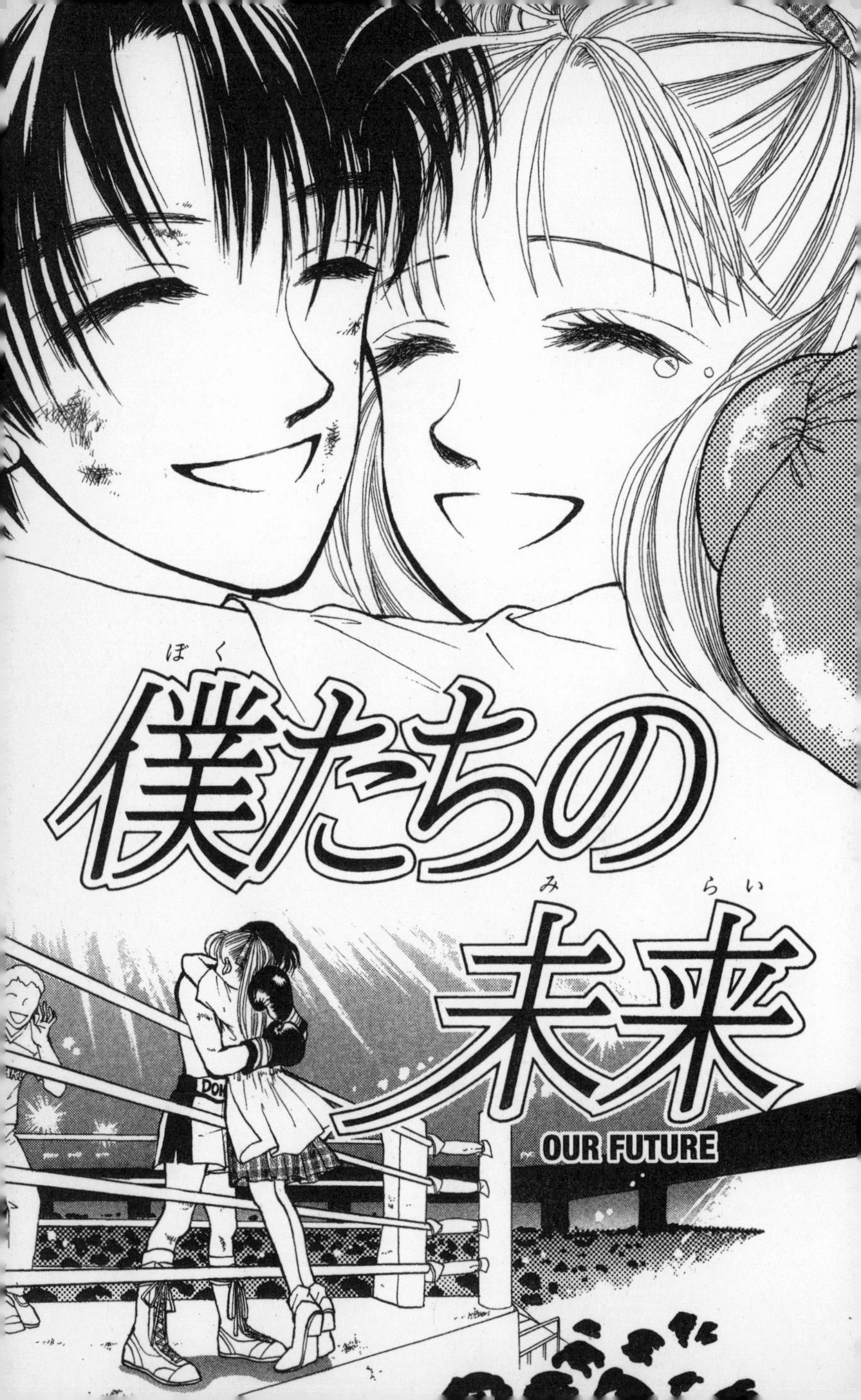

僕(ぼく)たちの未来(みらい)
OUR FUTURE

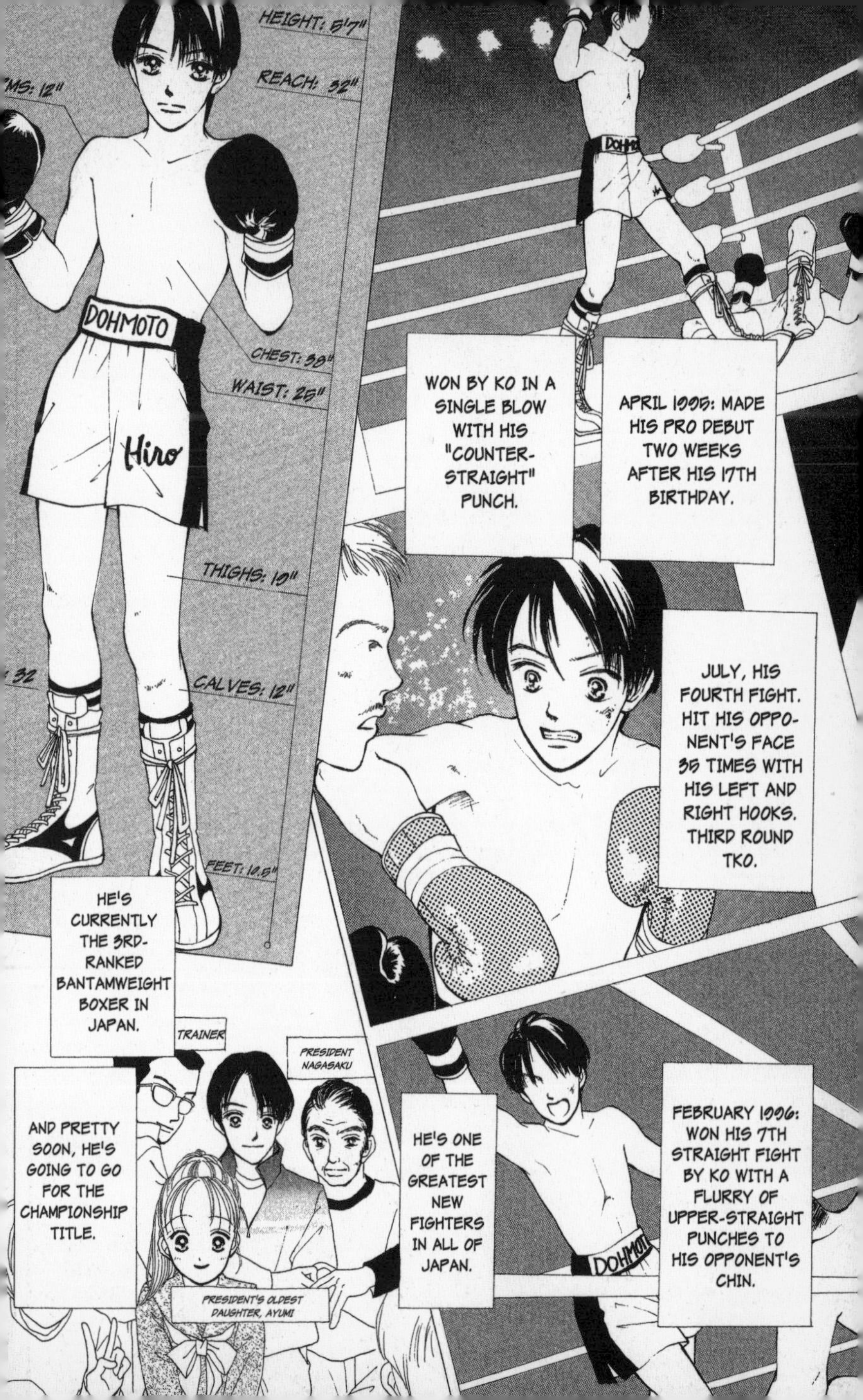
APRIL 1995: MADE HIS PRO DEBUT TWO WEEKS AFTER HIS 17TH BIRTHDAY.
WON BY KO IN A SINGLE BLOW WITH HIS "COUNTER-STRAIGHT" PUNCH.
DOHMOTO
JULY, HIS FOURTH FIGHT. HIT HIS OPPONENT'S FACE 35 TIMES WITH HIS LEFT AND RIGHT HOOKS. THIRD ROUND TKO.
FEBRUARY 1996: WON HIS 7TH STRAIGHT FIGHT BY KO WITH A FLURRY OF UPPER-STRAIGHT PUNCHES TO HIS OPPONENT'S CHIN.
HE'S ONE OF THE GREATEST NEW FIGHTERS IN ALL OF JAPAN.
DOHMOTO
HEIGHT: 5'7"
REACH: 32"
MS: 12"
CHEST: 38"
WAIST: 25"
DOHMOTO
Hiro
THIGHS: 19"
32
CALVES: 12"
FEET: 10.5"
HE'S CURRENTLY THE 3RD-RANKED BANTAMWEIGHT BOXER IN JAPAN.
TRAINER
PRESIDENT NAGASAKU
AND PRETTY SOON, HE'S GOING TO GO FOR THE CHAMPIONSHIP TITLE.
PRESIDENT'S OLDEST DAUGHTER, AYUMI

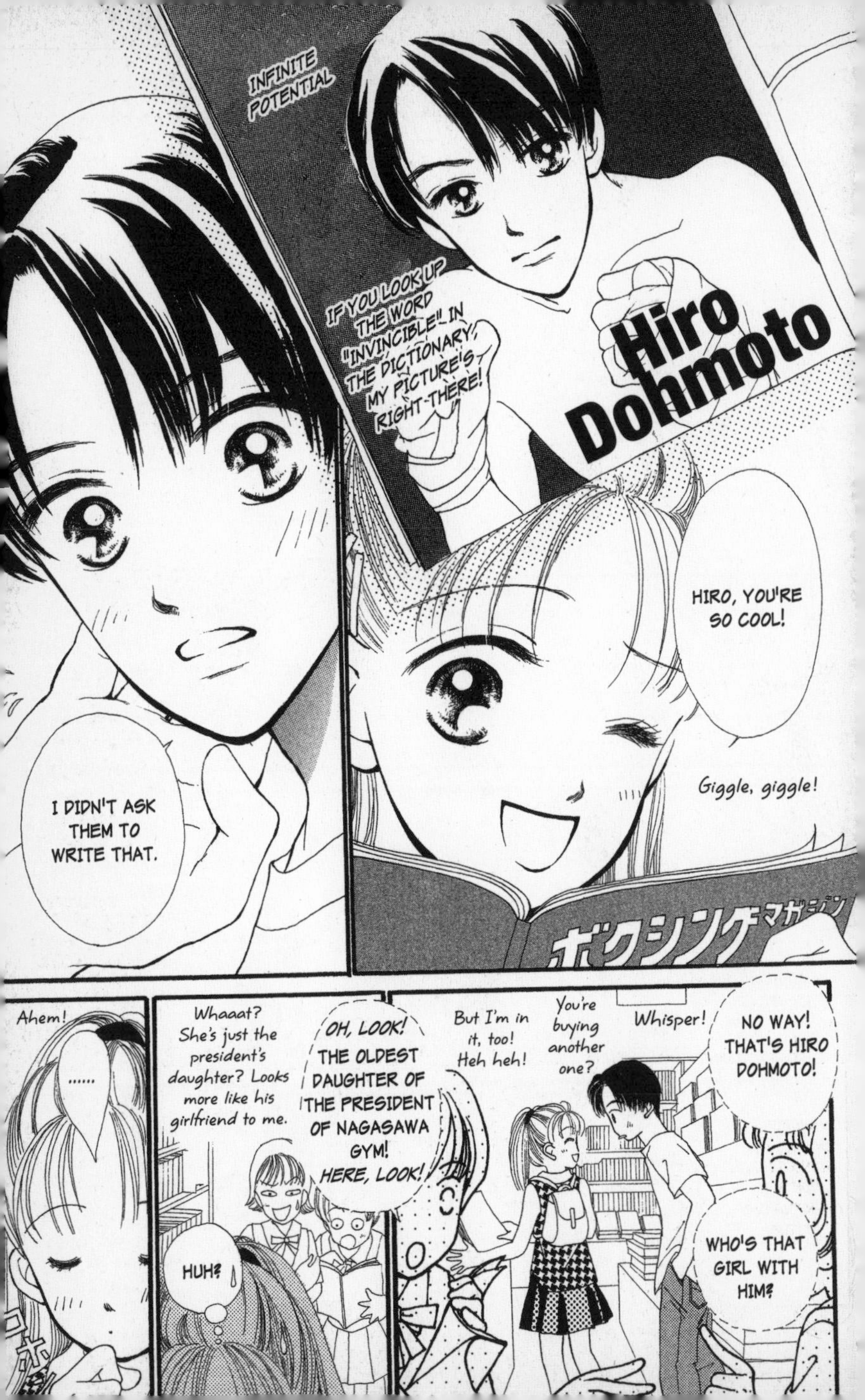
INFINITE POTENTIAL
IF YOU LOOK UP THE WORD "INVINCIBLE" IN THE DICTIONARY, MY PICTURE'S RIGHT THERE!
Hiro Dohmoto
HIRO, YOU'RE SO COOL!
Giggle, giggle!
ボクシングマガジン
I DIDN'T ASK THEM TO WRITE THAT.
NO WAY! THAT'S HIRO DOHMOTO!
Whisper!
You're buying another one?
But I'm in it, too! Heh heh!
WHO'S THAT GIRL WITH HIM?
OH, LOOK! THE OLDEST DAUGHTER OF THE PRESIDENT OF NAGASAWA GYM! HERE, LOOK!
Whaaat? She's just the president's daughter? Looks more like his girlfriend to me.
HUH?
Ahem!
......

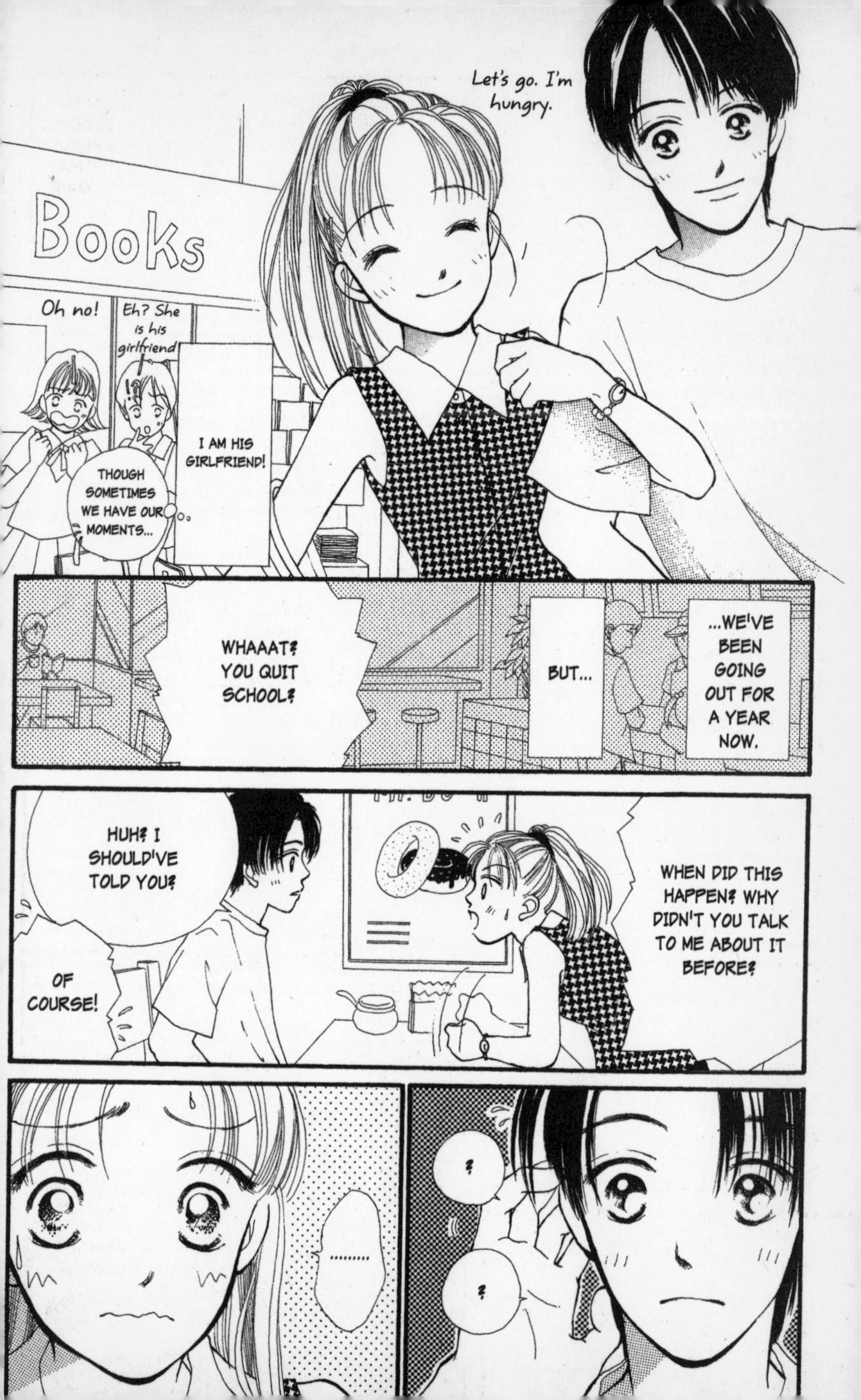
Let's go. I'm hungry.
Eh? She is his girlfriend!
Oh no!
I AM HIS GIRLFRIEND!
THOUGH SOMETIMES WE HAVE OUR MOMENTS...
...WE'VE BEEN GOING OUT FOR A YEAR NOW.
BUT...
WHAAAT? YOU QUIT SCHOOL?
WHEN DID THIS HAPPEN? WHY DIDN'T YOU TALK TO ME ABOUT IT BEFORE?
HUH? I SHOULD'VE TOLD YOU?
OF COURSE!
?
?
....

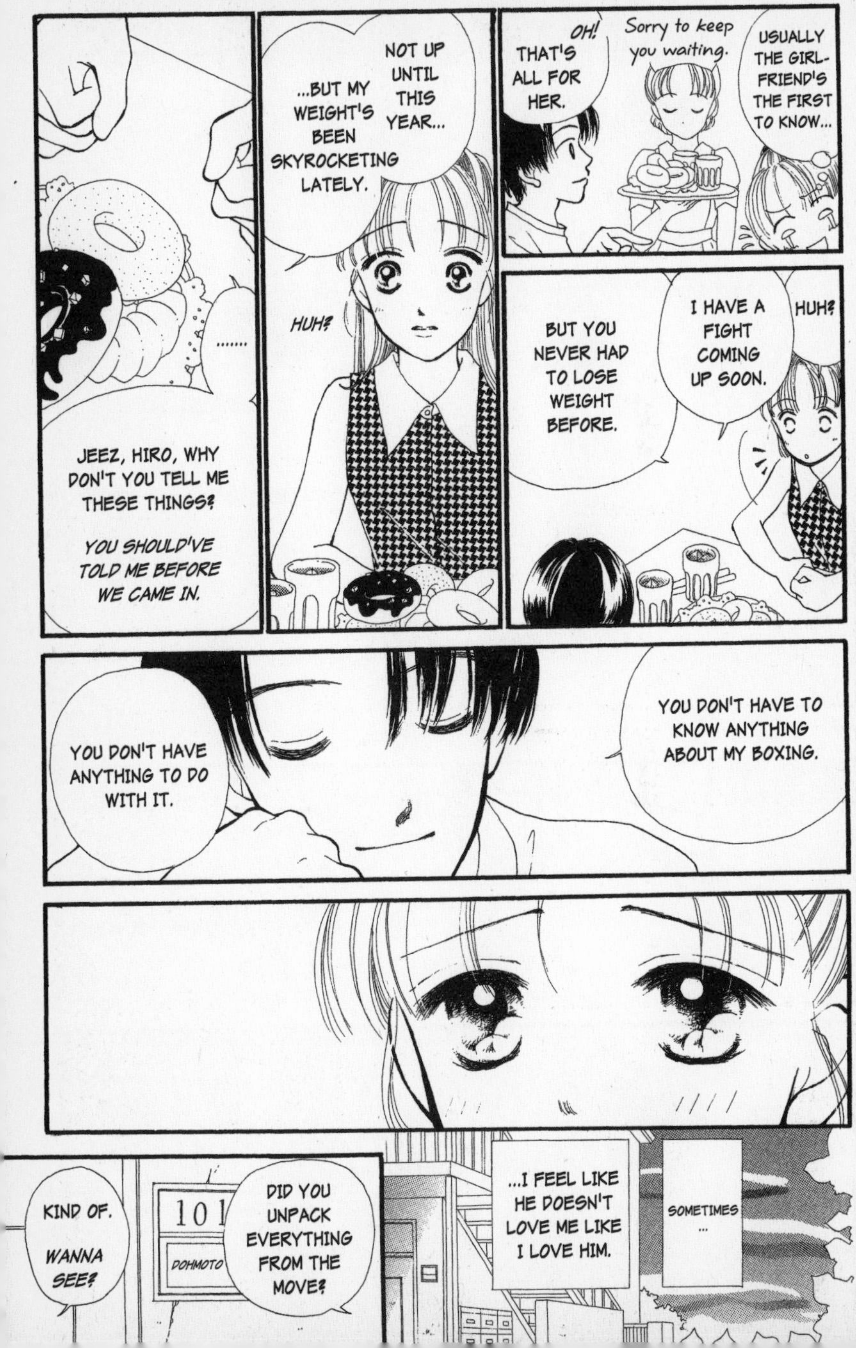
USUALLY THE GIRL-FRIEND'S THE FIRST TO KNOW...
Sorry to keep you waiting.
OH! THAT'S ALL FOR HER.
HUH?
I HAVE A FIGHT COMING UP SOON.
BUT YOU NEVER HAD TO LOSE WEIGHT BEFORE.
NOT UP UNTIL THIS YEAR...
...BUT MY WEIGHT'S BEEN SKYROCKETING LATELY.
HUH?
....
JEEZ, HIRO, WHY DON'T YOU TELL ME THESE THINGS?
YOU SHOULD'VE TOLD ME BEFORE WE CAME IN.
YOU DON'T HAVE TO KNOW ANYTHING ABOUT MY BOXING.
YOU DON'T HAVE ANYTHING TO DO WITH IT.
SOMETIMES...
...I FEEL LIKE HE DOESN'T LOVE ME LIKE I LOVE HIM.
DID YOU UNPACK EVERYTHING FROM THE MOVE?
101
DOHMOTO
KIND OF.
WANNA SEE?

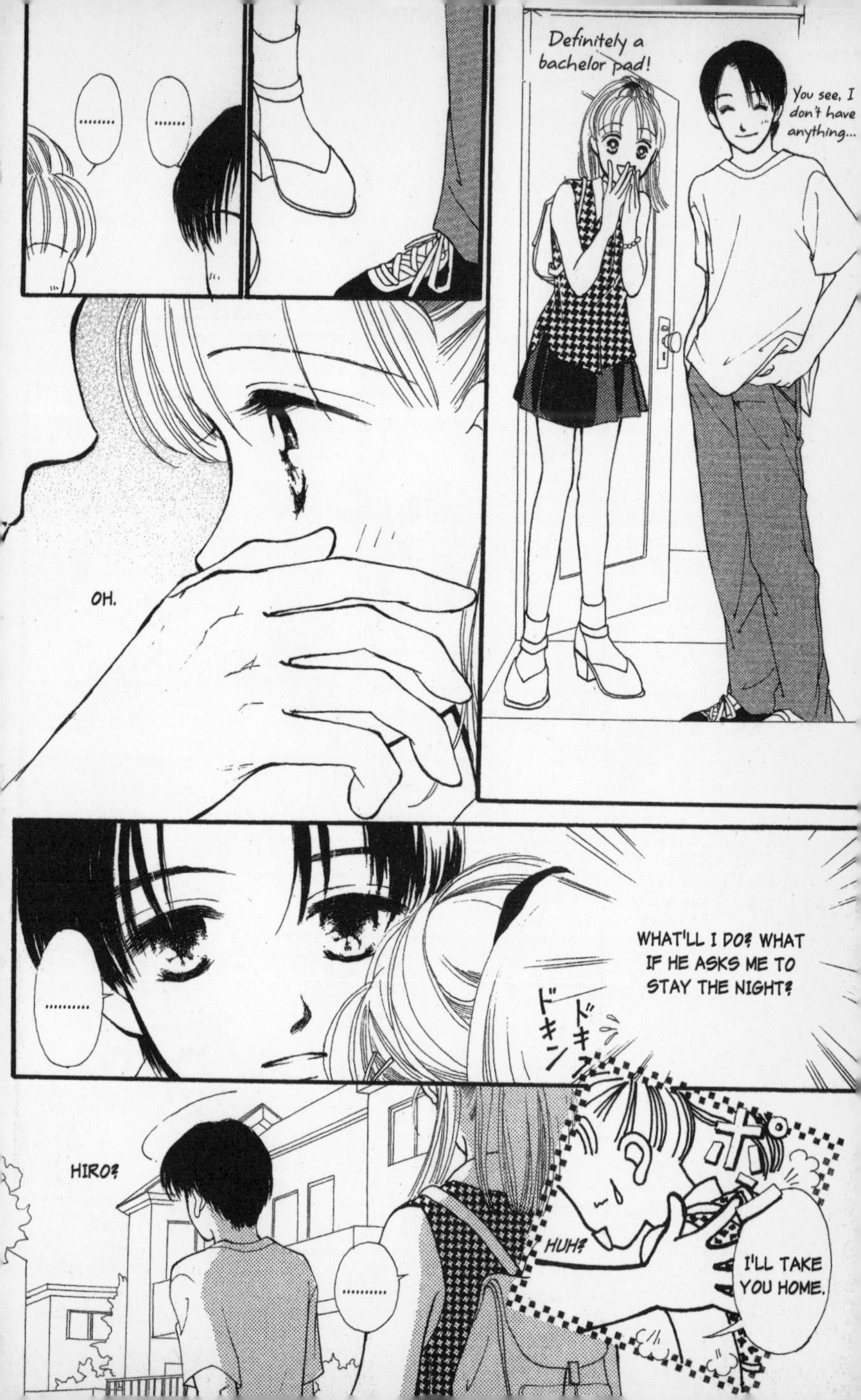
You see, I don't have anything...
Definitely a bachelor pad!
....
....
OH.
WHAT'LL I DO? WHAT IF HE ASKS ME TO STAY THE NIGHT?
ドキンドキン
....
ポ
I'LL TAKE YOU HOME.
HUH?
....
HIRO?

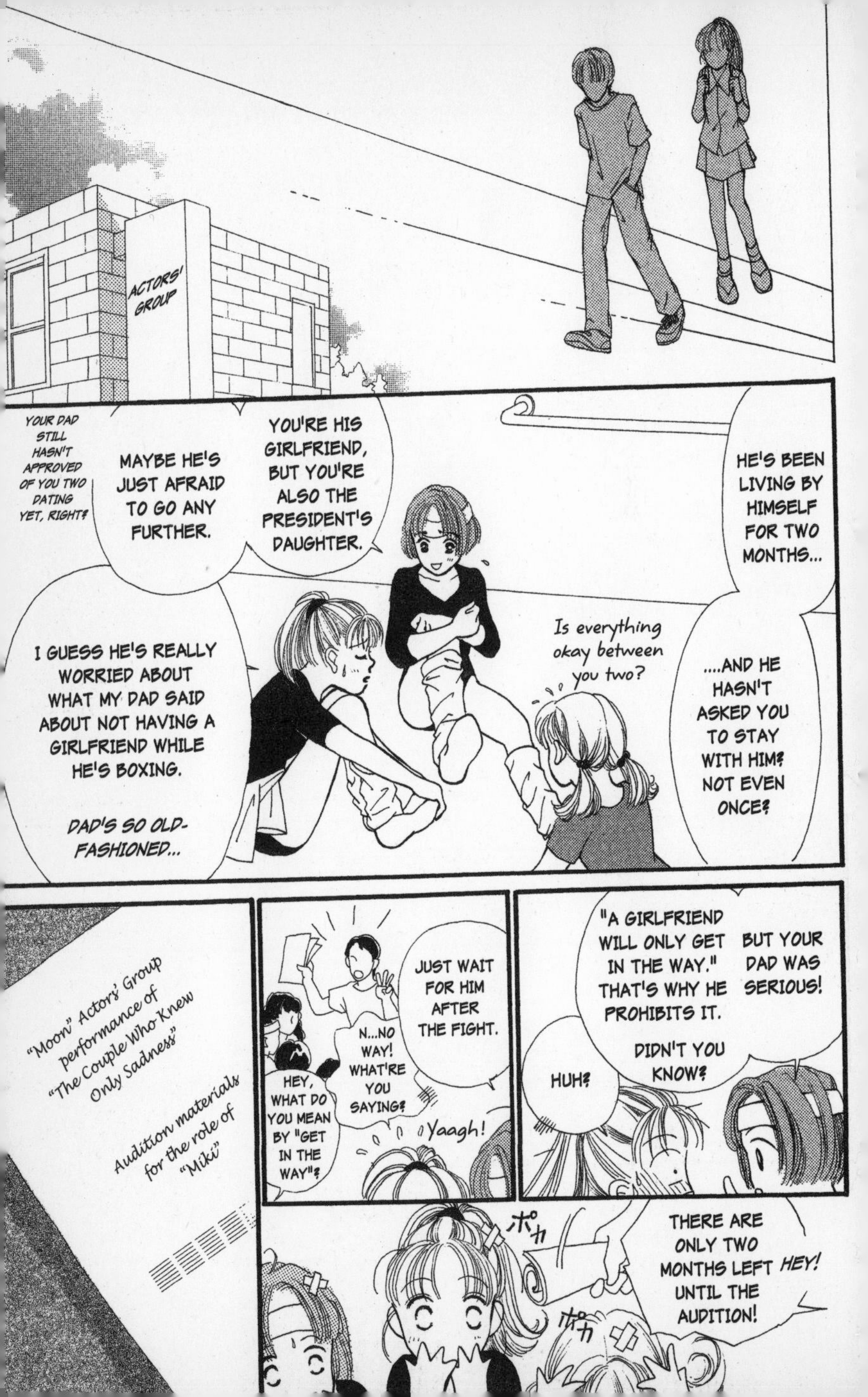
ACTORS' GROUP
HE'S BEEN LIVING BY HIMSELF FOR TWO MONTHS...
....AND HE HASN'T ASKED YOU TO STAY WITH HIM? NOT EVEN ONCE?
Is everything okay between you two?
YOU'RE HIS GIRLFRIEND, BUT YOU'RE ALSO THE PRESIDENT'S DAUGHTER.
MAYBE HE'S JUST AFRAID TO GO ANY FURTHER.
YOUR DAD STILL HASN'T APPROVED OF YOU TWO DATING YET, RIGHT?
I GUESS HE'S REALLY WORRIED ABOUT WHAT MY DAD SAID ABOUT NOT HAVING A GIRLFRIEND WHILE HE'S BOXING.
DAD'S SO OLD-FASHIONED...
BUT YOUR DAD WAS SERIOUS!
"A GIRLFRIEND WILL ONLY GET IN THE WAY." THAT'S WHY HE PROHIBITS IT.
DIDN'T YOU KNOW?
HUH?
JUST WAIT FOR HIM AFTER THE FIGHT.
N...NO WAY! WHAT'RE YOU SAYING?
HEY, WHAT DO YOU MEAN BY "GET IN THE WAY"?
Yaagh!
HEY!
THERE ARE ONLY TWO MONTHS LEFT UNTIL THE AUDITION!
ポカ
ポカ
"Moon" Actors' Group performance of "The Couple Who Knew Only Sadness"
Audition materials for the role of "Miki"

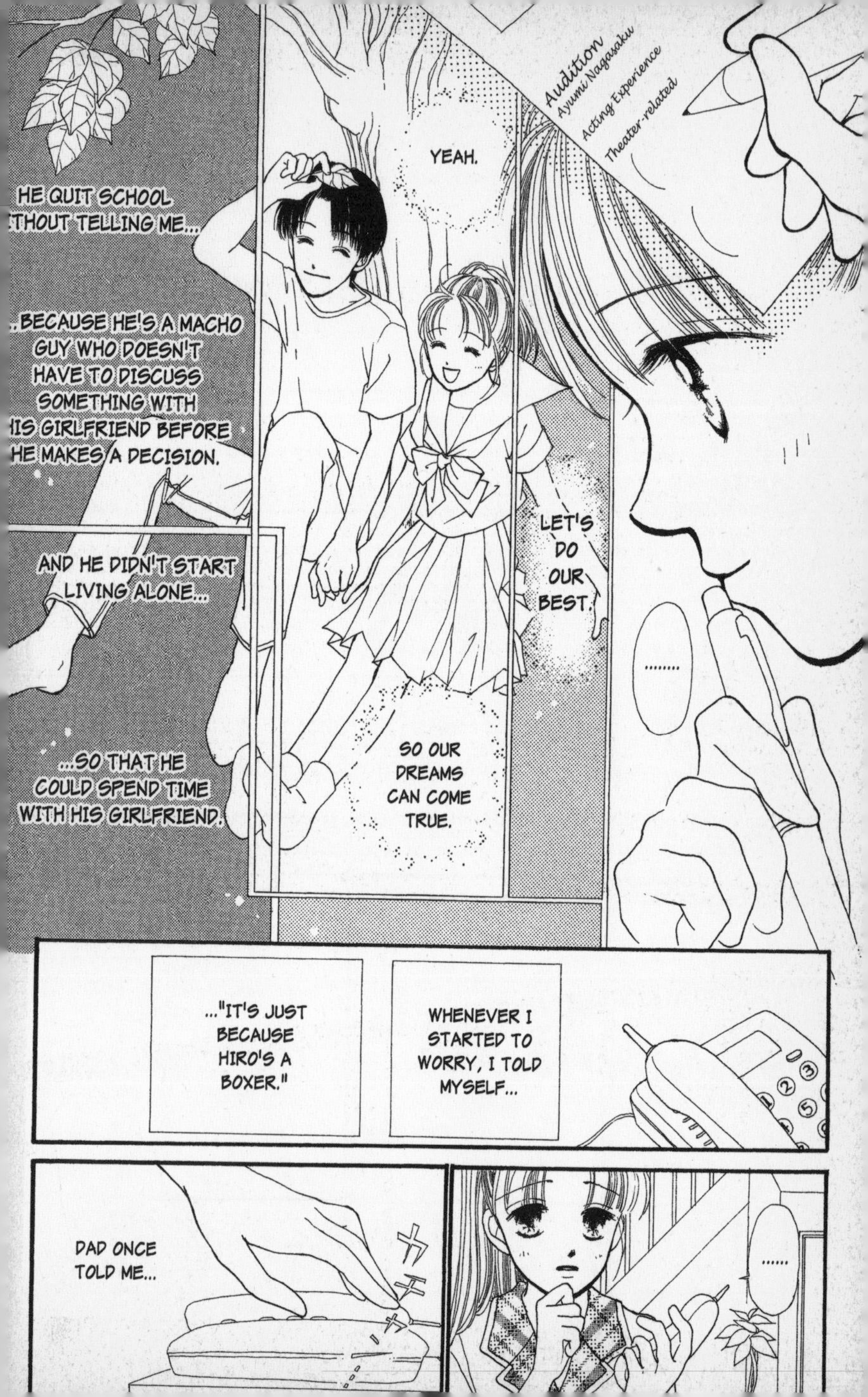

Audition
Ayumi Nagasaku
Acting Experience
Theater-related
....
YEAH.
LET'S DO OUR BEST.
SO OUR DREAMS CAN COME TRUE.
HE QUIT SCHOOL ITHOUT TELLING ME...
..BECAUSE HE'S A MACHO GUY WHO DOESN'T HAVE TO DISCUSS SOMETHING WITH IS GIRLFRIEND BEFORE HE MAKES A DECISION.
AND HE DIDN'T START LIVING ALONE...
...SO THAT HE COULD SPEND TIME WITH HIS GIRLFRIEND.
WHENEVER I STARTED TO WORRY, I TOLD MYSELF...
..."IT'S JUST BECAUSE HIRO'S A BOXER."
......
DAD ONCE TOLD ME...

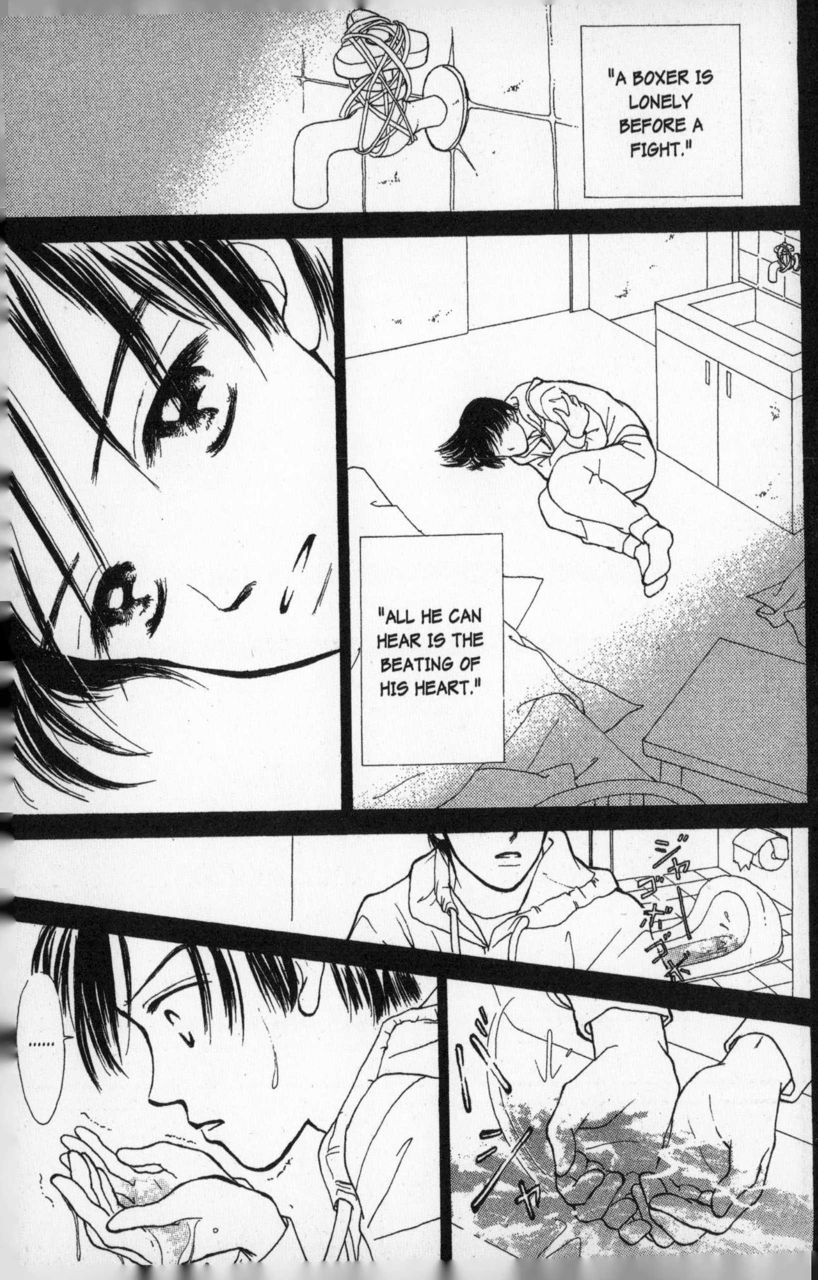
"A BOXER IS LONELY BEFORE A FIGHT."
"ALL HE CAN HEAR IS THE BEATING OF HIS HEART."
......

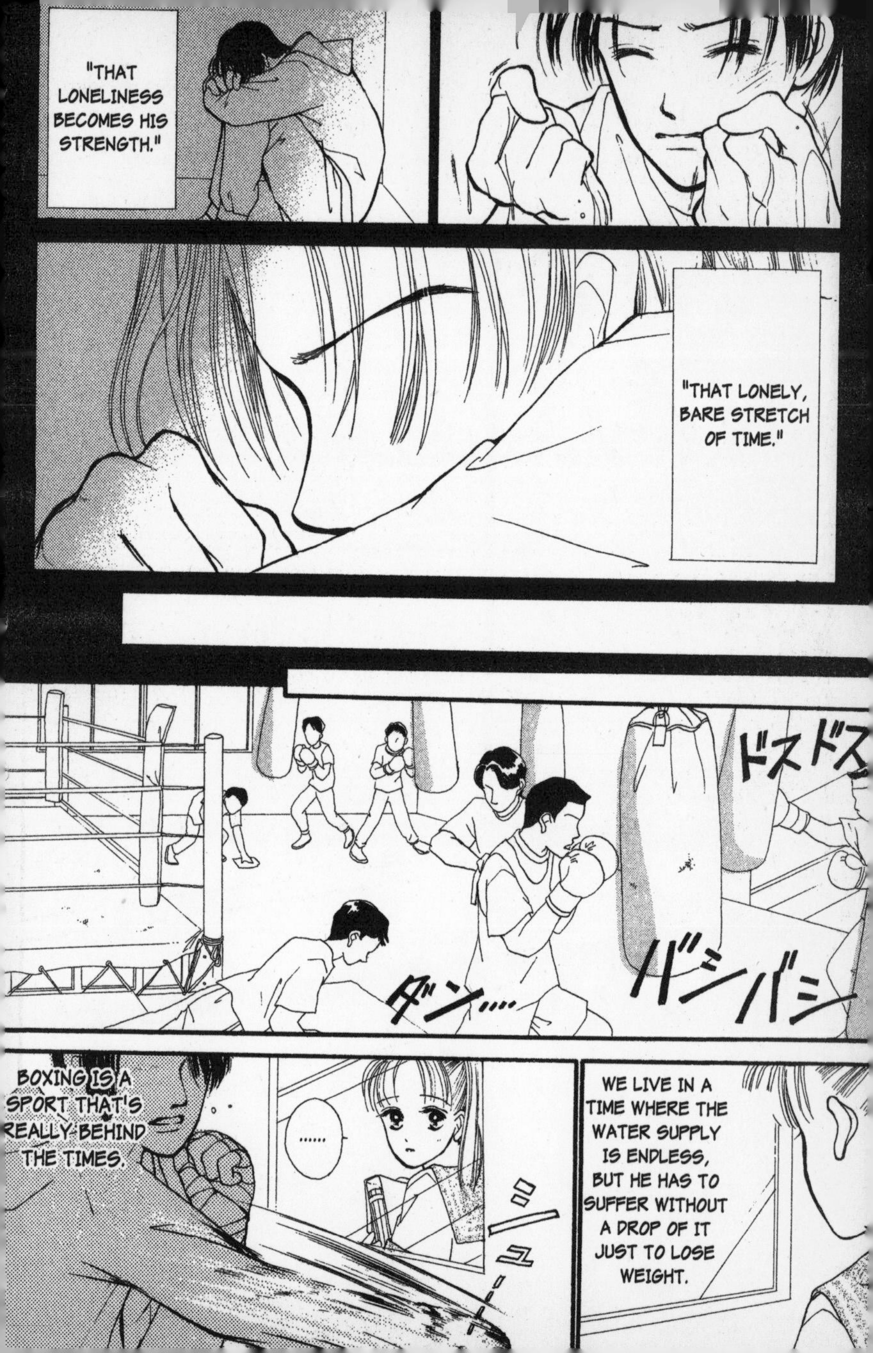
"THAT LONELINESS BECOMES HIS STRENGTH."
"THAT LONELY, BARE STRETCH OF TIME."
ドスドス
バシバシ
ダン....
WE LIVE IN A TIME WHERE THE WATER SUPPLY IS ENDLESS, BUT HE HAS TO SUFFER WITHOUT A DROP OF IT JUST TO LOSE WEIGHT.
......
BOXING IS A SPORT THAT'S REALLY BEHIND THE TIMES.

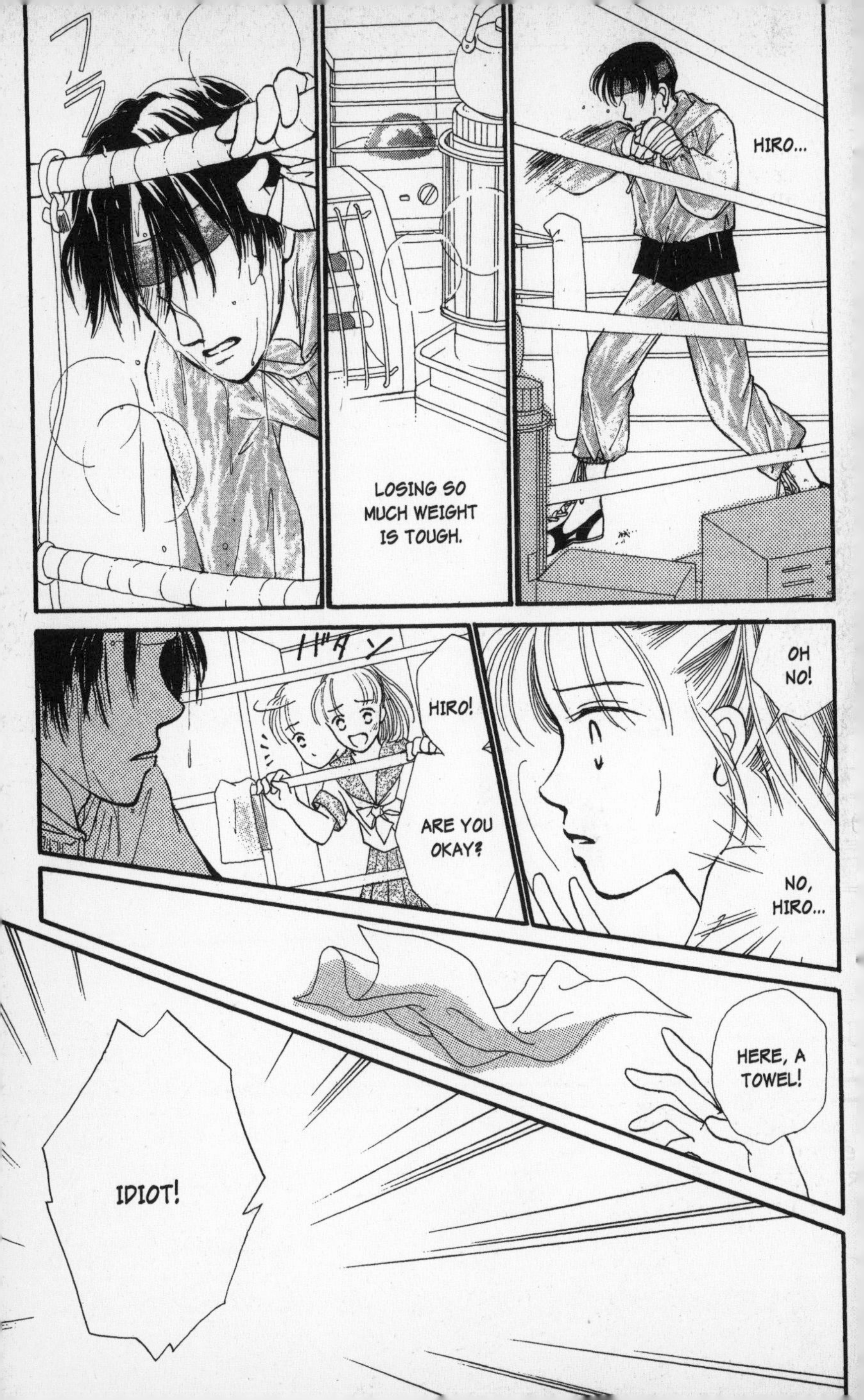
HIRO...
LOSING SO MUCH WEIGHT IS TOUGH.
フラ
OH NO!
NO, HIRO...
バタン
HIRO!
ARE YOU OKAY?
HERE, A TOWEL!
IDIOT!

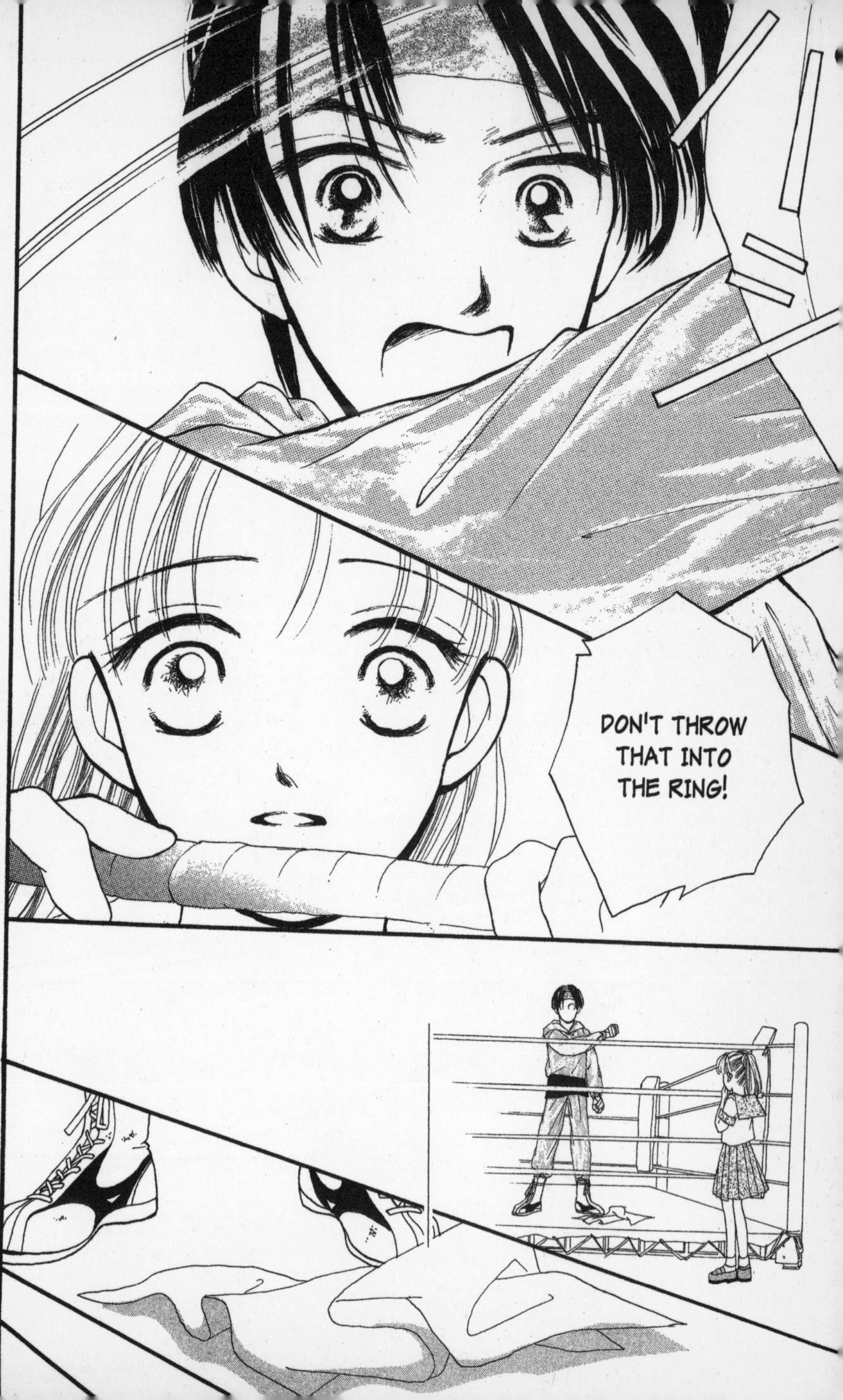
DON'T THROW
THAT INTO
THE RING!

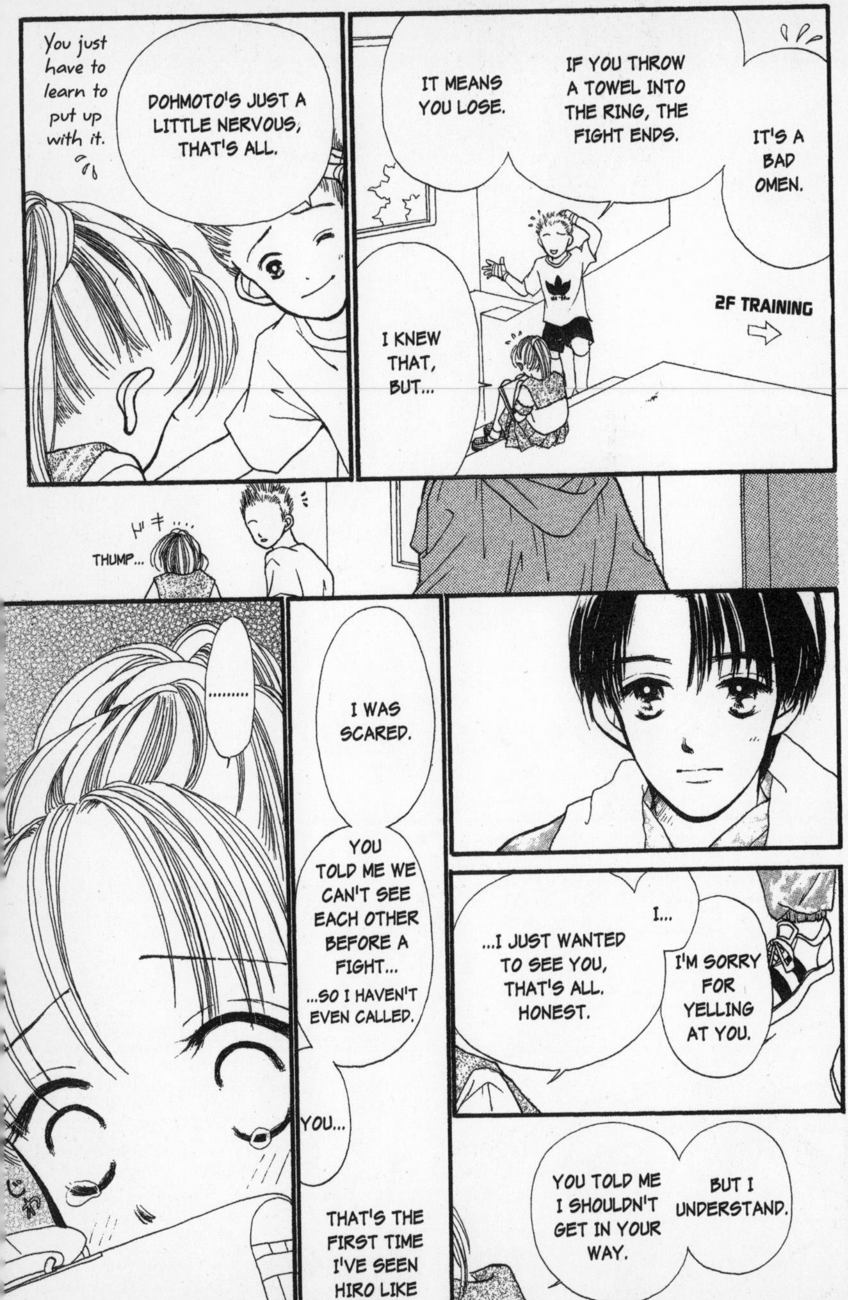
IF YOU THROW A TOWEL INTO THE RING, THE FIGHT ENDS.
IT MEANS YOU LOSE.
IT'S A BAD OMEN.
2F TRAINING
I KNEW THAT, BUT...
DOHMOTO'S JUST A LITTLE NERVOUS, THAT'S ALL.
You just have to learn to put up with it.
ドキ...
THUMP...
I...
I'M SORRY FOR YELLING AT YOU.
...I JUST WANTED TO SEE YOU, THAT'S ALL. HONEST.
BUT I UNDERSTAND.
YOU TOLD ME I SHOULDN'T GET IN YOUR WAY.
I WAS SCARED.
YOU TOLD ME WE CAN'T SEE EACH OTHER BEFORE A FIGHT...
...SO I HAVEN'T EVEN CALLED.
YOU...
THAT'S THE FIRST TIME I'VE SEEN HIRO LIKE THAT.
....
じわ

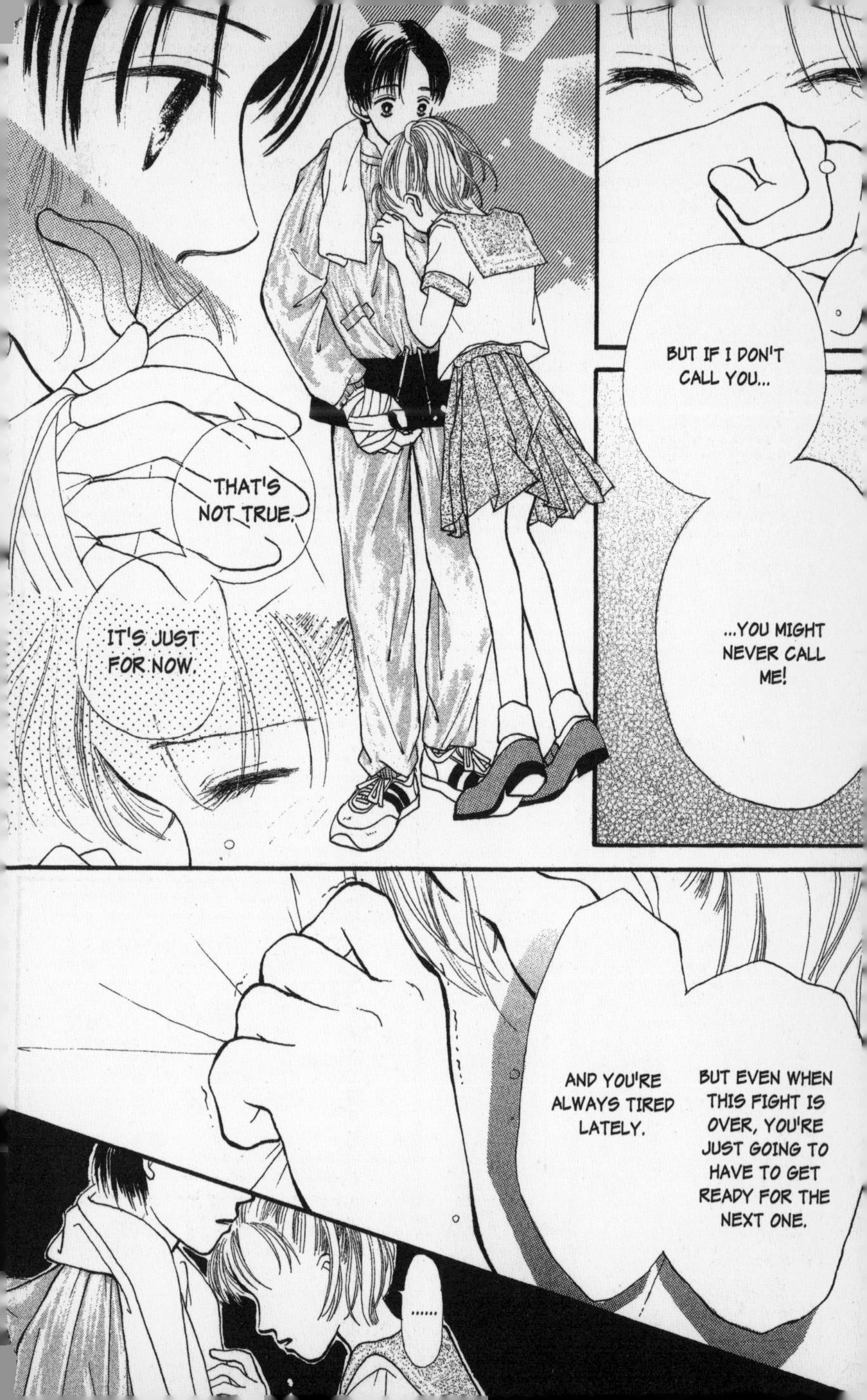
BUT IF I DON'T CALL YOU...
...YOU MIGHT NEVER CALL ME!
THAT'S NOT TRUE.
IT'S JUST FOR NOW.
BUT EVEN WHEN THIS FIGHT IS OVER, YOU'RE JUST GOING TO HAVE TO GET READY FOR THE NEXT ONE.
AND YOU'RE ALWAYS TIRED LATELY.
......

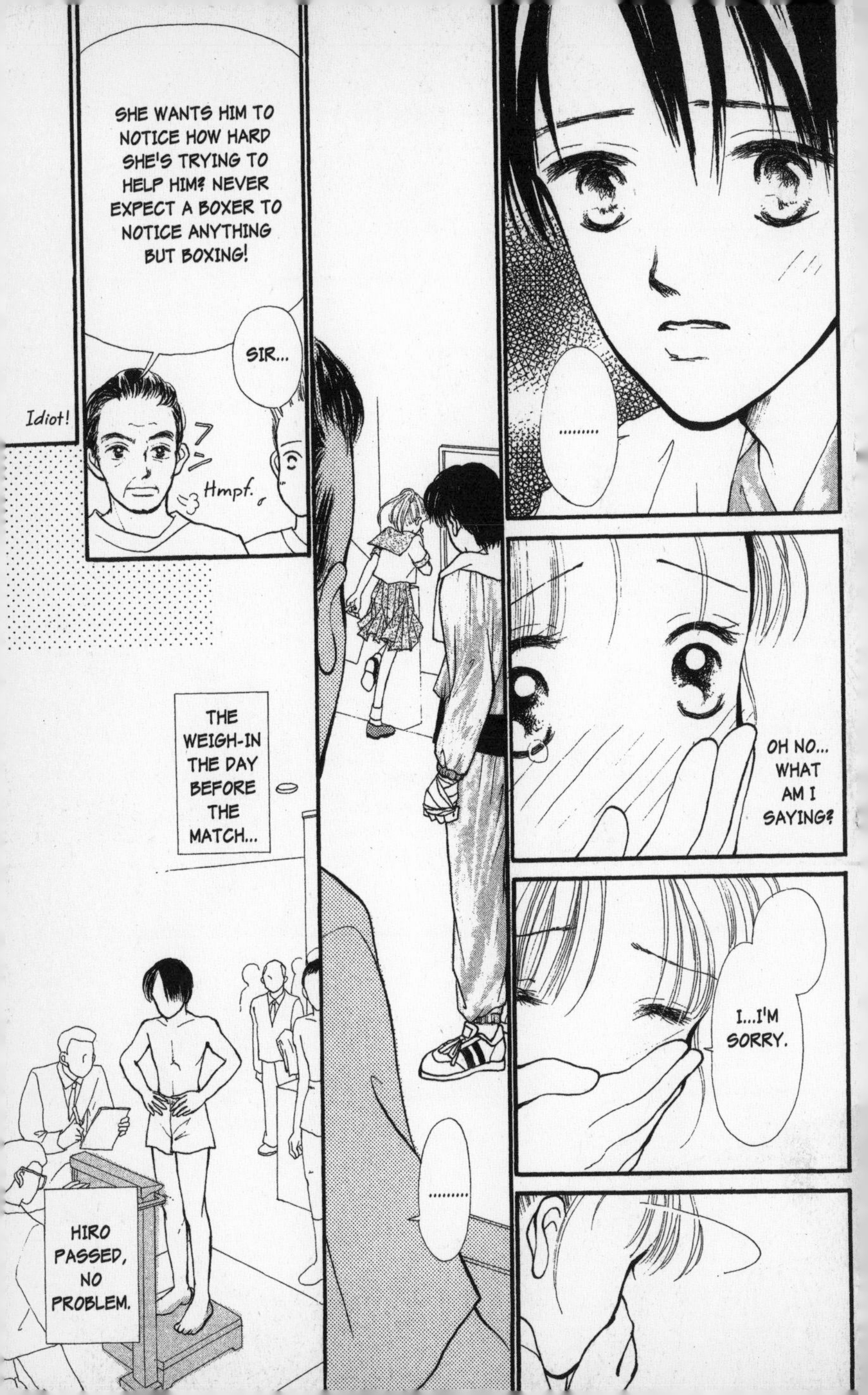
....
OH NO... WHAT AM I SAYING?
I...I'M SORRY.
....
SHE WANTS HIM TO NOTICE HOW HARD SHE'S TRYING TO HELP HIM? NEVER EXPECT A BOXER TO NOTICE ANYTHING BUT BOXING!
SIR...
Idiot!
Hmpf.
THE WEIGH-IN THE DAY BEFORE THE MATCH...
HIRO PASSED, NO PROBLEM.

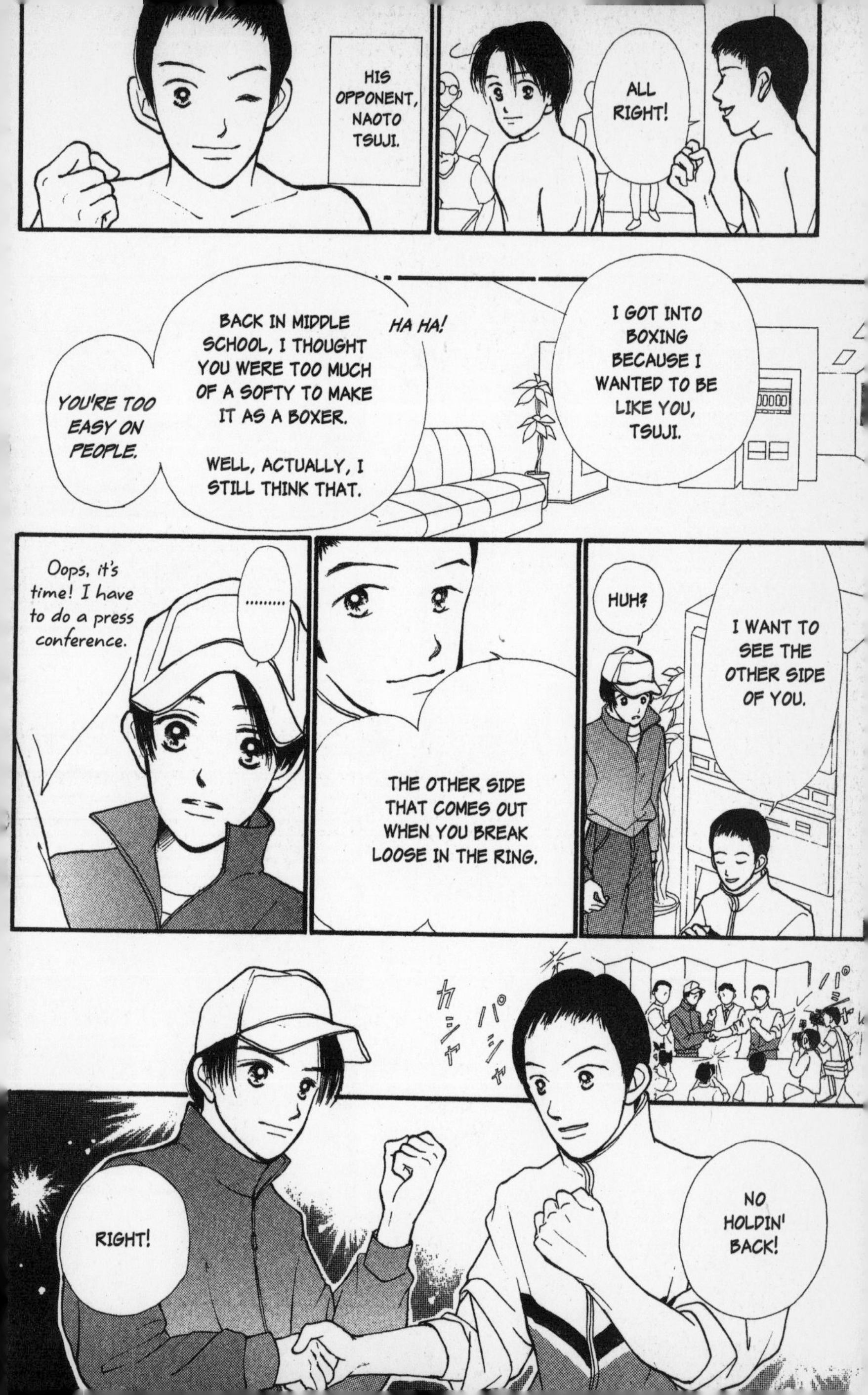
ALL RIGHT!
HIS OPPONENT, NAOTO TSUJI.
I GOT INTO BOXING BECAUSE I WANTED TO BE LIKE YOU, TSUJI.
HA HA!
BACK IN MIDDLE SCHOOL, I THOUGHT YOU WERE TOO MUCH OF A SOFTY TO MAKE IT AS A BOXER.
WELL, ACTUALLY, I STILL THINK THAT.
YOU'RE TOO EASY ON PEOPLE.
HUH?
I WANT TO SEE THE OTHER SIDE OF YOU.
THE OTHER SIDE THAT COMES OUT WHEN YOU BREAK LOOSE IN THE RING.
....
Oops, it's time! I have to do a press conference.
カシャ
パシャ
NO HOLDIN' BACK!
RIGHT!

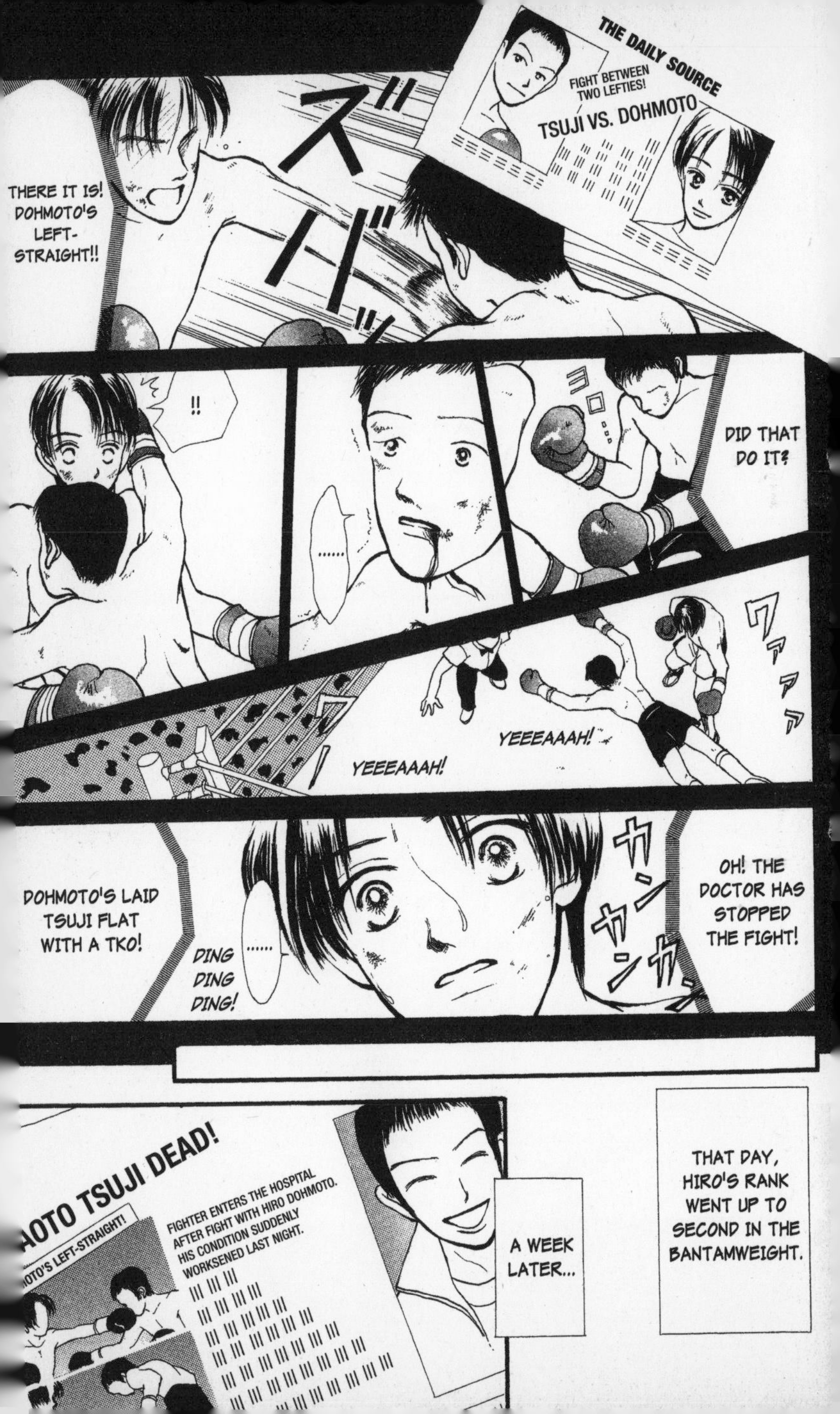
THE DAILY SOURCE
FIGHT BETWEEN TWO LEFTIES!
TSUJI VS. DOHMOTO
ズバッ
THERE IT IS! DOHMOTO'S LEFT-STRAIGHT!!
DID THAT DO IT?
ヨロ
......
!!
ワァァァ
YEEEAAAH!
YEEEAAAH!
OH! THE DOCTOR HAS STOPPED THE FIGHT!
カーンカーンカーン
DING DING DING!
......
DOHMOTO'S LAID TSUJI FLAT WITH A TKO!
THAT DAY, HIRO'S RANK WENT UP TO SECOND IN THE BANTAMWEIGHT.
A WEEK LATER...
AOTO TSUJI DEAD!
FIGHTER ENTERS THE HOSPITAL AFTER FIGHT WITH HIRO DOHMOTO. HIS CONDITION SUDDENLY WORKSENED LAST NIGHT.
MOTO'S LEFT-STRAIGHT!

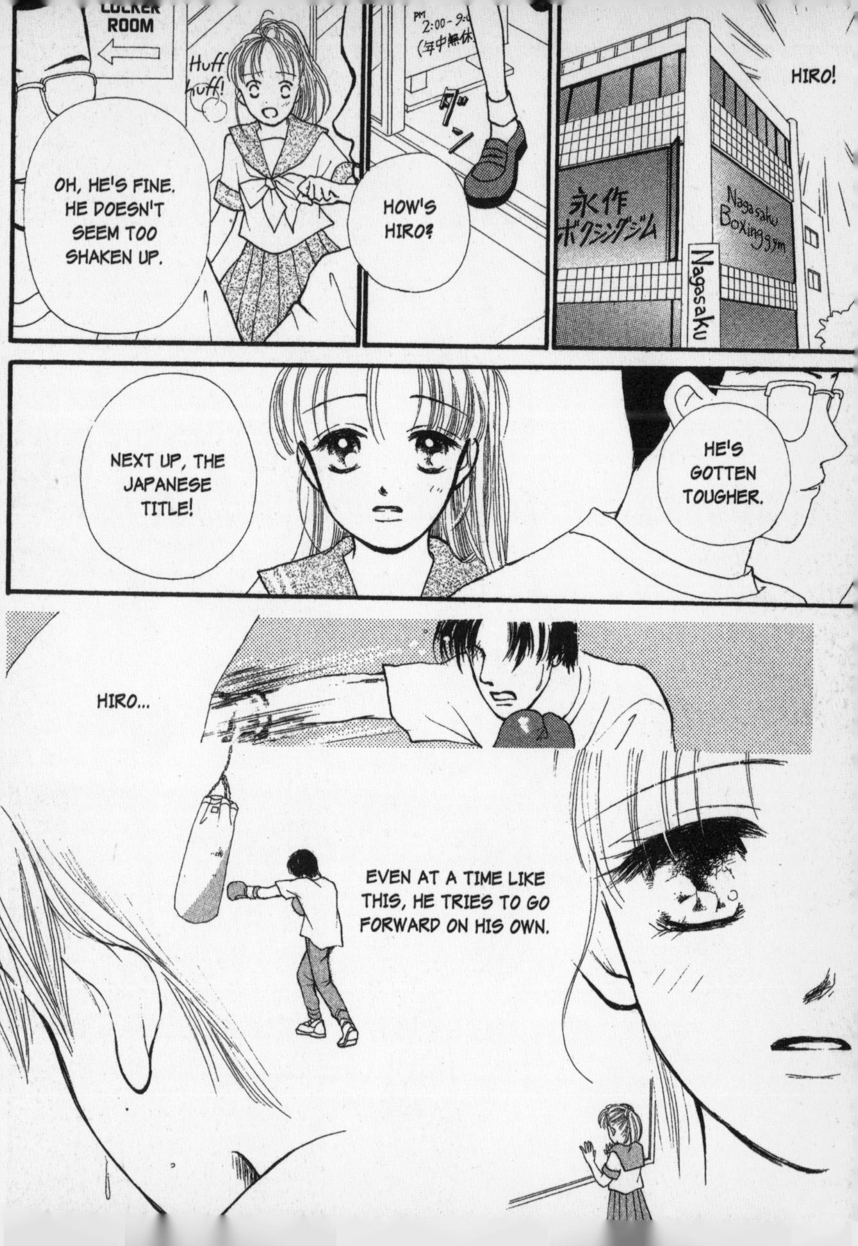
HIRO!
永作 ボクシングジム
Nagasaku Boxing gym
Nagasaku
HOW'S HIRO?
LOCKER ROOM
Huff huff!
OH, HE'S FINE. HE DOESN'T SEEM TOO SHAKEN UP.
HE'S GOTTEN TOUGHER.
NEXT UP, THE JAPANESE TITLE!
HIRO...
EVEN AT A TIME LIKE THIS, HE TRIES TO GO FORWARD ON HIS OWN.

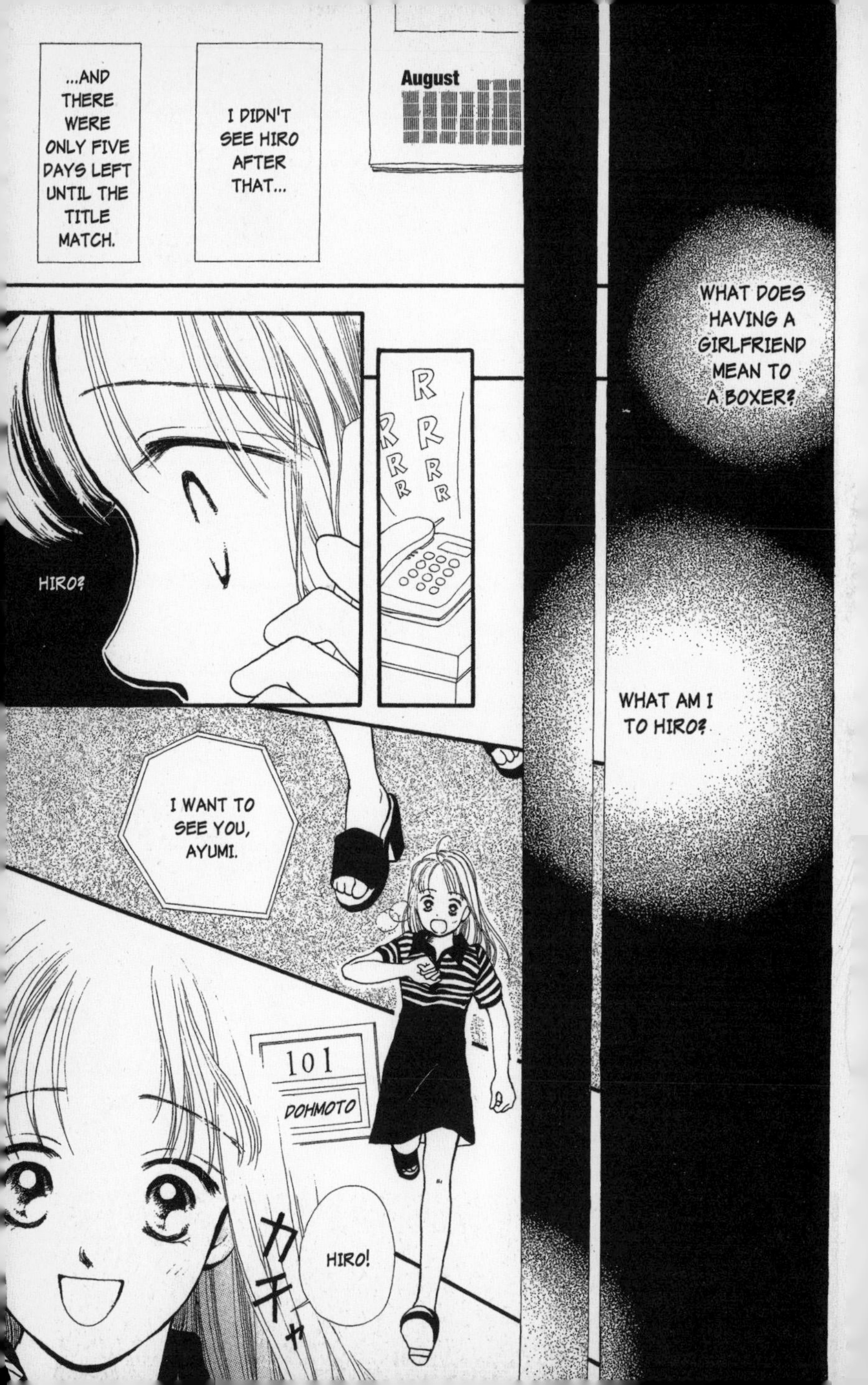
WHAT DOES HAVING A GIRLFRIEND MEAN TO A BOXER?
WHAT AM I TO HIRO?
August
I DIDN'T SEE HIRO AFTER THAT...
...AND THERE WERE ONLY FIVE DAYS LEFT UNTIL THE TITLE MATCH.
RRRRRRRRR
HIRO?
I WANT TO SEE YOU, AYUMI.
101
DOHMOTO
HIRO!
カチャ

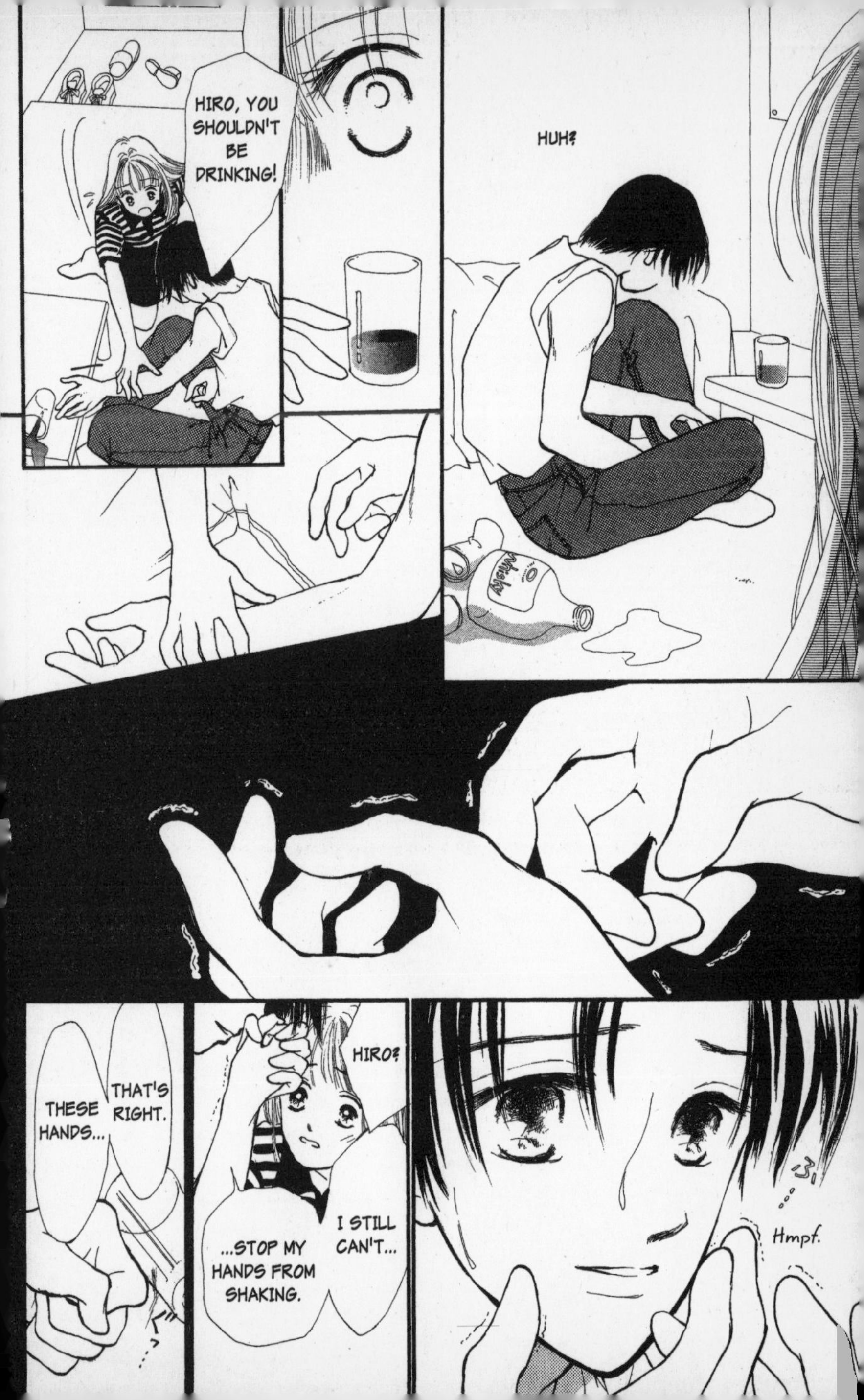
HUH?
Whisky
HIRO, YOU SHOULDN'T BE DRINKING!
Hmpf.
HIRO?
I STILL CAN'T...
...STOP MY HANDS FROM SHAKING.
THAT'S RIGHT.
THESE HANDS...

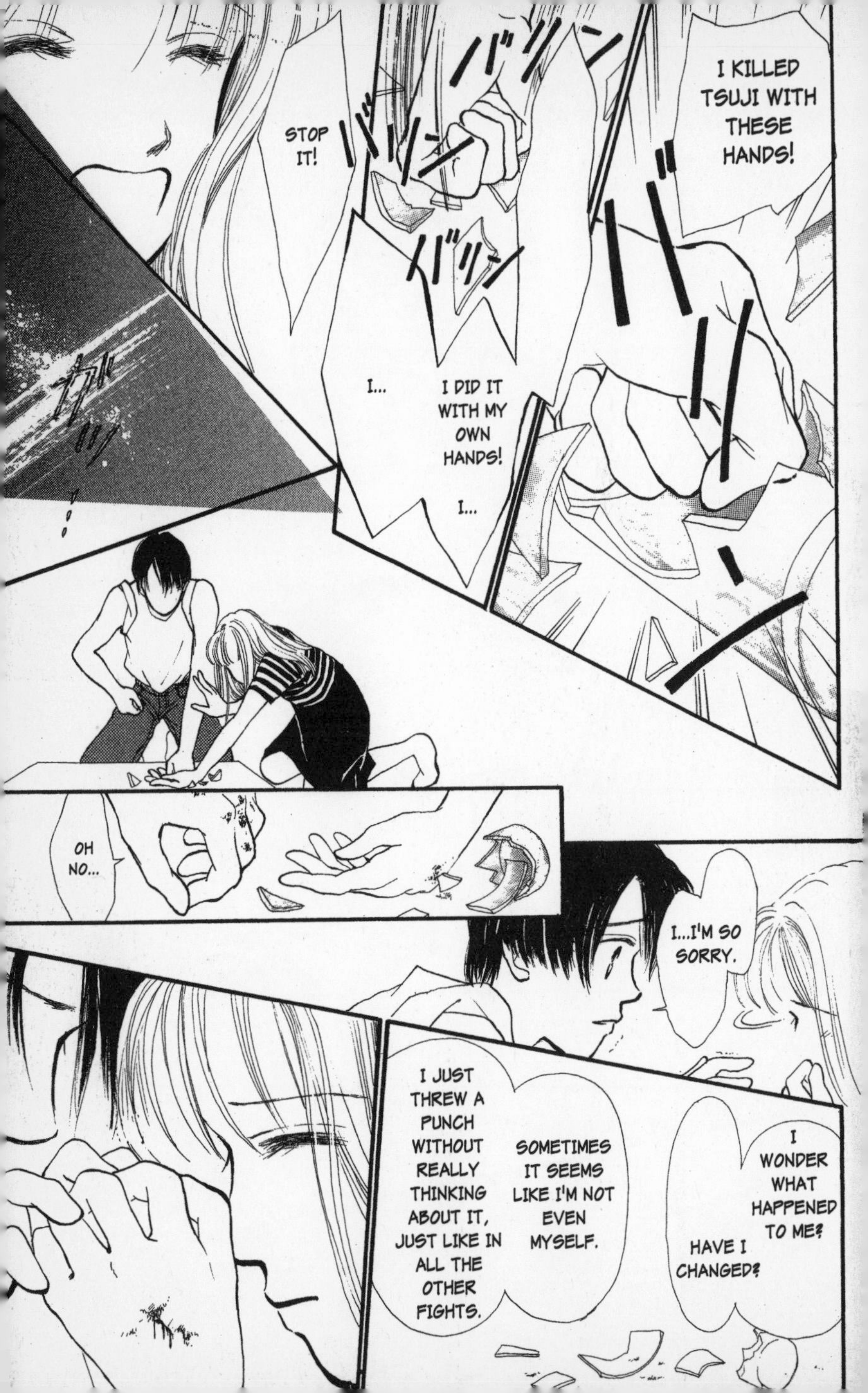
I KILLED TSUJI WITH THESE HANDS!
I DID IT WITH MY OWN HANDS!
I...
I...
STOP IT!
OH NO...
I...I'M SO SORRY.
I WONDER WHAT HAPPENED TO ME?
HAVE I CHANGED?
SOMETIMES IT SEEMS LIKE I'M NOT EVEN MYSELF.
I JUST THREW A PUNCH WITHOUT REALLY THINKING ABOUT IT, JUST LIKE IN ALL THE OTHER FIGHTS.

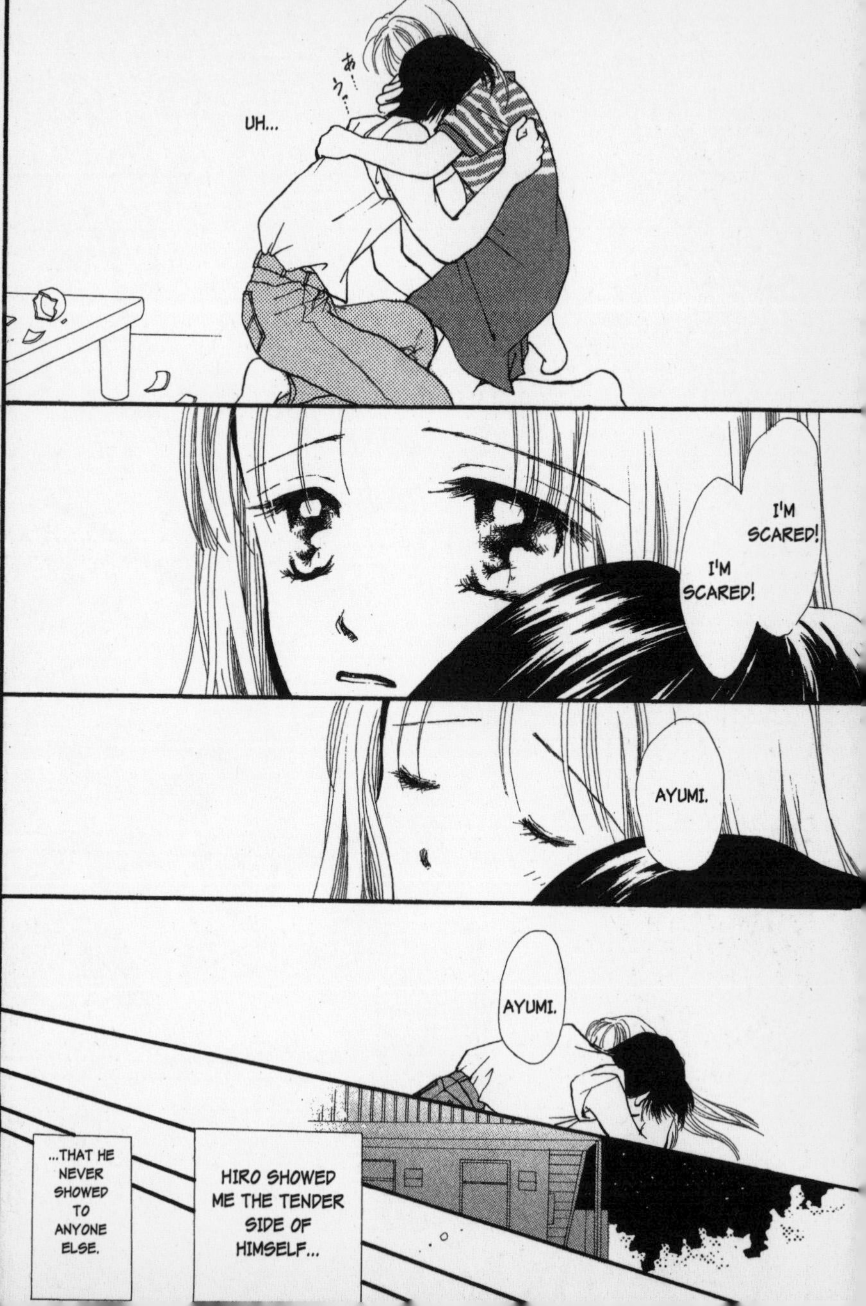
あ…う…
UH...
I'M SCARED!
I'M SCARED!
AYUMI.
AYUMI.
HIRO SHOWED ME THE TENDER SIDE OF HIMSELF...
...THAT HE NEVER SHOWED TO ANYONE ELSE.

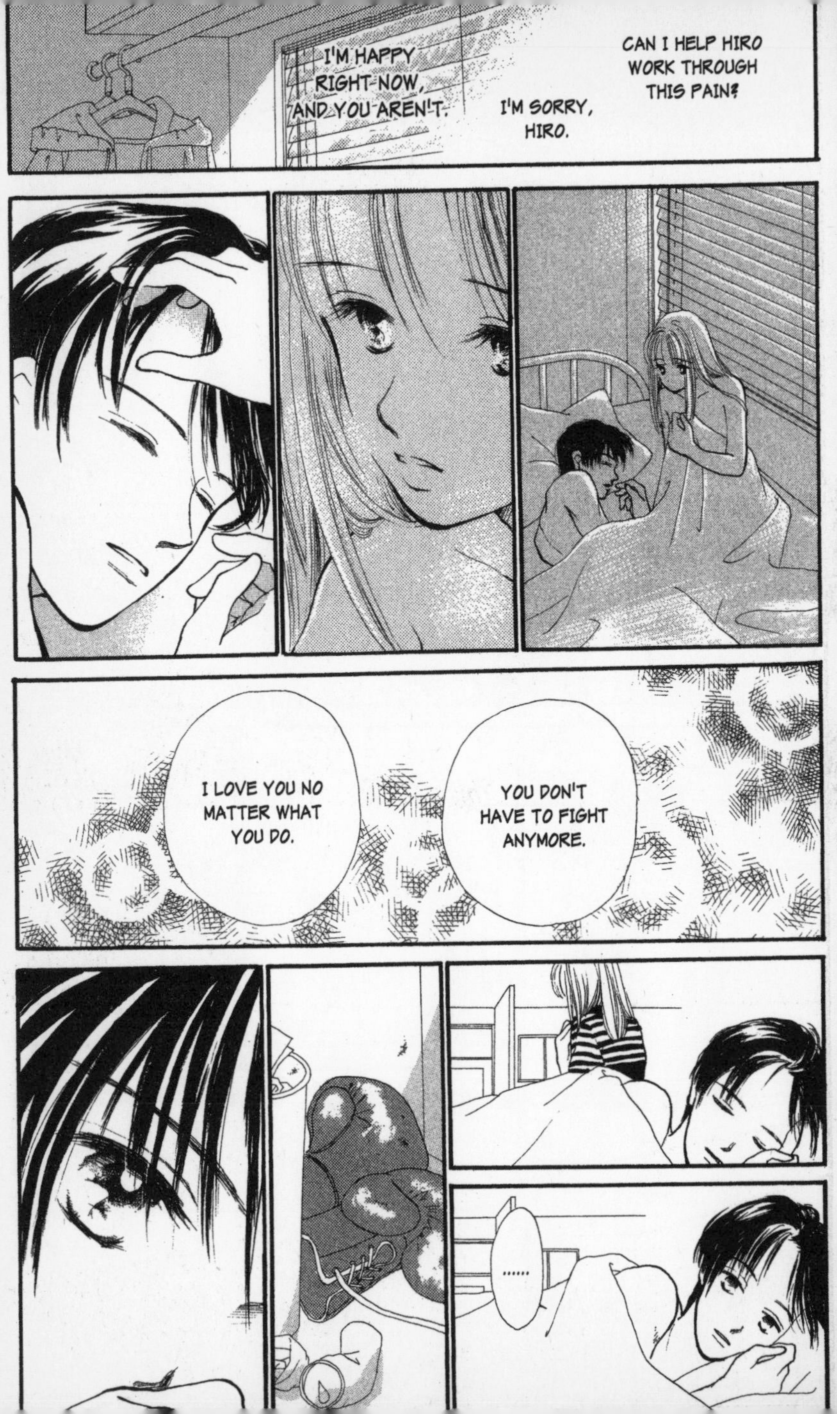
CAN I HELP HIRO WORK THROUGH THIS PAIN?
I'M SORRY, HIRO.
I'M HAPPY RIGHT NOW, AND YOU AREN'T.
YOU DON'T HAVE TO FIGHT ANYMORE.
I LOVE YOU NO MATTER WHAT YOU DO.
......

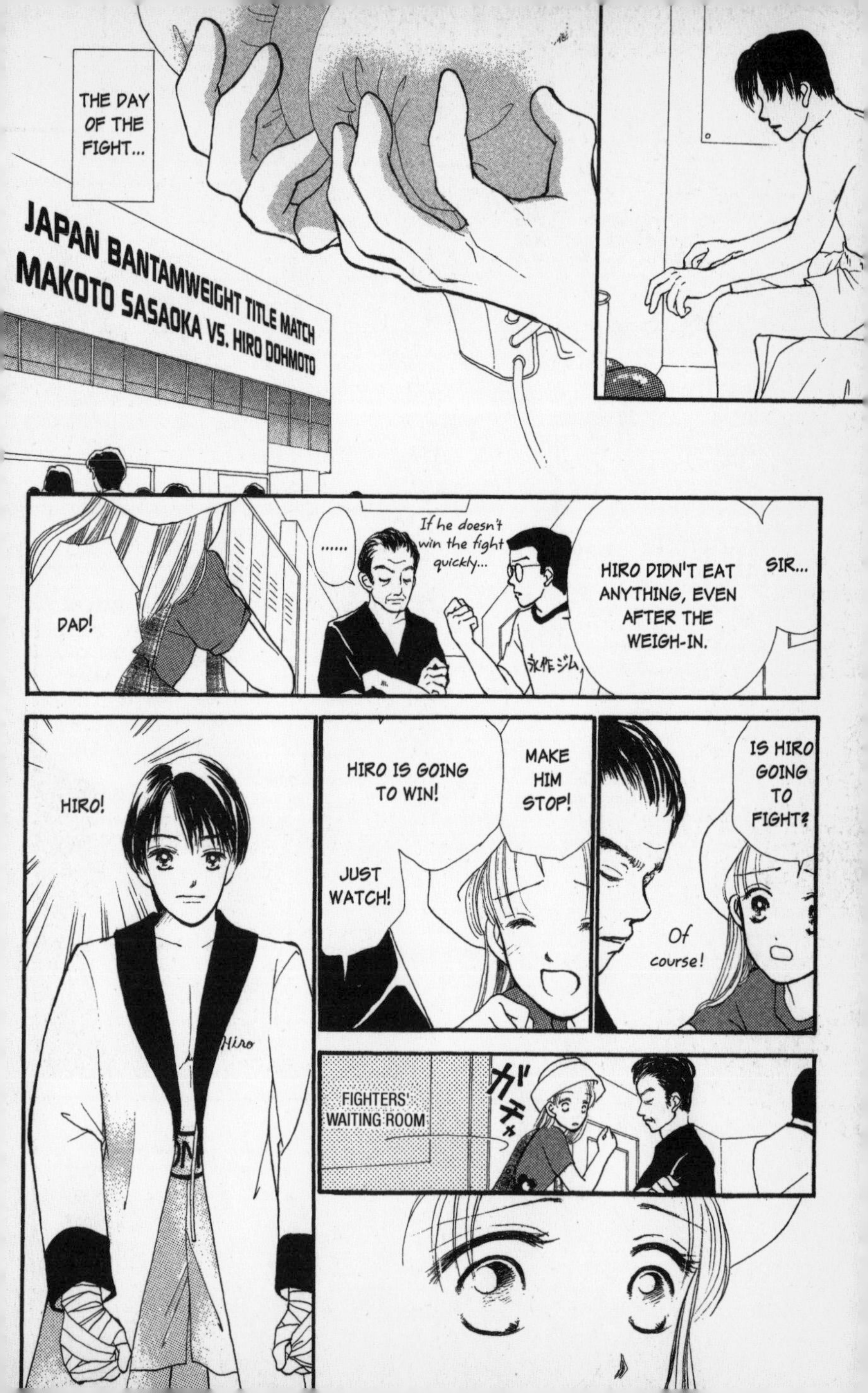
THE DAY OF THE FIGHT...
JAPAN BANTAMWEIGHT TITLE MATCH
MAKOTO SASAOKA VS. HIRO DOHMOTO
SIR...
HIRO DIDN'T EAT ANYTHING, EVEN AFTER THE WEIGH-IN.
永作ジム
If he doesn't win the fight quickly...
......
DAD!
IS HIRO GOING TO FIGHT?
Of course!
MAKE HIM STOP!
HIRO IS GOING TO WIN!
JUST WATCH!
ガチャ
FIGHTERS' WAITING ROOM
Hiro
HIRO!

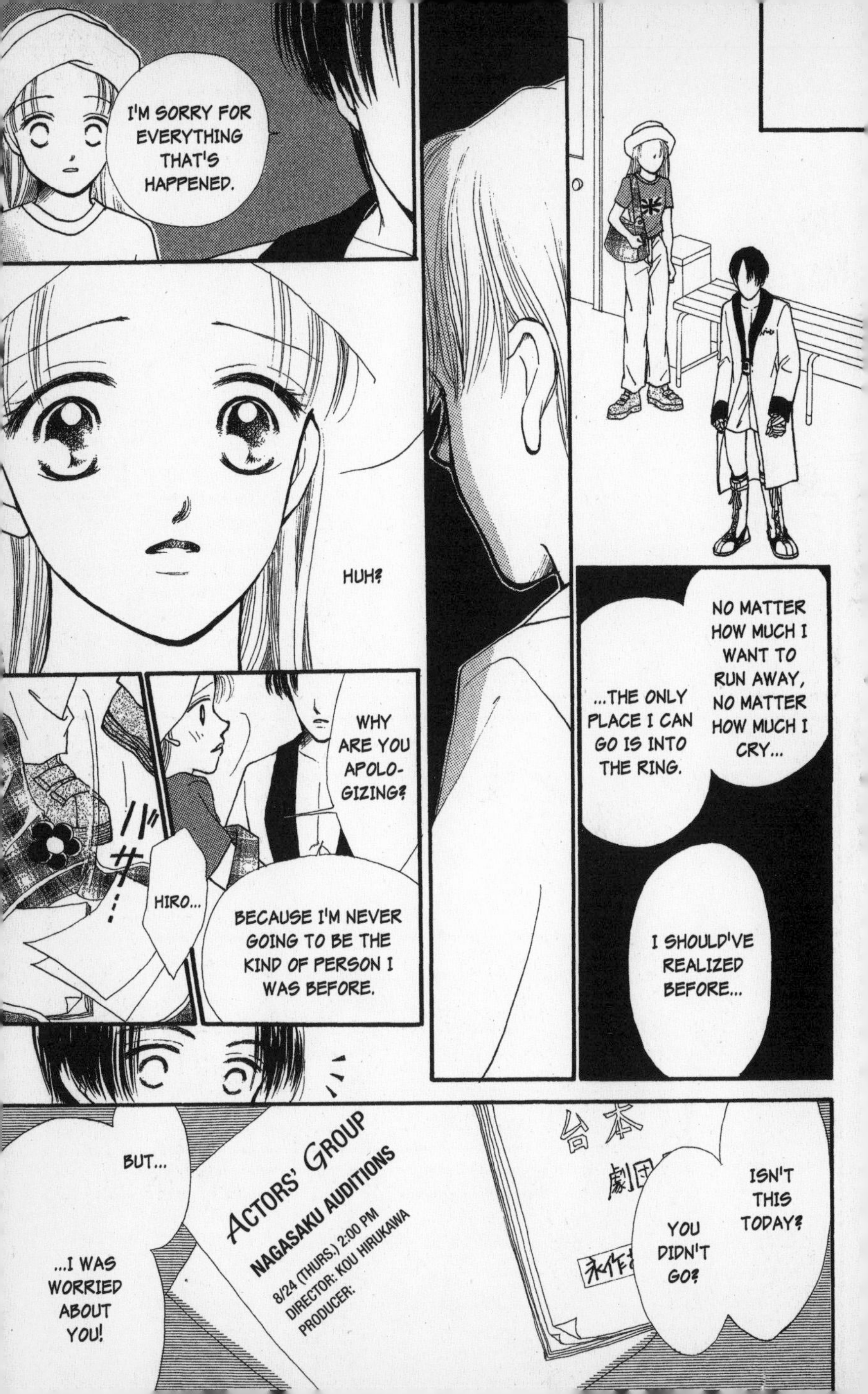
NO MATTER HOW MUCH I WANT TO RUN AWAY, NO MATTER HOW MUCH I CRY...
...THE ONLY PLACE I CAN GO IS INTO THE RING.
I SHOULD'VE REALIZED BEFORE...
I'M SORRY FOR EVERYTHING THAT'S HAPPENED.
HUH?
WHY ARE YOU APOLOGIZING?
BECAUSE I'M NEVER GOING TO BE THE KIND OF PERSON I WAS BEFORE.
HIRO...
ISN'T THIS TODAY?
YOU DIDN'T GO?
台本
劇団
ACTORS' GROUP
NAGASAKU AUDITIONS
8/24 (THURS.) 2:00 PM
DIRECTOR: KOU HIRUKAWA
PRODUCER:
BUT...
...I WAS WORRIED ABOUT YOU!

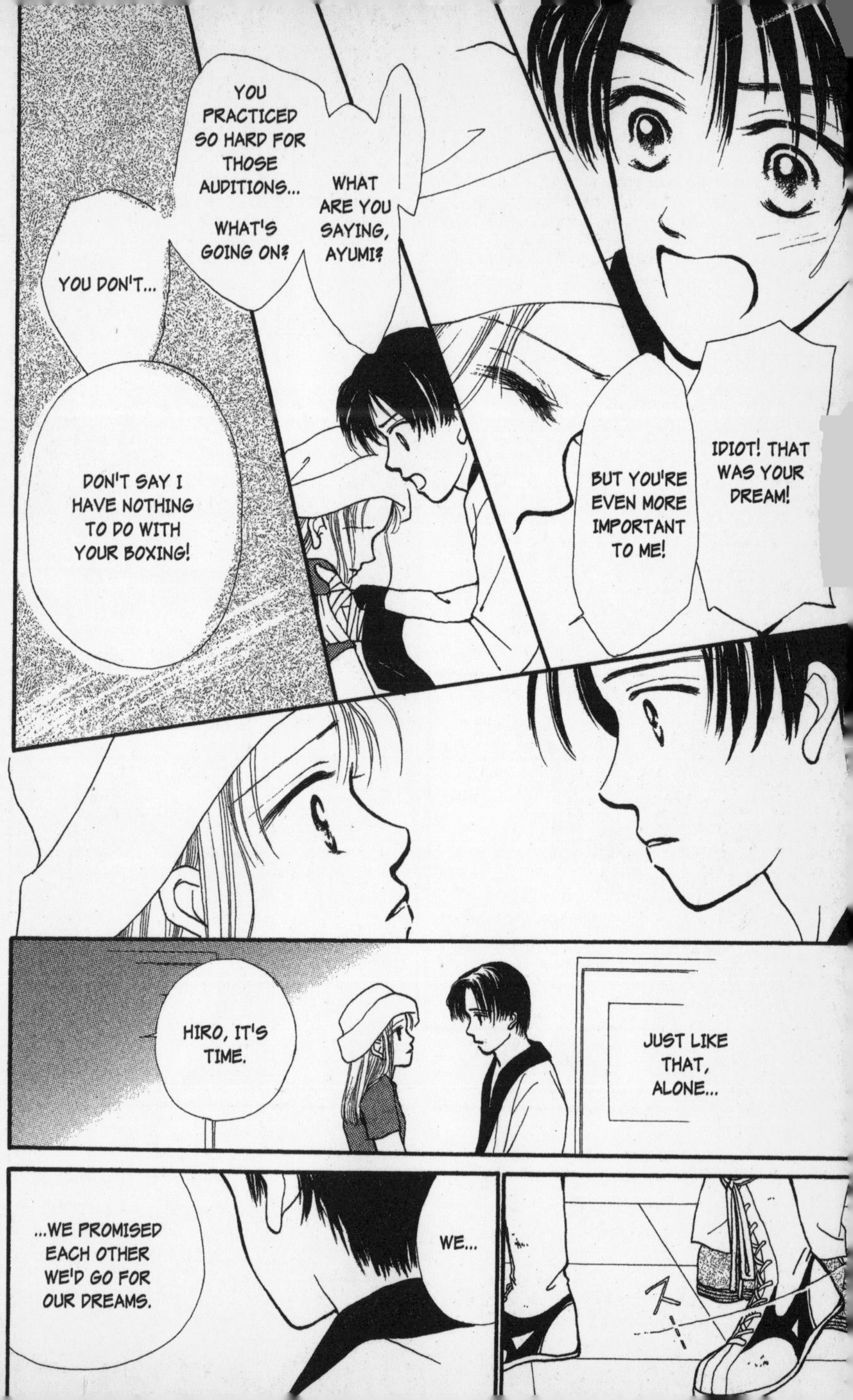
WHAT ARE YOU SAYING, AYUMI?
YOU PRACTICED SO HARD FOR THOSE AUDITIONS...
WHAT'S GOING ON?
IDIOT! THAT WAS YOUR DREAM!
BUT YOU'RE EVEN MORE IMPORTANT TO ME!
YOU DON'T...
DON'T SAY I HAVE NOTHING TO DO WITH YOUR BOXING!
JUST LIKE THAT, ALONE...
HIRO, IT'S TIME.
ス...
WE...
...WE PROMISED EACH OTHER WE'D GO FOR OUR DREAMS.

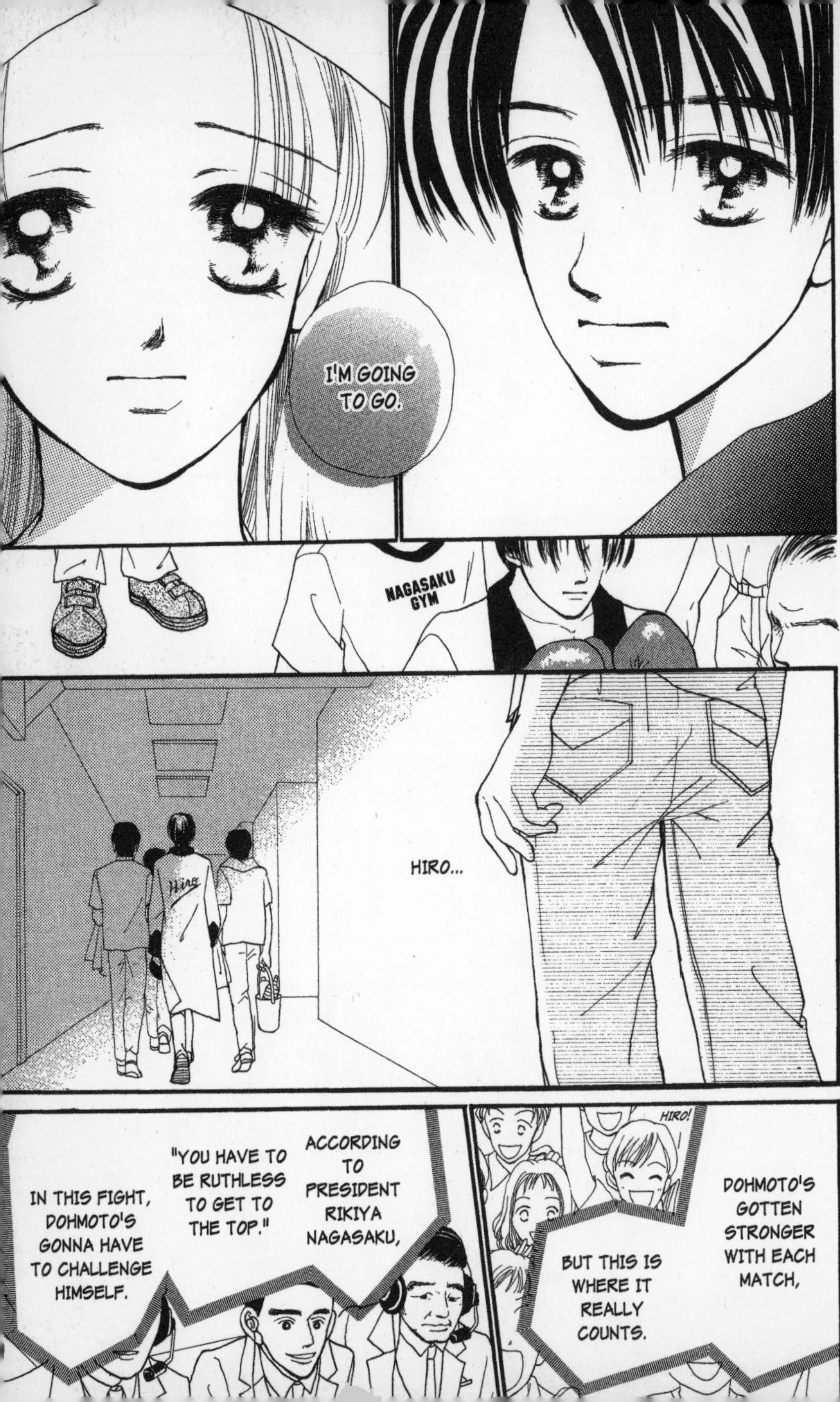
I'M GOING TO GO.
NAGASAKU GYM
HIRO...
HIRO!
DOHMOTO'S GOTTEN STRONGER WITH EACH MATCH,
BUT THIS IS WHERE IT REALLY COUNTS.
ACCORDING TO PRESIDENT RIKIYA NAGASAKU,
"YOU HAVE TO BE RUTHLESS TO GET TO THE TOP."
IN THIS FIGHT, DOHMOTO'S GONNA HAVE TO CHALLENGE HIMSELF.

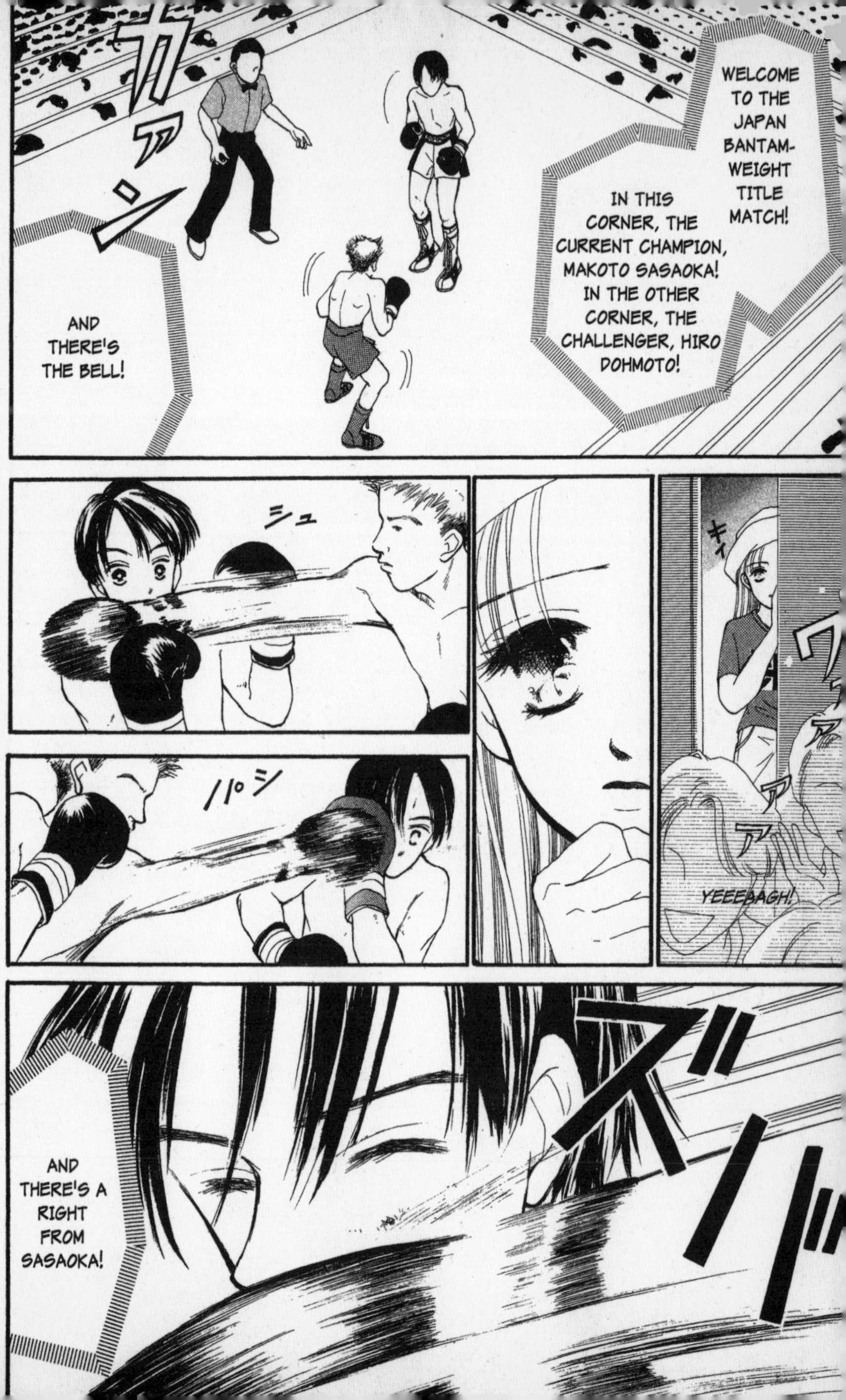
WELCOME TO THE JAPAN BANTAMWEIGHT TITLE MATCH!
IN THIS CORNER, THE CURRENT CHAMPION, MAKOTO SASAOKA! IN THE OTHER CORNER, THE CHALLENGER, HIRO DOHMOTO!
カァン
AND THERE'S THE BELL!
キィ
YEEEAAGH!
シュ
パシ
ズド
AND THERE'S A RIGHT FROM SASAOKA!

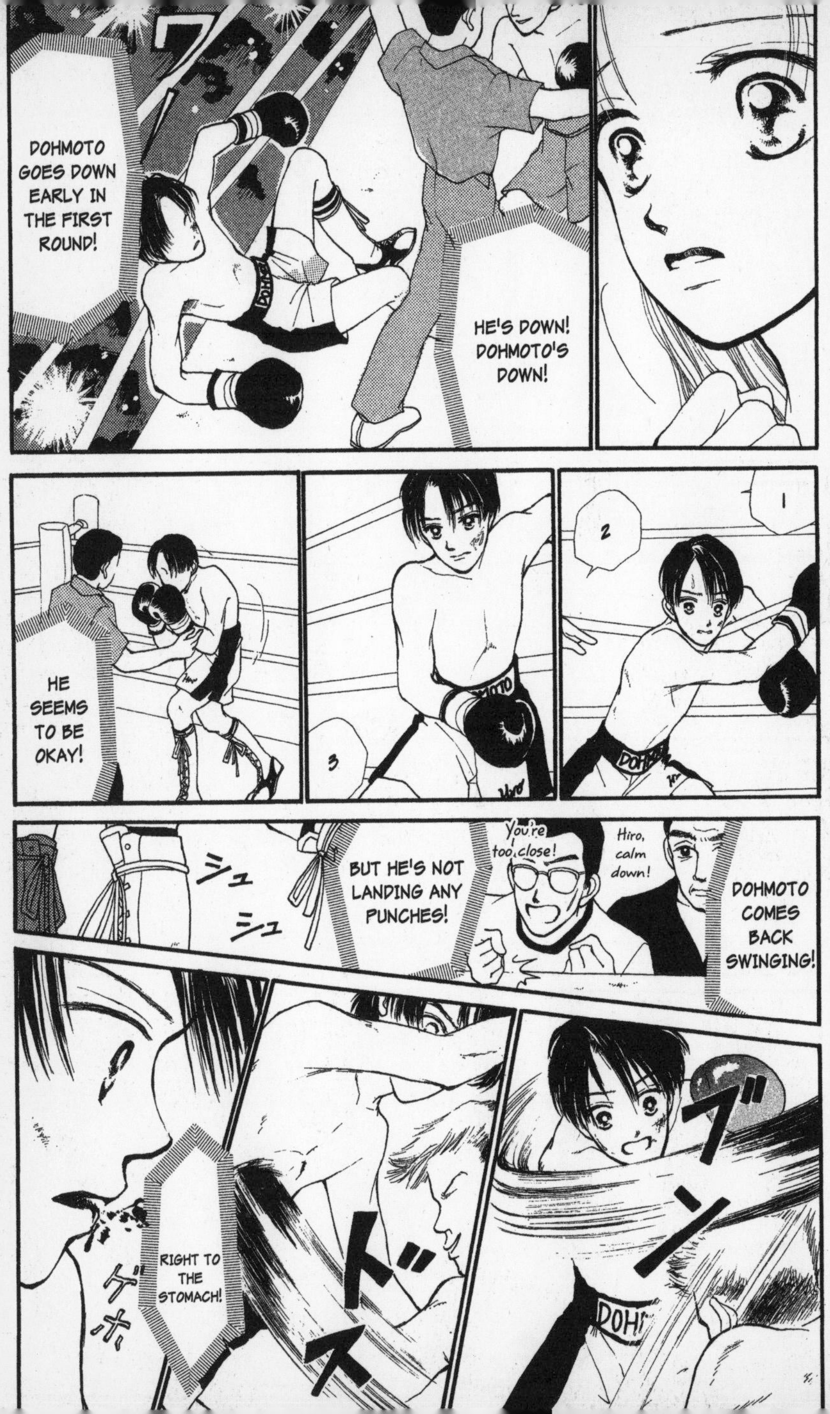
DOHMOTO GOES DOWN EARLY IN THE FIRST ROUND!
HE'S DOWN! DOHMOTO'S DOWN!
1
2
3
HE SEEMS TO BE OKAY!
DOHMOTO COMES BACK SWINGING!
Hiro, calm down!
You're too close!
BUT HE'S NOT LANDING ANY PUNCHES!
シュ
シュ
ブーン
ドス
RIGHT TO THE STOMACH!
ゲホ

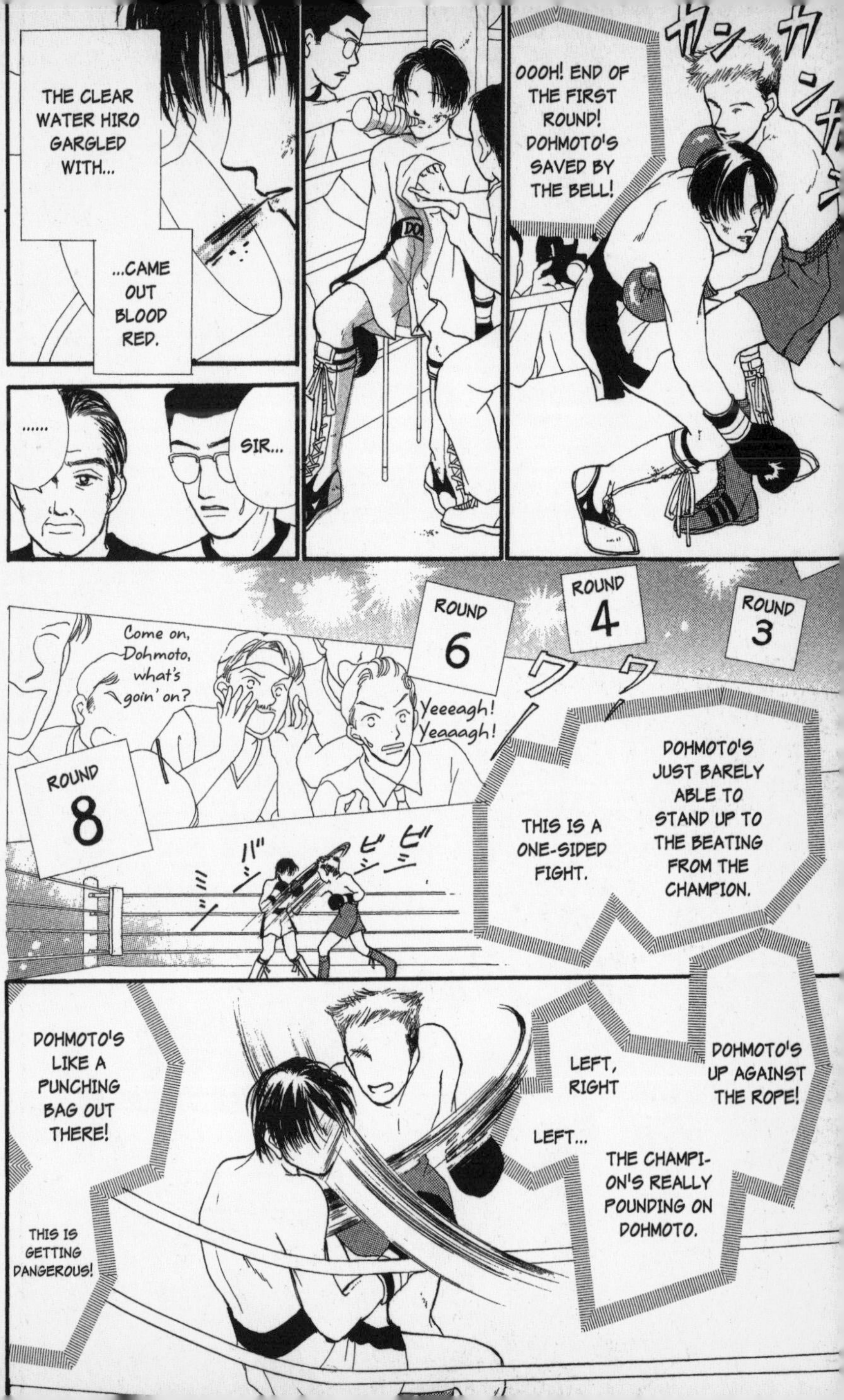
OOOH! END OF THE FIRST ROUND! DOHMOTO'S SAVED BY THE BELL!
THE CLEAR WATER HIRO GARGLED WITH...
...CAME OUT BLOOD RED.
SIR...
......
ROUND 3
ROUND 4
ROUND 6
DOHMOTO'S JUST BARELY ABLE TO STAND UP TO THE BEATING FROM THE CHAMPION.
THIS IS A ONE-SIDED FIGHT.
Yeeeagh! Yeaaagh!
Come on, Dohmoto, what's goin' on?
ROUND 8
DOHMOTO'S UP AGAINST THE ROPE!
LEFT, RIGHT
LEFT...
THE CHAMPI-ON'S REALLY POUNDING ON DOHMOTO.
DOHMOTO'S LIKE A PUNCHING BAG OUT THERE!
THIS IS GETTING DANGEROUS!

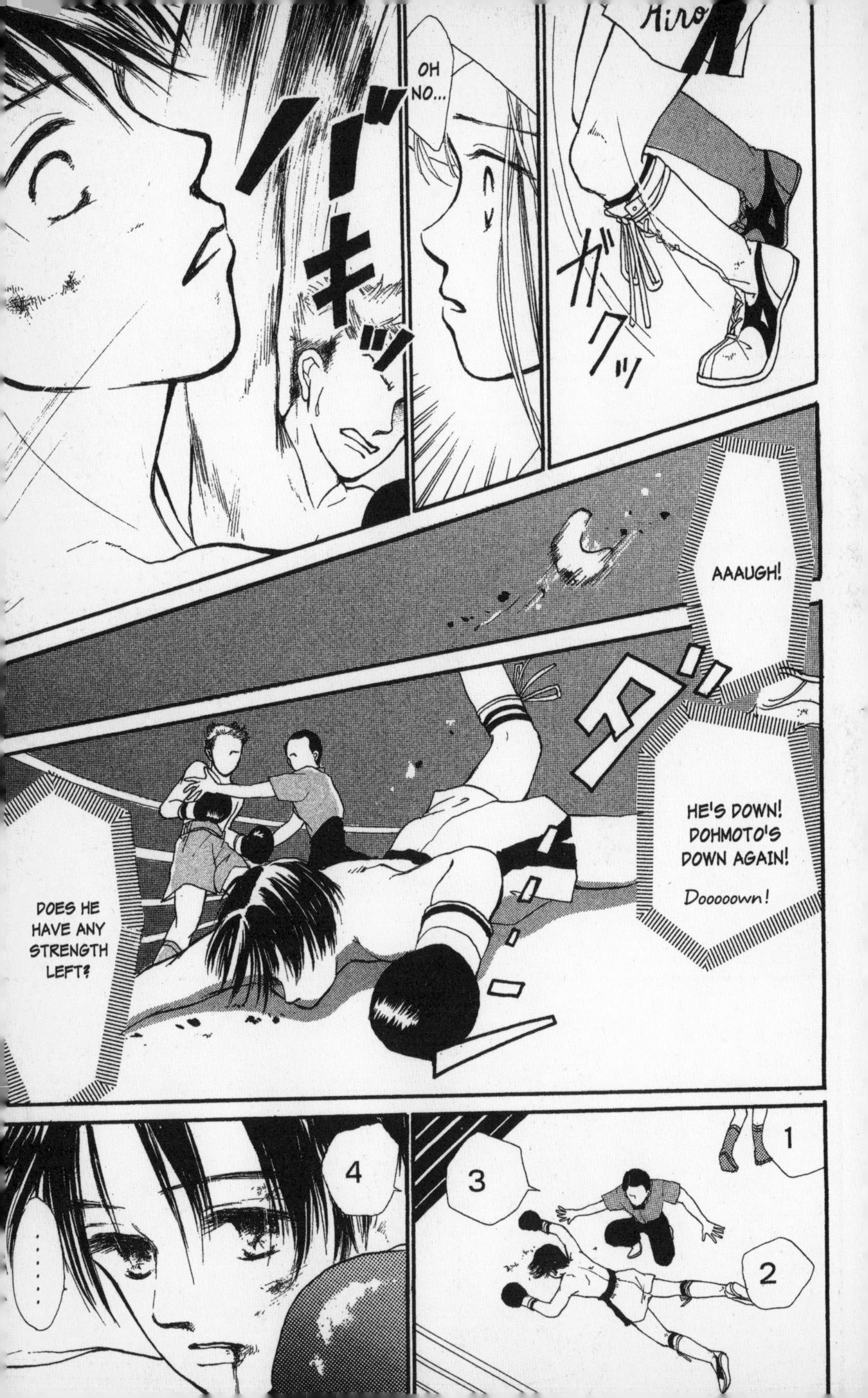
Hiro
ガクッ
OH NO...
AAAUGH!
ダーン
HE'S DOWN! DOHMOTO'S DOWN AGAIN!
Doooown!
DOES HE HAVE ANY STRENGTH LEFT?
1
2
3
4
......

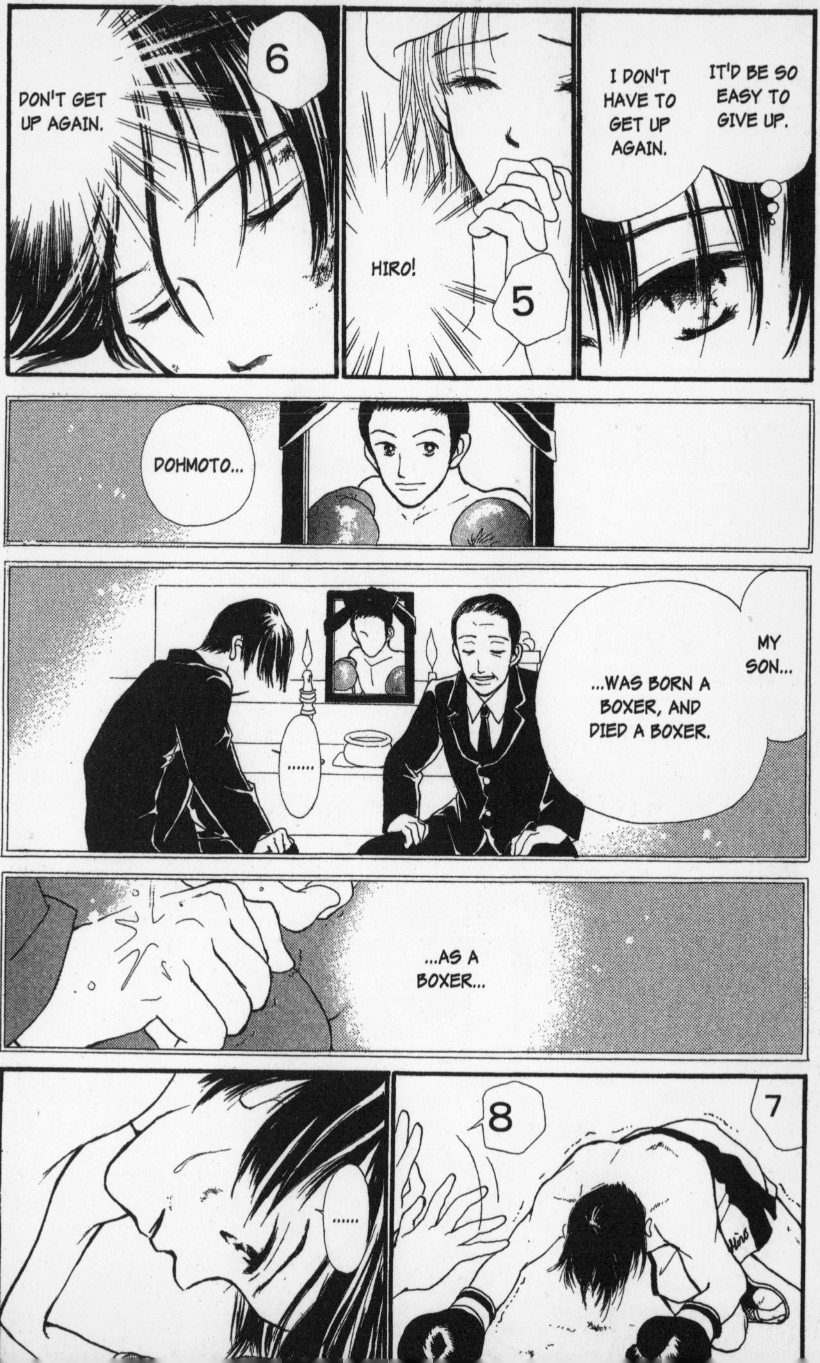
IT'D BE SO EASY TO GIVE UP.
I DON'T HAVE TO GET UP AGAIN.
HIRO!
5
6
DON'T GET UP AGAIN.
DOHMOTO...
MY SON...
...WAS BORN A BOXER, AND DIED A BOXER.
......
...AS A BOXER...
7
8
......

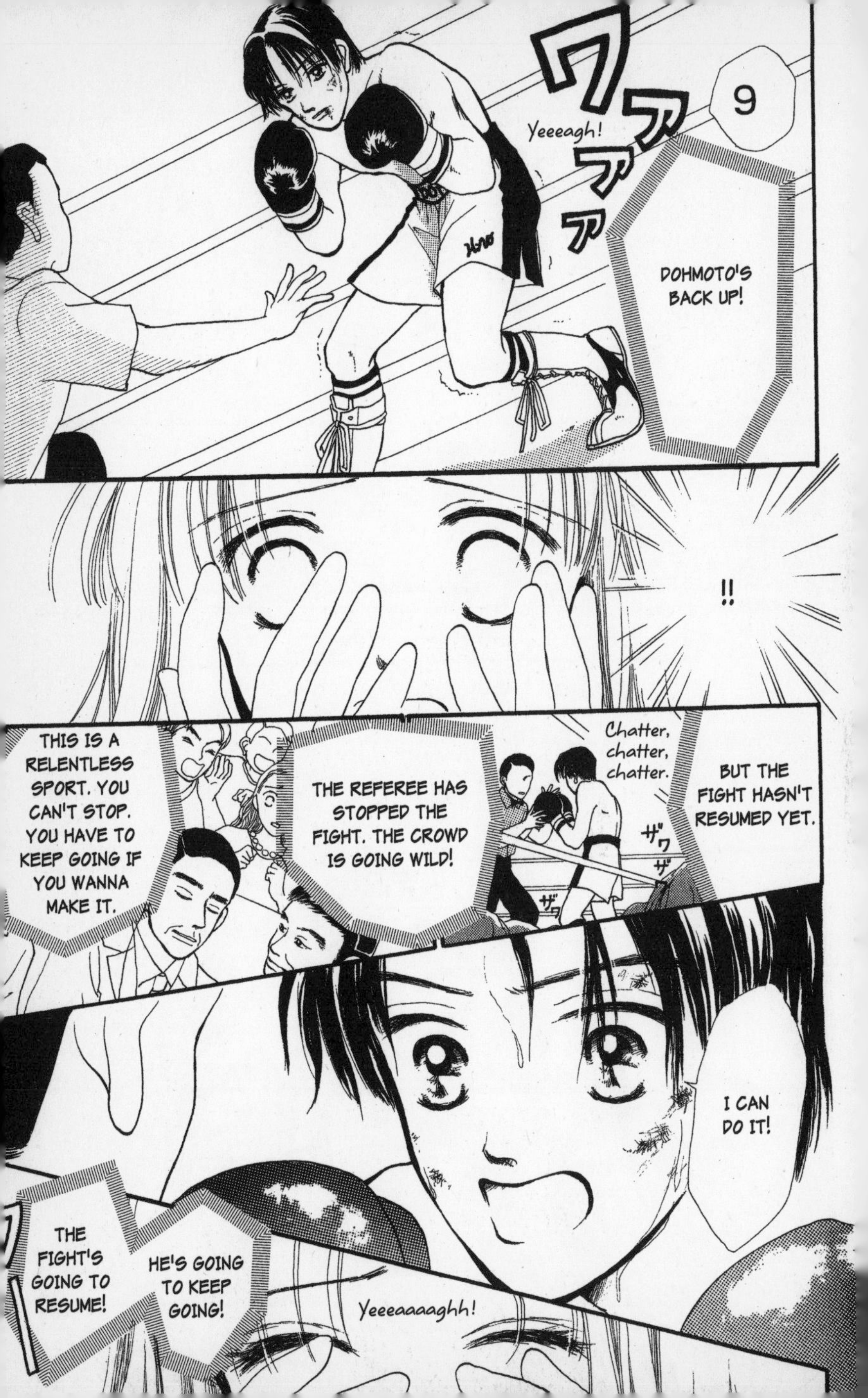
9
DOHMOTO'S BACK UP!
ワァァァ
Yeeeagh!
!!
BUT THE FIGHT HASN'T RESUMED YET.
Chatter, chatter, chatter.
ザワ ザ
ザワ
THE REFEREE HAS STOPPED THE FIGHT. THE CROWD IS GOING WILD!
THIS IS A RELENTLESS SPORT. YOU CAN'T STOP. YOU HAVE TO KEEP GOING IF YOU WANNA MAKE IT.
I CAN DO IT!
Yeeeaaaaghh!
HE'S GOING TO KEEP GOING!
THE FIGHT'S GOING TO RESUME!

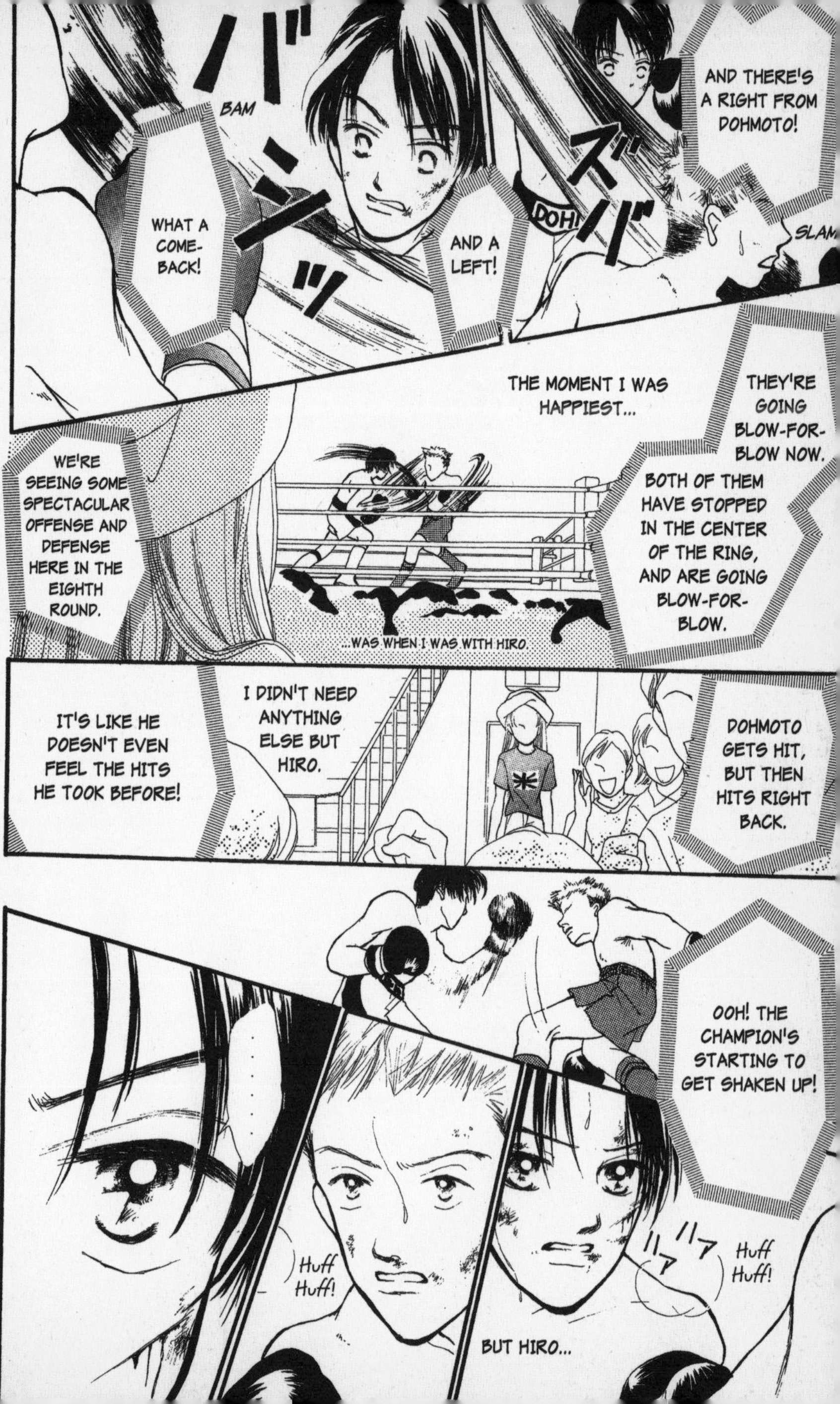
AND THERE'S A RIGHT FROM DOHMOTO!
ズバ
SLAM
DOH
AND A LEFT!
WHAT A COME-BACK!
バシッ
BAM
THEY'RE GOING BLOW-FOR-BLOW NOW.
THE MOMENT I WAS HAPPIEST...
BOTH OF THEM HAVE STOPPED IN THE CENTER OF THE RING, AND ARE GOING BLOW-FOR-BLOW.
WE'RE SEEING SOME SPECTACULAR OFFENSE AND DEFENSE HERE IN THE EIGHTH ROUND.
...WAS WHEN I WAS WITH HIRO
DOHMOTO GETS HIT, BUT THEN HITS RIGHT BACK.
I DIDN'T NEED ANYTHING ELSE BUT HIRO.
IT'S LIKE HE DOESN'T EVEN FEEL THE HITS HE TOOK BEFORE!
OOH! THE CHAMPION'S STARTING TO GET SHAKEN UP!
ハァ ハァ
Huff Huff!
BUT HIRO...
Huff Huff!
......

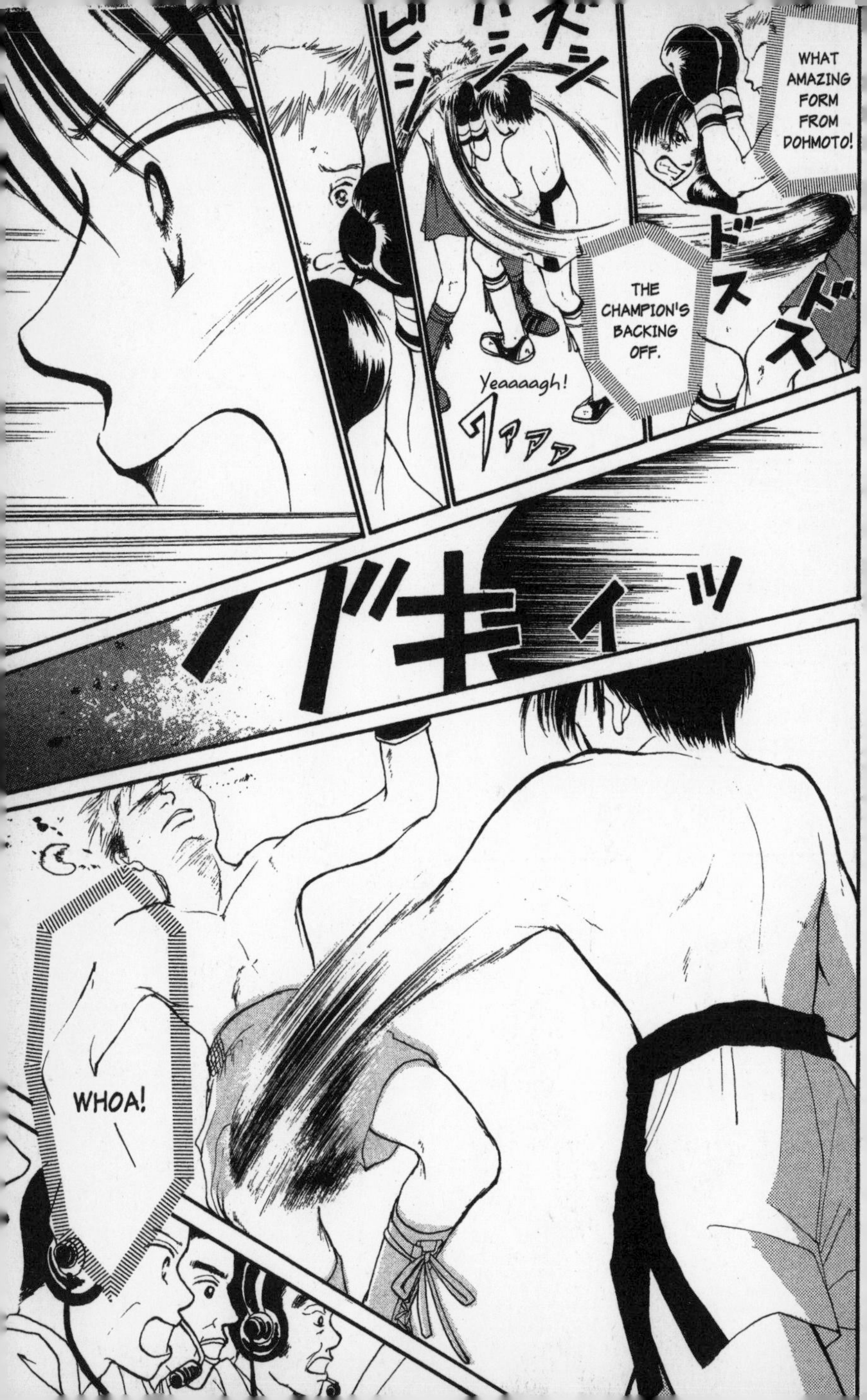

WHAT AMAZING FORM FROM DOHMOTO!
ドス
ドス
THE CHAMPION'S BACKING OFF.
ズシ
ハシ
ビシ
Yeaaaagh!
ワァァァ
ドキィッ
WHOA!

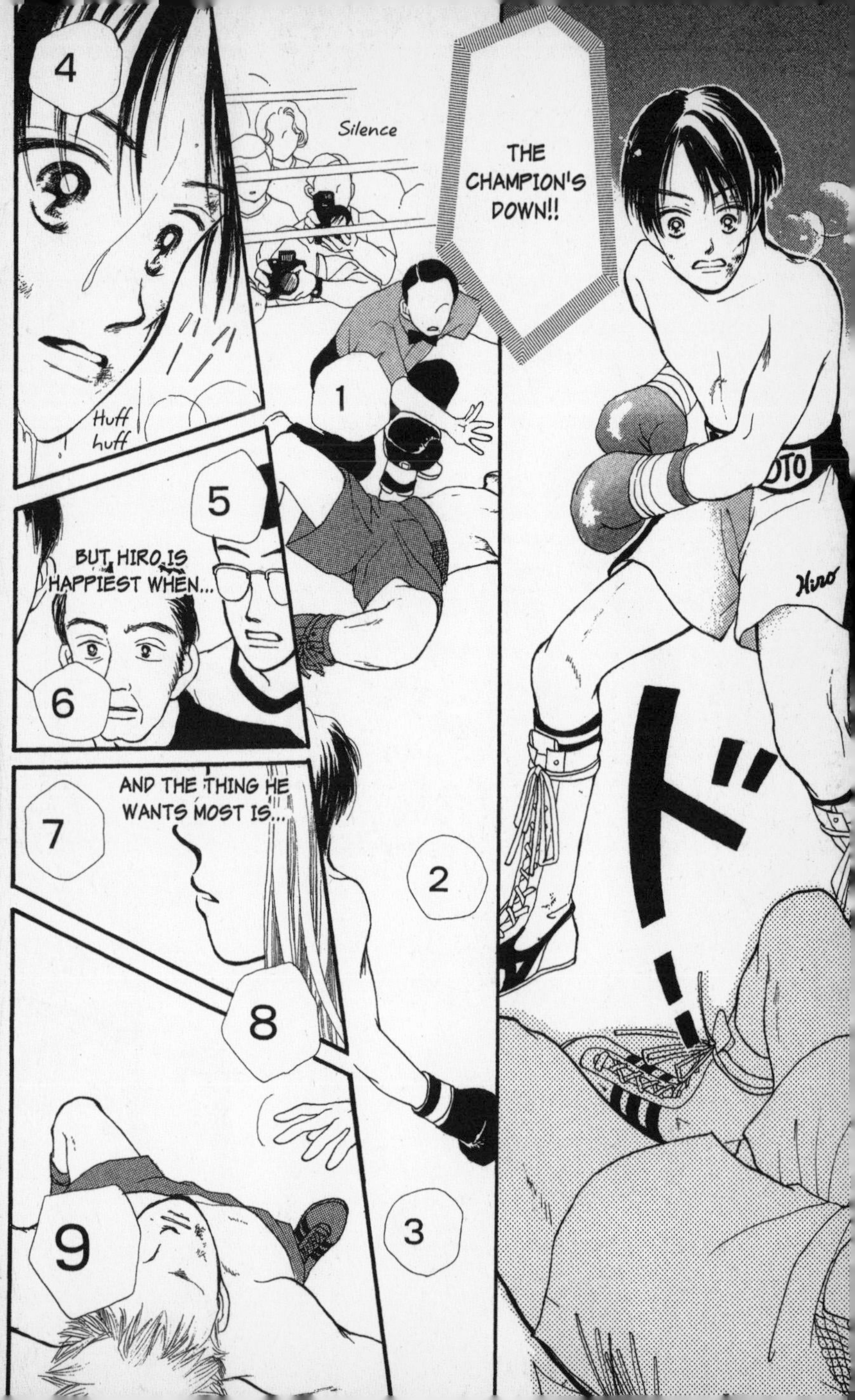
THE CHAMPION'S DOWN!!
ド
1
2
3
Silence
4
Huff huff
5
BUT HIRO IS HAPPIEST WHEN...
6
AND THE THING HE WANTS MOST IS...
7
8
9

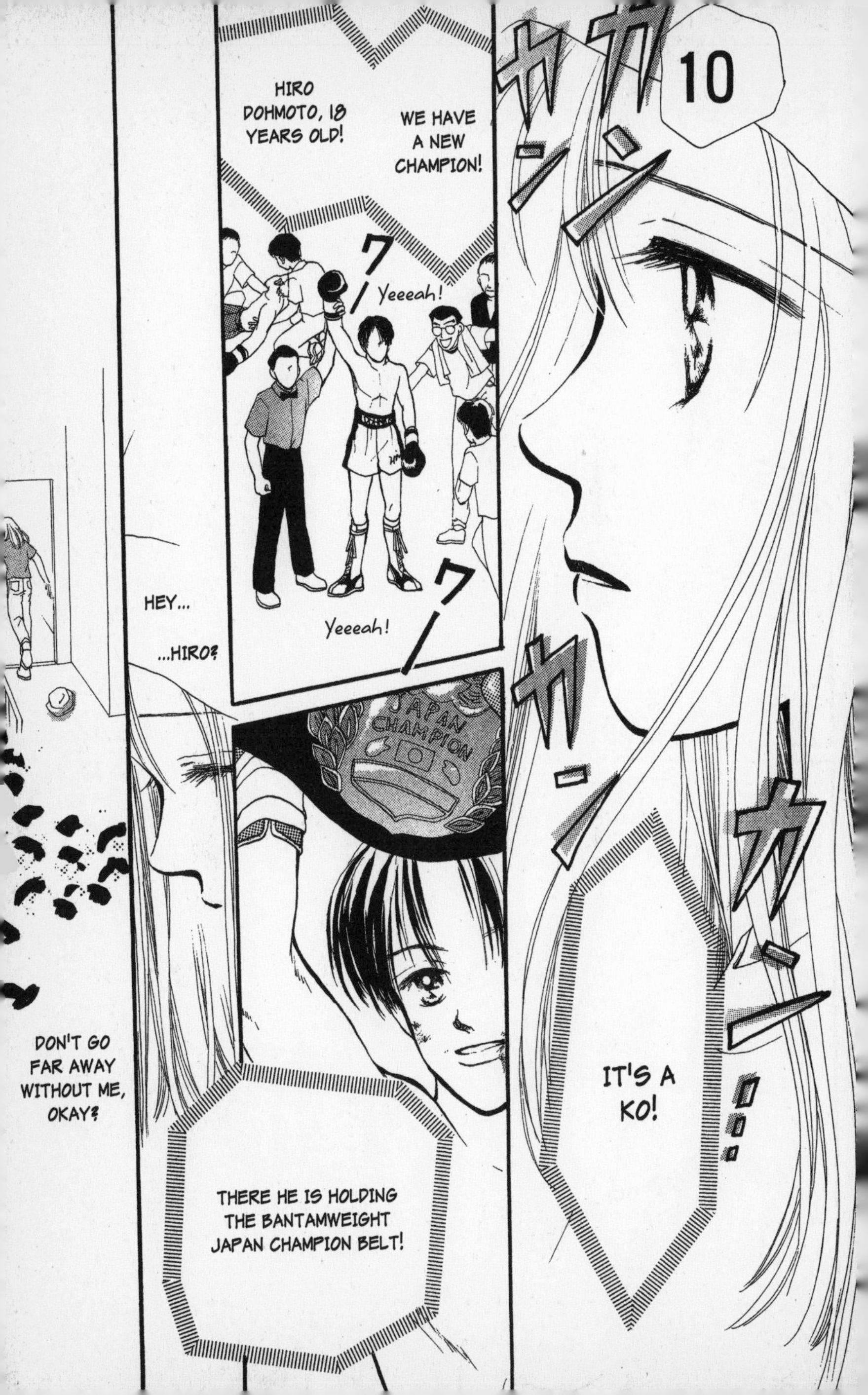
10
IT'S A KO!
WE HAVE A NEW CHAMPION!
HIRO DOHMOTO, 18 YEARS OLD!
Yeeeah!
Yeeeah!
JAPAN CHAMPION
THERE HE IS HOLDING THE BANTAMWEIGHT JAPAN CHAMPION BELT!
HEY...
...HIRO?
DON'T GO FAR AWAY WITHOUT ME, OKAY?

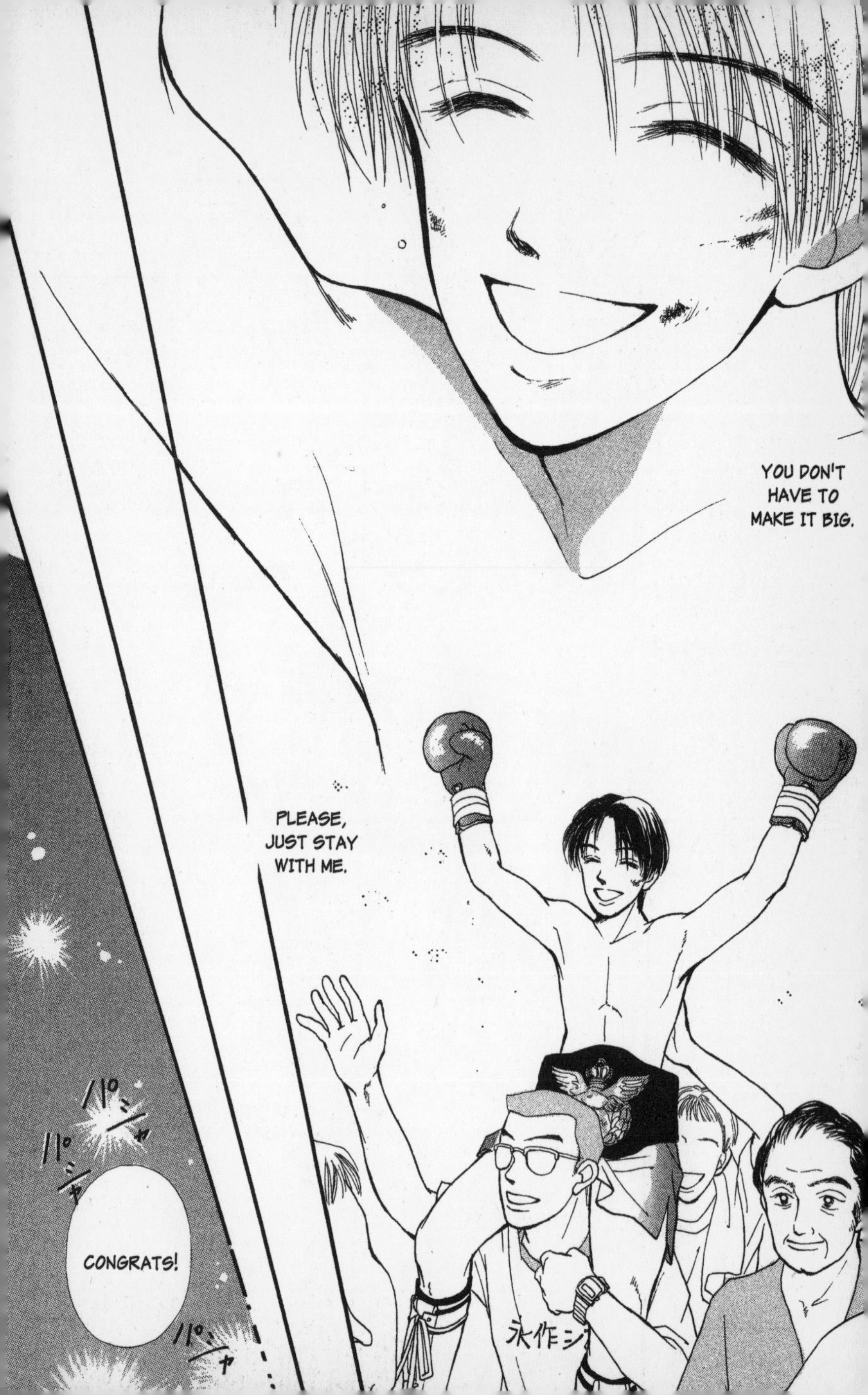
YOU DON'T HAVE TO MAKE IT BIG.
PLEASE, JUST STAY WITH ME.
永作ジ
パシャ
パシャ
CONGRATS!
パシャ

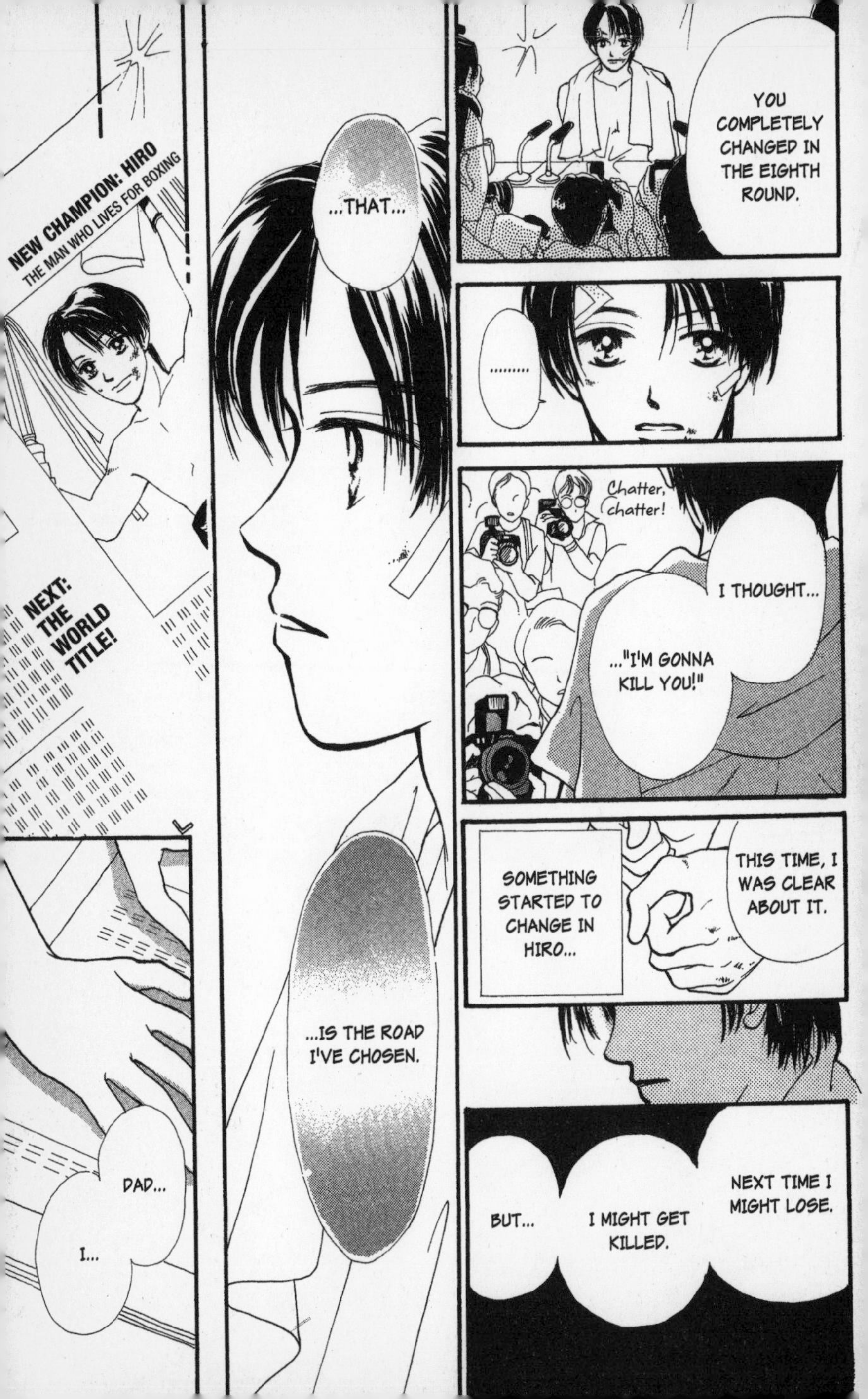
YOU COMPLETELY CHANGED IN THE EIGHTH ROUND.
....
Chatter, chatter!
I THOUGHT...
..."I'M GONNA KILL YOU!"
THIS TIME, I WAS CLEAR ABOUT IT.
SOMETHING STARTED TO CHANGE IN HIRO...
NEXT TIME I MIGHT LOSE.
I MIGHT GET KILLED.
BUT...
...THAT...
...IS THE ROAD I'VE CHOSEN.
NEW CHAMPION: HIRO
THE MAN WHO LIVES FOR BOXING
NEXT: THE WORLD TITLE!
DAD...
I...

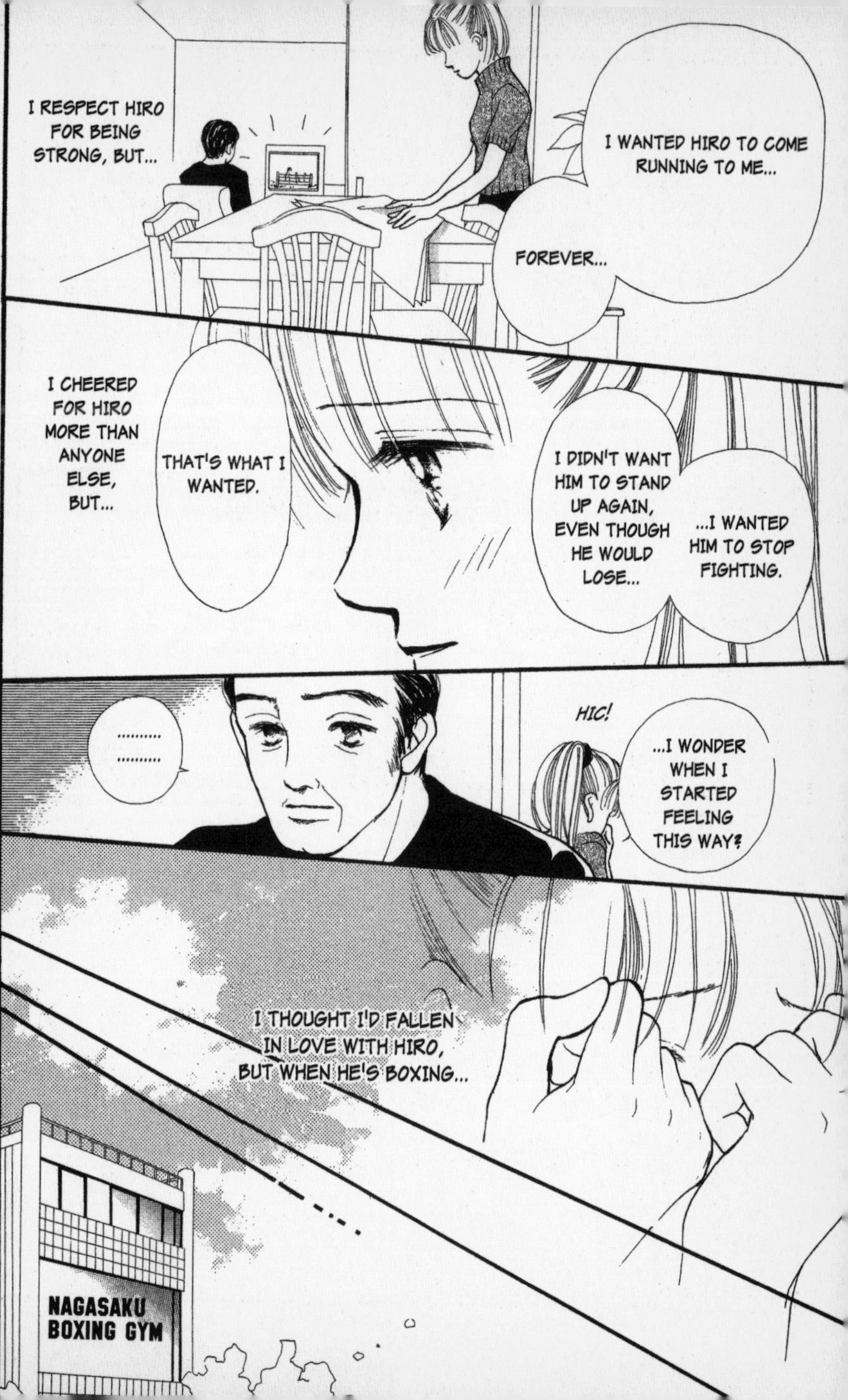
I WANTED HIRO TO COME RUNNING TO ME...
FOREVER...
I RESPECT HIRO FOR BEING STRONG, BUT...
...I WANTED HIM TO STOP FIGHTING.
I DIDN'T WANT HIM TO STAND UP AGAIN, EVEN THOUGH HE WOULD LOSE...
THAT'S WHAT I WANTED.
I CHEERED FOR HIRO MORE THAN ANYONE ELSE, BUT...
HIC!
...I WONDER WHEN I STARTED FEELING THIS WAY?
....
I THOUGHT I'D FALLEN IN LOVE WITH HIRO, BUT WHEN HE'S BOXING...
NAGASAKU BOXING GYM

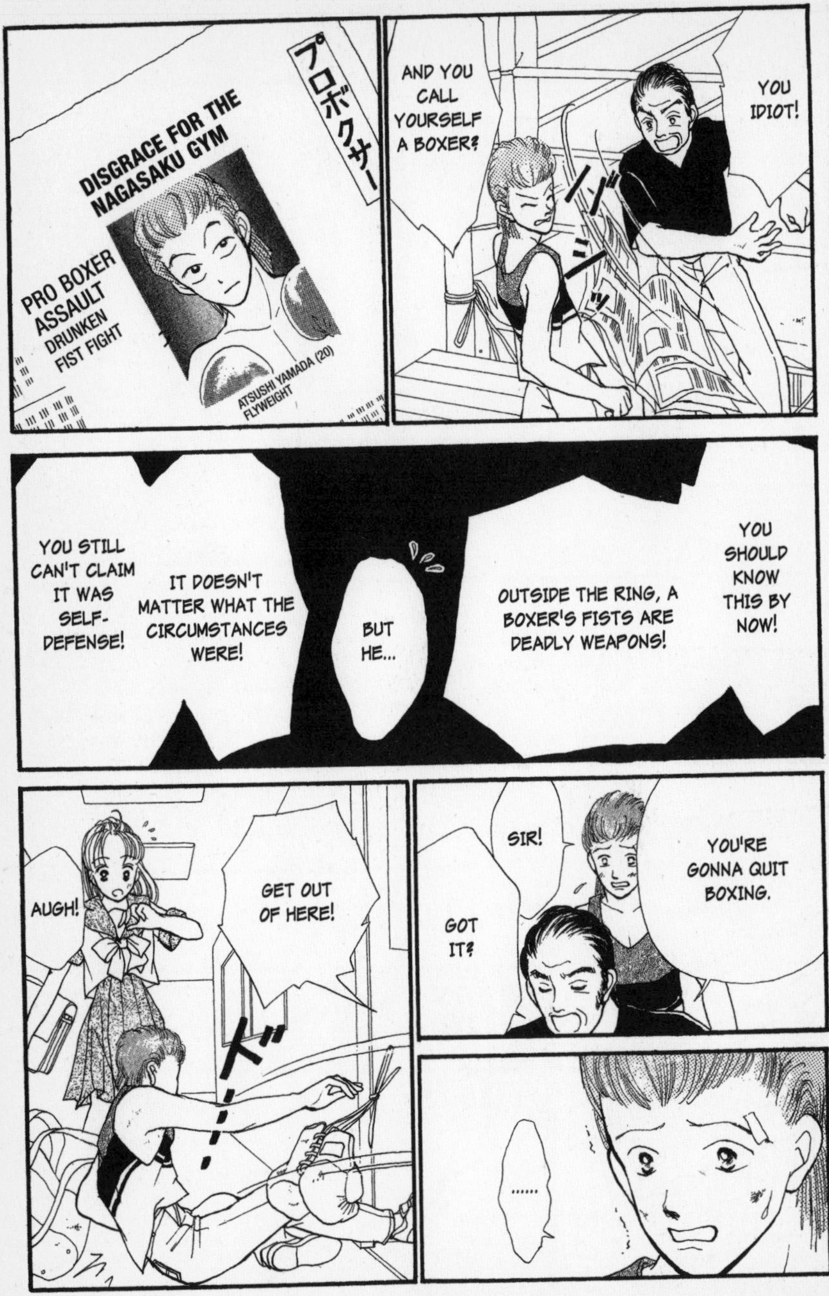

YOU IDIOT!
AND YOU CALL YOURSELF A BOXER?
プロボクサー
DISGRACE FOR THE NAGASAKU GYM
PRO BOXER ASSAULT
DRUNKEN FIST FIGHT
ATSUSHI YAMADA (20) FLYWEIGHT
YOU SHOULD KNOW THIS BY NOW!
OUTSIDE THE RING, A BOXER'S FISTS ARE DEADLY WEAPONS!
BUT HE...
IT DOESN'T MATTER WHAT THE CIRCUMSTANCES WERE!
YOU STILL CAN'T CLAIM IT WAS SELF-DEFENSE!
YOU'RE GONNA QUIT BOXING.
SIR!
GOT IT?
......
GET OUT OF HERE!
AUGH!

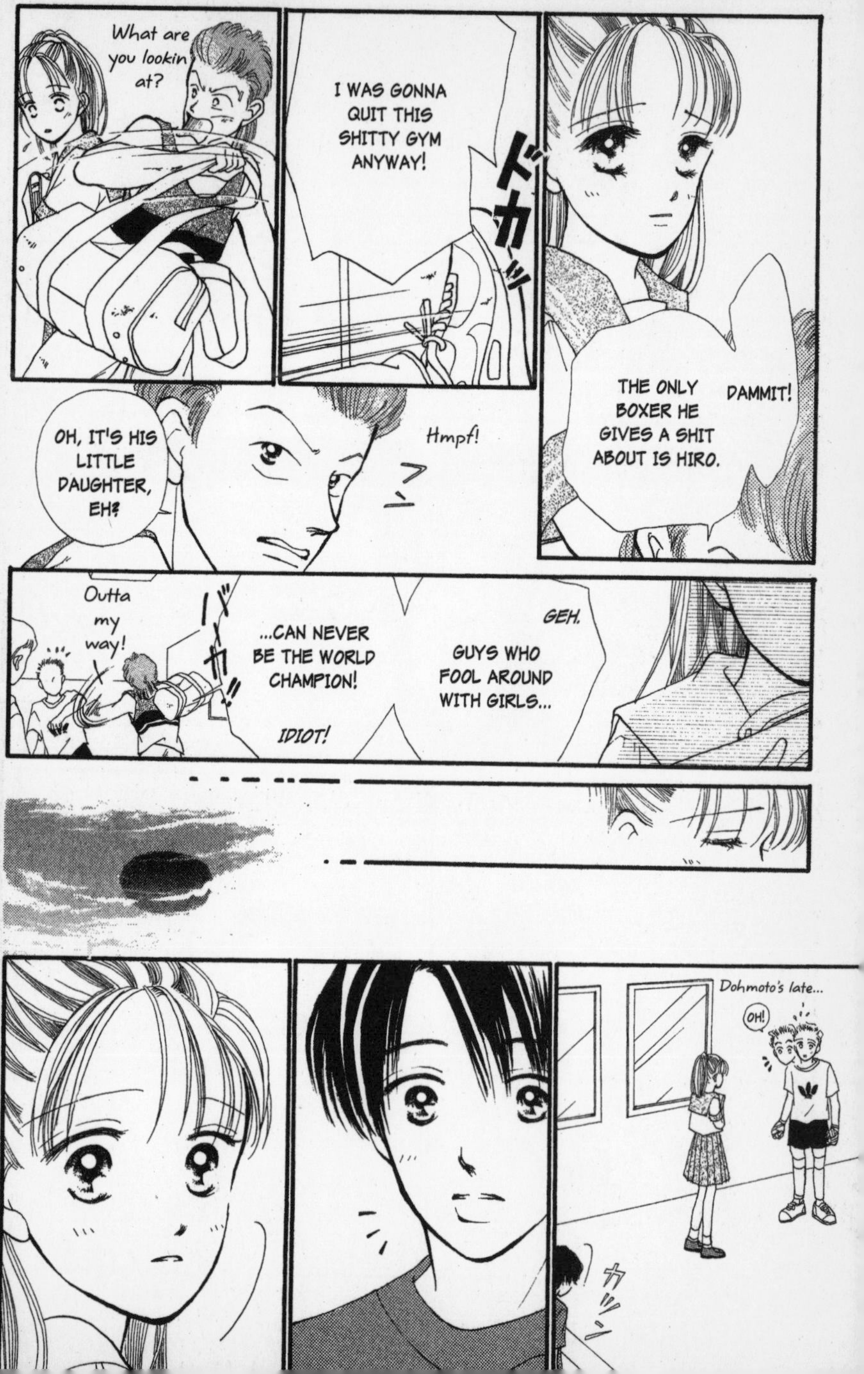
DAMMIT!
THE ONLY BOXER HE GIVES A SHIT ABOUT IS HIRO.
I WAS GONNA QUIT THIS SHITTY GYM ANYWAY!
ドカーッ
What are you lookin at?
OH, IT'S HIS LITTLE DAUGHTER, EH?
Hmpf!
GEH.
GUYS WHO FOOL AROUND WITH GIRLS...
...CAN NEVER BE THE WORLD CHAMPION!
IDIOT!
ドガッ!!
Outta my way!
Dohmoto's late...
OH!
カツー

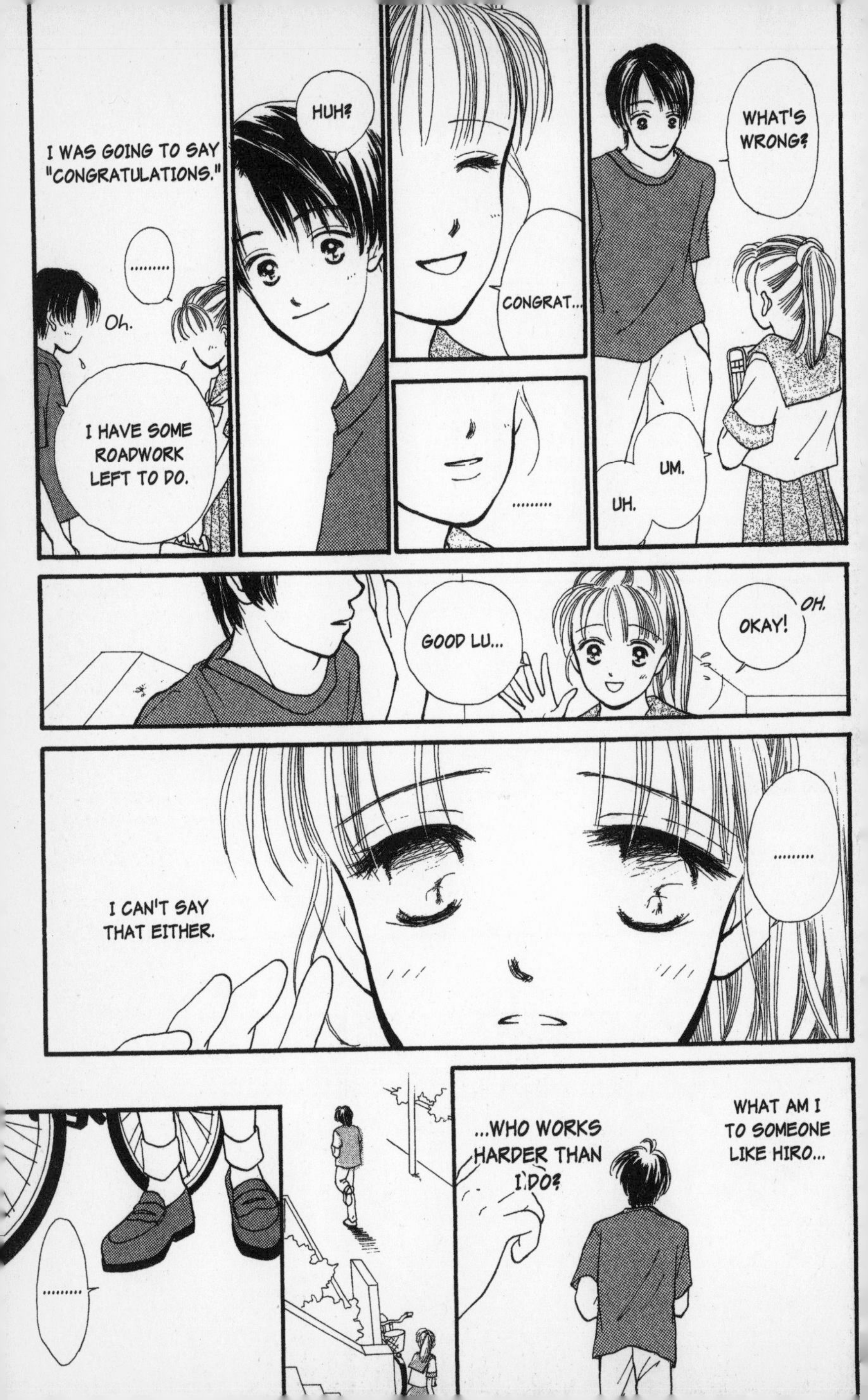
WHAT'S WRONG?
UM.
UH.
CONGRAT...
....
HUH?
I WAS GOING TO SAY "CONGRATULATIONS."
....
Oh.
I HAVE SOME ROADWORK LEFT TO DO.
OH.
OKAY!
GOOD LU...
....
I CAN'T SAY THAT EITHER.
WHAT AM I TO SOMEONE LIKE HIRO...
...WHO WORKS HARDER THAN I DO?
....

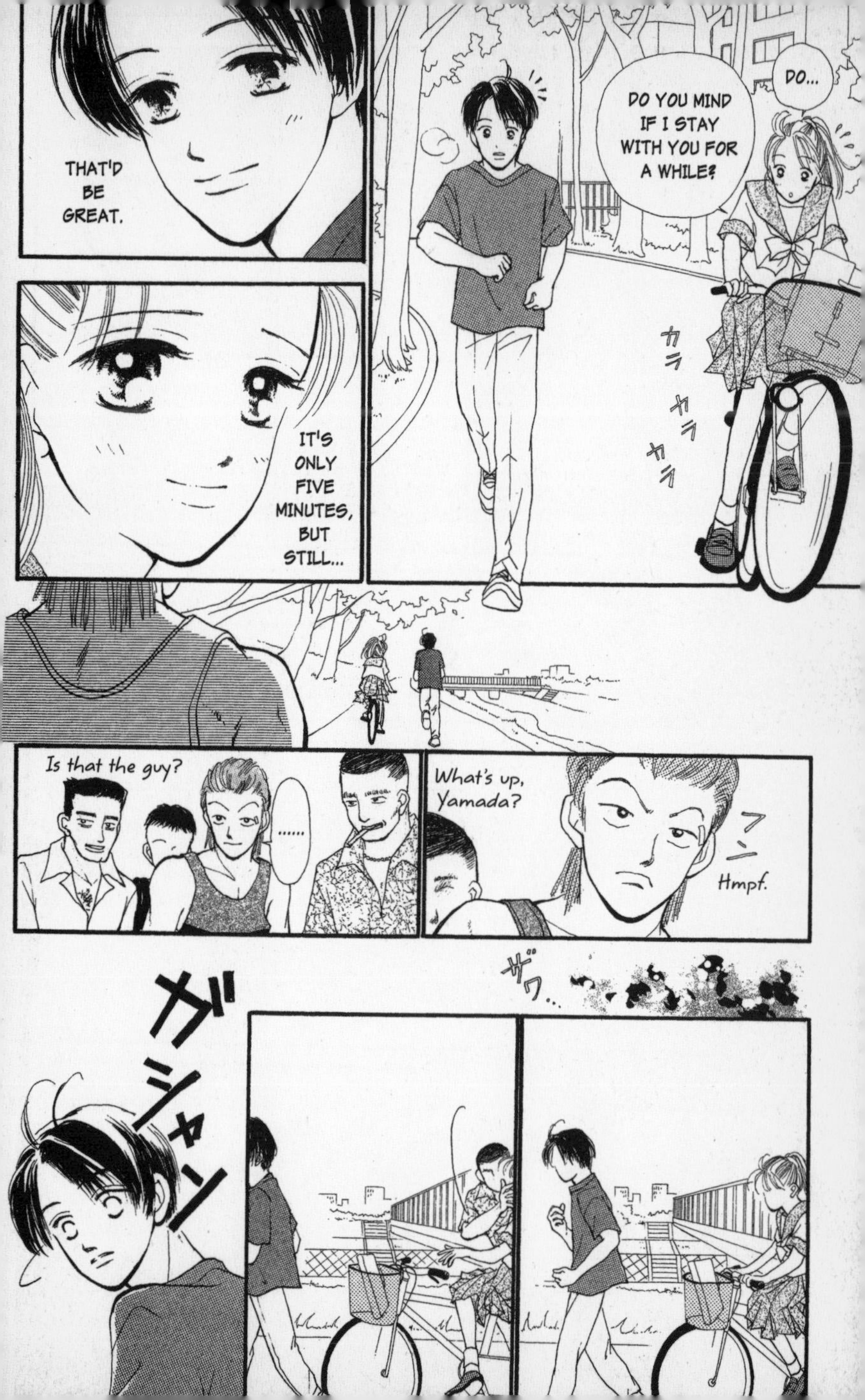
DO...
DO YOU MIND IF I STAY WITH YOU FOR A WHILE?
カラ カラ カラ
THAT'D BE GREAT.
IT'S ONLY FIVE MINUTES, BUT STILL...
What's up, Yamada?
フン
Hmpf.
Is that the guy?
......
ザワ...
ガシャン

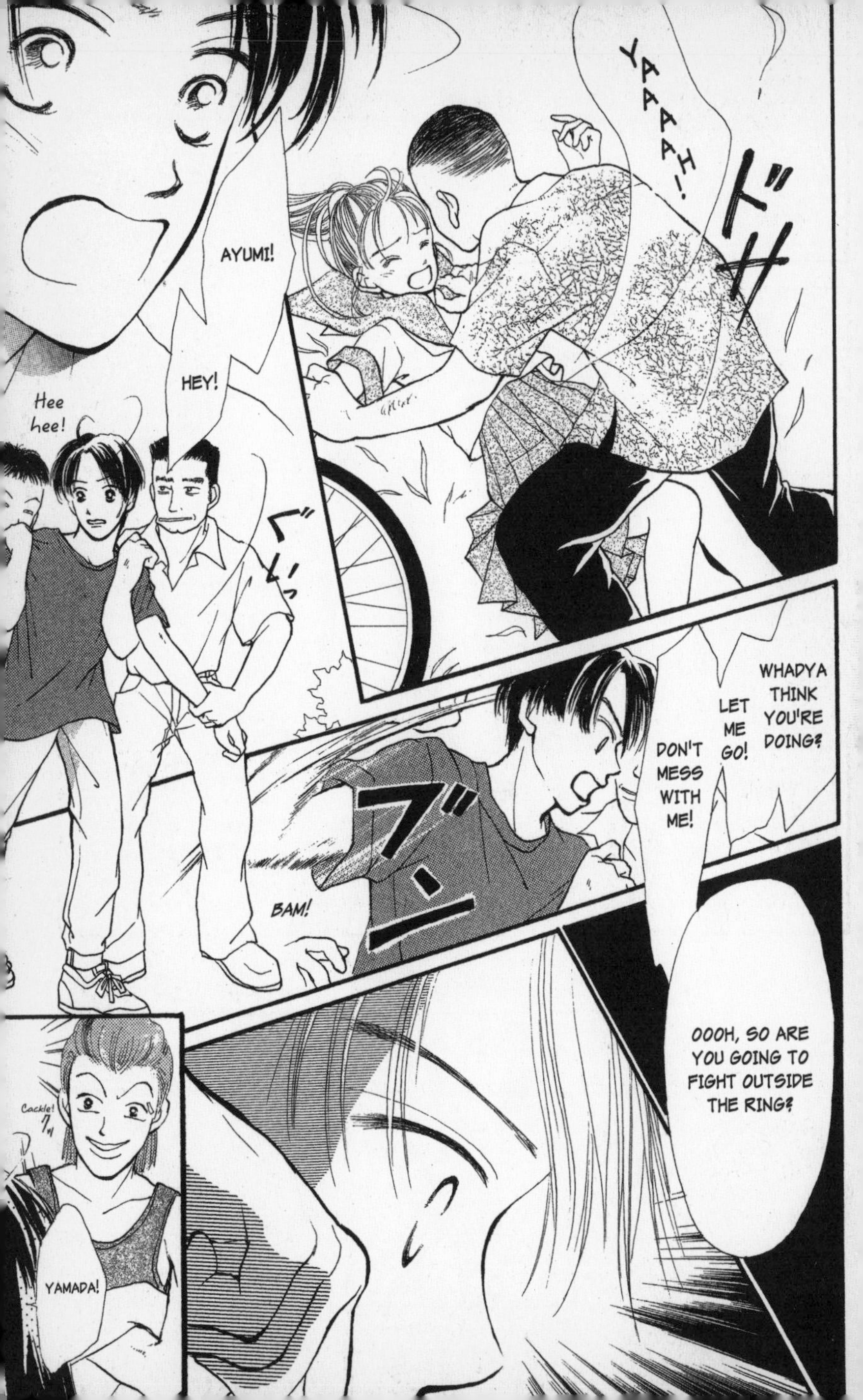
YAAAAAH!
ドサ
AYUMI!
WHADYA THINK YOU'RE DOING?
LET ME GO!
DON'T MESS WITH ME!
ブン
BAM!
HEY!
ぐいっ
Hee hee!
OOOH, SO ARE YOU GOING TO FIGHT OUTSIDE THE RING?
Cackle!
YAMADA!

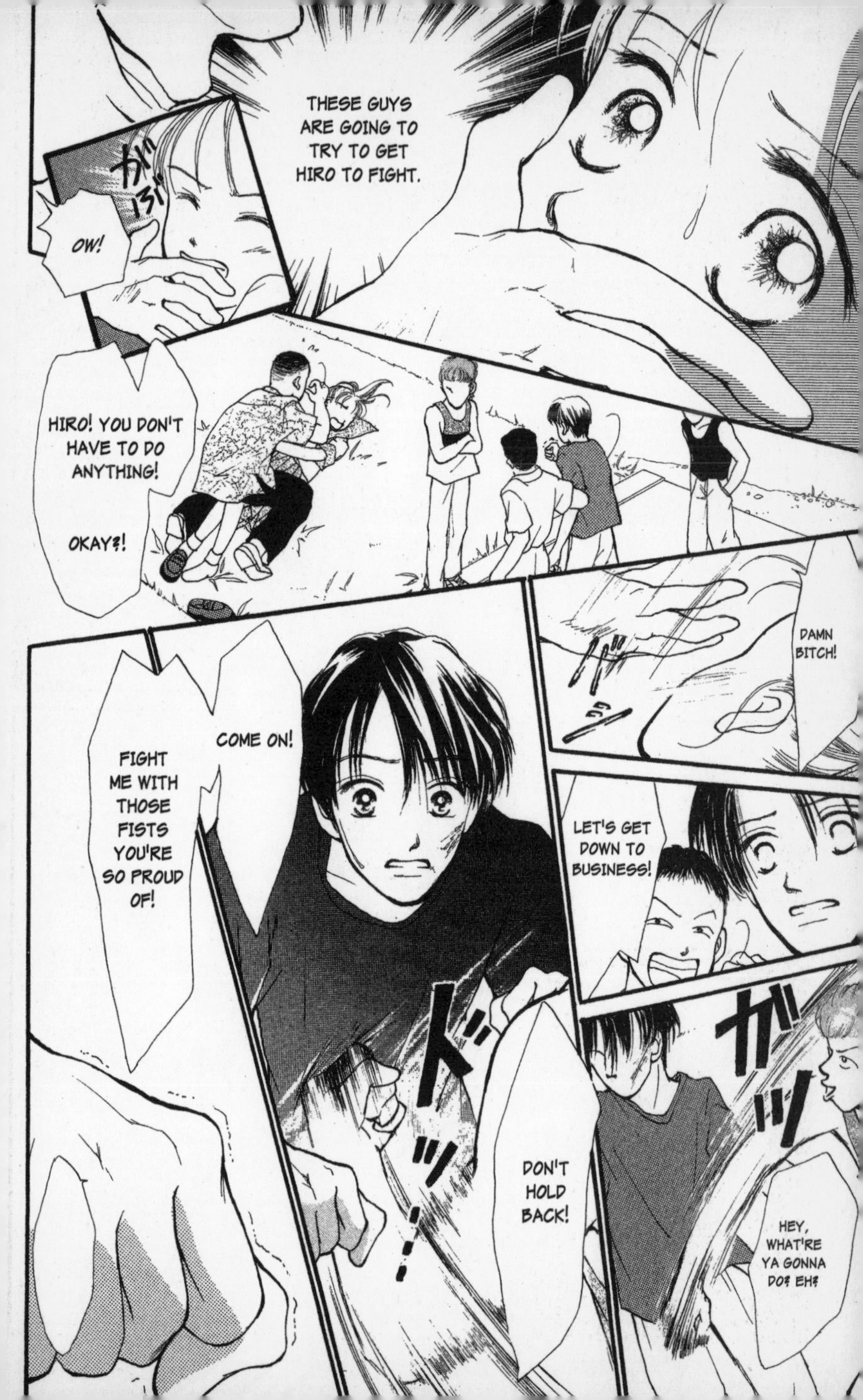
THESE GUYS ARE GOING TO TRY TO GET HIRO TO FIGHT.
OW!
HIRO! YOU DON'T HAVE TO DO ANYTHING!
OKAY?!
DAMN BITCH!
LET'S GET DOWN TO BUSINESS!
HEY, WHAT'RE YA GONNA DO? EH?
COME ON!
FIGHT ME WITH THOSE FISTS YOU'RE SO PROUD OF!
DON'T HOLD BACK!

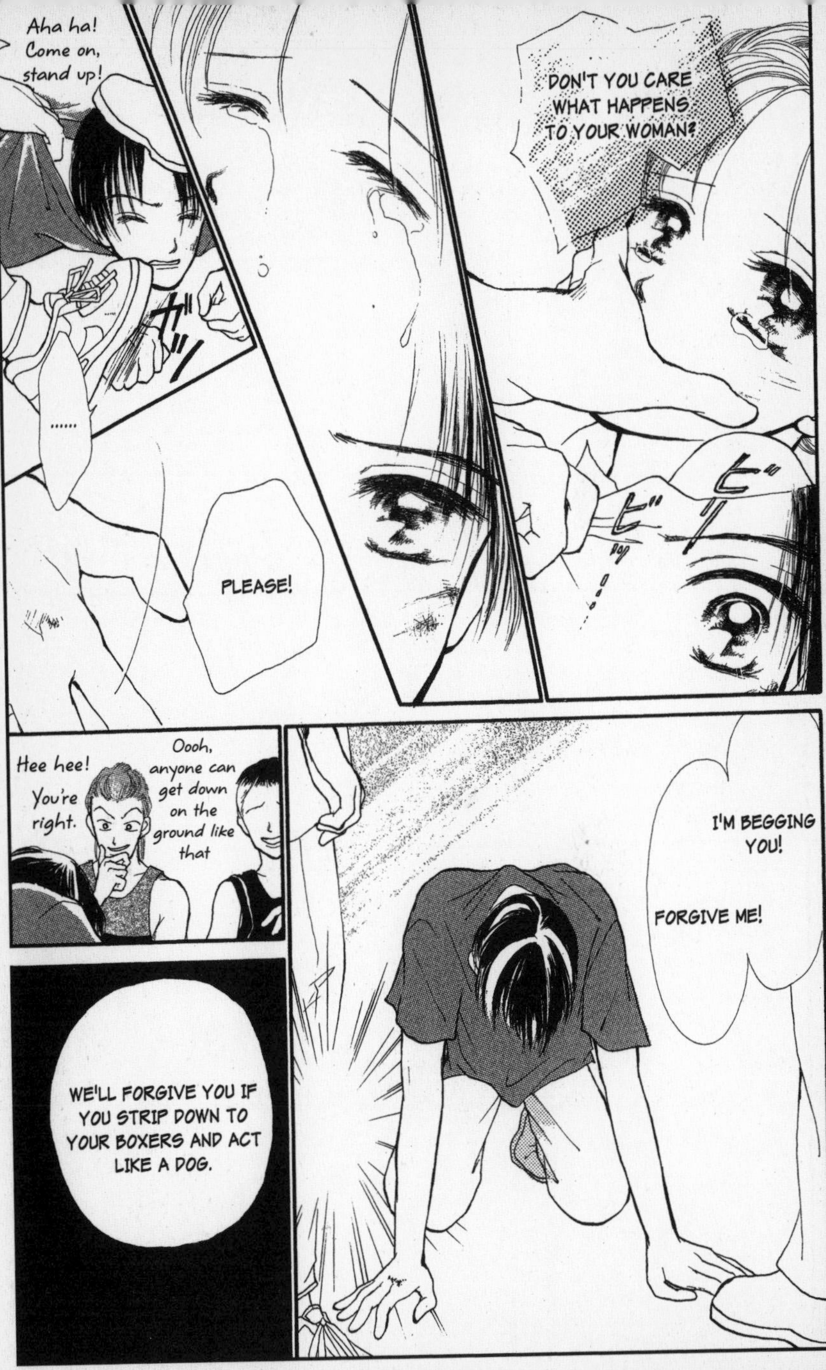
DON'T YOU CARE WHAT HAPPENS TO YOUR WOMAN?
Aha ha! Come on, stand up!
......
PLEASE!
I'M BEGGING YOU!
FORGIVE ME!
Oooh, anyone can get down on the ground like that
Hee hee! You're right.
WE'LL FORGIVE YOU IF YOU STRIP DOWN TO YOUR BOXERS AND ACT LIKE A DOG.

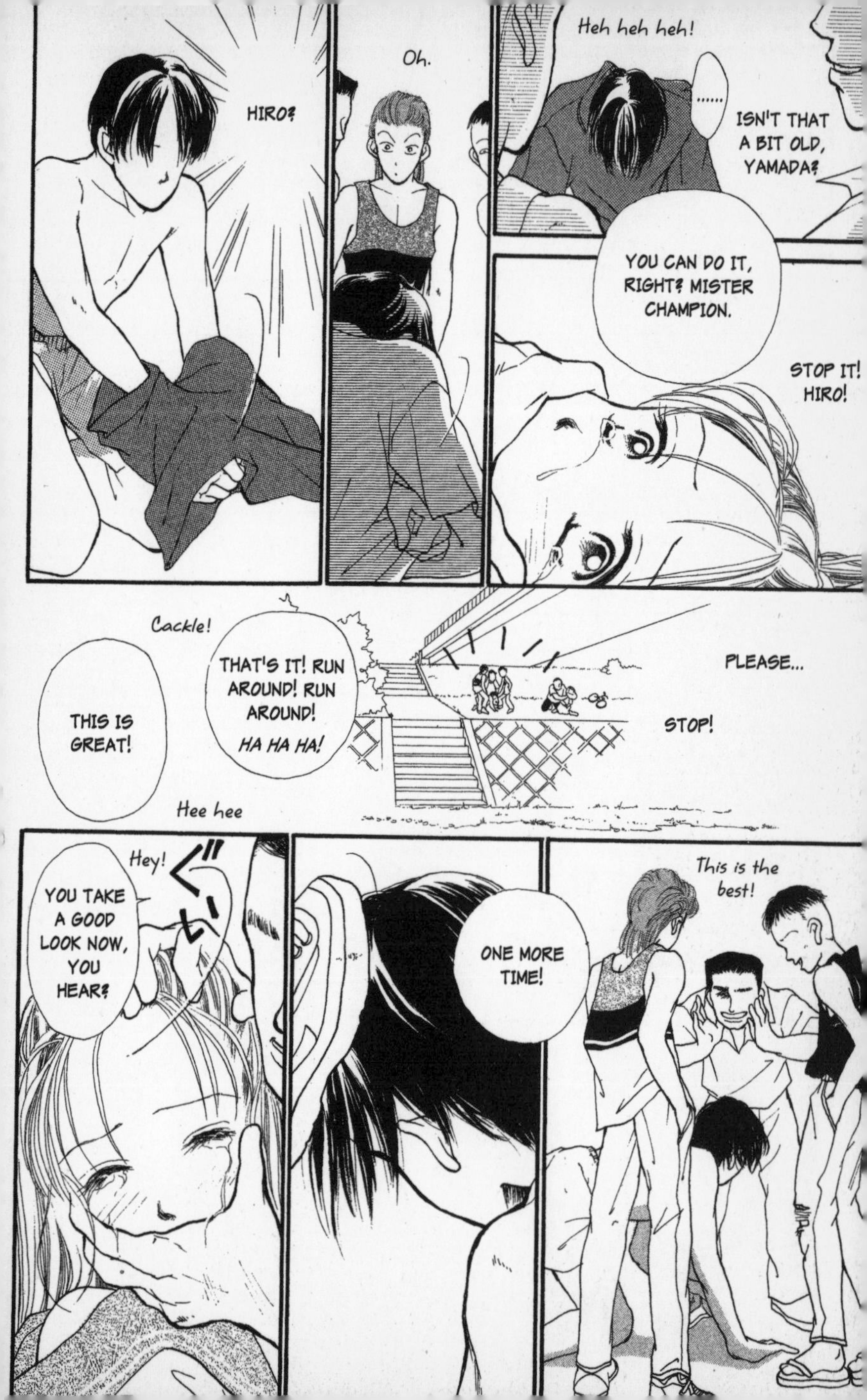
Heh heh heh!
......
ISN'T THAT A BIT OLD, YAMADA?
YOU CAN DO IT, RIGHT? MISTER CHAMPION.
STOP IT! HIRO!
Oh.
HIRO?
PLEASE...
STOP!
THAT'S IT! RUN AROUND! RUN AROUND! HA HA HA!
Cackle!
THIS IS GREAT!
Hee hee
This is the best!
ONE MORE TIME!
Hey!
YOU TAKE A GOOD LOOK NOW, YOU HEAR?

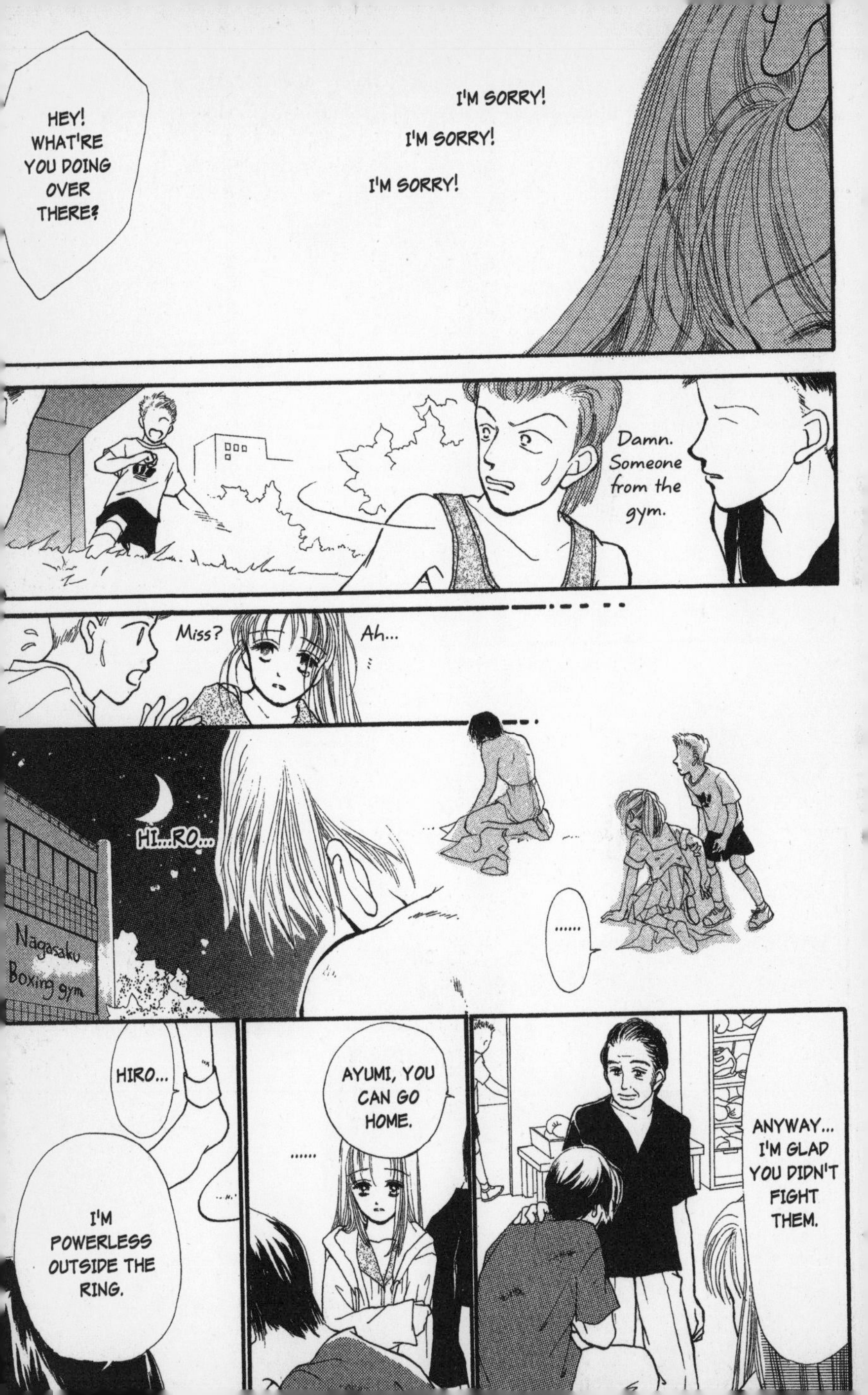
I'M SORRY!
I'M SORRY!
I'M SORRY!
HEY! WHAT'RE YOU DOING OVER THERE?
Damn. Someone from the gym.
Ah...
Miss?
......
HI...RO...
Nagasaku Boxing gym
ANYWAY... I'M GLAD YOU DIDN'T FIGHT THEM.
AYUMI, YOU CAN GO HOME.
......
HIRO...
I'M POWERLESS OUTSIDE THE RING.

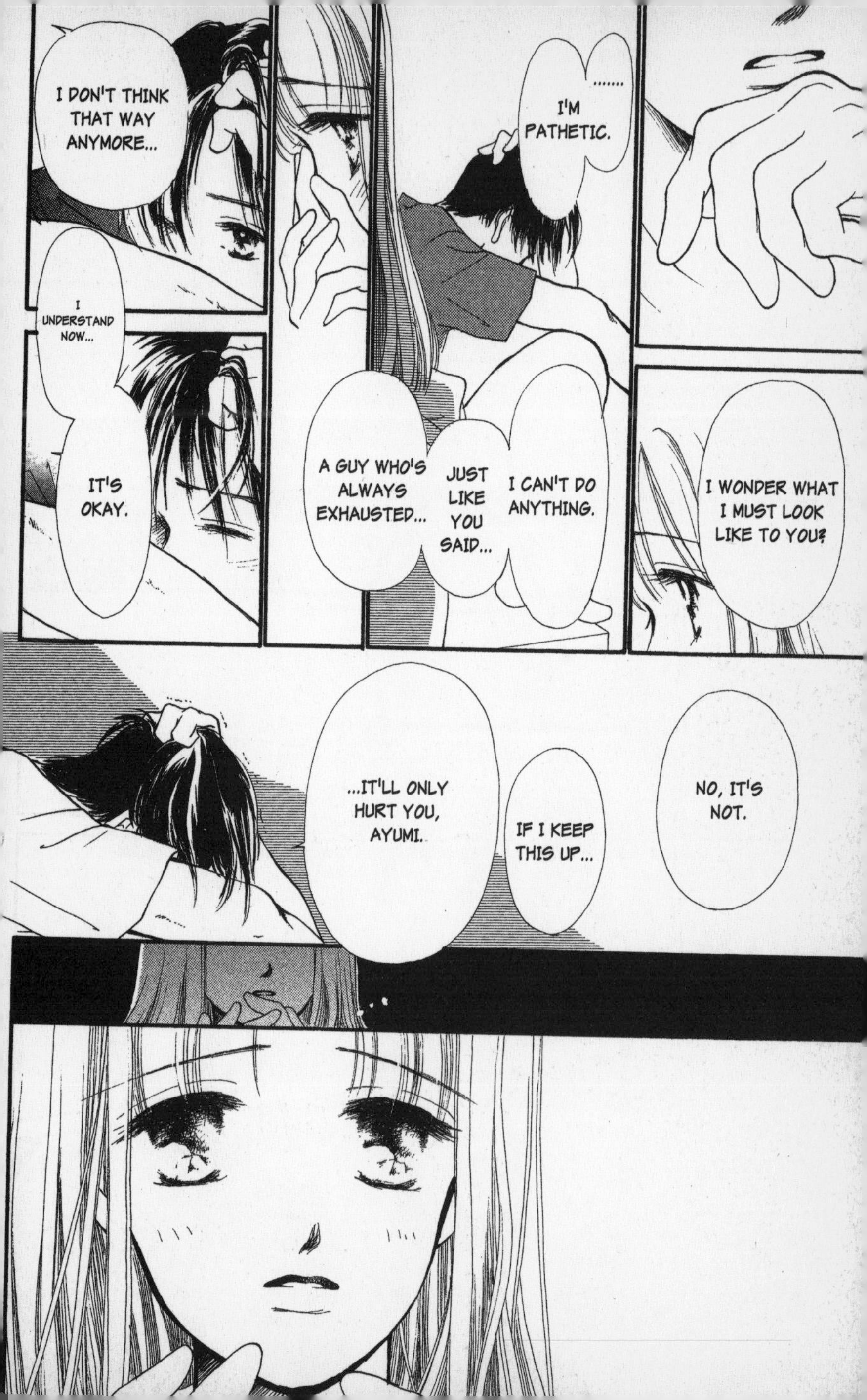
I WONDER WHAT I MUST LOOK LIKE TO YOU?
....
I'M PATHETIC.
I CAN'T DO ANYTHING.
JUST LIKE YOU SAID...
A GUY WHO'S ALWAYS EXHAUSTED...
I DON'T THINK THAT WAY ANYMORE...
I UNDERSTAND NOW...
IT'S OKAY.
NO, IT'S NOT.
IF I KEEP THIS UP...
...IT'LL ONLY HURT YOU, AYUMI.

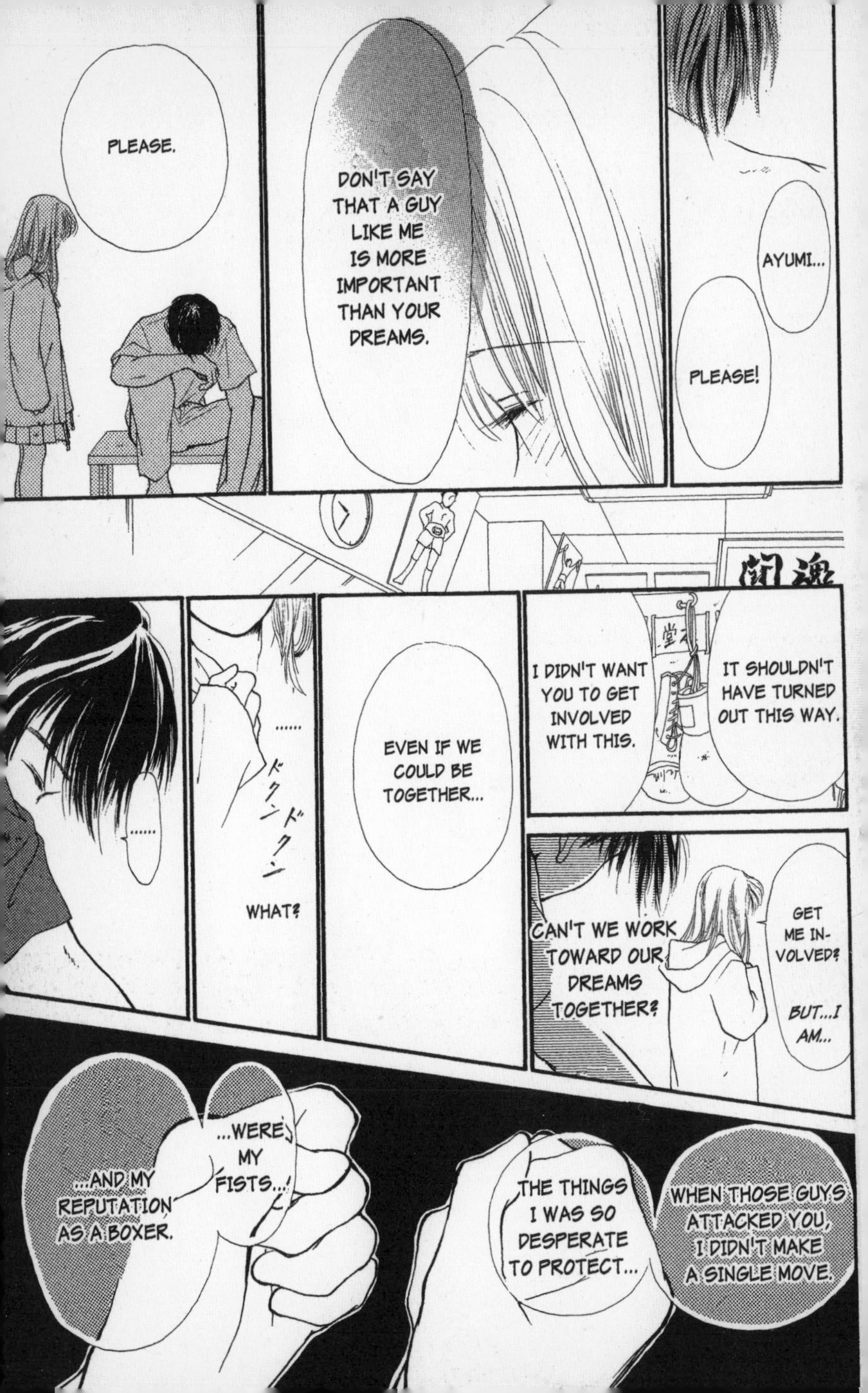
AYUMI...
PLEASE!
DON'T SAY THAT A GUY LIKE ME IS MORE IMPORTANT THAN YOUR DREAMS.
PLEASE.
IT SHOULDN'T HAVE TURNED OUT THIS WAY.
I DIDN'T WANT YOU TO GET INVOLVED WITH THIS.
GET ME IN-VOLVED?
BUT...I AM...
CAN'T WE WORK TOWARD OUR DREAMS TOGETHER?
EVEN IF WE COULD BE TOGETHER...
......
ドクン ドクン
WHAT?
......
WHEN THOSE GUYS ATTACKED YOU, I DIDN'T MAKE A SINGLE MOVE.
THE THINGS I WAS SO DESPERATE TO PROTECT...
...WERE MY FISTS...
...AND MY REPUTATION AS A BOXER.

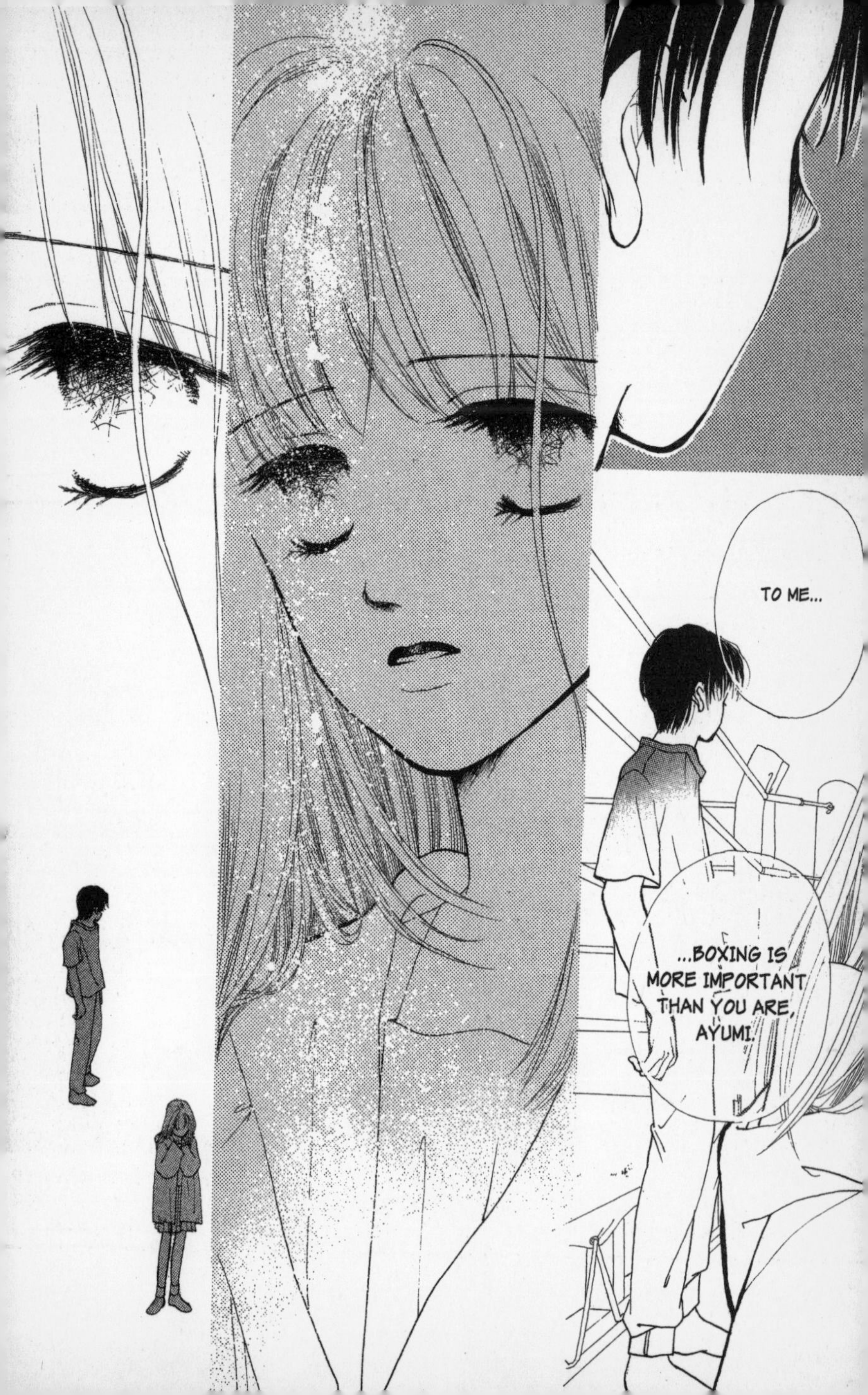
TO ME...
...BOXING IS MORE IMPORTANT THAN YOU ARE, AYUMI.

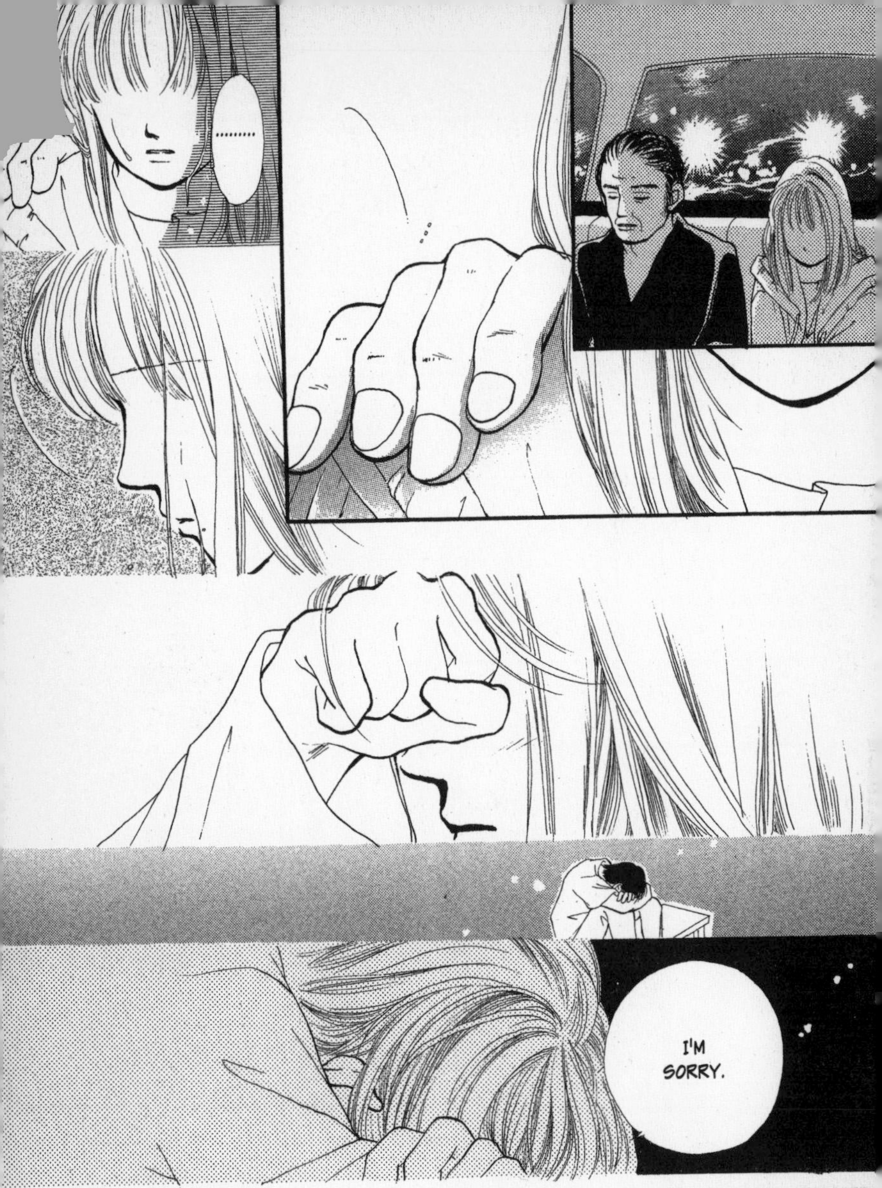
......
I'M SORRY.
WHEN WE BOTH REALIZED THAT HIRO WAS A BOXER AND NOTHING ELSE...
...NEITHER OF US...
...COULD SAY A SINGLE THING.

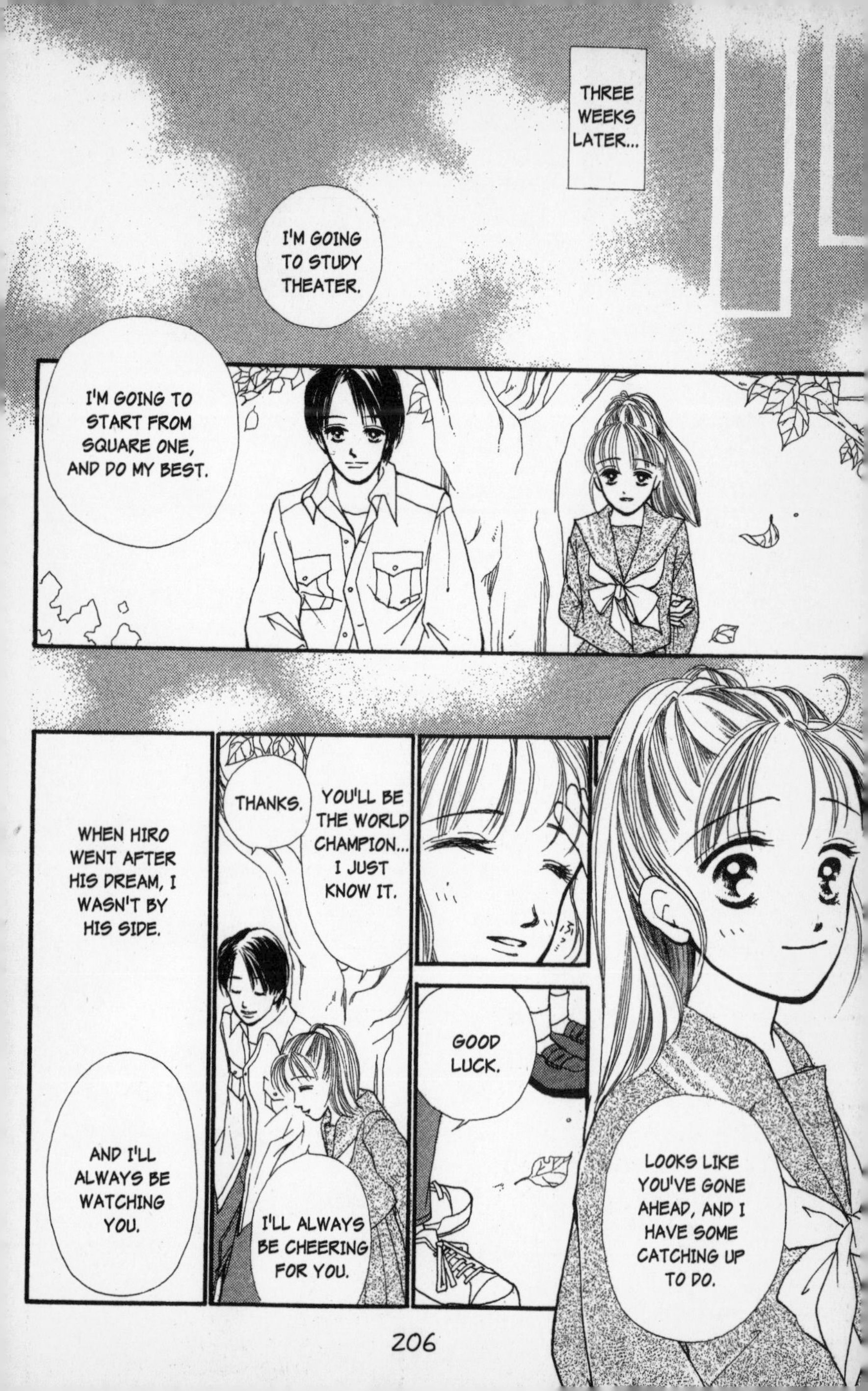
THREE WEEKS LATER...
I'M GOING TO STUDY THEATER.
I'M GOING TO START FROM SQUARE ONE, AND DO MY BEST.
LOOKS LIKE YOU'VE GONE AHEAD, AND I HAVE SOME CATCHING UP TO DO.
GOOD LUCK.
YOU'LL BE THE WORLD CHAMPION... I JUST KNOW IT.
THANKS.
I'LL ALWAYS BE CHEERING FOR YOU.
WHEN HIRO WENT AFTER HIS DREAM, I WASN'T BY HIS SIDE.
AND I'LL ALWAYS BE WATCHING YOU.

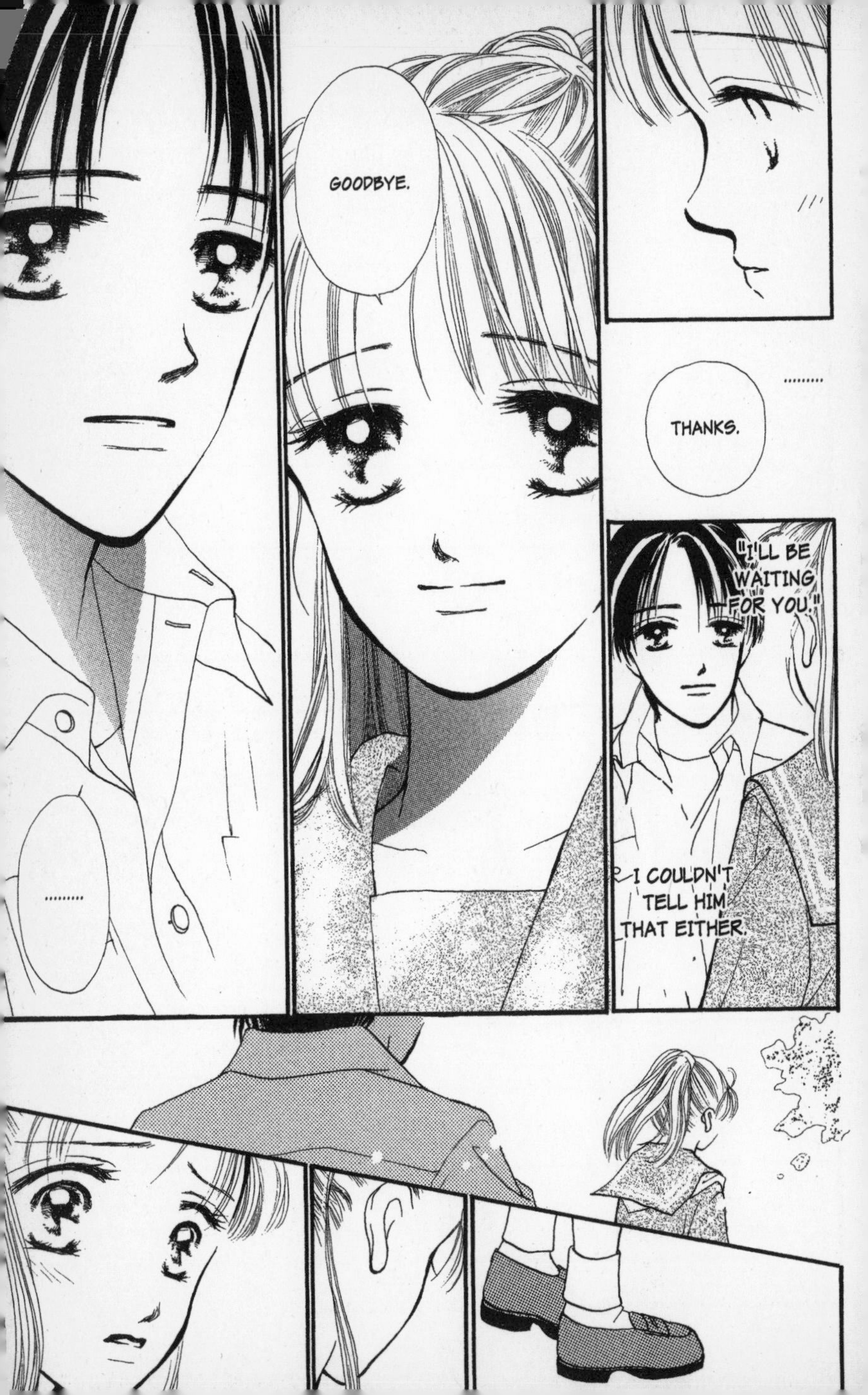
....
THANKS.
"I'LL BE WAITING FOR YOU."
I COULDN'T TELL HIM THAT EITHER.
GOODBYE.
....

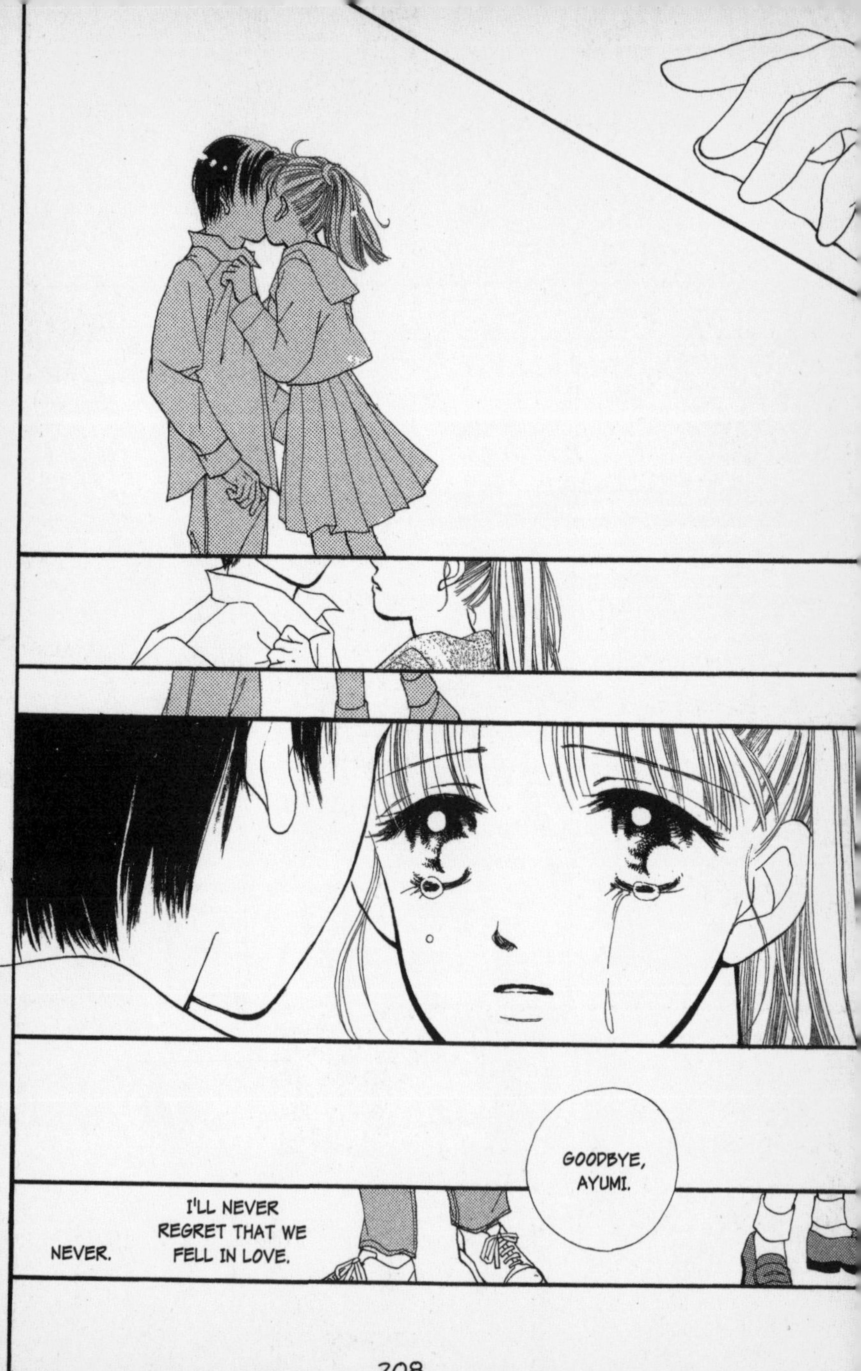
GOODBYE, AYUMI.
I'LL NEVER REGRET THAT WE FELL IN LOVE.
NEVER.

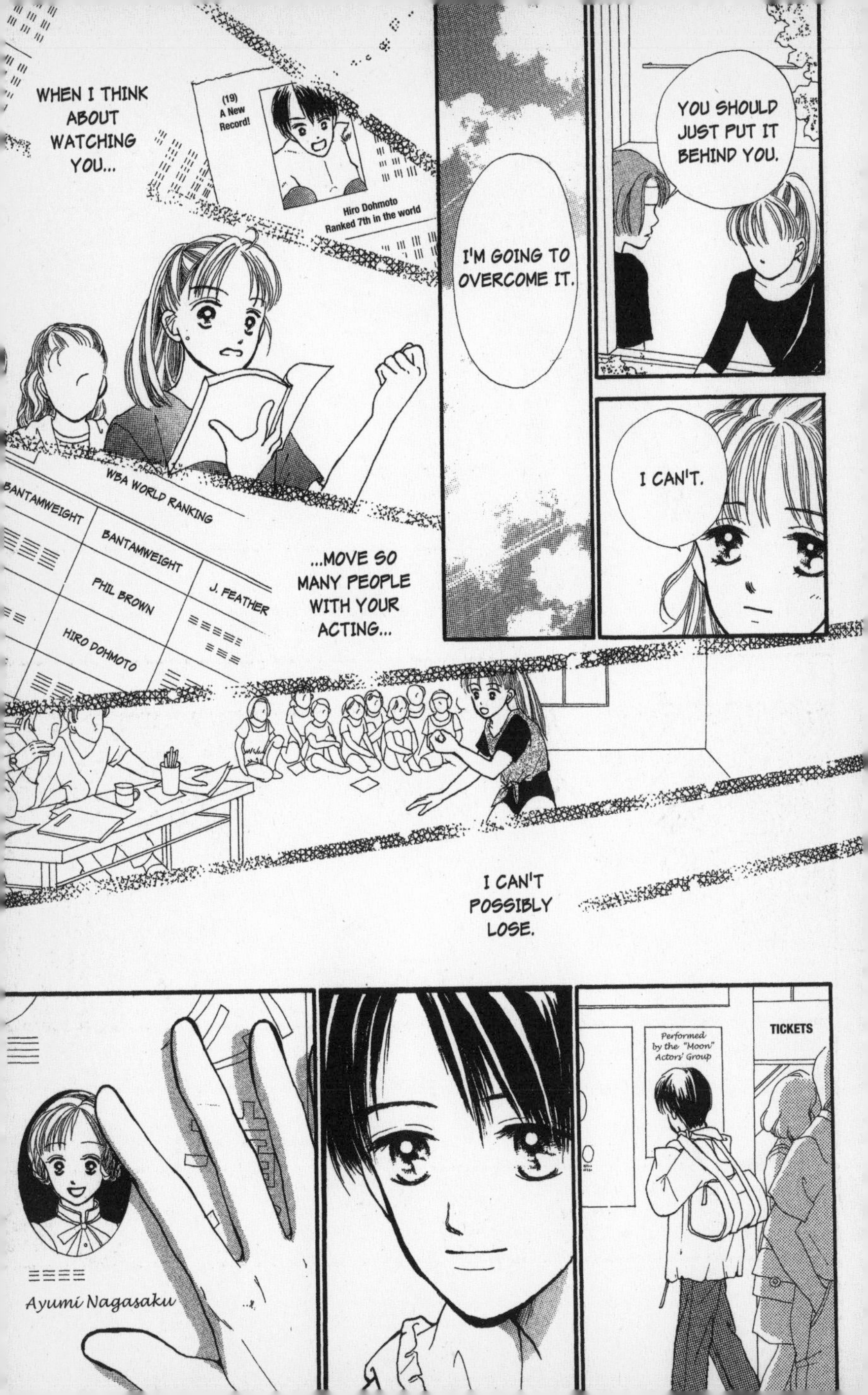
YOU SHOULD JUST PUT IT BEHIND YOU.
I CAN'T.
I'M GOING TO OVERCOME IT.
WHEN I THINK ABOUT WATCHING YOU...
(19)
A New Record!
Hiro Dohmoto Ranked 7th in the world
WBA WORLD RANKING
BANTAMWEIGHT
BANTAMWEIGHT
J. FEATHER
PHIL BROWN
HIRO DOHMOTO
...MOVE SO MANY PEOPLE WITH YOUR ACTING...
I CAN'T POSSIBLY LOSE.
TICKETS
Performed by the "Moon" Actors' Group
Ayumi Nagasaku

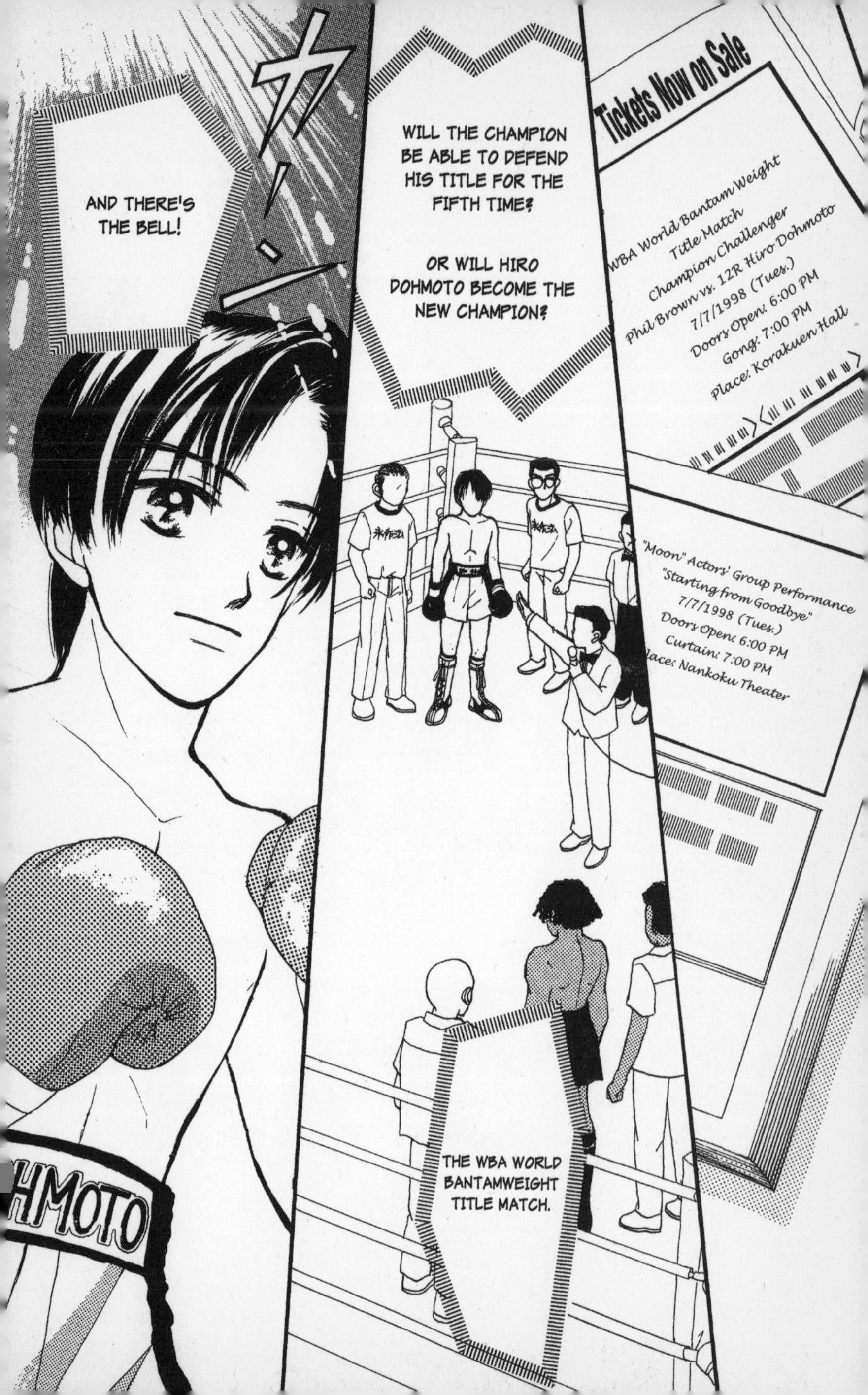
Tickets Now on Sale
WBA World Bantam Weight
Title Match
Champion Challenger
Phil Brown vs. 12R Hiro Dohmoto
7/7/1998 (Tues.)
Doors Open: 6:00 PM
Gong: 7:00 PM
Place: Korakuen Hall
"Moon" Actors' Group Performance
"Starting from Goodbye"
7/7/1998 (Tues.)
Doors Open: 6:00 PM
Curtain: 7:00 PM
lace: Nankoku Theater
WILL THE CHAMPION BE ABLE TO DEFEND HIS TITLE FOR THE FIFTH TIME?
OR WILL HIRO DOHMOTO BECOME THE NEW CHAMPION?
THE WBA WORLD BANTAMWEIGHT TITLE MATCH.
AND THERE'S THE BELL!
HMOTO